TWENTIETH-CENTURY THEATRE

A unique and invaluable collection, *Twentieth-Century Theatre* offers a wide range of original writings on theatre by its most creative practitioners – directors, playwrights, performers and designers – from the start of the century to the present.

Setting theory beside practice, these writings bring alive a number of vital and continuing concerns, each of which is given full scope in a separate section of the book. Assembled and juxtaposed in this way, they explore and clarify the modernist, political and popular bearings of theatre in our century and its inner and global dimensions. The wide range of writers and texts not only provides illuminating perspectives on past history, but also throws fresh light on the sources and development of theatre today.

Introductions to the different sections of the book indicate the broad lines of development that underlie its varied contents, while notes on the contributors and their writings clarify difficulties and add helpful contextual information. The volume provides direct access to the thinking behind much of the most stimulating theatre the century has had to offer, as well as guidelines to its present most adventurous developments. It not only makes an essential and versatile coursebook for students at all levels, but also offers a feast of ideas for anyone interested in or engaged in theatre.

Richard Drain teaches part time at York University and is currently writing an opera libretto for composer Trevor Wishart. His plays have been performed by various companies and on BBC radio. He has also directed numerous devised shows which have toured to theatres, schools, community centres and prisons.

TWENTIETH-CENTURY THEATRE

A sourcebook

Edited by Richard Drain

London and New York

First published 1995
by Routledge
11 New Fetter Lane, London EC4P 4EE

Simultaneously published in the USA and Canada
by Routledge
29 West 35th Street, New York, NY 10001

Reprinted 1998, 1999, 2001

Routledge is an imprint of the Taylor & Francis Group

© 1995 Richard Drain

Typeset in 10/12pt Garamond
by J&L Composition Ltd, Filey, North Yorkshire

Printed and bound in Great Britain by Clays Ltd, St Ives plc

British Library Cataloguing in Publication Data
A catalogue record for this book is available from the British Library

Library of Congress Cataloguing in Publication Data
Twentieth-Century Theatre: A sourcebook / edited by Richard Drain.
p.   cm.
Includes bibliographical references.
1. Theatre.   2. Drama.   I. Drain, Richard.
PN2020.R46   1994
792—dc20
94–40136

ISBN 0–415–09619–7 (hbk)
ISBN 0–415–09620–0 (pbk)

It is particularly important that the theatre, the most transient of all the arts, which leaves nothing behind but a few inadequate photographs and vague memories, be caught in print if it makes claim to historical significance and progressive development. For that reason the theoretical discoveries that have been made deserve to be recorded just as much as the facts and events.

Erwin Piscator

CONTENTS

CONTENTS

CONTENTS

Part III The Popular Dimension

CONTENTS

Part IV The Inner Dimension

CONTENTS

CONTENTS

PREFACE

This is a collection of writings on theatre by those involved in theatre, whether as directors, performers, writers or designers. It is concerned with significant innovations in modern stage practice; and aims to illuminate the ideas behind them. Its span is wide: from the onset of this century to the present. So it cannot hope to be comprehensive, and has no illusion of being so. Numerous important figures are omitted, and it deals with five aspects of theatre only. These five aspects, however, have had deep and lasting importance, and offer perspectives into a range of key developments throughout the period.

These developments are not the work of one or two people, even if they come to seem so later. Here, key texts by renowned figures are placed in the context of other important writings: they are part of a running debate involving many. It is a debate on the aims and means of theatre ranging widely across national frontiers, conducted intensively throughout the century, and continuing actively into our own time. This precludes more than a short sampling of their work, but may help illuminate it from other angles. The selection aims to hold a balance between theory and practice, and suggest the importance of one to the other; and to highlight the continuing attempts to renew theatre that have been so important to its modern history, and remain so vital to its future.

The status of theatre has been uncertain throughout the century. If the low artistic reputation with which it began has been redeemed, its role within culture at large has diminished sharply with the growth of the media. But this precarious status has had one good outcome. As these writings witness, it has meant that theatre people have engaged throughout in a questioning of its role and purposes. The various answers offered in response to this have prompted the transformations that make up its modern history. Displaced from the centre of the larger cultural stage, theatre has sought fresh ways to engage with society. It has fought to be something more than entertainment for the privileged, or escapism for the many. Those at its cutting edge have used it as a form of intervention, whose function is to challenge preconceptions. This challenge has been signalled in the invention of new forms and styles. But it will not do to read the history of modern theatre simply in terms of form and style, as these are rooted in deeper issues. This volume gives space to these, as its authors do.

Nor can the history of modern theatre be confined to theatres. Theatre has been pursued outside the institutional frame and allocated edifices that stand ready to contain it, and in the process the concept of theatre has widened. Anthropological and global perspectives have widened it still more. This sets this volume a difficult task, but it is not adequate to limit the boundaries of theatre by an outdated conventional measure. To do so would be to run counter to the spirit of all those who speak here, for it is they who challenged and are challenging such boundaries.

Theatre is live performance. The human encounter it involves between audience and performers, and the emotional dynamic that results, are essential to it. In consequence, theatre, unlike literature or film, cannot be preserved. This gives the writings collected here a special value. While they may be secondary to their creative stage work for their authors, for us they are primary: primary documents in theatre history, and a means of understanding at first hand the course of that history.

But these writings do not simply sketch a history; they make up a resource. Theatre is of its time, but the ideas voiced in these pages live on in the work of those who follow, finding new forms and fresh relevance. In the world of the theatre, they are freely passed on, to be freely redeveloped and freshly realised. This volume shows that process at work and is dedicated to its continuance.

PROLOGUE

ANDRÉ ANTOINE
FROM The Free Theatre (1890)

As the hoped-for emergence of a new generation of dramatists and dramatic works takes place, it may be affirmed that this rebirth will necessitate new means of expression. For works that are all observation and study, actors are needed who are spontaneous and authentic, in touch with reality through and through.

These long-awaited works, conceived according to a more spacious and flexible aesthetic and no longer circumscribing their characters; this new theatre, no longer based like its predecessor on five or six agreed types who are always the same, reappearing again and again under different names, in different plots, in different milieux; one cannot doubt that in this new theatre the multiplicity and complexity of the stage characters will bring about the rise of a new generation of actors flexible enough to take on any role. Young leading players, for example, will no longer all be cut from the same cloth, but will become in turn good, wicked, elegant, common, strong, weak, valiant, cowardly – in short, they will become living beings, diverse and variable.

The art of the actor, then, will no longer depend, as in previous repertories, on physical qualities or natural gifts; it will gain its life from truth, observation, and the *direct* study of nature. . . .

Since the theatrical style of the new plays tends to keep close to daily conversation, the actor must no longer '*speak*' in the classic theatrical sense; he must *talk* – which without doubt will be just as difficult.

What is meant at present by the phrase *the art of speaking*, consists solely in endowing the student with an exaggerated articulation and concocting a voice for him: a peculiar *specialised* organ quite different from the one he really has. For sixty years, all actors have uniformly spoken *through the nose*, solely because this way of speaking has to be adopted for them to be heard by the audience in our theatres, which are either *much too big* or have *poor acoustics*; and also because this nasal voice is resistant to the passing years and does not age.

PROLOGUE

In present-day theatre, all the characters gesticulate and express themselves in the same fashion, whether they are old or young, sick or healthy. All the actors, by *speaking well*, renounce those infinitely numerous nuances which can throw light on a character and give it a more intense life. . . .

The same transformation must be carried through in other areas of dramatic art: once the scenery is scaled back down to the dimensions current in contemporary milieux, the characters will express their emotions in credible settings, without continually concerning themselves to strike pictorial poses and form *tableaux*. The audience will enjoy an intimate drama, with natural and fitting moves, and with unaffected gestures and movements appropriate to a modern man, living our normal daily life.

Moves that are part of the blocking will be modified: no longer will the actor continually come out of his frame to pose in front of the audience; he will move around among the furniture and props, and his acting will be filled out with the thousand nuances and thousand details now indispensable to the establishing and logical composition of a character.

Purely mechanical movement, and effects of the voice, along with flamboyant and redundant gestures, will disappear with the simplification of theatrical action and its return to reality; and the actor will revert to natural gestures, and replace *effects* made *only* with the voice with a *composition* of elements: his expression of things will gain support from familiar, real objects, and a pencil revolved or a cup tipped over will have as much significance and as intense an effect on the audience as the grandiloquent exaggerations of the romantic theatre.

Translated by Richard Drain and Micheline Mabille

Part I

THE MODERNIST DIMENSION

May naturalism in the theatre die!
Evgeny Vakhtangov

INTRODUCTION

1

The remarks of André Antoine that preface this selection, dating from 1890, signal the effective initiation of modern theatre; and propose lines of development for it which his own work in Paris with the Théâtre Libre did much to establish. They follow up Zola's advocacy of a stage reformed on naturalistic principles, vigorously elaborated ten years before. Antoine's aim was to realise such ideas in practice, and so enable theatre, in effect, to catch up with literature, where realism and its offspring naturalism were deeply established. Indeed, readers of Balzac and Flaubert might have said that the achievement of Antoine and his few fellow-spirits elsewhere was at last to drag theatre into the nineteenth century, some ten years before it ended.

Antoine's proposed reforms were gradually implemented. This meant not just changes in staging methods and the training of actors, but acceptance of the concept and practice of ensemble work. This was vital to the development both of a living inter-relationship of characters on stage, and of what Antoine calls 'composition' – the relation of things to a total effect. Ensemble work in its turn required a breakdown of hierarchy, a diminishing of the power of the 'great' actor, or actor-manager. Technically, Antoine *was* an actor-manager. But his innovations pointed the way to a shift in power from the actor to the director – that shift whose most eloquent advocate was Gordon Craig. In all this, a new concept was being born: of the director as artist, and theatre as an art form. But a 'composition' does not have to be in the realist manner, and an ensemble can be orchestrated in many styles. Fine art was developing from Manet to Matisse. Why should theatre not do likewise? So it is that hardly had the stage discovered how to become lifelike than it grew impatient of being so. By the start of the twentieth century, with Chekhov's *The Cherry Orchard* not yet written and the full implementation of realism in the theatre only beginning to be achieved, advanced ideas were turning their back on the whole project, urging theatre in quite other directions.

These ideas at first owed much to symbolism. The symbolists saw theatre as a potential crucible in which the arts of poetry, painting, music and dance might be harmoniously fused. Then it might manifest the dreams and

3

yearnings of human life, freed from its mere material conditions. Such ideas predate modernism proper, and are largely reserved for Part IV of this volume. But the vital part played by this early movement in establishing the artistic credentials of theatre cannot be entirely passed over here; for this is the base from which much theatrical modernism operates. Hence the inclusion here of Adolphe Appia and Gordon Craig. Appia is a crucial pioneer, seeking a theatre sensitive to 'the spirit of music', and a stage that could offer equivalent qualities of rhythm, tone and harmony in the unfolding movement of its actors in a space architecturally conceived, the whole freely moulded and accented by the play of variegated lighting. Such considerations were not only foreign to theatres of the time, but impossible to realise without a wholesale rethinking of current stage practice, and indeed equipment. Appia carried this through, preparing the way for Craig and others, and implicitly introducing the stage to the concept of abstract form.

But modernism is an umbrella term covering a number of tendencies, and some have a very different character. In the world of the arts, many were keen to clear the air of what Tristan Tzara called 'the fumes of symbolism',[1] which for them were as musty and redolent of the previous age as naturalism. Delighting in parody and outrage, and championing the 'lowest' forms of popular entertainment, they fought a guerilla war against bourgeois culture, seeing it as a pervasive mess of reactionary values and nauseating sentiments. The first twentieth-century wave of this onslaught comes with the futurists; and is soon followed by Dada. But the great pioneer of these tactics is Alfred Jarry. Before the nineteenth century was out, Jarry had succeeded in achieving a *succès de scandale* with his scabrous and grotesque creation, Ubu, and the crude puppet-like staging of his sub-Shakespearean adventures. Much more than a jape, as Jarry's article here shows, Ubu and the toilet brush he brandished were a rude signal of things to come.

The futurist movement was launched a decade later in 1909, and initiated on many fronts the impact of modernist ideas on the arts. The futurists aimed to jerk the buried heads of all concerned out of the sands of establishment 'culture', uproot the arts from their pre-industrial past, and connect them to the age of the dynamo and the combustion engine. Significantly their ideas flourished best in two countries still at the time deeply agrarian – Italy and Russia. In Italy, where the movement began, the machine spelt dramatic advance – exemplified for F. T. Marinetti, its best-known spokesman, in Italy's thriving car industry with its new internationally competitive racing models.[2]

While futurism sought to revolutionise all the arts, Marinetti was particularly concerned with theatre. His withering analysis of its current forms is coupled with provocative suggestions for hijacking and rerouting it. Other futurists moved into theatre work from painting and the visual arts – notably

Fortunato Depero and Enrico Prampolini. Their revolutionary scenographic concepts may have taken their start from Gordon Craig, who was already based in Italy, exploring the idea of a theatre of mobile architectural forms. Prampolini and Depero outreached him, liberating scenography from the dramatic text, and devising spectacles geared to a musical or sound score, composed of moving shapes and changing light. They open a road which branches out to the constructivists, Tadeusz Kantor, 1960s' happenings, Robert Wilson, and other developments in performance art. The futurists' playwriting ventures point another way. A series of cabaret squibs or staged jokes, they ridicule the conventions of both society and stage. With their chopped-up or derailed parody of social behaviour and dramatic histrionics, they initiate many aspects of what is now known as absurdism.

This spirit flourished further with the anarchic intervention of Dada – represented here by Tristan Tzara. Dada was launched in Zurich in 1916: in the middle of the First World War, and yet outside it, for Switzerland remained neutral. From there, the mass slaughter of a generation that was taking place across the border in France was seen to make a bitter or farcical mockery of European values – hitherto seen as the values of civilisation. In Dada, bitterness and farce are mixed. Tzara and its other founders strongly opposed the war. But rational protest from the safe haven of Switzerland was condemned in advance to an inevitable futility. The lasting and sobering significance of Dada was that it first faced up to the ineffectuality of the artist and the intellectual, and of all that till then had prided itself on constituting 'culture'. It put Art with a capital letter under a lasting question mark.[3] It did so partly by offering no answers, deliberately contradicting its own assertions and abolishing itself before they could be codified.

Dada denied its own modernism, and no doubt would have objected to its inclusion here.[4] Dada preferred non-Western cultures to 'modern' culture; and was against all -isms, including modernism, seeing them as symptoms of dogmatic programme, or worse, academic classification. Dada favoured spontaneity and a cabaret environment – which it proceeded to create by setting up its Cabaret Voltaire. Its first '*grande soirée*' included poems (read simultaneously in two or three languages), dialogues, songs, dance, cubist paintings and cacophonous music. The cabaret format reflects the continuing endorsement by artists and writers of a whole field of performance outside the formalities of straight theatre. This is heralded in painting by Lautrec, by Wedekind's enthusiasm for circus and cabaret, and by Jarry's taste for *guignol* – the French equivalent of our Punch and Judy. It is witnessed by Picasso's early clowns and acrobats, and cheered on by Marinetti in his manifesto, 'The Variety Theatre'. The 'modernist' stage emerged out of this background. It quits the drawing room and raids the kitchen, stocking up with common fare including custard pies. Much modernist theatre is the offspring of the cross-over. It weds its advanced

aesthetics with the popular. This realm is too large to be adequately represented here, but will be explored further in Part III.

Tzara acknowledged Jarry as a main precursor of Dada, suggesting a
double connection: 'the will to scandalise', and 'auto-mockery'.[5] Jarry,
writes Tzara, 'opens the way to the new spirit of Apollinaire', to the new
world from which 'all the fumes of Symbolism have been swept'.[6] Guillaume
Apollinaire knew and admired Jarry. In the prologue to his play, he repeats
Jarry's attack on 'the stupidity of trompe l'œil'; and in a preface coins the
term 'surrealist' to describe what he is doing. The word is adopted by Yvan
Goll in the preface to his play Methusalem, whose factory-owning protagonist is a grotesque blood brother of Ubu. The surrealist 'movement' under
Breton's leadership begins soon after. Its members too admired Jarry, not
least Artaud, whose earlier ventures went under the name of the 'Alfred Jarry
Theatre'. While the rich possibilities of a surrealist theatre were resisted by
Breton, who expelled Artaud from the movement, a line of surrealist plays
followed, leading down to Ionesco's.

Next to this Dada might not seem more than a cabaret diversion, lacking
the status of legitimate theatre; but Dada strews tintacks on the highway of
Art, and both legitimacy and status end up badly punctured. It points an
alternative way, across open country, where disruptive activities become
theatre, and theatre becomes a disruptive activity. Its reverberations run
through the twentieth century, to Artaud, Arrabal, Kantor, the 'happenings'
of the 1960s, and much else.

2

Dada took root also in Germany, but in a different context; for there the stage
was powerfully affected by expressionism. Like their symbolist predecessors, the expressionists sought a theatre which might speak via non-
naturalistic forms direct to the human spirit. But in a country at war first
with the allied powers and then with itself, the forms it developed were, not
surprisingly, conflicting or tormented rather than harmonious. Expressionist
drama, while rejecting naturalism, had no wish to renounce naturalism's
drive to lay bare unpalatable truths. In this it was faithful to its two most
influential predecessors, Strindberg and Wedekind.

Though the movement began before 1914, the large extension of expressionism into theatre comes in the war years. It is represented here by Walter
Hasenclever and Ivan Goll (who, coming from Alsace, had roots in both
French and German culture). Hasenclever's The Son, written in 1914, was
not the first expressionist play, but was the first to make its mark with a wide
public. Its expressionist features include its subjective rendering of characters, who are portrayed as seen by the protagonist; and a theme involving, in
Hasenclever's words, 'the struggle of the spirit against reality'. His essay
here explaining his ideas calls upon Einstein's theory of relativity. Relativity is

a key modernist notion, invoked also by Tzara and the futurists. It is used to deflate the status of 'objective' truth, license multiple viewpoints, and release them from the judgement of a final authority. In that sense it backs the rebellion of sons against the father, the subject of Hasenclever's play. His denial that a play must be understandable, and his wish that his audience 'may lose the logic of their century', echoes Dada, as does the 'alogic' proposed by Ivan Goll. More widely, his hope that they feel in their heart 'the magic chain of love, hate, fury, greed, power, money and lies' bridges the way from Strindberg and Wedekind to Artaud.

The fullest fruition of modernist ideas in the theatre is seen in Germany and Russia in the 1920s. In Germany it continued up to the accession of Hitler in the 1930s, when modernist work was suppressed. Increasingly from the mid-1920s it took political forms, notably in Piscator and Brecht. In Russia the same is true, though there revolutionary *élan* and futurist audacity combine to give it a more celebratory character. These developments are traced largely in Parts II and III; but passages by El Lissitsky and Sergei Radlov are included here to register the impulse towards more abstract forms that flourished in stage design and movement.

Also included is a manifesto of the remarkable but short-lived Oberiu group, of Leningrad. The Oberiu, together with Stanislas Ignacy Witkiewicz, introduce us to the powerful absurdist work of eastern Europe, disturbing and premonitory. Witkiewicz was artist as well as writer; and his 'Introduction to the Theatre of Pure Form' of 1920 is a reminder that the contribution of art to theatre has not been confined to providing it with sets and costumes. It has also been a rich source of ideas. In Witkiewicz, the idea of 'pure form' drawn from art is carried over into theatre, and applied to characters and action. This prises them away from consistency and likelihood, into the free world of 'autonomous' theatre – a word that looks back to the 'Synthetic Theatre' manifesto of the futurists, and forward to his Polish compatriot, Tadeusz Kantor. The word applies well too to the two remarkable plays produced by the Oberiu, whose principles as expounded by Daniil Kharms are very much in line with Witkiewicz's ideas.

These ideas mark a significant step in modernist thinking. Hitherto modernism had been opposed to realism largely on the grounds that it fails to cope with twentieth-century reality. For the expressionists, it cannot articulate its distortions and anguish. For the futurists it cannot convey the kinetic energies that animate it, nor the swift montage of sights and sounds that are everyday urban experience. Witkiewicz's theory of 'pure form' cuts this connection with the real. Theatre is envisaged as an alternative world, guided by laws relating only to itself, like the forms and colours in a Picasso painting. In contrast, under Piscator and Brecht the same decade sees the start of a major attempt to bring modernist ideas into relation with realism. Both ventures have their risks. A modernism wedded to 'realism' risks recuperation; while a modernism which seeks no inspiration in modern reality risks becoming an introverted exercise. None the less, from then on modernist theory tends to be split between these two faiths, the defenders of one unwilling to give a hearing to the other.

3

This parting of the ways is left hanging as European modernism of either kind undergoes the double assault of fascism and Stalinism. Its surviving practitioners are reduced to refugee status in countries whose theatres, if not cultures, are broadly alien to it. Their energies are consumed in trying to take root, or make a living, rather than in developing their work. Alienation becomes a major theme, and for many there is every temptation to cultivate in their art an alternative world to those to which they are exiled. More recently, as we may see here, Eugene Ionesco echoes Witkiewicz in calling for theatre to 'invent a unique event . . . create an inimitable universe foreign to all others'. This project gained a further dimension in performance art. As Richard Foreman puts it: 'this new art is not extracted from the flux of life . . . but is a parallel phenomenon to life itself.'[7]

We arrive here in post-modernist territory, and some may question whether such recent work should be placed in a modernist perspective. But readers here may check this out for themselves. The boundary separating these two sprawling domains, never that clear, in theatre seems more one of chronology than principle. This is not because theatre lags behind, but rather the reverse. Many of the features commonly identified as post-modernist in the other arts are in one sense or another 'theatrical'; and they already have a long history in modernist theatre. The play of styles, pastiche, the celebration of artifice; the disclosure of fictional happenings as fictive; the open display of structural devices, or their dismantling and reassembly; the abandonment of artistic unity; the cross-over with popular modes: all these accepted trademarks of the post-modern are common features in modernist theatre of the opening decades of the century.

In more recent work, the continuity with modernism is perhaps clearest in the work of Kantor, if only because of the clear consciousness in his writings of his significant predecessors: Craig, Dada, the constructivists and the surrealists. From his awareness of these springs a concern with scenic materiality, and with images that fuse, below the conscious level, memory, personal archetypes and the 'impossible'. Following Dada, Kantor rejected the 'work of Art' in its traditional sense; and sought to incorporate elements alien to it. A parallel could be drawn with Beckett, who, in a rare pronouncement on his work, is reported as saying, 'My little exploration is that whole zone of being that has always been set aside by artists as something unusable – as sounding by definition incompatible with art.'[8] In Kantor this zone takes in not only 'found' objects and detritus, but chance and accident.

Such work, while creating certainly an 'inimitable universe', does not

divorce itself from elements in the real universe. It is a 'parallel phenomenon' perhaps, but the word parallel entails a relationship. The purist stance
of those who invoked 'Pure Form' in the 1920s has given way to an appetite
for elements in real life ignored by 'Art'. This was true in the 'happenings' of
the 1960s, devised in the States by Kaprow and fellow artists. A hidden
formal element was retained in these: actions within them were frequently
governed by a tight if arbitrary system. In this sense, happenings were less
given over to the 'flux of life' than their name might suggest. But the
elements deployed in them were none the less frequently matters of everyday experience – car tyres and a brand of breakfast cereal in the example
Allan Kaprow offers here – commodities split from their usual context, but
undeniably drawn from the flux of life as people in the West now experience
it.

A principle shared by much of this recent work is its freedom to be 'non-
matrixed' – a word coined by Michael Kirby to describe happenings. Its
elements, that is, do not cohere to create an imagined reality where given
characters, with a presumed life-history, are found at a particular time in a
particular place. Coherence of this kind is discarded in favour of modernist
collage (in Kantor and in happenings); free association (Robert Wilson); or of
lateral hops of the musing intelligence (Richard Foreman). Things that
commonly go together are dissociated. In Foreman's earlier work, dialogue
is separated from performers by being put on tape. In Wilson's, what one
sees does not accord with what one hears. As he has explained: 'it designs
choreographies which have nothing to do with what the actors say. And
what they say has nothing to do with the scenery and costumes.'[9] The
modernist impulse toward the separation and fresh recombination of elements is here pushed to a far point.

To understand fully the modernist background to this American work, it is
helpful to look back to Gertrude Stein, a reference point for both Wilson and
Foreman. Her essay 'Plays' offers characteristically original suggestions
towards a new form of theatrical experience. Her notion that a play might
be a form of 'landscape' reduces dramatic conflict and climax to a minimum.
These qualities have ceaselessly been pronounced the lifeblood of theatre;
but then, most pronouncements on theatre have been by men, who may
have a predisposition to them. It is worth remembering that forms of
performance that succeeded in dispensing with these supposedly indispensable factors were pioneered in the early years of the century by women in
the field of dance, notably Loïe Fuller and Isadora Duncan; and that Stein
celebrates this in an early piece of writing, 'Orta, or One Dancing',[10] which is
a continuous flow of rhythmic repetitions and variations like the free dance
that is its subject. This may have nourished her later sense of what she
wanted from the theatre. It is only recently, in work like Robert Wilson's and
Richard Foreman's, that these qualities of 'landscape' and free dance, along
with something akin to the non-linear 'field composition' explored by

9

Charles Olson in poetry,[11] have flourished in new forms of stage practice. In ways like these, the heritage of modernism is not yet inert, but still a source of new creative work.

NOTES

1 Tristan Tzara, *Œuvres Complètes*, vol. 5, Paris, Flammarion, 1982, p. 357.
2 See Reyner Banham, *Theory and Design in the First Machine Age*, London, Architectural Press, 1960, pp. 99–105.
3 See 'Dada contre l'Art', Tzara, op. cit., p. 353.
4 Ibid., pp. 335–6.
5 Ibid., p. 363.
6 Ibid., p. 360.
7 Richard Foreman, 'Ontological-Hysteric Manifesto 1 (April, 1972)', in *Plays and Manifestos*, New York University Press, 1976, p. 73.
8 Israel Shenker, 'Moody Man of Letters', *New York Times*, 6 May 1956, Section 2, p. 3.
9 Translated from 'Bob Wilson', *L'Avant-scène, Ballet/Danse 2*, April–July 1980, p. 89.
10 Published in *Two: Gertrude Stein and Her Brother, and Other Early Portraits*, New Haven, CT, Yale University Press, 1951.
11 See Charles Olson, 'Projective Verse', in Donald Allen and Warren Tallman (eds), *The Poetics of the New American Poetry*, New York, Grove Press, 1973.

1

ALFRED JARRY

FROM Of the Uselessness to Theatre of the Theatre (1896)

'Let us note that there are many theatre audiences, or at least two: that of the intelligent, small in number, and that of large number...' So wrote Jarry in reply to a questionnaire in 1896. He speaks again here for the former, whose number he now puts at five hundred.

What follows is an index of certain things that are notoriously horrid and incomprehensible to these five hundred spirits, and that encumber the stage uselessly: above all the *scenery* and the *actors*.

The scenery is hybrid, neither natural nor artifice. If it looked the same as nature it would be a superfluous duplicate. . . . It is not artifice in the sense that it does not offer the artist a realisation of the outside world seen through himself, or better created by himself. . . .

There are two kinds of setting: interiors and open air. They claim to represent rooms or natural fields. We shall not go back over the question of the stupidity of *trompe l'œil*;[1] it is agreed upon once and for all. Let us simply say that the said *trompe l'œil* creates an illusion for those who see crudely, that is to say, do not see, and shocks and offends those who see in an intelligent and discriminating fashion, by presenting them with a caricature by someone with no understanding. Zeuxis deceived brute beasts, they say, and Titian an innkeeper. . . .

We have tried *heraldic* scenery,[2] that is to say, designing the whole of a scene or act in a unified and uniform hue, the characters passing harmonically on the field of a coat of arms . . . each entering into the *locality* desired, or better, if the author has known what he wanted, into the true scenery which appears on stage by a process of exosmosis.[3] The signboard brought on according to changes of location avoids the periodic recall from the world of the mind caused by physical changes of scenery – scenery one perceives above all at the moment one sees it to be different.

In these conditions, every part of the scenery that meets a special need – a window that is opened, a door that is burst through – is a prop, and can be brought on like a table or a torch.

With make-up the actor assumes the character's face and should assume his body. Expressions, the play of the visage etc., are various contractions and extensions of the facial muscles. People have not considered that under the assumed face and the make-up the muscles remain the same, and that Mounet[4] and Hamlet do not have the same zygomatic formation,[5] although anatomically they are believed to be one man – or the difference is said to be negligible. By means of an enclosing *mask*, the actor should substitute for his head that of the CHARACTER in effigy. This would not have, as in the antique world, the appearance of tears or laughter (which are not characters) but the character of the part: the Miser, the Hesitant One, the Covetous, piling up his crimes...

And if the eternal character of the part is included in the mask, there is a simple means, similar to a kaleidoscope or even more a gyroscope, to highlight, one by one or severally, chance moments. . . . By slow movements of the head, from up to down and down to up, and librations[6] from side to side, the actor moves the mask's shadows over its whole surface. And experience proves that the six main positions (and the same for the profile, though these are less distinct), are sufficient for every expression. We do not give instances, because they vary according to the original essence of the mask; and because all those who have known how to look at a Guignol[7] could verify them.

As they are simple expressions, they are universal. The grave error of present pantomime is that it ends up with a conventional mime language, tiresome and incomprehensible. An example of this convention: a vertical ellipse around the face with the hand and a kiss on that hand to express beauty are supposed to suggest love. – Example of a universal gesture: the puppet shows his amazement by a violent recoil and by banging his head against the wings.

Through all these incidental happenings the intrinsic expression subsists, and in many scenes the best thing is the impassivity of the mask as it dispenses its hilarious or solemn words. This can be compared only to the inorganic nature of the skeleton concealed under the flesh, whose tragicomic quality has been recognised throughout the ages.

It goes without saying that the actor must have a special *voice*, which is the voice of the role, as if the mouth cavity of the mask could emit only what the mask would say if its lip muscles were supple. It is best for them not to be supple, and for the delivery throughout the play to be monotone.

Translated by Richard Drain and Micheline Mabille

NOTES

1 Painting that 'deceives the eye'.
2 The original version of *King Ubu* was the third act of a four-act work, *Caesar*

Anti-Christ. Each act shows the further metamorphosis of this Anti-Christ, from a golden cross into a heraldic band or fess, and then into the fleshly incarnation of Ubu himself. The second act is entitled 'The Heraldic Act'; each of its scenes is envisioned in terms of heraldry, and some consist simply of a heraldic motif, e.g. 'Scene II. Sable, a unicorn passant argent.' Here as elsewhere, his visual concept of theatre is of a kind of animated iconography.

3 *Exosmosis:* Jarry's notable erudition is evidenced in his frequent use of scientific terms. Exosmosis denotes the passing of a liquid etc. through a membrane from a region of high concentration to low. Jarry seems to suggest that the writer will bring the scene into being for the audience as if through the evenly-painted canvas 'membrane' of the set. In practice, the set for *Ubu*, whose production was in the hands of Aurelien Lugné-Poe, was painted to represent at the same time interiors and exteriors as well as different climatic zones, so that snow, blossoming apple trees, palm trees and a fireplace were all depicted. (See Arthur Symons' description in Roger Shattuck's *The Banquet Years*, London, Faber & Faber, 1959, p. 161). But Jarry had recommended a plain backdrop and no scenery, on the principle of the 'uniform . . . field' he recommends here.

4 Paul Mounet, one of the 'awe-inspiring *Shades*' whose memory still haunted the Comédie-Française when Jean-Louis Barrault joined it in the early 1940s. 'And in the Café de la Régence there survives the thundering Shade of Paul Mounet.' (Jean-Louis Barrault, *Reflections on the Theatre*, London, Rockliff, 1951, p. 92).

5 The zygomatic arch comprises the cheekbones and the front of the skull.

6 Again a scientific term: the librations of the moon denote the way it seems to oscillate as its 'edge' is alternately perceptible and imperceptible. Jarry seems to be suggesting that very slight turns of the mask could alter its outline back and forth.

7 A puppet character, who originated in Lyon. Like Punch, Guignol is often in trouble with the police. The word is also used generically to mean the puppet shows in which he features; hence 'Grand-Guignol': violent and gruesome melodrama.

Alfred Jarry (1873–1907), French writer and artist. This article by Jarry was written some three months before the staging of his play *King Ubu* in December 1896, and outlines the thinking from which it sprang. Written according to Jarry as a 'Guignol', the play broke drastically with the kind of scenery and acting that Jarry lambastes here, and with all other accepted theatrical norms of the time. Yeats, who saw its first performance, wrote: 'The players are supposed to be dolls, toys, marionettes, and now they are all hopping like wooden frogs, and I can see for myself that the chief personage, who is some kind of King, carries for Sceptre a brush of the kind that we use to clean a closet . . . after all our subtle colour and nervous rhythm, after the faint mixed tints of Condor, what more is possible? After us the Savage God.' (*The Autobiography of W. B. Yeats*, London, Macmillan, 1955, p. 233).

13

2

ADOLPHE APPIA

FROM A New Art-Material (c. 1902)

At present, theatrical technique is about one thing only: scenic illusion. With very rare exceptions, everything is sacrificed to the pursuit of this illusion. The important development of scene-painting on vertical canvases, the parallel aligning of those canvases, the construction of the stage with the single end in view of enabling them to be handled, and the almost total dedication of the lighting to the task of showing them off to best advantage – all this leaves no doubt that someone is wanting to make us believe in the reality of the scenic picture.

But...the Actor? Is it painted canvases that determine the drama? A play without an actor is a diorama. That plastic, living, moving form . . . how much care is taken over that? Where do we place it? Ah, that's it! – the actor is a most inconvenient necessity for our scene painters; they do not exactly resent him, but they make him feel how out of place his presence is in front of their fine painting. Every bit of the painted scenery designed to accommodate the real solid form of the actor, is called 'practicable'; these are the concessions that painting is willing to make to the free human body. Let us admit for the moment that reasonable concessions have been made. Here then is the actor in front of painting generously cut out on his behalf. To enhance himself, what is there left to him? A plastic form, whatever it may be, exists only by virtue of the light. How is the actor lit? Alas, not at all; the painting has taken all the lighting for itself. Those long rows of electric lamps which run parallel to the slices of scenery, or which even run right round the stage, are designed to let us see the painting clearly. No doubt they also let us see the actor clearly, lit from all sides at once . . . But is that *Lighting*? Would a sculptor have thought of lighting in this way his bronze or marble dreams? . . .

However, if we leave aside painting for a moment and attempt really to light the actor...what happens? All the vast apparatus of the stage would suddenly lose its *raison d'être*, and the actor would suddenly find himself in excruciating emptiness, in a veritable void. What is called twilight and night lighting on our stages witnesses to that with a crudity we know.

We must therefore conclude that our scene-painting is based on a principle of immobility in contradiction with the presence of the actor, and the decorative factor which gives this away is: *the Lighting*.

It is useless to wish for movement without light, without real lighting that creates forms, and it is useless to seek to have light that creates forms if one remains under the tyranny of dead painting. This follows rigorously.

But in that case, some will say, how is the scenic illusion to be maintained?

Is this illusion then to be so cared about that anything and everything is sacrificed to it? In the presence of the actor, everyone knows that the most beautiful scenery is nothing more than an assembly of painted canvases; and if, perhaps accidentally, a particularly favourable arrangement for deceiving the spectator happens to be found, will not the following arrangement immediately destroy its effect? Now, an illusion which is not constant simply does not exist. Our eyes, tricked, do us a disservice here; and yet the first indispensable conviction we must acquire where representation is concerned is that illusion, not only does not exist on our stages, but that it is impossible and...*must* not be possible.

Yes, drama must not, any more than independent paintings or sculpture, seek to deceive the eye.

FROM How to Reform Our Staging Practices (1904)

An attempt of this kind[1] cannot fail to teach us the path to follow in order to transform our rigid and conventional staging practices into an *artistic* material, living, supple and fit to realise no matter what dramatic vision. It will even come to surprise us that we neglected for so long such an important branch of art, and abandoned it, as if unworthy of our direct attention, to people who are not artists. Our aesthetic feeling is thus positively anaesthetised where theatrical production is concerned; he who would not tolerate in his apartment an object of less than exquisite taste, finds it natural to book an expensive seat in a theatre, already ugly and built in defiance of good sense, to spend hours at a show beside which the garish prints sold at the fair are delicate works.

The procedures of staging, like other artistic procedures, are founded on forms, light and colour; now these three elements are in our control and we can in consequence arrange them in the theatre as elsewhere in an artistic fashion. Until now it has been believed that staging must achieve the highest possible degree of illusion; and it is this principle (unaesthetic though it is) which has barred our progress. I strive to show in these pages that scenic art must be based on the one reality worthy of theatre: the human body.

Translated by Richard Drain and Micheline Mabille

NOTE

1   This passage follows the discussion on staging a scene from Wagner's *Siegfried* that will be found in Part IV.

The 'new art-material' of the first (unfinished) article is, as the second suggests, what Appia believed theatre might become: a medium no longer blocking artistic expression, but giving it free scope.

Adolphe Appia (1862–1928), Swiss designer and theatre reformer. The groundwork for these ideas was fully laid in his *Music and Staging* (1899). Their aim, which he had been developing since 1888, anticipates that which Craig announced in 1905: 'The theatre has been, and should be, a medium for artists' (*The Art of the Theatre*, Edinburgh and London, T. N. Foulis, 1905, p. 11). But he differs from Craig in basing his aesthetic throughout the different phases of his thinking upon the human performer.

3

GORDON CRAIG

From Rearrangements (1915)

Inquiring into these results we find that the body of the modern Theatre is composed of strangely contradictory elements; of the organic and the inorganic hopelessly clinging together.

Regard for a moment this bunch of confusion; and first regard that side where all the stage conventions and inventions are clustered.

We find:

1　On the poet's part, an unnatural mode of speech – verse or prose.
2　On the actor's part, a natural, even colloquial mode of utterance.
3　Scenes imitating nature in paint and canvas.
4　Actors of flesh and blood.
5　Movements half natural, half artificial.
6　Light always failing in an attempt to simulate Nature's light.
7　The faces painted and disguised.
8　The facial expression always attempting to come through the paint and disguise.

Thus in 1, 2, 4, and 8 – the words, actors, their speech and facial expression are organic.

3 and 7 – the scenes and the disguised faces are inorganic.

5 and 6 – the light and movement are half one thing and half the other.

It is with this material that the modern Theatre fatuously believes it can fashion a work of art. And it is against this material that the nature of all art rebels and prevails.

Let us rearrange and change parts of this conglomeration and then see whether things are not more of a piece. And against those items which we rearrange or change we will place a sign (§), so that it will be seen at a glance.

1　The poet's work to be as it is – an unnatural mode of speech, or verse.
§2　The actor's work to be an unnatural mode of delivery.
§3　The scene to be a non-natural invention, timeless, and of no locality.
§4　Actors to be disguised beyond recognition, like the marionette.
§5　Movements conventionalised according to some system.

§6 Light frankly non-natural, disposed so as to illuminate scene and actors.

§7 Masks.

§8 Expression to be dependent on the masks and the conventional movements, both of which are dependent on the skill of the actor.

Now we find that without having to eliminate any one of the eight factors, we have been able to harmonise their conflicting purposes by altering some of them. . . .

I would propose, therefore, that we familiarise ourselves and our assistants with these seemingly new suggestions until we realise their *value*; and that where, by the addition and application of one or more of these suggestions we can increase the value of the whole Art of the Theatre, we should not be held up by an over-sensitive lack of confidence in our power to apply them, or by lack of faith in the power of the spectators to accept them.

This is one method of advancing our institution to a position which may influence the distinguished traducers of our work to reconsider their verdict that the Art of the Theatre is an *inferior* art.

Gordon Craig (1872–1966), English actor, designer, director and modern theatre pioneer, also offers in this article an alternative 'rearrangement' whereby theatre could become consistently 'organic' or natural – with idiomatic speech colloquially delivered, natural movements, the setting a facsimile of nature, perhaps with real objects, etc. But his preference for the more provocative option of the 'inorganic' is clear, and this is in line with the most notorious of all his proposals, that actors be replaced by marionettes. But Craig, initially an actor himself, backed off from this proposal afterwards – as befitted the son of a renowned actress (Ellen Terry), and an admirer of Henry Irving, his first employer. From 1897 he worked as designer and director, for Beerbohm Tree, Otto Brahm (of the Berlin *Freie Buhne*), Max Reinhardt, Eleonora Duse, and Stanislavski. At the same time he furthered his fertile ideas on theatre through his magazine *The Mask* (1908–29), and his numerous articles and books. His volume *The Art of the Theatre* (1905) and the extended *On the Art of Theatre* (1911) where the marionette is extolled, were landmarks, rapidly translated into all the major European languages.

4

F. T. MARINETTI, E. SETTIMELLI AND B. CORRA

FROM The Futurist Synthetic Theatre (1915)

Our Futurist theatre will be

Synthetic. That is, very brief. To compress into a few minutes, into a few words and gestures, innumerable situations, sensibilities, ideas, sensations, facts, and symbols.

The writers who wanted to renew the theatre (Ibsen, Maeterlinck, Andreyev, Claudel, Shaw) never thought of arriving at a true synthesis, of freeing themselves from a technique that involves prolixity, meticulous analysis, drawn-out preparation. Before the works of these authors, the audience is in the indignant attitude of a circle of bystanders who swallow their anguish and pity as they watch the slow agony of a horse that has collapsed on the pavement. The sigh of applause that finally breaks out frees the audience's stomach from all the indigestible time it has swallowed. Each act is as painful as having to wait patiently in an antichamber for the minister (*coup de théâtre*: kiss, pistol shot, verbal revelation, etc.) to receive you. All this passéist or semi-Futurist theatre, instead of synthesising fact and idea in the smallest number of words and gestures, savagely destroys the variety of place (source of dynamism and amazement), stuffs many city squares, landscapes, streets, into the sausage of a single room. For this reason this theatre is entirely static.

We are convinced that mechanically, by force of brevity, we can achieve an entirely new theatre perfectly in tune with our swift and laconic Futurist sensibility. Our acts can also be moments [*atti – attimi*] only a few seconds long. With this essential and synthetic brevity the theatre can bear and even overcome competition from the *cinema*.

Atechnical. . . . With our synthetist movement in the theatre, we want to destroy the Technique that from the Greeks until now, instead of simplifying itself, has become more and more dogmatic, stupid, logical, meticulous, pedantic, strangling. THEREFORE:

1   *It's stupid to write one hundred pages where one would do*, only because the audience through habit and infantile instinct wants to see character in a play result from a series of events, wants to fool itself into thinking that the character really exists in order to admire the beauties of Art, meanwhile refusing to acknowledge any art if the author limits himself to sketching out a few of the character's traits.

2   *It's stupid* not to rebel against the prejudice of theatricality when life itself (which consists *of actions vastly more awkward, uniform, and predictable* than those that unfold in the world of art) is for the most part *antitheatrical* and even in this offers *innumerable possibilities* for *the stage.* EVERYTHING OF ANY VALUE IS THEATRICAL.

3   *It's stupid* to pander to the primitivism of the crowd, which, in the last analysis, wants to see the bad guy lose and the good guy win.

4   *It's stupid* to worry about verisimilitude (absurd because talent and worth have little to do with it).

5   *It's stupid* to want to explain with logical minuteness everything taking place on the stage, when even in life one never grasps an event entirely in all its causes and consequences, because reality throbs around us, bombards us *with squalls of fragments of interconnected events, mortised and tenoned together, confused, mixed up, chaotic.* E.g., it's stupid to act out a contest between two persons *always* in an orderly, clear, and logical way, since in daily life we nearly always encounter mere *flashes of argument* made *momentary* by our modern experience, in a tram, a café, a railway station, which remain cinematic in our minds like fragmentary dynamic symphonies of gestures, words, lights, and sounds.

6   *It's stupid* to submit to obligatory *crescendi, prepared effects, and postponed climaxes.*

7   *It's stupid* to allow one's talent to be burdened with the weight of a technique that *anyone* (even imbeciles) *can acquire by study, practice, and patience.*

8   IT'S STUPID TO RENOUNCE THE DYNAMIC LEAP IN THE VOID OF TOTAL CREATION, BEYOND THE RANGE OF TERRITORY PREVIOUSLY EXPLORED.

Dynamic, simultaneous. That is, born of improvisation, lightninglike intuition, from suggestive and revealing actuality. We believe that a thing is valuable to the extent that it is improvised (hours, minutes, seconds), not extensively prepared (months, years, centuries).

We feel an unconquerable repugnance for desk work, a priori, that fails to respect the ambience of the theatre itself. THE GREATER NUMBER OF OUR WORKS HAVE BEEN WRITTEN IN THE THEATRE. The theatrical ambience is our inexhaustible reservoir of inspirations: the magnetic circular sensation invading our tired brains during morning rehearsal in an empty gilded theatre; an actor's intonation that suggests the possibility of constructing a cluster of paradoxical thoughts on top of it; a movement of scenery that hints at a symphony of lights; an actress's fleshiness that fills our minds with genially full-bodied notions. . . .

Autonomous, alogical, unreal. The Futurist theatrical synthesis will not be subject to logic, will pay no attention to photography; it will be *autonomous*, will resemble nothing but itself, although it will take elements from reality and combine them as its whim dictates. Above all, just as the painter and composer discover, scattered through the outside world, a narrower but more intense life, made up of colours, forms, sounds, and noises, the same is true *for the man gifted with theatrical sensibility, for whom a specialized reality exists that violently assaults his nerves*: it consists of what is called THE THEATRICAL WORLD.

THE FUTURIST THEATRE IS BORN OF THE TWO MOST VITAL CURRENTS in the Futurist sensibility, defined in the two manifestos 'The Variety Theatre' and 'Weights, Measures, and Prices of Artistic Genius', which are: (1) our frenzied passion for real, swift, elegant, complicated, cynical, muscular, fugitive, Futurist life; (2) our very modern cerebral definition of art according to which no logic, no tradition, no aesthetic, no technique, no opportunity can be imposed on the artist's natural talent; he must be preoccupied only with creating synthetic expressions of cerebral energy that have THE ABSOLUTE VALUE OF NOVELTY.

The *Futurist theatre* will be able to excite its audience, that is, make it forget the monotony of daily life, by sweeping it through *a labyrinth of sensations imprinted on the most exacerbated originality and combined in unpredictable ways.*

Every night the *Futurist theatre* will be a gymnasium to train our race's spirit to the swift, dangerous enthusiasms made necessary by this Futurist year.

CONCLUSIONS

1 TOTALLY ABOLISH THE TECHNIQUE THAT IS KILLING THE PASSÉIST THEATRE.

2 DRAMATIZE ALL THE DISCOVERIES (no matter how unlikely, weird, and antitheatrical) THAT OUR TALENT IS DISCOVERING IN THE SUBCONSCIOUS, IN ILL-DEFINED FORCES, IN PURE ABSTRACTION, IN THE PURELY CEREBRAL, THE PURE-LY FANTASTIC, IN RECORD-SETTING AND BODY-MADNESS. (E.g., *Vengono*, F. T. Marinetti's first drama of objects,[1] a new vein of theatrical sensibility discovered by Futurism.)

3 SYMPHONIZE THE AUDIENCE'S SENSIBILITY BY EXPLORING IT, STIRRING UP ITS LAZIEST LAYERS WITH EVERY MEANS POSSIBLE; ELIMINATE THE PRECONCEPTION OF THE FOOTLIGHTS BY THROWING NETS OF SENSATION BETWEEN STAGE AND AUDIENCE; THE STAGE ACTION WILL INVADE THE ORCHESTRA SEATS, THE AUDIENCE.

4 FRATERNIZE WARMLY WITH THE ACTORS WHO ARE AMONG THE FEW THINKERS WHO FLEE FROM EVERY DEFORMING CULTURAL ENTERPRISE.

5   ABOLISH THE FARCE, THE VAUDEVILLE, THE SKETCH, THE COMEDY, THE SERIOUS
     DRAMA, AND THE TRAGEDY, AND CREATE IN THEIR PLACE THE MANY FORMS OF
     FUTURIST THEATRE, SUCH AS: LINES WRITTEN IN FREE WORDS, SIMULTANEITY,
     COMPENETRATION, THE SHORT, ACTED-OUT POEM, THE DRAMATISED SENSATION,
     COMIC DIALOGUE, THE NEGATIVE ACT, THE REECHOING LINE, 'EXTRALOGICAL'
     DISCUSSION, SYNTHETIC DEFORMATION, THE SCIENTIFIC OUTBURST THAT CLEARS
     THE AIR.

6   THROUGH UNBROKEN CONTACT, CREATE BETWEEN US AND THE CROWD A CUR-
     RENT OF CONFIDENCE RATHER THAN RESPECTFULNESS, IN ORDER TO INSTILL IN
     OUR AUDIENCES THE DYNAMIC VIVACITY OF A NEW FUTURIST THEATRICALITY.

These are the *first* words on the theatre. Our first eleven theatrical
syntheses (by Marinetti, Settimelli, Bruno Corra, R. Chiti, Balilla
Pratella) were victoriously imposed on crowded theatres in Ancona,
Bologna, Padua, Naples, Venice, Verona, Florence, and Rome, by Ettore
Berti, Zoncada, and Petrolini. In Milan we shall soon have the great metal
building, enlivened by all the electromechanical inventions that alone will
permit us to realize our most free conceptions on the stage.

Translated by R. W. Flint

NOTE

1   *They are Coming.* The objects are principally a table and a number of chairs,
     arranged and rearranged by two servants at the sometimes nonsensical orders
     of a major-domo for guests who fail to arrive; and which finally make their own
     exit. A translation of the two-page text, which foreshadows the drama of objects
     practised by Beckett and Ionesco and particularly Ionesco's *The Chairs*, is in
     Futurist Performance by Michael Kirby (New York, Dutton, 1971).

Filippo Tomasso Marinetti (1876–1944), Italian poet, playwright and pro-
moter of the Futurist cause, produced manifestos from 1909 to 1921. The
influence of Jarry has been argued (by R. W. Flint in *Marinetti: Selected
Writings*, London, Secker & Warburg, 1972). His first play, *Il re baldoria*, was
written in 1905 and staged in France in 1909. A collection of his plays was
published in 1920 (*Elettricita sessuale*). From 1914, he was a friend of
Mussolini and fascist enthusiast. It is hard to argue any inherent connection
between futurism and fascism, however, since the Russian futurists
embraced the soviet revolution with equal enthusiasm. Bruno Corra, author
of *Per l'arte nuova della nuova Italia* (1918), and Emilio Settimelli both wrote
futurist sketches, and both signed the Manifesto of Futurist Cinema (1916).
Corra and his brother pioneered the technique of painting directly on film in
1910. Settimelli appeared in one of the lost futurist films, *Vita Futurista*, and
wrote *Marinetti, Man and Artist* (1921).

5

ENRICO PRAMPOLINI

FROM Futurist Scenography (1915)

To us, scenography is a monstrous thing. Today's scenographers, sterile whitewashers, still prowl around the dusty and stinking corners of classical architecture. We must rebel and assert ourselves and say to our poet and musician friends: this action demands this stage rather than that one.

Let us be artists too, and no longer merely executors. Let us create the stage, give life to the text with all the evocative power of our art. It is natural that we need plays suited to our sensibility, which imply a more intense and synthetic conception in the scenic development of subjects.

Let's renovate the stage. The absolutely new character that our innovation will give the theatre is *the abolition of the painted stage.* The stage will no longer be a coloured backdrop but a *colourless electromechanical architecture, powerfully vitalised by chromatic emanations from a luminous source,* produced by electric reflectors with multicoloured panes of glass, arranged, coordinated analogically with the psyche of each scenic action.

With the luminous irradiations of these beams, of these planes of coloured lights, the dynamic combinations will give marvellous results of mutual permeation, of intersection of lights and shadows. From these will arise vacant abandonments, exultant, luminous corporalities.

These assemblages, these unreal shocks, this exuberance of sensations combined with dynamic stage architecture that will move, unleashing metallic arms, knocking over plastic planes, amidst an essentially new modern noise, will augment the vital intensity of the scenic action.

On a stage illuminated in such a way, the actors will gain unexpected dynamic effects that are neglected or very seldom employed in today's theatres, mostly because of the ancient prejudice that one must imitate, represent reality.

And with what purpose?

Perhaps scenographers believe it is absolutely necessary to represent this reality? Idiots! Don't you understand that your efforts, your useless realistic preoccupations have no effect other than that of diminishing the intensity and emotional content, which can be attained precisely through the interpretive equivalents of these realities, i.e., abstractions?

Let's create the stage. In the above lines we have upheld the idea of a *dynamic stage* as opposed to the static stage of another time; with the fundamental principles that we shall set forth, we intend not only to carry the stage to its most advanced expression but also to attribute to it the essential values that belong to it and that no one has thought of giving it until now.

Translated from the Italian by Victoria Nes Kirby

Enrico Prampolini (1894–1956), Italian painter and sculptor, considered the most important of the second generation of futurists. An admirer of Balla and Boccioni, he joined forces with them in 1912, and exhibited in the large 1914 futurist exhibition in Rome. He believed with Balla that the concept of art overrode the boundaries between the different arts; and with Boccioni that it was linked with cultural action. He wanted to abolish all its psychological, literary and subjective elements, to arrive at an art work that was concrete and autonomous. In 1923 he was one of those who signed the Futurist Machine Art Manifesto, and carried its aims into theatre by replacing the actor with mechanised scenery, lifts, phonographs and other elements. Shows were presented in Paris in 1925 and 1927. In the 1930s he became interested in exploiting the biological presence of matter and its autonomous chemical or other changes. There is some parallel here with Kurt Schwitters' ideas for a 'Merz-Theatre': this was to involve 'solid, liquid and gaseous bodies, such as white wall, man, barbed wire entanglement, blue distance . . .'. (See Henning Rischbieter's *Art and the Stage in the Twentieth Century*, Greenwich, Connecticut, New York Graphic Society, 1968, p. 171, or the collection, Kurt Schwitters, *Poems Performances Pieces Proses Plays Poetics*, Philadelphia, Temple University Press, 1993).

6

TRISTAN TZARA

Speech from *The First Celestial Adventure of Mr Antipyrine* (1916)

TRISTAN TZARA: Dada is our intensity; it fixes bayonets without consequence the German baby's Sumatran head; Dada is art without slippers or parallel; it is against and for unity and decidedly against the future; we know wisely enough that our brains will turn into comfortable cushions that our anti-dogmatism is as narrow as a petty official that we are not free and that we shout freedom. Severe necessity without discipline or morals and spit on humanity. Dada remains within the European frame of weaknesses, it's shit all the same, but to decorate the zoo-garden of art from now on we want to shit in various colours, of all the flags on the consulates clo clo bong heeho aho heeho aho We are circus managers and whistle in the winds of fairs, among convents prostitutions theatres realities feelings restaurants Hoho-hohihihioho Bang Bang. We declare that the motor car is a sentiment that has molly-coddled us enough with its dragging abstractions, and transat-lantic liners and noises and ideas. However we externalise the facile we seek the central essence and we're glad we can hide it; we don't want to count the windows of the marvellous elite because Dada exists for no-one, and we want everyone to understand that is Dada's balcony, believe me – from which you can hear military machines and whizz down through the air like a seraph into the sea of people to take a piss and understand the parable or the parabola Dada isn't madness – nor wisdom – nor irony look at me, dear bourgeois.

Art was a game . . . art isn't serious, I assure you, and if we show the South in order to say learnedly: negro art without humanity it's to give you pleasure, good listeners, I love you so, I love you so, I assure you I adore you

The Secret of the *Handkerchief of Clouds* (1925)

Handkerchief of Clouds is an ironic tragedy or a tragic farce in fifteen short acts, each separated by a commentary. The action, which draws on the world of the fiction serial and the cinema, takes place on a platform in the middle of the stage. The play is performed without break from beginning to end. 'It is the interval that has killed off the theatre', says one of the play's commentators. These commentaries, at first of no great significance, develop little by little, and by the end have taken on the dimensions of another play, parallel to that acted on the stage platform.

There are only three characters who keep their identity throughout the whole play. The six commentators play seventeen different roles. They make up and change costumes on stage. Their names are the same on stage as they are in life. Otherwise the whole play is based on the fiction of theatre. I do not want to hide from the audience that what they are seeing is theatre. That is also why Miss Loïe Fuller's[1] lighting crew are on stage with their reflectors, and why the stage-hand lets down the scenery in full view of everyone. The settings are not there to give the illusion of a reality, but to establish where the action is taking place. An on-screen enlargement of a picture postcard goes with each act.

I shall not recount the subject of the play, because it is more complicated than a film serial.

Translated by Richard Drain and Micheline Mabille

NOTE

1 See Part IV, ch. 61.

Tristan Tzara (1896–1963), Romanian writer, moved to Zurich in 1915; a year later, barely 20, he and a group of friends founded Dada. His play, *The First Celestial Adventure of Mr Antipyrine*, was the first work to be printed under Dada's aegis. *Antipyrine*: a drug against fever, which Tzara then happened to be taking. Meanwhile Europe's fever was the war. Tzara recalled: 'by 1916–17, the war seemed to have installed itself for good. . . . All the forms of civilisation that are called modern, and even its basis, logic and reason, aroused disgust' (radio interview, May 1950). The revolt against logic and language are obvious in the speech-cum-manifesto above. The mention of the South and of negro art reflects Tzara's enthusiasm for the arts of Africa and Polynesia (as distinct from 'the forms of civilisation that are called modern'). He used their musical rhythms in his writing. It is unlikely that any slur was intended by his phrase 'without humanity'. Rather the reverse: humanity at the time was demonstrating its values by slaughtering itself on battlefields. Tzara's play was staged in full when he moved to Paris in 1920, along with its sequel. *Handkerchief of Clouds* was written a year after he had pronounced in an article 'The End of Dada', and was accounted by Aragon 'the most remarkable dramatic image of modern art' (*Les Collages*, 1965). After Dada, Tzara took the short step onwards to surrealism.

7

GUILLAUME APOLLINAIRE

FROM Prologue to *The Breasts of Tiresias* (1917)

THE DIRECTOR OF THE THEATRE COMPANY:
So here I am back again amongst you
Back with my same enthusiastic troupe
And with a stage as well
But sadly I find still
Theatrical art without integrity or grandeur
Such that killed off long evenings before the war
A slandering and pernicious art
Which showed the sin not the redeemer. . . .

IT IS HIGH TIME TO LIGHT THE STARS AGAIN[1]
. . . So here I am back amongst you

Don't get impatient, actors

Wait for it audience don't be impatient

I bring you a play that aims to reform people's ways
It's about children in a family setting
It's a domestic subject
That's why it's treated in a colloquial fashion
The actors aren't going to put on some spine-chilling tone
They'll appeal quite simply to your common sense
And above all be concerned to entertain you
So you'll be readily prepared to profit
From all the teachings that the play contains
And the earth gleam everywhere with the gazing eyes
                              of new-born babes
Till they outnumber even the glittering stars

Listen you people of France to the lesson of war
And make babies you that hardly make any more

We're attempting here to infuse the theatre with a new spirit
A joy a sensuousness an integrity
To replace this more-than-a-century-old pessimism
Which is distinctly ancient for something so boring
The play's been designed for an old-style stage
Because who would have built us a new theatre
A circular theatre with two stages
One in the middle the other forming a ring
Around the audience to give full scope
To the exercise of our modern theatrical art
Which often with no apparent link
Just as in life marries together
Sounds gestures colours cries noises
Music dance acrobatics poetry painting
Choruses actions and multiple settings

You'll find here actions
Added on to the main drama embellishing it
Switches of tone from the touching to the burlesque
And a moderate use of the unbelievable
Along with actors in chorus style or otherwise
Who aren't necessarily samples of humanity
But of the whole universe
For theatre must not be an art of *trompe l'œil*[2]

It's quite all right for the dramatist to make use
Of all the mirages he has available
Like Morgana the enchantress on Mount Gibel
And to make crowds or lifeless objects speak
If he wants
And to take no more count of time
Than he does of space

His universe is his play
And in it he is god the creator
Who disposes at his pleasure
Sounds gestures moves volumes colours
Not with the aim of simply
Photographing a so-called slice of life
But to bring rising up in all its truth
Life itself
For the play must be a complete universe
With its creator
That's to say nature itself
And not only

The representation of a little bit
Of what surrounds us or once did

Excuse me friends my troupe of actors

Excuse me dear audience
For having talked to you at some length
It's so long since I was last with you

But over there there's still a fierce blaze
Where they're shooting down the stars in smoke
And those who light them again ask you
To raise yourselves up to those sublime fires
And flame too

Oh audience
Be the unquenchable torch of the new fire

Translated by Richard Drain and Micheline Mabille

NOTES

1 The stars have been put out, the Director has explained, by the gunfire of the war from which he has come back.
2 Cf. Jarry, p. 11 and Appia, p. 14. *Trompe l'œil* suggests to the French not simply painting that 'deceives the eye', but analogous forms of bluff, lies and window dressing.

Guillaume Apollinaire (1880–1918), French poet and playwright, friend and admirer of Alfred Jarry, began writing *The Breasts of Tiresias* in the year they first met, 1903, but completed it only much later, during the war (1917), shortly before he was killed in action. Jarry's influence shows in its spirited anti-realism – for which Apollinaire coined the term 'surrealist'. For Apollinaire's view of the theatre world, see his burlesque account in the title story of *The Poet Assassinated*, chapter 11, where the protagonist 'fearlessly walked into the hall where the Theatres, their acolytes, hired killers, and lackeys were gathered'.

8

WALTER HASENCLEVER

The Task of Drama (1920)

This play[1] has no other aim than to bind together the world of the living and the dead. The life and death of each human being is as incomprehensible as the world itself: starting from this supposition, the author is not concerned with the notion that by the end of the play the audience should understand the happenings on stage. Though elsewhere certitude reigns, the special attitude of the human spirit towards questions of being may here stir up opposition. The end of art is not to induce agreement, but to shake foundations.

More than ever, the task of the dramatist who grasps the world in its mobile state must be to win recognition on stage for the changed conception of its nature. The laws handed down from centuries of tradition are shattered. The attempts of chemistry to convert all the elements back into one are nearer to alchemy than public opinion wishes to admit. The collapse in physics of concepts of space and time, of energy and matter, and the conception in mathematics of the fourth coordinate, confirm the teaching of the occult sciences. The results of medical research into the phenomena of mediums and somnambulism make the day seem not too distant when a changed physical world will correspond to a changed mental world. Astrology and the occult are on the way to becoming scientifically proved. We stand on the threshold of the fourth dimension.

The end of Newton in mechanics means the end of Aristotle in drama. If it is true that within the flux of space a straight line cannot be conceived; if each solid body manifests itself not as absolute but only as relative: then the same discovery holds good too in the realm of tragedy. For his part, the dramatist too stands obliged to admit the relativity of events; at every point of the action he must reveal its link with the total action.

This play attempts to create this new dimension on stage. The single human being has no destiny; human destiny is the destiny of all. As if between words and gesture, light and shadow, space and time, there unfolds on an invisible trajectory the action of human spirits intertwined in a common life; it is the tragic world of spirits assembled in a magic spectacle.

The poet has the right to invent; he may create the word and mould the language in order to achieve an ultimate concentration; rhythm to him is

31

what the formula is to the mathematician. This play is written in rhythm from the first word to the last. The stage directions belong to the text as the speeches belong with the stage directions; both are only part of the whole; this is spoken, that is played. To liken this to film or mime would be as inadequate as to take Shakespeare for a spiritualist because he makes appear the ghost of Hamlet's father. Restraint is not poverty of ideas.

What happens in this play? A murdered being rises from the grave, a human being in the profoundest sense of the word, an unredeemed and imperfect being, a debtor in the world's huge book of defaulters. If he had perfected his life, he could not have died by the knife; his guilt was that he could die. He walks laden with the head his murderer presents to him, his own, to expiate the crime in place of the murderer, a double who walks the world until he finds eternal rest. The play begins 'I have killed.' And ends, 'I love.'

May the spectator sitting in the theatre try to transmute himself into the play. May he feel on his own body the magic chain of blood and madness, love, hate, violence and hunger, domination, money and deceit. May he sense at the sight of these sufferings the curse of birth, the despair of death. May he lose the logic of his century; may he see into the human heart.

Translated by Richard Drain and Anna Millan

NOTE

1 *Humanity* (1918). For the play in translation, see Walter Sokel's *Anthology of German Expressionist Drama*, Ithaca, NY, Anchor, 1963.

Walter Hasenclever (1890–1940), German expressionist playwright and poet. His play *The Son* (written 1914, staged 1916), seized the public imagination as an onslaught against patriarchal authority, was played throughout Germany, and brought expressionist drama, whose prototype it is, to a wide audience. Meanwhile Hasenclever had volunteered for military service, was wounded, and joined the growing opposition to the war. Part-Jewish, he continued to write plays through the 1920s and early 1930s, but fled Germany when the Nazis came to power in 1933. His fate was to be interned by the French in 1939, and when Germany invaded France he committed suicide.

9

VALESKA GERT

From I am a Witch (1950)

Valeska Gert is writing here of her work in the 1920s and 1930s.

I performed theatre, I longed for the dance; I danced, I longed for the theatre. I was in conflict until the idea occurred to me to combine them: I wanted to dance human characters. I invented an intricate fabric, one of whose strands was modern dance-pantomime; another strand was abstract dance; other strands were satiric dances, dances to sounds, expressionistic dances. I exploded a bundle of stimuli on the world; other dancers would make a whole programme out of a single strand, but for me they were loud, whizzing little rockets, shooting around the world.

My dances were short and clear. I did no variations as other dancers do. For me the only important things were attack, tragic or comic climax, subsidence, nothing more. Because I didn't like solid citizens, I danced those whom they despised – whores, procuresses, down-and-outers, and degenerates.

. . . So far, streetwalkers had not been portrayed on the dance stage. People were too noble, though later it became an epidemic. But other dancers only endorsed the society I condemned. I called the character *Canaille*;[1] without my being aware of it, it was the first socially critical dance-pantomime.

I wiggle my hips provocatively, hoist the black, very short skirt, and for an instant show white flesh above long, black stockings, pink garters, and high-heeled shoes (a scandal at a time when dancers, if they weren't dancing ballet, hopped across the stage barefoot). I am an ultra-refined whore. My movements are sleek and voluptuous. My white face is almost entirely covered by strands of black hair falling over my forehead. I bow my head deeply; my chin disappears up to the garish red mouth in a red collar which hangs loosely round my neck. Then I bend my knees slowly, spread my legs wide and sink down. In a sudden spasm, as if bit by a tarantula, I twitch upwards. I sway back and forth. Then my body relaxes, the spasm dissipates, the jerking becomes ever gentler, ever feebler, the intervals longer, the excitement ebbs away, one last twitch, and I'm down to earth again. What's been happening to me? I've been exploited. My body's been abused because

33

I need money. Wretched world! I spit one disdainful step to the right and one to the left; then I shuffle off.

I was dancing coitus, but I "alienated" it, as people say nowadays. Art is always an alienation of reality. My *Procuress* was the whore grown old, capable of doing business only with the bodies of the young. Still, she spurted keen venomous lust, clutched her fat belly, staggered in drunkenness, and mumbling, begged for money, all together.

Brecht invited me to Munich. He presented an evening at the Kammerspiele: Ringelnatz[2] recited, glass in hand; Brecht played the lute and recited his ballads. I danced *Canaille* to organ music. . . . At the Romanesque Café there was a lot of talk about modern dance. One scrawny girl with a pockmarked face and sharply jutting cheekbones said, "We want the 'outlandish' in dance." That's what I wanted too. What's outlandish? Birth, love, death. Nobody had previously dared to portray them barefaced and truthfully. I wanted to do it.

Translated by Laurence Senelick

NOTES

1   Scum.
2   Joachim Ringelnatz wrote poems about the violent and seamy sides of the life he knew as a sailor.

Valeska Gert (1892–1978), German cabaret dancer, made her first stage appearance in 1916 in Berlin. She performed in the mixed media evenings of the Dadaist group, in Kokoschka's expressionist play *Hiob* (1918), and Toller's *Transfiguration* (1919). In the inter-war years she danced often to an accompaniment of 'concrete music', a collage of recorded sounds involving sharp changes of tempo. *Izvestia* commented: 'The city is the source of her social fantasy . . . . The fantastic shapes of procuresses, drug addicts and cast-offs of society distort themselves in terrifying forms before the deeply stricken audience. The entire century of capitalism dances in her dances' (see Ann Teresa de Keersmaeker, 'Valeska Gert', *Drama Review*, vol. 25, no. 3, Fall 1981, p. 55). She worked in various cabarets, including her own, toured Europe and Soviet Russia, and acted in films, playing Mrs Peachum in Pabst's *The Threepenny Opera*. She has been credited with inventing grotesque dance-pantomime, and seen as a precursor of Pina Bausch. For a further statement on her work, see her piece 'Dancing' in *Schrifttanz: a view of German dance in the Weimar Republic*, eds Valerie Preston Dunlop and Susanne Lahusen, London, Dance Books, 1990, pp. 13–16.

10

STANISLAS IGNACY WITKIEWICZ

FROM On a New Type of Play (1920)

Theatre, like poetry, is a *composite art*, but it is made up of even more elements not intrinsic to it; therefore, it is much more difficult to imagine Pure Form on the stage, essentially independent, in its final result, of the content of human action.

Yet it is not perhaps entirely impossible.

. . . The idea is to make it possible *to deform either life or the world of fantasy with complete freedom so as to create a whole whose meaning would be defined only by its purely scenic internal construction, and not by the demands of consistent psychology and action according to assumptions from real life.* . . .

The theatre of today impresses us as being something hopelessly bottled up which can only be released by introducing what we have called *fantastic psychology and action*. The psychology of the characters and their actions should only be the pretext for a pure progression of events: therefore, what is essential is that the need for a psychology of the characters and their actions to be consistent and lifelike should not become a bugbear imposing its particular construction on the play. We have had enough wretched logic about characters and enough psychological "truth" – already it seems to be coming out of our ears. Who cares what goes on at 38 Wspólna Street, Apartment 10, or in the castle in the fairy tale, or in past times? In the theatre we want to be in an entirely new world in which the fantastic psychology of characters who are completely implausible in real life, not only in their positive actions but also *in their errors*, and who are perhaps completely unlike people in real life, produces events which by their bizarre interrelationships create a performance in time not limited by any logic except the logic of the form itself of that performance. What is required is that we accept as inevitable a particular movement of a character, a particular phrase having a realistic or only a formal meaning, a particular change of lighting or décor, a particular musical accompaniment, just as we accept as inevitable a particular part of a composition on a canvas or a sequence of chords in a musical work. We must also take into account the fact that such characters' thoughts and feelings are completely unfettered and that they react with complete freedom to any and all events, even though there is no justification for any of this. Still, these elements would have to be suggested on the same level of formal necessity as all the other elements of performance on the stage mentioned above. Of course, the public would have to be won over to this fantastic psychology, as with the square leg in the painting by Picasso. The public has already laughed at the deformed shapes on the canvases of contemporary masters; now they will also have to laugh at the thoughts and actions of characters on the stage, since for the time being these cannot be completely explained. We believe that this problem can be resolved in exactly the same way as it has been in contemporary painting and music: by understanding the essence of art in general and by growing accustomed to it. Just as those who have finally understood Pure Form in painting can no longer even look at other kinds of painting and cannot help understanding correctly paintings which they laughed at before as incomprehensible, so those who become used to the theatre we are proposing will not be able to stand any of the productions of today, whether realistic or heavily symbolic. . . .

Of course, even assuming that a certain segment of the public interested in serious artistic experiences will come to demand plays written in the style described above, such plays would still have to result from a *genuine creative necessity* felt by an author writing for the stage. If such a work were only a kind of *schematic nonsense*, devised in cold blood, artificially, without real need, it would probably arouse nothing but laughter, like those paintings with a bizarre form of subject matter which are created by those who do not suffer from a real "insatiable pursuit of new forms," but who manufacture them for commercial reasons or *pour épater les bourgeois*. Just as the birth of a new form, pure and abstract, without a direct religious basis, took place only through deforming our vision of the external world, so the birth of Pure Form in the theatre is also possible only through deforming human psychology and action.

We can imagine such a play as having complete freedom with respect to absolutely everything from the point of view of real life, and yet being extraordinarily closely knit and highly wrought in the way the action is tied together. The task would be to fill several hours on the stage with a performance possessing its own internal, formal logic, independent of anything in "real life." An invented, *not created*, example of such a work can only make our theory appear ridiculous, and, from a certain point of view, even absurd (for some, even infuriating or, to put it bluntly, *idiotic*), but let us try.

Three characters dressed in red come on stage and bow to no one in particular. One of them recites a poem (it should create a feeling of urgent necessity at this very moment). A kindly old man enters leading a cat on a string. So far everything has taken place against a background of a black screen. The screen draws apart, and an Italian landscape becomes visible.

Organ music is heard. The old man talks with the other characters, and what they say should be in keeping with what has gone before. A glass falls off the table. All of them fall on their knees and weep. The old man changes from a kindly man into a ferocious "butcher" and murders a little girl who has just crawled in from the left. At this very moment a handsome young man runs in and thanks the old man for murdering the girl, at which point the characters in red sing and dance. Then the young man weeps over the body of the little girl and says very amusing things, whereupon the old man becomes once again kindly and good-natured and laughs to himself in a corner, uttering sublime and limpid phrases. The choice of costumes is completely open: period or fantastic – there may be music during some parts of the performance. In other words, an insane asylum? Or rather a madman's brain on the stage? Perhaps so, but we maintain that, *if the play is seriously written and appropriately produced*, this method can *create works of previously unsuspected beauty*; whether it be drama, tragedy, farce, or the grotesque, all in a uniform style and unlike anything which previously existed.

Translated by Daniel Gerould and C. S. Durer

Stanislas Ignacy Witkiewicz (1885–1939), Polish playwright, novelist, painter, art critic and essayist, and leading exponent of 'catastrophism' in Polish literature. Educated at home in an artistic milieu, he hand-printed his first volume of plays at the age of 8. Service in the Tzar's army at the outbreak of war (Poland was under Russian rule) took him to Moscow, where he encountered paintings of Picasso, to which he refers here. Returning to Poland he associated with a group of artists known as the Formists, and developed his own theory of 'Pure Form'. He began too to write a series of extraordinary plays, which were received with a good deal of hostility. He set up with friends the Formist Theatre in Zakopane, which lasted from 1925 to 1927. In Britain his work was long ignored, and many encountered it for the first time in Kantor's revelatory production of *The Water Hen*, devised in Krakow in 1967 and later toured to Edinburgh.

11

IVAN GOLL

Preface to *Methusalem* or *The Eternal Bourgeois* (1922)

Aristophanes, Plautus, Molière, had an easy time of it; they got their best effects by the simplest means in the world: beatings. We have lost this sort of naïveté. The clown in the circus and Charlie Chaplin in the cinema still hand out kicks and punches, etc., but these are the points where the audience laughs least. Lack of primitive naïveté? Or is our more refined ethos to blame? This is certainly the case: but is the plebs also so refined? Even in army barracks physical punishment is frowned upon: this was not the case in the times of Aristophanes and Molière. And besides, modern man is now-a-days much more liable to have a gun than a stick. But a gun-shot is not so funny as a simple beating.

So the modern satirist must look for new stimuli. These he has found in Surrealism and Alogic. Surrealism is the most forceful negation of realism. Surface reality is stripped away to reveal the Truth of Being. 'Masks': crude, grotesque, like the emotions they express. No more 'heroes', just people, no more characters, just naked instincts. Quite naked. To know an insect you must dissect it. The dramatist is research-scientist, politician and legislator; as surrealist he reports on these things from a distant realm of truth. These things he learns by listening at the impenetrable walls of the world.

Alogic is to-day the most intellectual form of humour, and therefore the best weapon against the empty clichés which dominate all our lives. Almost invariably the average man opens his mouth only to set his tongue, not his brain, in motion. What is the point of talking so much and taking it all so seriously? Moreover the average man is so sensitive that he takes any highly flavoured word for an insult and will throw death into the scales to avenge it. Dramatic alogic must ridicule all our banalities of language, exposing the basic sophistry of mathematical logic and even dialects. At the same time alogic will serve to demonstrate the multi-hued spectrum of the human brain, which can think one thing and say another and leap with mercurial speed from one idea to another without the slightest ostensibly logical connection.

But to avoid being a moaner, a pacifist and Salvation Army type, the author must perform a few somersaults, that you all may become as little children once more. For what is he after: to present you with dolls, to teach you to play, and then to scatter the sawdust from the broken dolls to the four winds again.

Plot of the drama? Events are so powerful in themselves that they contain their own intrinsic drive. A man is run over: an experience hurled hard and irrevocable into the stream of life. Why is only the death of man called tragic? A conversation five sentences long with an unknown woman can well become far more tragic for you in eternity. Drama should be without beginning or end, like everything else here on earth. But sometime it has an end – why? No, life goes on, everyone knows that. The drama stops because you have tired, grown old in a single hour, and because truth, the most potent poison for the human heart, may only be swallowed in very small doses.

Berlin 1922

Translated by J. M. Ritchie

This piece prefaces a play whose protagonist, Methusalem, 'the original bourgeois', is a worthy descendant of Jarry's Ubu, transported to the age of cinematic montage and harsh political struggle.

Ivan Goll (1891–1950), from Lorraine, was 'by fate a Jew, born by chance a Frenchman, made by the whim of a rubber stamp a German'. He made the best of his borderland background by writing in both German and French, and fusing in his work expressionism and surrealism. Goll was a warm admirer of Apollinaire, and his dark satire is propelled by an exuberant inventiveness. The ideas expressed here are a development of those put forward in his 1918 preface 'Two Superdramas' (included in Walter Sokel's *Anthology of German Expressionist Drama*, Ithaca, NY, Anchor, 1963), where he calls for the magnification of reality, denatured masks, 'oversized ears, white eyes, stilts' – the grotesque enlisted to disturb 'reasonable attitudes'. 'It is not the object of art to make life comfortable for the fat bourgeois.'

12

EL LISSITZKY

FROM The Painter on the Stage Progresses Towards Architecture (1922)

A great store of creative energy had accumulated which could not be released in architecture because there was no building. This energy found its release in the theatre. Originally the painters found satisfaction in the theatre because it afforded opportunities for painting decorative canvases on a large scale and having them enriched by the effects of artificial light. Examples were the stage settings of Lentulov, Fedotov, and others, but this did not satisfy them for long. Soon the painters themselves began, in accordance with the evolution of painting, to push forward three-dimensional, spatial ideas of decoration. The painter on the stage progressed toward architecture. . .

The basic principles of the artists in creating the décor were as follows:
Firstly: the scenic, acrobatic movements of the actors modify the apparatus of the play.
Secondly: the apparatus, which is itself modified as a result of its mechanical construction, conditions the movements of the actors which are deduced from this.
Thirdly: these factors simultaneously give to the whole structure the illusion of reality.
An attempt was made to transfer the theatre from its enclosed space out into the street. In Petersburg and other towns the architectural features of the town were supplemented by means of specially erected buildings and used for the magnificent staging of open-air plays, which were attended by thousands upon thousands of people.

Translated by Michael Bullock

El Lissitzky (1890–1941), Russian architect, artist and art critic, co-founder of constructivism. 'There was no building' because the Soviet state, still fighting for survival, continued to be in financial crisis. Architecture's loss was theatre's gain, and constructivism strongly affected Soviet theatre design in the 1920s, where it provided a kind of mobile scenic gymnasium for the new athletic modes of performance developed by Meyerhold, Eisenstein and Radlov, as outlined in the next piece and by Eisenstein in Part II. Constructivist principles included the functional use of modern materials, the discarding of ornament, and a concern for structural efficiency and architectural engineering, and the geometric forms that were natural to these. Examples of Constructivist designs by Lissitzky and Tatlin can be found in Henning Rischbieter's *Art and the Stage in the Twentieth Century* (Greenwich, Connecticut, New York Graphic Society, 1968), and many examples of Constructivist work are discussed and illustrated in Nancy van Norman Baer's *Theatre in Revolution: Russian Avant-Garde Stage Design 1913–1935* (London, Thames & Hudson, 1991). For further writings of the Constructivists, see *The Tradition of Constructivism*, a valuable collection of key texts edited by Stephen Bann (New York, Viking Penguin, 1974), which includes writing by Lissitzky.

13

SERGEI RADLOV

FROM On the Pure Elements of the Actor's Art (1923)

After the naively grave assertions that in the theatre the main thing is the innermost thought of the author,

the naively thoughtless pretensions of the designer and the naively monarchical encroachments of the director,

all at once somehow it became clear that the main thing in theatre always was, is and will be –

THE ACTOR

It is striking that people of the most diverse directions and factions arrived simultaneously at this sensation; that this particular truth, like a cork exploded from a bottle, instantly struck a universal consciousness; that it became suddenly, *a priori*, an acknowledged axiom. It seems that the stormy seven years 1914–1921 raised anew a heroic human being, a maker of history, to an eminence long forfeited by him, and we felt the main value of theatre in the physical contemplation of a person laying bare before us the artistically-ordered nature of his being.

So far, everything is clear, lofty and excellent. But isn't it time to consider what constitutes the sphere of powers, rights, and responsibilities of the actor? What is his art? What does it express, how does it express, and for whom?

. . . We had considered the art of transformation as the chief and most sacred responsibility of the actor. To stop resembling himself (that is, to conceal, to dissemble, to depersonalise the material of his art), to express something other, strange, not like himself – seemed his principal aim. In the face of this, the spectator became somewhat like the stupid birds from the unfortunate old anecdote, who began pecking painted grapes.

Unhappy theatre art! Even painting finally freed itself from the absurd demand to deceive viewers. From the sonnet, after all, or the octave, it seems no one ever demanded that they resemble anything but themselves. Even composers only now and then sought to give the illusion of sea surf, of the beloved's voice, and the creak of a wagon. Only theatre must for some reason without fail deceive and not dare to be itself.

However, even here besides, in the most highly developed forms of theatrical art – operatic singing and ballet – we are seeing an obvious weakening of the desire to "transform" and to imitate man. A ballerina dances, in general, quite abstractly, not troubling herself that she is portraying a swan, a flower, or a woman, concretely studying only her own body and the possibilities concealed in it. Operatic singing frequently has nothing to do with likeness to human speech.

> *The further goes the development of a given branch of human, acting mastery,*
>
> *the greater the number of beautiful forms in sound and body arising and crystallizing in it,*
>
> *the more grows with every step, as an onerous and tiresome burden, the problem of representation of a concrete, real human being.*
>
> *Let the actor endlessly complicate and enrich the visual and oral forms created by him, in order to reflect with their help the most intricate and subtle temporal and spatial forms of our disposition,*
>
> *and then he himself will refuse the dubious and dismal joy of being able to imitate a drunken, amorous, angry, lisping and hiccuping man. . . .*

But of just what, more precisely, might this abstract art consist? Here I must set down in words – necessarily vague, and inexpressive – the principal functions of the new actor.

Movement of his body evokes in the spectator first of all spatial sensations. On his mastery depends the creation in the viewer of the most concrete feeling of the three-dimensionality of this space. A cube of air surrounding a human body begins to live, being cut by the lines of his movements. These lines, temporarily extended, are perceived by our memory as existing in the present. Imagine that you are watching a man who at dusk took a torch in his hands and is rapidly moving it through the air. You see circles, figure-eights, ellipses, but are not able to determine where, at any given moment, the hand is holding the light. So, too, the actor carves in space the various, simplest forms, living in the air. Using this, and training his body in a given direction, he will create before us a performance of circles, undulating lines, diamonds and every possible sort of angular form. Constructivist movements and the visual richness of them amplify the demands we make on the new actor's body. And through movement, we evoke even temporal sensations. To replace a spatial problem with a temporal, and to let not the ear but the eye of the spectator feel the flow of time, to plunge him into temporal emotion, is an undertaking of fantastic difficulty. Decelerations, accelerations, repetitions of movements, violent changes in speed achieve this.

But these temporal sensations, of course, are created far more easily through sound. Not only by the sound of the voice, but also by the tread of feet, by the clatter of objects in the actor's hands, he lets us listen to the passing of time. A thing is not just seen, but also sounds under the magic touch of his hand.

As for the voice, it is the bearer of pure forms of sound. Freed of words — for the actor is not obliged to utter one semantic word! — the actor will give us richly articulated, now high, now low, now slowed, now accelerated pure sound. In this wordless speech of his the actor sounds freely, like a bird. Emotion — without thematic, dramaturgical foundation — appears before the spectator in its purest, unalloyed form. The greatest and sharpest contrasts are possible. Beyond word (but within sound) are possible strength, tension, and the pressure of emotion, inaccessible either to the always more languid pantomime, or to the contemporary, urban, cloaked word. Instead of neurasthenic weeping — Byzantine dirge, instead of pallid joy — heroic rejoicing. The soul of the actor is no less trained than the leg muscles or the thorax.

The actor enters into wholly new relations with the set. All volumes of either planes, cubes or cylinders, inclined or vertical, are "played up," accentuated and revealed thanks to movement constructivistically fitted to them. The very materials of scenic construction find their expression always through penetrating, three-dimensional acting. If Tatlin[1] "places his eye under the control of touch," then the new actor will allow it to be controlled by hearing. Wooden, brass, and iron parts of scenic construction will resonate in their own ways in answer to the running, knocking, and falling of the actors. This deliberate manifestation of materials and system of acting, coordinated with the fundamentals of scenic construction, will create a more organic and serious "constructivism" in theatre, than the present giddy conglomeration of stairs, little machines, and wheels.

In conclusion — there are the insidious questions from my reader. Is not such art an esthetic diversion? Won't it be created only as a conversation piece for the sated snobbism of over-cultivated people? I will speak frankly. I am not attempting to state what should constitute national art. But I lack the regrettable courage to believe Spengler,[2] that we are living in a post-cultural epoch of civilisation, not capable of the creation of art. However, except for this path, the path of creation of form, I don't see any road at all for the formally-impoverished, straggling art of theatre. I am almost ready to think that only this creative art of the purest elements of acting skill puts the actor in the position of free and active artist, and lets theatre drink of the water of life.

Translated by Lynn Ball

NOTES

1 Vladimir Tatlin, leading constructivist, whose extraordinary design for a monumental leaning tower with revolving segments has a distinguished place among the Great Unbuilt of modern architecture. For his account of his stage production of Khebnikov's experimental poem *Zangesi* see *The Tradition of Constructivism,* op. cit., p. 41.
2 Oswald Spengler 1880–1936, who propounded a cyclic view of history and a sombre view of the present in *The Decline of the West* (1918), invoked later by the Nazis in their attacks of 'decadence'.

Sergei Radlov (1892–1958), Soviet theatre director, is here close in spirit to constructivism. Compare Rodchenko's belief that the designer 'must be able to make "all possible combinations of diverse systems, kinds and applications" through understanding the fundamentals of formal "construction"'; and Okhitovich on town planning: 'We ask ourselves how shall we resettle all the urban populations and economic activities? Answer . . . according to the principle of maximum freedom, ease and speed of communication' (see Andreas Papadakis, Catherine Cooke and Andrew Benjamin, *Deconstruction*, London, Academy Editions, 1989, pp. 31 and 17). To work out all possibilities and realise them in maximum freedom of movement is Radlov's aim. For further constructivist influence on music and dance (Meyerhold's biomechanics, Foregger's *tye-fe-trenage* and *Machine Dances*, etc., see Nancy van Norman Baer, *Theatre in Revolution: Russian Avant-Garde Stage Design 1913–1935* (London, Thames & Hudson, 1991). Earlier, Radlov was a student of Meyerhold's, and had directed theatre brigades and mass spectacles; he then ran the Popular Comedy Troupe of Petrograd, which used time-honoured techniques of fairground theatre to convey agit-prop points. He also staged productions influenced by expressionism. Later, in Stalinist times, he became renowned for his productions of Shakespeare.

14

OSKAR SCHLEMMER

FROM New Stage Forms (1928)

A: Can you tell me what the lines on the stage mean?[1]

B: They are the axes of the stage, then the diagonals, and inside the resulting square, a circle is drawn. Apart from the centre-point marked by the lines on the floor, the central point of the space has also been fixed by stretching light-coloured strings from the corners of the stage; a surprising effect which somehow brings the space to life.

A: But what for? Are the actors so stupid they need such aids to orient themselves?

B: No. But because the geometry and stereometry of the stage space are in this way 'revealed', and the the notion of the dimensions awakened, the space acquires a specific character it did not have before. Its accordance with laws becomes perceptible, the actor, performer or dancer is 'bewitched' by this spatial system which otherwise he would be unaware of, and he moves within it differently than he would in the indeterminate fluidity of space.

A: But doesn't such an exaggerated principle kill off what is best in a dancer: the unconscious, the self-surrender, the exaltation? Doesn't it rob him of his soul? After all, the dancer isn't a gym teacher or a traffic warden. It is just this quality of soul and ecstasy we demand of the artist.

B: Certainly, and I would be the last to want to see that stifled. Let me remind you of Goethe's phrase 'freedom within law', and remind you further that in all art, and particularly in the highest art, there reigns an operation of laws that we experience as form and style. Let me remind you of the music of J. S. Bach, which is a wondrous work of adherence to contrapuntal laws, and equally of course a wonder of sensibility. Or to take an example from the pictorial arts: the book of proportions of Albrecht Durer, that exceptional work on measure, of the human form in particular, where the secrets of number are sought with a fanatical zeal. Law and number have hindered either of these two great artists from revealing a spiritual content, indeed, they attained this only through consummated form. To return to our stage: why should measure and law be banned here, where they advance upon us in the proportions of the space, the proportions of man, and in every form, just as they do in colour, in light and in the passage of time, etc.?

Translated by Richard Drain and Anna Millan

NOTE

1   Photos show four strings rising from the stage corners and crossing diagonally at a single point, centre stage, apparently some eight foot in the air. This device may have inspired the use of strings in Richard Foreman's work some forty years later.

Oskar Schlemmer (1888–1943), German painter, designer and creator of performance pieces, first engaged in theatre work in 1912. His geometrical *Triadic Ballet* was performed in full in 1922, but the conception dated back to 1916, when he staged an initial section of it. Design of scenery and costumes for various productions followed. He taught at the Bauhaus from 1920, and in 1925 turned down the offer of a permanent job at the Volksbuhne with Piscator to create a Bauhaus experimental theatre. A series of experimental creations followed. In 1929, following political criticism of his work, he left the Bauhaus to work at the Breslau Academy. In 1930, the Nazis destroyed a series of mural paintings he had done at Weimar. They shut down the Breslau Academy two years later, and then an exhibition of his work in Stuttgart. In 1937, he figured in the Nazi exhibition of 'Degenerate Art' in Munich. Along with some other involuntary exhibitors, he ended up in a factory doing lacquer work.

15

DANIIL KHARMS

The Oberiu Theatre (1928)

Suppose two people walk out on the stage, say nothing, but tell each other something by signs. While they are doing that, they are solemnly puffing out their cheeks. The spectators laugh. Is this theatre? Yes, it is. You may say it is *balagan*.[1] But *balagan* is theatre.

Or suppose a canvas is let down on the stage. On the canvas is a picture of a village. The stage is dark. Then it begins to get lighter. A man dressed as a shepherd walks onstage and plays on a pipe. Is that theatre? Yes.

A chair appears on the stage; on the chair is a samovar. The samovar boils. Instead of steam, naked arms rise up from under the lid.

All these – the man and his movements on the stage, the boiling samovar, the village painted on the canvas, the light getting dimmer and getting brighter – all these are separate elements of theatre.

Until now, all these elements have been subordinated to the dramatic plot – to the play. A play has been a story, told through characters, about some kind of event. On the stage, all have worked to explain the meaning and course of that event more clearly, more intelligibly, and to relate it more closely to life.

That is not at all what the theatre is. If an actor who represents a minister begins to move around on the stage on all fours and howls like a wolf, or an actor who represents a Russian peasant suddenly delivers a long speech in Latin – that will be theatre, that will interest the spectator, even if it takes place without any relation to a dramatic plot. Such an action will be a separate item; a series of such items organised by the director will make up a theatrical performance, which will have its plot line and its scenic meaning.

This will be a plot which only the theatre can give. The plots of theatrical performances are theatrical, just as the plots of musical works are musical. All represent one thing – a world of appearances – but depending on the material, they render it differently, after their own fashion.

When you come to us, forget everything that you have been accustomed to seeing in all theatres. Maybe a great deal will seem ridiculous. We take a dramatic plot. We develop it slowly at first; then suddenly it is interrupted by seemingly extraneous and clearly ridiculous elements. You are surprised. You want to find that customary logical sequence of connections which, it

48

seems to you, you see in life. But it is not there. Why not? Because an object and a phenomenon transported from life to the stage lose their lifelike sequence of connections and acquire another – a theatrical one. We are not going to explain it. In order to understand the sequence of connections of any theatrical performance one must see it. We can only say that our task is to render the world of concrete objects on the stage in their interrelationships and collisions. We worked to solve this task in our production of "Elizabeth Bam."

"Elizabeth Bam" was written on commission for the theatrical section of Oberiu by one of the members, D. Kharms. The dramatic plot of the play is shattered by many seemingly extraneous subjects which detach the object as a separate whole, existing outside its connection with others. Therefore the dramatic plot does not arise before the spectator as a clear plot image; it glimmers, so to speak, behind the back of the action. The dramatic plot is replaced by a scenic plot which arises spontaneously from all the elements of our spectacle. The centre of our attention is on it. But at the same time, separate elements of the spectacle are equally valuable and important to us. They live their separate lives without subordinating themselves to the ticking of the theatrical metronome. Here a corner of a gold frame sticks out – it lives as an object of art; there a fragment of a poem is recited – it is autonomous in its significance, and at the same time, independent of its will, it advances the scenic plot of the play. The scenery, the movement of an actor, a bottle thrown down, the train of a costume – they are actors, just like those who shake their heads and speak various words and phrases.

Translated by George Gibian

NOTE

1   Knock-about puppet show; booth show at a fair.

The Oberiu Group, or Association for Real Art, was rescued from oblivion for English-language readers by George Gibian in 1971, with the publication of a selection of the surviving work of Daniil Kharms (1905–42), and Alexander Vvedensky (1904–41), much of which they had never been able to have published. The Oberiu group to which they belonged was formed in Leningrad in 1926, its best known member the poet Nikolay Zabolotsky. Broadly futurist in tendency, though critical of *zaum*, the 'transrational' language explored by futurist poets (a splintered and reinvented language of emotive speech sounds), the Oberiu put on various readings and performances, wishing to be active in theatre and film as well as poetry and fiction. Its production of Kharms' play *Elizabeth Bam* in 1928, however, together with the publication of its manifesto (whose section on theatre was apparently written by Kharms), incurred the disapproval of the authorities, and their programme of performances did not survive past 1930. Kharms and Vvedensky were both arrested in 1941; Vvedensky was shot, in obscure circumstances, soon after; Kharms died of starvation in the Leningrad blockade.

16

GERTRUDE STEIN

FROM Plays (1935)

In the first place at the theatre there is the curtain and the curtain already makes one feel that one is not going to have the same tempo as the thing that is there behind the curtain. The emotion of you on one side of the curtain and what is on the other side of the curtain are not going to be going on together. One will always be behind or in front of the other. . . .

In a real scene, naturally in a real scene, you either have already very well known all the actors in the real scene of which you are one, or you have not. More generally you have than you have not . . . . Would it make any difference in a real scene if they were all strangers, if they had never known each other. Yes it would, it would be practically impossible in the real scene to have a really exciting scene if they were all strangers because generally speaking it is the contradiction between the way you know the people you know including yourself act and the way they are acting or feeling or talking that makes of any scene that is an exciting scene an exciting scene. . . .

But now how about the theatre.

It is not possible in the theatre to produce familiarity which is of the essence of acquaintance because, in the first place when the actors are there they are there and they are there right away.

When one reads a play and very often one does read a play, anyway one did read Shakespeare's plays a great deal at least I did, it was always necessary to keep one's finger in the list of characters for at least the whole first act, and in a way it is necessary to do the same when the play is played. One has one's programme for that and beside one has to become or has become acquainted with the actors as an actor and one has one's programme too for that. And so the introduction to the characters on the stage has a great many different sides to it. And this has again a great deal to do with the nervousness of the theatre excitement. . . .

I had before I began writing plays written many portraits. I had been enormously interested all my life in finding out what made each one that one and so I had written a great many portraits.

I came to think that since each one is that one and that there are a

51

number of them each one being that one, the only way to express this thing each one being that one and there being a number of them knowing each other was in a play. And so I began to write these plays. And the idea in What Happened, A Play was to express this without telling what happened, in short to make a play the essence of what happened. I tried to do this with the first series of plays that I wrote. . . .

Then I began to spend my summers in Bilignin in the department of the Ain and there I lived in a landscape that made itself its own language. I slowly came to feel that since the landscape was the thing, I had tried to write it down in Lucy Church Amiably and I did but I wanted it even more really, in short I found that since the landscape was the thing, a play was a thing and I went on writing plays a great many plays. The landscape at Bilignin so completely made a play that I wrote quantities of plays.

I felt that if a play was exactly like a landscape then there would be no difficulty about the emotion of the person looking on at the play being behind or ahead of the play because the landscape does not have to make acquaintance. You may have to make acquaintance with it, but it does not with you, it is there and so the play being written the relation between you at any time is so exactly that that it is of no importance unless you look at it. . . .

The landscape has its formation and as after all a play has to have formation and be in relation one thing to the other thing and as the story is not the thing as any one is always telling something then the landscape not moving but being always in relation, the trees to the hills the hills to the fields the trees to each other any piece of it to any sky and then any detail to any other detail, the story is only of importance if you like to tell or like to hear a story but the relation is there anyway. And of that relation I wanted to make a play and I did, a great number of plays.

Gertrude Stein (1874–1946), American writer. The piece she refers to here, *What Happened, a Five Act Play*, was the first of her 'plays', written in 1913. Few of them are recognisable as works for the stage, but their rhythmic speeches, internal rhymes, repetitions and development anticipate Beckett's comment to Jean Reavey, 'Drama is following music' (see Dougald McMillan and Martha Fehsenfeld, *Beckett in the Theatre*, London, John Calder, and New York, Riverrun, 1988, p. 16), and have attracted composers as much as directors – notably Virgil Thompson, who scored the all-black Broadway production of *Four Saints in Three Acts* in 1934. The opening production of Judith Malina and Julian Beck's Living Theatre was of her *Dr. Faustus Lights the Lights* (1938) – a work also mounted more recently by Robert Wilson, who like Richard Foreman has acknowledged the influence of her work on his own.

17

EUGENE IONESCO

Notes on the Theatre (1953)

Pure drama, or shall we say tragic action, is then the following: an action of universal significance, serving as a pattern or prototype, which embraces and reflects all the particular stories and actions that belong to the same category as the model action represented. (Universality or permanence is rejected in our own Heraclitic-Hegelian-Marxist period. I am, however, convinced that in reaction to our own period, as is customary, a later period governed by a new intellectual fashion will one of these days rehabilitate universal ideas.)

As for me, sometime I should like to be able to strip dramatic action of all that is particular to it: the plot, the accidental characteristics of the characters, their names, their social setting and historical background, the apparent reasons for the dramatic conflict, and all the justifications, explanations and logic of the conflict. This conflict would have to exist, or else there would be no drama, but no-one would know the reason for it. One may speak of the dramatic quality of a painting, or representational works like those of Van Gogh, or of non-representational works. This dramatic quality quite simply springs from a clashing of forms and lines, from abstract antagonisms, without psychological motivation. One speaks of the dramatic quality of a musical work. One can also say that a natural phenomenon (storms) or a landscape is dramatic. The importance and the truth of this "dramatisation" reside in the fact that it cannot be explained. In the theatre one looks for a motive. And in the theatre of to-day it is being increasingly looked for. In this way the theatre is being devalued.

With spoken choruses and a central mime as soloist (perhaps assisted by two or three others at the most), one could by means of set gestures, a few words and pure movement succeed in expressing pure conflict, pure drama in its essential truth, and reproduce the permanently destructive and self-destructive pattern of existence itself: pure reality, non-logical and non-psychological (transcending what to-day is called absurd and non-absurd), impellent and expellent forces.

But how does one manage to represent the non-representable? How do you represent the non-representational and *not* represent the representational?

It is all very difficult. Let us try at least to "particularise" as little as possible, to dematerialise as much as we can, or else do something different: invent

53

a unique event, unlike and unconnected with any other event; create an inimitable universe, foreign to all the others, a new cosmos within the cosmos with its own laws and consistencies, an idiom that could belong to nothing else: a world that could be nothing but *my own*, irresolvable but still in the end able to be communicated, substituted for that other world with which other people could identify themselves (I fear none of this is really possible).

It is, however, true that self in the absolute is the universal.

Above all make no effort to achieve what is called the "popular" theatre. Drama "for the people" should be rejected for the same reasons as so-called "bourgeois" or "boulevard" drama. Why? Because "popular" theatre as well as "bourgeois" theatre is "non-popular" theatre. Both are equally cut off from the profound springs of the human soul. Both are the products of people who live confined in their own little world, prisoners of their ideological obsessions, which express nothing but their own schizophrenia, although they mistake them for fundamental truths that must irrevocably be passed on to the whole world. In reality, their "popular" theatre is a theatre of edification and political instruction.

Boulevard theatre, which is accused of being bourgeois, that is to say of belonging to a minority, is however, curiously enough, accepted quite spontaneously by the great public drawn from every class.

A boulevard play pleases a banker, a civil servant, a little clerk, my own concierge, and a working man, etc.

I am in favour of anti-theatre in so far as it could be an anti-bourgeois and anti-popular theatre (assuming one understands by popular[1] theatre this didactic drama we have just mentioned). Deliberately to try and popularise the theatre is in the long run to vulgarise it, to simplify it and turn it into something rudimentary. Bourgeois drama too is vulgar and facile drama...because it is "popular".

But drama that really came from the "people", by that I mean from the supra-social depths of the mind, would in the present state of affairs be accepted neither by the bourgeois or the socialists, nor by the intellectuals who swarm through the newspaper offices and the cafés of Saint-Germain-des-Prés.

What we need is mythical drama: *that* would be universal. The drama of ideas is also, in spite of itself, a drama of myths...but degraded ones: ideas that are not equivalent to an Idea.

A drama that really sprang from the soul of the people would be primitive and rich; pseudo-popular, didactic drama is merely primary, elementary. I am all for primitive drama, and against primary drama.

Of course everyone cannot succeed in writing for everyone. It is no simple matter to reach those springs of the mind that are common and universal. One must write for oneself, for it is in this way that one may reach others.

Translated by Donald Watson

NOTE

1 Changed from the translator's 'anti-popular' which follows the printed French text, as the latter seems to be in error.

Eugene Ionesco (1912–94), French playwright, was born in Romania and later studied in Bucharest, but spent his childhood in France and returned to live there in 1938. His father was Romanian, his mother French, and French was his first language. His career as a playwright started late but in post-war Paris his work, though first derided, soon found a responsive audience. Those persuaded, by logic, experience or existentialism, that the situation of humanity was philosophically absurd, discovered at last that this could be comic as well as tragic. A production of *The Bald Prima Donna* (1950), a piece partly composed of sentences out of an English phrase book, became a perennial feature of the Latin Quarter scene in Paris, running for many years; and his work was widely performed abroad, establishing theatrical absurdism in countries (like Britain) previously resistant to it. He became a natural target of criticism for the newly converted Brechtians who abounded at that time. These included the leading English theatre reviewer Kenneth Tynan. Ionesco offers a wry depiction of himself harried by multiple critics in his play *L'Impromptu à l'Alba* (1955).

18

ALLAN KAPROW

From Events (1966)

We generally mean by "formal" art (the fugues of Bach, the sonnets of Shakespeare, Cubist paintings) an art that is primarily manipulative. As in a chess game, the manipulation is intellectual, whereby elements of the work are moved according to strict, sometimes self-imposed regulations. The weaving of these elements into groupings, regroupings; the losing and finding of themes, sub-themes, and counterthemes, seemingly disparate yet always dominated by the relentless inevitability that they shall resolve at the end, is the peculiar fascination of such an art.

Formal art must be made of a substance that is at once stable and general in meanings. A formalist cannot easily use the horrifying records of Nazi torture chambers, but he can use a simple statement like "the sky is blue," abstract shapes such as circles and squares, the raising and lowering of an arm that does nothing else. The impact of the imagery, the "what," is not as important as the intricacy and subtlety of the moves the imagery is put through.

A formalist who wishes to make a Happening must choose with discretion situations that can be freely manipulated without jarring the overtones of the imagery within them. A group of men all in white doing calisthenics, a ticking metronome, a sheet of paper being moved variously across the floor are obviously easily formalised. But for this to become truly great, I think that some time must elapse. The media are still too undigested for us to feel at home with them. This is essential: to be profitably involved in an activity of arrangements, the materials arranged must not command attention. At present, the media are all rather unstable because their meanings in their new context tend to arise more quickly than anything else. Kleenex may be a commonplace, but collected in quantity in a Happening would immediately push into relief all that we have only half-consciously thought about Kleenex and its intimate uses.

Therefore, in making a Happening, it is better to approach composition without borrowed form theories, and instead to let the form emerge from what the materials can do. If a horse is part of a work, whatever a horse does gives the "form" to what he does in the Happening: trotting, standing, pulling a cart, eating, defecating, and so forth. If a factory of heavy

56

machinery is chosen, then the clanging of motorised repetition might easily cause the form to be steadily repetitive. In this way a whole body of nonintellectualized, nonculturized experience is opened to the artist and he is free to use his mind anew in connecting things he did not consider before.

Think of the following items: tires, doughnuts, Cheerios cereal, Life Savers candy, life preservers, wedding rings, men's and women's belts, band saws, plastic pools, barrel hoops, curtain rings, Mason jar gaskets, hangman's nooses – one could go on almost indefinitely. They are all obviously united by a common circular shape (an observation that could be made by a botanist or a standard auto parts salesman as well as by any painter; for the recognition and use of physical resemblances is not the special talent of artists alone, even if the tradition of form analysis would seem to tell us so). By juxtaposing any half dozen of these items, an idea for a Happening could emerge. And from this combination meanings not normally associated with such things could be derived by minds sensitive to symbols. Here is the score for an unperformed Happening I have written as an illustration:

> Naked women eat giant bowls of Cheerios and milk atop a mountain of used tires. Children disgorge barrels of whitewash over the mountain. A hundred yards away, men and women swimmers in brightly colored plastic pools continually leap out of the water to catch with their mouths rubber gaskets festooned with Life Saver candies that hang from chains of men's belts. The mountain is taken down, tire by tire, and moved into the pools, and the water spills out. The children tie the adults together with the belts. They pour whitewash over the now still heaps of bodies. Then they buckle dozens more of the belts around their necks, waists, and legs. They take the remaining Life Savers to a factory-fresh tire shop and offer them for sale in laughy voices.

In performance, this would be first and foremost a rough, fast-moving affair. But on reflection, the overtones of salvation implicit in the Life Saver theme combine with the supposed nourishment of the cereal, the "pleasure of life" in the candies, the baptismal-sacrificial symbol of the whitewash (milk) bath and the bathing pools (where swimmers leap for Life Savers) and with the tire as the "wheel of progress and fortune." The "death" of this last object (it is *used*, i.e. useless) is built up by combination with others into a strong mound image, thus alluding to the phoenix idea of life-out-of-death. The mound is then destroyed as it is dumped, piecemeal, into the pools whose waters of life are displaced. The children, as direct regeneration images, leave the dying adults tied (united) in death by their belts, and carry on in gentle fun among the living in the brand-new tire shop.

The whole work has a humorous, almost slapstick immediacy about it, in spite of the underlying symbolism, because the imagery is drawn from daily life and juxtaposed in unexpected ways. Cheerios, Life Savers, and tires (which resemble life preservers) are an amusing group, whatever they reveal to depth psychology.

Allan Kaprow (b. 1927) studied art history at Columbia and music under John Cage – from whom he may have derived his interest in incorporating chance and indeterminacy into his work. Kaprow argued for using perishable materials (first in 1958 in *Art News*), an idea put forward by Prampolini in the 1930s. Kaprow has a good claim to be considered the originator of 'happenings'. His first major show, '18 Happenings in 6 Parts', took place in a New York gallery in 1959. Happenings followed the development by artists of the 'assemblage', which the spectator regards from outside, and the 'environment', which the spectator looks around from inside. Happenings could incorporate both these forms, but no longer as static entities; both could be changed as the happening unfolded by its performers or participants.

19

ROBERT WILSON

FROM Speech Introducing *Freud* (1969)

I guess almost anyone setting out to do a play about Sigmund Freud the man[1] would have become overly (and overtly?) concerned about the role of his studies and intellectual life – his mind, and what I was thinking about was that those things are popularly familiar – everyone knows them. The things that impressed me most though about Freud as a person being and having these ideas which seemed to have influenced just about everything when reading about him was the fact that he was very human – intensely ordinary and very sort of bourgeois in one sense – and that was precisely part of his enigmatic brilliance. Yet while we know that attention is hardly ever given to that side of him, history has recorded him as someone who was particularly motivated by having theories – theories which, by the way, structurally and systematically seem to defy just what we mean by the words structure and system and logic. This piece though, as a kind of hybrid "dance play" doesn't deal with any big ideas – it just pays inordinate attention to small, *detail* things. Although we do see him plotting and making charts, notes, undoubtedly the most moving event in his life was when his prized grandchild, Heinerlie, died – he never got over that – something within him was smothered for the rest of his life. He said that. A very simple emotional experience. A death. And suddenly all of his ideas about living and theorizing about feeling were suspended, rendered meaningless.

There are a lot of reversals in this piece, such as the ending, a tableau in a cover with all those animals. It's like going back. Going back to some indefinable time or memory too hazy to specify in exact particulars. That is, in another sense though, I suppose, the same as moving continually ahead. Isn't that called *retroactive*? No, not actually. I mean it's going back as well as in the same time forward. That is, Freud is plotting and scheming up these charts and yet what we *see* happening – the stage activity, is very human-like – someone running and someone sitting, another making small talk, someone pouring a drink, someone dancing, people doing ritualistic exercises. The activities are just very mundane and thus in that way pointedly human.

Another thing that happens is that the stage is divided into zones –

stratified zones one behind another that extend from one side of the stage horizontally to the other. And in each of these zones there's a different "reality" – a different activity defining the space so that from the audience's point of view one sees through these different layers, and as each occurs it appears as if there's no realization that anything other than itself is happening outside that particularly designated area. People might associate this with Freud and the layers of consciousness – different levels of understanding but that kind of obvious intention has been erased or eradicated from this production. I see it more simply as a collage of different realities occurring simultaneous like being aware of several visual factors and how they combine into a picture before your eyes at any given moment. Awareness in that way occurs mostly through the course of experience of each layer rendering the others transparent. And this might, at first of course, confuse some people, because we are so being used to going to the theater and having the play explicitly narrated to us in verbal direct(ed)ness. Like Shakespeare. Like Shaw. Like Tennessee Williams. Those kinds of plays are primarily constructed *with* words, although other elements are included. On the other hand in dance people as diverse as Jerome Robbins, Merce Cunningham and Yvonne Rainer focus the intention of their work on the formal presentation of movement. The focus here is neither verbal nor concerned with specifying the physicality of people in virtual space. It's simply more visual. And people are just beginning to return again to discerning visual significances as a primary mode – or method – of communicating in a context where more than one form, or "level" exists. In that sense of overlays of visual correspondences we can speak of multi-dimensional realities. . . . See, we're not particularly interested in literary ideas, because having a focus that encompasses in a panoramic visual glance all the hidden slices ongoing that appear in clear awareness as encoded fragments seems to indicate theater has so much more to do than be concerned with words in a dried out, flat, one-dimensional literary structure. I mean The Modern World has forced us to outgrow that *mode* of seeing. We're interested in *another* thing – another *kind* of experience that happens when encoded fragments and hidden detail become without words suddenly transparent. Unfortunately, the usual bill of theater – like all those year-in-year-out tired Broadway productions mounted (and, destroyed) each season is that they are dealing with all those stories, and those are the same old stories over and over. The same stories Shakespeare told. The same stories that the soap operas tell on television. The same stories that Tennessee Williams is telling. And they're o.k.; they're interesting, but like, you get that – you know that instantly you're just being handed the same thing over and over differently disguised and I always say, well so what? You see we're interested here in a theater that deals totally with another sort of thing, even though we're not sure exactly what that is. I feel that when theater really connects with an audience or when a group of people really connect with one another that there are a lot of things involved. It's always a mystery, isn't it, when you have to stop to analyse it? I am now remembering something a little girl said to me about 4 years ago when I was her teacher. This child had a speech impediment and had a very difficult time speaking at every stage of learning to say a word. I was tongue-tied myself, and, so I was sympathetic with her. I could understand part of the problem though in an instant. She wanted desperately to sing but she couldn't get into the school choir, cause of course she couldn't say the words and she couldn't make those sounds. You know, like that. So I said, well, that doesn't make any difference you know, you can, you *can* sing. She said, well I can't carry a tune. She said, "I know I'd *like* to sing." So I said, well just go ahead and, you know – *sing*. So then she did and then after a couple of years of working with it she really developed an incredible thing with her voice and it was very moving to hear her sing. And eventually by gaining confidence in herself this way she learned in the same manner to talk. Two obstacles were removed. And then one day I heard her working with another child – and this child was singing along with a Bob Dylan recording or something like that. And that little girl, who originally had the speech impediment said emphatically OH NO! SHE SAYS, WHY DO YOU WANT TO SING THOSE SONGS? YOU KNOW, WHY DO YOU WANT TO LEARN MUSIC THAT WAY? You know she continued enthusiastically you can sing your own way. No; don't sing like the Beatles you know. Don't sing like Frank Sinatra. Don't sing like, you know. Sing your *own* way. And that's what interests me.

NOTE

1   *The Life and Times of Sigmund Freud*, 1969.

Robert Wilson (b. 1941), American artist and theatre director. Wilson's works include sculpture, installations and graphic work. His theatre work is visually conceived and involves many preliminary drawings. However, behind the studied art-work productions now internationally in demand lie the largely unprecedented theatre pieces which first made his name, which evolved from a personal history. When he was young, Wilson suffered from a speech impediment; at 17 this was cured by Ms Byrd Hoffman, a dancer, whom Wilson commemorated in the name of his company, the Byrd Hoffman School of Byrds. Wilson went on to work with brain-damaged and disturbed children, as well as working with the aged and terminally ill – work guided by his belief (based on his own experience) in helping people discover and assert their own vocabulary of movement and expression. This work fed directly into his first extraordinary theatre shows, as indeed did the brain-damaged and handicapped, who were part of his troupe. The first show to reach Europe was the revelatory *Deafman Glance* (1970), hailed by Aragon in a letter to André Breton as 'what we from whom surrealism was born dreamt would arise after us, beyond us . . . ' (Stefan Brecht, *The Theatre of Visions: Robert Wilson*, Frankfurt am Main, Suhrkamp Verlag, 1978, and London, Methuen, 1982, p. 434).

20

TADEUSZ KANTOR

From Impossible Theatre (1972)

Autonomous theatre.

That concept – an old one, known for some decades – retains the lost flavour of avant-gardes past and gone; it evokes the large hopes of our youth – a fascinating climate of radicalism, nonconformism, and unrelenting destruction of all that had gone rigid in the plastic arts, and in values at large.

From the start of our century, the theatre took it as its watchword. From time to time it was set aside for various reasons, some mean and petty, some powerful and menacing.

The idea of autonomous theatre, a theatre seeking only to justify the very fact of its existence, in opposition to a theatre in the service of literature, a theatre that copies life, and that irrevocably loses its theatrical instinct, its sense of liberty, and its own expressive force.

This second theatre, renouncing the laws of its own artistic existence, was obliged to submit itself to the conditions, the laws and the conventions of life; it became an institution – and creation was reduced to a mere production machine.

SINCE MARCEL DUCHAMP[1]

In seeking the autonomy of the theatre, one cannot restrict oneself to a limited professional field; one cannot attach the label of authentic theatre to some things, and expel others as unauthentic. This kind of 'chauvinism' and intolerance becomes doctrinal and academic.

One must go beyond the theatrical domain, and effect a break – in a sense, betray that domain.

Autonomy can be achieved only through close links with art as a whole, with the permanent risk that art represents, and with all its problems, dangers and surprises.

The reduction of artistic research merely to professional experiments generally leads to its losing itself in simplified and simple-minded automatic processes.

Following the period when theatre became more and more a reproduction of literature, it returns inevitably to the alternative: to a theatre of gesture, a theatre of rites and signs; to ceremonies, to celebrations, to magic practices of a highly doubtful kind.

All of that has nothing to do with the complex combination of problems that art poses today. Art since the time of Dada and Marcel Duchamp has abandoned the hallowed and secure ground reserved for centuries for 'the work of art'; art since the time of surrealism has aimed to appropriate reality as a whole.

THEATRE AND LITERATURE

In seeking an autonomous theatre, I do away with the reality of the text.

I am not at all convinced that in rejecting the expression or pursuit of a new dramatic form that might manage to save the theatre from stagnation, one guarantees its autonomy.

To deprive theatre of its complexity means quite simply avoiding difficulties, and retreating before that essential imperative of art, 'unity'. It means dodging the 'impossible'.

To replace literary expression with manipulated gesturings, animated by what pretend to be spiritual impulses, represents no more than a purely academic solution. If language has become a mask, one must tear off that mask. To eliminate it, however, or degrade it, would signify a breach with the mental faculties.

That would signify equally a breach with humour, criticisms, risk and danger – notions that imply necessarily the intervention of those faculties.

The reality of the text effects – in relation to life – a singular condensation of acts, events and situations. It has its own structure and fiction which belong to it alone. It brings to the theatre multiple mental perspectives.

The invention of collage and the concept of the 'ready-made' object, without endangering the autonomy of the theatre work, has restored to it the outside element which language too can be.

The theatre, like the other arts, should not fear the intervention of extra-theatrical realities.

The theatre, to evolve and become alive, must come out of itself – must cease to be a theatre.

It is not for literature to trespass on the territory of theatre; it is for theatre to take risks – to venture, as things stand, beyond its own sphere: to trespass on the territory of literature. . . .

A NEW REALITY

The notion of freedom in art, defined and affirmed for the first time in surrealism, in its programme for a total and indivisible reality, is the very principle of new art.

The work of art, confined within its structure, offspring of the creative act, of inner expression, and representation – unique, isolated and finally institutionalised: the work of art has become the principal obstacle, the barrier one must break through.

I should like to pause briefly on certain moments in the past which represent important landmarks in my theatrical orientation.

In 1968 I took part in the symposium *Principle-Collage*, at Nuremburg. Characteristically, theatre was represented only by artists belonging to other disciplines.

The great good sense of the collage method is that it re-opens to question the exclusive right of the creator to shape the work; no longer is the creator the only one to form, to imprint, and to express.

The admittance of foreign reality, unconstructed, found or readymade, throws an objective light on the artist's romantic role as godly demiurge of form; it shifts the centre of gravity from sensual and artisan values back to intellectual and imaginative values.

Art has begun to annex fields and objectives which hitherto were forbidden to it.

In the shows realised at the Cricot 2 Theatre in the years 1955–1957, the collage method was carried through into all the material used. The principle: to link up the segments of the text and the precise notions contained in them with completely different, or even contrary, situations and behaviour taken from current reality or 'the stuff of life': a condition deprived of all illustrative or symbolic function. Everything was based on the break-up of logical links; the process was to superimpose, to 'tot up', in order to create a new reality.

Translated by Richard Drain and Micheline Mabille

NOTE

1 Marcel Duchamp, taken here to mark a crucial artistic watershed, was active at the time of cubism and Dada, to which he subscribed. He disrupted aesthetic conceptions by introducing ready-made objects into art exhibitions, and further challenged them with his conceptually based constructed assemblages. Both these aspects of his work are relevant to Kantor's activities.

FROM Elementary School of Theatre (1986)

The following is the twelfth *Insegnamento* or 'teaching' from a series of lessons given to student actors at the Paolo Grassi Drama School, Milan, in 1986, which led up to a short two-part show, *A Wedding*, 'in constructivist and surrealist style'.

Only now do we realise that what we were doing is the first 'Act' of the show called *A Wedding*, and that the rehearsal of the nuptial ceremony we have watched was the substance of this 'Act'.

An act that is sufficiently ambiguous:

in fact we don't very well know if

the play (the drama) represents a theatre milieu and a troupe of actors who are preparing a show entitled *A Wedding* –

We have already seen the first act: it shows us a rehearsal; there is every likelihood then that the second will present us with the actual show –

there could be another possibility though, of the 'illusion' kind:

in this case, the play would present (in the first act) two families, perhaps known for their little oddities, who, to ensure a perfectly smooth unfolding of the ceremony, carry out, with the agreement of the liberal-minded bishop, a rehearsal of the *rites*. After which the 'real' wedding would take place (in the second act).

The first scenario would seem to have most chance of carrying our enterprise through to an epilogue.

We agree then that the play is about a WEDDING performed by ACTORS.

or more precisely: about a TROUPE OF ACTORS who prepare and perform a show with the title, *A WEDDING*.

But this agreement will be continually prone to the ambiguity already mentioned.

And that's the most interesting thing.

So the actors of the elementary School play the role of actors from some theatre or other, who in their turn are rehearsing and performing the show entitled *A Wedding*. But as always happens in the theatre, the coherence of the notional convention (of the commedia dell'arte kind) from time to time disappears from view, and transforms itself into an 'illusion of life'. So we shall see, at the same time:

now the actors playing actors

and now, suddenly, actors playing figures from real life.

In my view, that's fine!

We come at this point to the substance of our twelfth teaching:

I should like to talk about the notion of the 'real', of *truth*.

In art, in the work of art.

The problem is the following.

After the scene, 'Rehearsal of the wedding', there should logically follow the scene of the 'prepared wedding' – that's to say, the real wedding.

That is, we'd have to watch the repetition of the first scene, but this time, so to say, 'polished up'.

That would be boring and stupid and couldn't make the basis of a '*drama*'.

We realise that very well.

So now there begin to form prospects and turns of events not 'from life' but that are 'constructed'.

That is, CONTRARY to categories of life.

The surrealists would have taken over this situation for their own ends and according to their own ideas, and would straight away have begun talking of oneiric vision, the vision of dreams.

Today that doesn't trouble us.

We are living nearly seventy years after the Constructivist Revolution.

A REAL WEDDING! ALL PREPARED!

HOW MANY BIZARRE AND UNFORSEEN THINGS COULD HAPPEN IN THE ALL-PREPARED PERFORMANCE OF A 'REAL' WEDDING!

How much that's 'IMPOSSIBLE' and 'UNKNOWN' could intervene, emanating from mysterious REGIONS OF THE IMAGINARY!

As if a violent wind crossed the stage, demolishing and sweeping away everything that is real and presumed to be TRUE.

IN ART TRUTH IS OTHERWISE!

Translated by Richard Drain and Micheline Mabille

Tadeusz Kantor (1915–90), Polish artist, scenographer and theatre director, studied at the Cracow Arts Academy where his courses included one on scenography under Karol Frycz, friend and admirer of Gordon Craig. He began underground experimental theatre work during the occupation, and following the war did scenography and costumes for nearly a hundred productions. He founded the Cricot group in 1955, and worked with them thereafter on numerous striking examples of 'autonomous theatre', including a piece based on *The Water Hen* of Witkiewicz, and also *The Dead Class* and *Wielopole/Wielopole* (the name of his birthplace), which contrived a transposition of Polish experience into a non-realist mode as dense and evocative as Bruno Schulz (friend of Witkiewicz), with whom his later work has distinct affinities. His considerable theoretic writings, most of them only now becoming available in English, are among the most important recent attempts to work out a new theatrical rationale and synthesis. 'Impossible Theatre' is one of two essays of that name. It is in ten sections, of which four are included here. It will be seen that some of the principles he outlines are embodied in the production exercise that follows.

21

RICHARD FOREMAN

FROM Unbalancing Acts (1992)

Society teaches us to represent our lives to ourselves within the framework of a coherent narrative, but beneath that conditioning we *feel* our lives as a series of multidirectional impulses and collisions. We're trained to see our lives as a series of projects, one following the next along the road of experience, and our "success" depends upon how well we progress from project to project. But traveling this narrow road shuts out a multitude of suggestive impulses and impressions – the ephemeral things that feed our creative insight and spiritual energy. It's as if we were wearing blinders to restrict our emotional field, making us spiritually and physically uneasy with the normal ambiguity of our everyday experience. So we compensate. We make self-righteous demands that noncontradiction be the basis of our value systems, but that inevitably means the suppression of all sensory richness. It reinforces our denial of the ambiguity inherent in life, which, when suppressed, makes the world seem rigid and frightening.

I like to think of my plays as an hour and a half in which you see the world through a special pair of eyeglasses. These glasses may not block out all narrative coherence, but they magnify so many other aspects of experience that you simply lose interest in trying to hold on to narrative coherence, and instead, allow yourself to become absorbed in the moment-by-moment representation of psychic freedom. . . .

No work of art is absolutely truthful about life, but is a strategic maneuver performed on coagulated consciousness. As Picasso said, art is a lie that tells the truth. And it's a lie that tells the truth because it's a chosen, strategic maneuver, which is not the truth. No art could ever be "the truth," because it has to leave out ninety percent of life. But since even life's tiniest detail is an integral part of the interwoven whole, if you're not talking about all of life you're not really talking about the truth – you're talking about a selective distortion. Art is a perspective; all perspectives are lies about the total truth; so art is a lie that, if it is strategically chosen, wakes people up. Art is a lever to affect the mind. The truth of art is in the audience's, the individual's, awakened perceptions. It is not in the work of art.

*

In my plays I try to separate the impulse from the object that seems to evoke it, and in doing so, clarify the quality of the impulse itself. One strategy I use is to overdetermine each specific, manifest impulse, so that its origin is no longer traceable to a single object that would falsely paint it with its own qualities. For instance, in a scene where the character says, "I have difficulty getting out of the room," I try to offer several reasons why, not just one. I baffle the impulse to leave the room: first, by tying the character's foot to a table; then by putting a wall between him and the door; and finally by blinding him so he cannot see his way out of the room. This strategy overloads the context. It focuses attention on the impulse to leave the room, blocking the spectator's normal tendency to think: I know how he can leave the room – he can walk through the door. If the spectator is offered a clear solution to imagine (exit through the door), his focus will be on the mundane object ("Will he get through the door?") rather than on what is happening to the character's body and soul, or on how the character's life is changed when it is filled with the impulse, "I want to leave the room."

Paradoxically, bafflement can clarify. Bafflement can force you to refocus your vision. It is the same as making the sun so bright you're forced to look away, but as you avert your eyes you see the delicate flower you've never observed before.

The playing space is an environment for the text to explore, a gymnasium for a psychic, spiritual, and physical work-out. It's an exercise room, a factory, an examination room, and a laboratory. If the mise-en-scène does not pay homage to all this, it castrates the full body of the theater.

All the materials we find available in the theater should be thrown together in full polymorphous play. Curtains, scenery, moving platforms, lights, noises, bodies – all add complexity to the stage space. In the same way, we find in the text a multitude of psychic materials with which to play. The text should be an open file system, so distributed in its references that all aspects of the world seem connected to it. The complexity of the lived world should be made available to the spectator by the text, setting, and articulated production; never fall prey to using this wealth of materials to convince the audience that they are seeing something "real," other than the dance of the accumulated riches of your artistic resonances in concrete, articulated form. As in music, a structural, rhythmical articulation of all the elements. . . .

The complexity of the scenery is a major resource that enables me to suggest the jump from one level of meaning to another during the moment-by-moment action of the play. For example, if an actor is at the back of the stage sitting in a chair against a suitably painted wall, the scene may seem to be realistically domestic. But if he then runs downstage to grab a handle at the end of a pole that rises from the floor and starts to spin it madly, since that pole is not something you would expect to find in a living room, it suggests that he must have left that domestic situation. Perhaps that action, which took place in *What Did He See?*, suggested a regression to childhood, but beyond that it suggests the wider notion of operating in a world gone mad. Had there been no bizarre pole in that living room set, and the actor had instead spun wildly around the post of a normal banister, it would not have referred to this wider level of meaning. It was only when the actor ran to manipulate the pole that he seemed to be entering another level of the set, one that subliminally evoked a demonic factory whose pole was strategically placed on the axis of the world. The next thing that character did in *What Did He See?* was to run to the top step of a platform and sit upon a throne, which invoked a third locale, added to the factory and living room. From that throne he looked down on the other characters, evoking overtones of manipulative power relationships. The physical resources of the set made possible the specific actions that enabled me to jump from psychological level to political level to metaphysical level, and so on. . . .

What my plays say, in effect, is that not all the problems of life can be resolved within the accepted terms of the materialist culture we've inherited; in fact, the *most* important ones cannot. This is an approach to art that puts it in direct opposition to the mythos of the mainstream, business-oriented culture of the late twentieth century. There's no question that serious twentieth-century art functions as an adversary to the going culture. That's why the powers-that-be have secretly – or not so secretly – considered adventurous (serious) art of the modern era subversive. It *is* subversive. It implies that the cultural choices we have made are wrong, which is, of course, a disturbing message. Mainstream art, on the other hand, even when it is seemingly critical on a specific issue, can only be revisionist at best. It may suggest that things have gone wrong, but can only point to options already existing within the culture. It has no deep way of evoking the possibility that the culture's deepest unconscious presuppositions might be the problem: that it might be desirable to reconstitute our very way of being human. Reactionary critics have a point, therefore, when they attack contemporary trends in art because they fear such art might undermine Western culture. In the long run, it well might. But they shouldn't worry. Something better is coming. My theater is one attempt among many to listen carefully, in order to hear the approaching footsteps.

Richard Foreman (b. 1937) founded his 'Ontological–Hysteric Theater' in 1968, initially choosing to work with non-actors. Ontology: the branch of metaphysical science concerned with the nature of being. His work, though, has also been called phenomenological – phenomenology being that other branch of enquiry which dispenses with theories of being and seeks to describe phenomena without them. Hysteric: Foreman views the bizarre situations depicted in his early work as 'normal bourgeois theatrical clichés, domestic triangles, things like that. That's why I called my theater "Ontological-Hysteric", because the basic syndrome controlling the structure was that of classic, middle-class, boulevard theatre, which I took to be hysteric in its psychological topology' (*Unbalancing Acts: Foundations for a Theater*, New York, Pantheon Books, 1992, p. 75).

Part II

THE POLITICAL
DIMENSION

I regard much current morality as to economic and sexual relations as disastrously wrong; and I regard certain doctrines of the Christian religion as understood in England today with abhorrence. I write plays with the deliberate object of converting the nation to my opinion in these matters.

George Bernard Shaw

INTRODUCTION

1

In a Europe whose politics lean towards the right, 'political theatre' is still generally understood to mean theatre of the left. This odd usage seems to imply that all other theatre is politically neutral. It would be naïve to think it is. But the left has figured much more strongly in the drive for change in theatre; the right has presumably been more content with it as it is. To that degree the left has stolen the limelight. So in a brief sampling of creative initiatives with political roots and purposes, the left can hardly not dominate.

Such initiatives constitute some of the most radical developments in stage practice the century has seen. The notion that all they involve is plying the audience with harangues and messages can be readily dismissed. They have entailed an attempt to rethink the nature and function of theatre in the light of the dynamics of society outside it, and of audience involvement within it. This has led to new modes of acting, staging and playwriting, and hence new ways of representing life on stage. Political consciousness has sparked off a critique of theatre's own structures and hierarchies, and brought about new working methods. It has energised the attempt to seek out new audiences,and has taken theatre, both literally and figuratively, into new territory.

This part samples some of the thinking and theory behind these ventures. It opens with Bernard Shaw. His preface to *Mrs Warren's Profession* is not only a classic attack on the censorship which had banned its public presentation, but a buoyant argument on behalf of a politicised theatre. This means for Shaw the 'problem play', a work designed to uncover the social and economic forces shaping its situations, and expose the sexual politics of its characters' exchanges. *Mrs Warren's Profession* is such a play, and its detailed settings signal its alliance with late nineteenth-century naturalism. But the accurate depiction of society is only part of its concern. Its chief purpose is to upset received ideas, as its preface makes clear. If, as Brecht was to argue, the effect of naturalism is to naturalise the unacceptable, Shaw is no naturalist. He depicts a recognisable world of assumptions and prejudices only so they may be questioned as fast as possible. In this way he sought to make his audience reconsider their stock responses, and take a fresh look at ingrained beliefs and habitual practices.

In all this, Shaw is a precursor of Bertolt Brecht, and it is no wonder that Brecht pays tribute to him.[1] 'My plays are built to induce,' writes Shaw, 'not voluptuous reverie but intellectual interest, not romantic rhapsody but humane concern.' This double emphasis, on the work as constructed artefact, and on the frame of mind it seeks to create in its audience, recurs repeatedly in discussion of political theatre. Despite Shaw and Brecht, however, there is no consensus on either matter. This becomes clear if we turn to Sergei Eisenstein's 'Montage of Attractions'. Again we find an emphasis on construction, or what Eisenstein calls *montage*. Again its *raison d'être* is the audience. 'The objective . . . is to guide the spectator in the desired direction (frame of mind)' by 'building "a construction that has impact".' But neither construction nor impact is conceived in terms of 'intellectual interest'. Eisenstein aims to shake his spectators into a new frame of mind by a series of 'aggressive' surprises that register on the senses. These may involve all kinds of variety show devices. The incongruous effects and exhilarating zaniness of futurist theatre here find themselves put to work to produce a modernist catharsis of backward habits of mind.

Vsevolod Meyerhold, under whom Eisenstein first worked, also turns away from Shaw. 'This ability to start the spectator's brain working is just one of theatre's properties' – and divorced from those which start the emotions working, it has little value for him. Theatre must not become 'a mere debating chamber'. Shaw was not worried about that, and he suggests abandoning 'the drama of pure feeling' to the opera composer. Meyerhold, by contrast, risks affronting those in power over him by pouring scorn on 'the mere exposition of thesis and antithesis', and enlists music, film and other arts into his concept of a 'total' theatre, fully engaging the spectator's senses and feelings.

2

It was in Germany, in the work of the expressionists, that a 'drama of feeling' had been pushed to its most extreme form. That these feelings involved disillusion with current society and ideology was evident. Here were plays dark with political storm signals. Yet what politics could rectify a world so bleak, or cure characters so crippled, benighted and perverse? The expressionists looked for a revolution, but believed it must first take place in the human soul.

The violent political conflicts of post-war Germany made such a view seem evasive. Critics accused the expressionists of indulging in an exacerbated subjectivism which left little foothold for hard political thought or constructive action. Such was Brecht's verdict, despite his respect for Kaiser.[2] A wave of expressionist influence abroad subsided; and since then a large and varied body of work has rarely been staged. It is our loss. The expressionists not only spearheaded an artistic revolt against capitalist values and the bourgeois order; they articulated this in a new theatre language akin to that of expressionist painting. Their theory springs from a radical vision of an integrated, total theatre. That their work was thought unconstructive in the midst of the anti-fascist struggle and the hard-line politics of 1920s' and 1930s' Germany is understandable. But its political bearing was recognised both by the Soviets, who staged a number of their plays, and the Nazis who banned them; and is overt in the plays of Ernst Toller, who represents expressionism in the pages that follow.

The most militant political theatre of these years comes however from Erwin Piscator and the new workers' groups. The latter turned their backs on the proscenium-arch theatres of the middle class, and went to perform in the street, at the factory gates or in workers' clubs. They were part of a workers' theatre movement that spread from the Soviet Union throughout Europe to the United States and Japan. They soon learnt that naturalism was not a form well suited to their purposes, nor to the rough conditions in which they performed, for reasons set out here in the document of the movement's British wing. They devised a new form: agit-prop – agitational propaganda (the latter word had not yet acquired its pejorative meaning). German groups, like the Red Troupe of Dresden, the Hamburg Riveters, the Red Rockets and Red Megaphones of Berlin, were particularly strong. Such work pre-dated Brecht's conversion to the didactic in the late 1920s, and it is unlikely these groups learnt from him; Brecht's stock with the political left was at first not high, as we can see here from Toller's article of 1928. They learnt rather from each other, and also from the Soviet Blue Blouse movement (whose 'Simple Advice' is in Part III), and perhaps from the 'music, songs, acrobatics, instant cartoons, sport, projections, films, statistics, sketches, speeches'[3] of Piscator's *Red Revue* (1924).

It was Piscator, as Brecht acknowledges, who first pioneered 'epic theatre'.[4] The term is now inseparably associated with Brecht, though in many ways it fits Piscator's work better. Piscator's view that the new 'hero' is not an individual but the epoch itself, led him to a theatre of epic sweep, where the epoch comes to dramatic life on stage. This is carried through with the help of all the technical means he can muster (or afford) to activate all dimensions of the theatrical space, effect panoramas, open up multiple perspectives, and foreground significant moments. The epoch for Piscator is not a mere chronicle of events, to be paraded on one spot. Each is to be seen in relation to wider forces. Like Meyerhold he seeks a total theatre that incorporates film. How better can the masses, that force central to the epoch, be brought on stage than by showing them on a screen?

Brecht's theatre is sparse by comparison. In theory he welcomes new film and stage technology, but in practice he has no great need for it. A traditional flat stage, clearly lit, and capable performers, are Brecht's requirements. When he looks to Russia, it is not to borrow futurist, constructivist or 'bio-mechanic' techniques; it is to adapt for the stage a solid example of socialist social realism, Gorki's novel, *The Mother.*

None the less Brecht's theory often seems to take its cue more from the progressive sciences than from the arts, which are suspected of lagging behind them – none further behind than the art of theatre, fixated in the wake of the misguided Aristotle on imitation, empathy and certain disabling emotions. In place of this, Brecht, like Eisenstein, presents his theatre as a kind of laboratory. But there the likeness stops. In Eisenstein's, the spectators are drawn in by 'attractions', which rouse, amuse, and shake them out of their preconceptions, showing them that everything is possible – as, in a Russia threatened by famine and breakdown, it needed to be. In Brecht's, the public strolls in and sits back. There are no fireworks. They proceed to observe demonstrations of the workings of social processes in the larger world outside. Passionate harangues on their injustice are generally conspicuous by their absence.

As political theatre, this hardly sounds inflammatory. Brecht's theory clarifies its rationale. His purpose is to persuade the audience to forgo the usual theatrical pleasure of empathy with the protagonists; and to enjoy instead an all-round view of them, seeing their interaction from new angles and relishing ironies. In this way the audience is enlisted as engaged critical observer rather than as the object of emotional or spectacular bombardment. Its members are enabled to grasp fully the social import of the scenes played inside the theatre, so they may act with a clear head in the scenes being played outside it. At the time, these last were turbulent enough to make a clear head imperative. Their background was the aggressive rise of fascism, and the bitter struggle of the left against it. It was easy to feel passionately, harder to weigh matters tactically. This helps explain the tone Brecht favoured. The message implicit in it for his audience is the message he gave his actors: don't get carried way.

The methods Brecht developed to bring about this frame of mind sought to create a *Verfremdungseffekt* – normally translated as 'alienation' effect. Brecht did not coin his term till the mid-1930s, but it fits a great deal of his earlier practice: see here, for instance, the prologue to his play *The Exception and the Rule*, where he asks us to find what it portrays 'estranging even if not very strange'; Brecht meant by his term just such a perspective.

To understand fully why he thought this kind of alienation necessary, we must understand his critique of naturalism – hitherto judged to be the most politically advanced form of realism. Brecht's attempt to view the arts in a scientific light is not foreign to naturalism. For Zola, who laid down natural-ism's theatrical programme, the word implied a link with the natural scien-ces. Both were forms of enquiry concerned not simply with the outward appearance of things, but with the inner laws (of survival and sexual repro-duction, for example) that inexorably governed them. How much of life is inexorable and how much is not, is, of course, a critical question for Marx-ists, as the possibility of revolution, or by another reckoning its inevitability, hangs on it. Brecht's work too is hung upon that question, showing as it does how things can hardly happen but as they happen, while also wishing to persuade us that under a different dispensation they need not. This partly hopeful contradiction we meet with too in naturalism. But the conventions of naturalism glue the spectator inflexibly to things as they are. They decree a seamless unfolding of perfectly simulated actuality. This leaves no space for radical alternatives to appear, or at least to appear realisable. They can feature only as wistful pipe-dreams, as they do, in fact, in numerous natur-alistic plays. Without abandoning the real, Brecht sought to devise tech-niques which could alter this, by prising apart the imprisoning illusion of an unquestionable reality that naturalism strove to create, and making spaces within it to let in some further light.

His success has sometimes led to the impression that he was the first to awaken theatre audiences from naturalistic illusion and keep them aware they were in a theatre. This only shows how short theatrical memory can be. The Russian director Tairov, looking back to his youth, recalls the credo of the 'stylized theatre' launched in 1905–6, in these terms: 'The spectator must never for a moment forget that he is in a theatre. . . . The actor must remember every second that he is on a stage.' Tairov recollects 'how painstakingly the actors shucked "contemptible feelings" from their souls, how they strove – God save us – not to experience emotional suffering, anger, love, hate, or joy, but only coldly and calmly *to represent them*.'[5] A member of the Habimah Studio who worked with Vakhtangov in 1922 wrote: 'It should appear as if the actor were saying to the spectator: "Now I am crying, but I, the actor, know about it. Look, I'm wiping my tears, and look, I'm not only wiping my tears, but notice how I'm doing it". . . . One must . . . *feel one's attitude to the character and to history as a whole*.'[6] This closely anticipates Brecht's precepts.

Brecht's originality lies not so much in ditching naturalism as in salvaging realism. No-one else had thought of wedding it so provocatively with the precepts of its arch-enemy, the theatre of style. The result was something new. Brecht's techniques are talked of as distancing, but the term slightly belies them. Effectively practised, they are space-making. They open up breathing spaces and thinking spaces. They do this by effecting separa-tions, which at the same time highlight distinctions: between the theatre and the real world; between components of the productions, such as words and music; between elements of the stage setting; between one scene and the next; between actors and the characters they perform; and between them and their audience. Western theatre, unlike eastern, prided itself on its hard-won success in yoking these elements unnaturally together, thereby serving as the shrine of make-believe. In the interests of a non-credulous political perspective, Brecht dismantled this tradition.

But his cultural politics were provocative to all parties. 'Alienation', the none-too-inviting term adopted by English translators in defiance of its very different use by Marx, tactfully screens us from one of the resonances of his own term *Verfremdung*. For this word, pinned firmly at the head of his theory and practice, was an only slightly disguised substitute for a term central to Russian formalist criticism, 'estrangement'. The formalists used it to pin-point how literature 'made strange' what it treated by showing it under a new light; and thus revised or enlarged its readers' notion of life and of the world. Brecht must have realised that his own work had the same aim; and that in effect he was engaged in the task of working out how the formalists' concept could be applied in the theatre to political ends.

But to acknowledge this, as his own term virtually does, was on the left to touch a sensitive nerve. The formalists' first proposition was to disentangle literature as an object of study from its historical and social context, in order to conduct an independent examination of its forms. This was deemed to run counter to Marx. Moreover, forms stood accused of distracting modern artists from 'content', and from reality. Formalism became a code-word for modernist experiment of all kinds, and under Stalin a cardinal sin punishable by the Gulag or worse. The correct communist mode became socialist realism – too often a form of touched-up naturalism guaranteed to set the proletariat in a rosy glow. Such a style was not for Brecht; and the suspicion this aroused of a formalist element in his work was for once strictly accurate. As a result, Brecht worked under fire from both sides – from the liberals who thought him doctrinaire, and the hard left on the lookout for deviations from the party line. To this prickly situation we owe in some measure the extent and elaboration of his theoretic writings.

On the Marxist left, Lukács was the most intellectually formidable figure he had to contend with. Brecht rejects his attempt to monopolise realism on behalf of nineteenth-century realist conventions, and claims to practise realism himself: a dialectical realism of the left, and of the twentieth century.[7] Earlier, Brecht had seemed to belong with those who aimed to dynamite the tracks of the realist–naturalist tradition. But this allows us to place him if we wish in line with it. We may see him as its sharp-eyed son, who restores to the once-pioneering enterprise its cutting edge by dispensing with old ways and customs, and streamlining its operations on modern principles. This reading of his role has prevailed. His realist credentials have excused his early appetite for discordant combinations and jagged edges, and his con-tinuing taste for fables and poetry; and served as his entry pass with writers and theatre groups trying to deal with the real world in a political way.

80

Brecht's influence on his successors was profound. The tours of his own remarkable productions for the Berliner Ensemble in the 1950s were the prelude to a wave of 'Brechtian' work throughout Europe. His ideas were applied not just to his own plays, but to the whole repertoire. Playwrights too were affected, notably in the wave of new British work in the 1960s and 1970s. Of the figures included here, Athol Fugard, Ariane Mnouchkine and Edward Bond were all affected by his influence. Elsewhere in the world, Brecht's ideas were congenial both to non-western theatrical traditions and to revolutionary aspirations. The work of Augusto Boal and Enrique Buenaventura (see Part V) illustrates how those ideas were put to creative use.

At the same time, this wide influence inevitably gave rise to a certain amount of inert imitation. This was perhaps encouraged by the 'Model Books', that were put out by Brecht, detailing with illustrations the Berliner's productions. As time went by, and as the 'Brechtian' spread with innocuous effect to western Europe's national theatres, to be applauded by the liberal middle class, there was increasing point in Heiner Müller's words: 'To make use of Brecht without criticising him is to betray him.'[8]

Brecht's writings concede a place for the emotions, but the passages where they do so are easily missed; whereas no-one can miss his emphasis on alienation. It is the distancing and lowering of temperature this involves that has aroused most argument amongst political theatre groups, concerned to make direct contact with their audiences and an impact upon them. Brecht's methods have been judged cold by groups aiming to achieve a closeness with their audience, and have been discarded or modified by many, from John McGrath (see Part III) to Edward Bond. Ironically, their furthest development has come outside the political sector, in avant-garde post-modernist work like that of Richard Foreman or the Wooster Group.

But this is not the whole story. Many of those on theatre's political frontline, working on material related to the life of their audience, material of the most potent emotional kind, have turned to Brecht to find a way of treating it. This is clear in the diary notes of Athol Fugard included here. Brecht offers ways of placing the personal case in a perspective and avoiding emotional exploitation. Also, since Brechtian theatre is not dependent on elaborate technical means, small groups with the smallest resources have been able to draw on his thinking – often to greater effect than major companies.

Many of them, however, have developed new working processes, as the contributions here of Fugard, Ariane Mnouchkine and others indicate. The hierarchy of writer, director, actor has come under fire, and collective creation in one or another form has been widely practised. While risks of conflicting purposes have been higher, the multiple release of creativity, inward command of material, committed attack and vibrant group interplay that distinguish this way of working at its best, have often made an impact on audiences that no other method could have achieved.

Groups have found themselves in a different world from Brecht's, working in different conditions to different ends. The strong allegiances of working-class and anti-fascist struggle have partly dissolved. While this is often lamented, it has meant that many groups have become more directly involved with their community and its different constituents, drawing their material from its specific concerns. It has also made room for a new consciousness of particular under-privileged groups. In response there has been a growth of theatre companies who define themselves in terms of gender, ethnicity and sexual orientation. The meaning of politics has widened to take in the concept of sexual politics. The bulk of the pieces that close this section, by Hélène Cixous, Judy Chicago, Carolee Schnee-mann, Suzanne Lacy and Leslie Labowitz, and Charles Ludlam, are concerned with the new developments that have sprung from this. The issues of ethnicity and cultural identity are largely held over till Part V, following a first airing by Kwesi Owusu in Part III.

NOTES

1 See, 'Three Cheers for Shaw' (1926), in Brecht on Theatre: The Development of an Aesthetic, London, Methuen, 1964, pp. 10–13.
2 For a discriminating account of Brecht's relation to expressionism, see John Willett, Brecht in Context, London, Methuen, 1984, ch. 5. For Brecht on Kaiser, see Brecht on Theatre, p. 31. A translation of the play Brecht refers to, Alcibiades Saved, is in Walter Sokel's Anthology of German Expressionist Drama, Ithaca, NY, Anchor, 1963.
3 Erwin Piscator, The Political Theatre, London, Eyre Methuen, 1980, p. 82.
4 Bertolt Brecht, The Messingkauf Dialogues, London, Methuen, 1965, p. 68. Brecht seems to have first developed his idea of epic theatre in 1926. See Brecht on Theatre, op. cit., p. 17.
5 Alexander Tairov, Notes of a Director, Coral Gables, Fla., University of Miami Press, 1969, pp. 48–9.
6 R. Ben-Ari, in Toby Cole and Helen Krich Chinoy (eds), Actors on Acting, New York, Crown, 1949, p. 444.
7 See for example 'The Popular and the Realistic' in Part III; and also further pieces by Brecht in Aesthetics and Politics: Debates between Ernst Bloch, Georg Lukács, Bertolt Brecht, Walter Benjamin, Theodor Adorno, London, New Left Books, 1977.
8 From his essay 'Fatzer±Keuner' (1980).

22

BERNARD SHAW

FROM Preface to *Mrs Warren's Profession* (1902)

As Mrs Warren's profession is organised prostitution, Shaw's play predictably fell foul of the Censor, or 'Examiner', who ruled it could only be privately performed.

This question of the Censorship reminds me that I have to apologise to those who went to the recent performance of Mrs Warren's Profession expecting to find it what I have just called an aphrodisiac. That was not my fault: it was the Examiner's. After the specimens I have given of the tolerance of his department, it was natural enough for thoughtless people to infer that a play which overstepped his indulgence must be a very exciting play indeed. . . . But I protest again that the lure was not mine. The play had been in print for four years; and I have spared no pains to make known that my plays are built to induce, not voluptuous reverie but intellectual interest, not romantic rhapsody but humane concern. . . . As to the voluptuaries, I can assure them that the playwright, whether he be myself or another, will always disappoint them. The drama can do little to delight the senses: all the apparent instances to the contrary are instances of the personal fascination of the performers. The drama of pure feeling is no longer in the hands of the playwright: it has been conquered by the musician, after whose enchantments all the verbal arts seem cold and tame. Romeo and Juliet with the loveliest Juliet is dry, tedious, and rhetorical in comparison with Wagner's Tristan, even though Isolde be both fourteen stone and forty, as she often is in Germany. Indeed, it needed no Wagner to convince the public of this. The voluptuous sentimentality of Gounod's Faust and Bizet's Carmen has captured the common playgoer; and there is, flatly, no future now for any drama without music except the drama of thought. The attempt to produce a genus of opera without music (and this absurdity is what our fashionable theatres have been driving at for a long time past without knowing it) is far less hopeful than my own determination to accept problem as the normal material of the drama.

. . . I am accused of ignoring, not stage logic, but, of all things, human feeling. People with completely theatrical imaginations tell me that no girl would treat her mother as Vivie Warren does, meaning that no stage heroine would in a popular sentimental play. They say this just as they might say that no two straight lines would enclose a space. They do not see how completely inverted their vision has become even when I throw its preposterousness in their faces, as I repeatedly do in this very play. Praed, the sentimental artist (fool that I was not to make him a theatre critic instead of an architect!) burlesques them by expecting all through the piece that the feelings of the others will be logically deducible from their family relationships and from his "conventionally unconventional" social code. The sarcasm is lost on the critics: they, saturated with the same logic, only think him the sole sensible person on the stage. Thus it comes about that the more completely the dramatist is emancipated from the illusion that men and women are primarily reasonable beings, and the more powerfully he insists on the ruthless indifference of their great dramatic antagonist, the external world, to their whims and emotions, the surer he is to be denounced as blind to the very distinction on which his whole work is built. Far from ignoring idiosyncrasy, will, passion, impulse, whim, as factors in human action, I have placed them so nakedly on the stage that the elderly citizen, accustomed to see them clothed with the veil of manufactured logic about duty, and to disguise even his own impulses from himself in this way, finds the picture as unnatural as Carlyle's suggested painting of parliament sitting without its clothes.

I now come to those critics who, intellectually baffled by the problem in Mrs Warren's Profession, have made a virtue of running away from it on the gentlemanly ground that the theatre is frequented by women as well as by men, and that such problems should not be discussed or even mentioned in the presence of women. With that sort of chivalry I cannot argue: I simply affirm that Mrs Warren's Profession is a play for women; that it was written for women; that it has been performed and produced mainly through the determination of women that it should be performed and produced; that the enthusiasm of women made its first performance excitingly successful; and that not one of these women had any inducement to support it except their belief in the timeliness and the power of the lesson the play teaches. Those who were "surprised to see ladies present" were men; and when they proceeded to explain that the journals they represented could not possibly demoralize the public by describing such a play, their editors cruelly devoted the space saved by their delicacy to reporting at unusual length an exceptionally abominable police case.

My old Independent Theatre manager, Mr Grein, besides that reproach to me for shattering his ideals, complains that Mrs Warren is not wicked enough, and names several romancers who would have clothed her black soul with all the terrors of tragedy. I have no doubt they would; but that is just what I did not want to do. Nothing would please our sanctimonious

British public more than to throw the whole guilt of Mrs Warren's profession on Mrs Warren herself. Now the whole aim of my play is to throw that guilt on the British public itself. Mr Grein may remember that when he produced my first play, Widowers' Houses, exactly the same misunderstanding arose. When the virtuous young gentleman rose up in wrath against the slum landlord, the slum landlord very effectually shewed him that slums are the product, not of individual Harpagons, but of the indifference of virtuous young gentlemen to the condition of the city they live in, provided they live at the west end of it on money earned by somebody else's labor. The notion that prostitution is created by the wickedness of Mrs Warren is as silly as the notion – prevalent, nevertheless, to some extent in Temperance circles – that drunkenness is created by the wickedness of the publican. Mrs Warren is not a whit a worse woman than the reputable daughter who cannot endure her. Her indifference to the ultimate social consequences of her means of making money, and her discovery of that means by the ordinary method of taking the line of least resistance to getting it, are too common in English society to call for any special remark. Her vitality, her thrift, her energy, her outspokenness, her wise care of her daughter, and the managing capacity which has enabled her and her sister to climb from the fried fish shop down by the Mint to the establishments of which she boasts, are all high English social virtues. Her defence of herself is so overwhelming that it provokes the St James's Gazette to declare that "the tendency of the play is wholly evil" because "it contains one of the boldest and most specious defences of an immoral life for poor women that has ever been penned." Happily the St James's Gazette here speaks in its haste. Mrs Warren's defence of herself is not only bold and specious, but valid and unanswerable. But it is no defence at all of the vice which she organizes. It is no defence of an immoral life to say that the alternative offered by society collectively to poor women is a miserable life, starved, overworked, fetid, ailing, ugly. Though it is quite natural and *right* for Mrs Warren to choose what is, according to her lights, the least immoral alternative, it is none the less infamous of society to offer such alternatives. For the alternatives offered are not morality and immorality, but two sorts of immorality. The man who cannot see that starvation, overwork, dirt, and disease are as anti-social as prostitution – that they are the vices and crimes of a nation, and not merely its misfortunes – is (to put it as politely as possible) a hopelessly Private Person.

Bernard Shaw (1856–1950), Irish playwright, joined the Fabian Society after moving to London, and turned to playwriting in his mid-thirties, in 1892. At the time he wrote this preface he was 46 and his first three plays – the 'Plays Unpleasant' as he dubbed them in response to the adverse reaction they had aroused – had had four performances between them. *Mrs Warren's Profession*, the third, written in 1894 and treating 'a profession which society officially repudiates as a metaphor for the way in which that larger society is really conducted', had been rejected even by the Independent Theatre in which he was involved, and which had staged two performances of his earlier *Widowers' Houses*. Its founder, J. T. Grein, thought it 'unfit for women's ears'. Shaw had to wait eight years to see it produced – by the Stage Society for two private performances in 1902. It had no public performance until 1925 in Britain, where censorship remained until 1968.

23

SERGEI EISENSTEIN

FROM A Personal Statement (1926)

In 1921 I entered the Proletcult organization[1] as a theatre designer. The Proletcult Theatre busily sought new art forms that would correspond to the ideology of the new Russian state structure. Our troupe was composed of young workers who wished to create genuine art; they brought to this aim a quite new kind of temperament and a new viewpoint on the world and on art . . . . The next years were a fierce struggle. In 1922 I became director of the First Moscow Workers' Theatre and completely broke with the views of the Proletcult administration. The Proletcult staff adhered to Lunacharsky's[2] position: to maintain old traditions and to compromise on the question of pre-revolutionary artistic efficiency. I was one of the most unbending supporters of LEF (Left Front), where we wanted *the new*, meaning works that would correspond to the new social conditions of art. We had on our side at that time all the young people and innovators, including the futurists Meyerhold and Mayakovsky; in the most rigid opposition to us were the traditionalist Stanislavsky* and the opportunist Tairov[3]. . . .

In 1922–23 I staged three dramas at the Workers' Theatre: in principle their staging was a mathematical calculation of the elements of affect,[4] which at that time I called "actions". In the first production, *The Sage*,[5] I tried to dissect cubistically a classical play into separately affective "attractions". The action took place in a circus. In the second production, *Do You Hear, Moscow?*, I used fundamentally technical means in trying to realize theatrical illusions with mathematical calculations. This was the first success of the new theatrical affects. The third production, *Gas Masks*, was staged in a gas factory, during working hours. The machines worked and the "actors" worked; for the first time this represented the success of an absolutely *real*, highly objective art.

---

* I have always been amused when the German press identified my anonymous actors, my "simple people", as artists of the Moscow Art Theatre, my "deadly enemy"!

Translated by Jay Leyda

NOTES

1 Founded 1917 to promote the cultural education of the workers, Proletcult's founding belief that proletarian culture could come only from the proletariat did not commit it to avant-garde styles.
2 See note, p. 93.
3 Alexander Tairov, director of the renowned Kamerny Theatre.
4 I.e., psychological response or feeling aroused by stimulus.
5 Elsewhere translated as *Wise Man*: see p. 90, and note p. 93.

FROM The Montage of Attractions (1923)

This term is being used for the first time. It requires explanation.

Theatre's basic material derives from the audience: the moulding of the audience in a desired direction (or mood) is the task of every utilitarian theatre (agitation, advertising, health education, etc.). The instrument of this process consists of all the parts that constitute the apparatus of theatre (Ostuzhev's 'chatter' no more than the colour of the prima donna's tights, a roll on the drums just as much as Romeo's soliloquy, the cricket on the hearth no less than a salvo under the seats of the auditorium[1]) because, despite their differences, they all lead to one thing – which their presence legitimates – to their common quality of *attraction*.

An attraction (in our diagnosis of theatre) is any aggressive moment in theatre, i.e. any element of it that subjects the audience to emotional or psychological influence, verified by experience and mathematically calculated to produce specific emotional shocks in the spectator in their proper order within the whole. These shocks provide the only opportunity of perceiving the ideological aspect of what is being shown, the final ideological conclusion. (The path to knowledge encapsulated in the phrase, 'through the living play of the passions', is specific to theatre.)

Emotional and psychological, of course, in the sense of direct reality as employed, for instance, in the Grand Guignol, where eyes are gouged out or arms and legs amputated on stage, or the direct reality of an actor on stage involved through the telephone with a nightmarish event taking place dozens of miles away, or the situation of a drunkard who, sensing his approaching end, pleads for protection and whose pleas are taken as a sign of madness. In this sense and not in the sense of the unravelling of psychological problems where the attraction is the theme itself, existing and taking effect *outside* the particular action, but topical enough. (Most agit-theatres make the mistake of being satisfied with attractions solely of that sort in their productions.)

I regard the attraction as being in normal conditions an independent and primary element in structuring the show, a molecular (i.e. compound) unity of the *effectiveness* of theatre and of *theatre as a whole*. It is completely analogous to Grosz's[2] 'rough sketches', or the elements of Rodchenko's[3] photo-illustrations.

'Compound'? It is difficult to distinguish where the fascination of the hero's nobility ends (the psychological moment) and where the moment of his personal charm (i.e. his erotic effect) begins. The lyrical effect of a whole series of Chaplin scenes is inseparable from the attractional quality of the specific mechanics of his movements. Similarly, it is difficult to distinguish where religious pathos gives way to sadistic satisfaction in the torture scenes of the mystery plays, and so on.

The attraction has nothing in common with the stunt. The stunt or, more accurately, the trick (it is high time that this much abused term was returned to its rightful place) is a finished achievement of a particular kind of mastery (acrobatics, for the most part) and it is only one kind of attraction that is suitable for presentation (or, as they say in the circus, 'sale'). In so far as the trick is absolute and complete *within itself*, it means the direct opposite of the attraction, which is based exclusively on something relative, the reactions of the audience.

Our present approach radically alters our opportunities in the principles of creating an 'effective structure' (the show as a whole) instead of a static 'reflection' of a particular event dictated by the theme, and our opportunities for resolving it through an effect that is logically implicit in that event, and this gives rise to a new concept: a free montage with arbitrarily chosen independent (of both the PARTICULAR *composition and any thematic connection with the actors) effects (attractions) but with the precise aim of a specific final thematic effect – montage of attractions.*

The path that will liberate theatre completely from the yoke of the 'illusory depictions' and 'representations' that have hitherto been the decisive, unavoidable and only possible approach lies through a move to the montage of 'realistic artificialities', at the same time admitting to the weave of this montage whole 'illusory sequences', and a plot integral to the subject, not something self-contained or all-determining but something consciously and specifically determined for a particular purpose, and an attraction chosen purely for its powerful effect.

Since it is not a matter of 'revealing the playwright's purpose', 'correctly interpreting the author' or 'faithfully reflecting an epoch', etc., the attraction and a system of attractions provide the only basis for an effective show. In the hands of every skilled director the attraction has been used intuitively in one way or another, not, of course, on the level of montage or structure but at least in a 'harmonic composition' (from which a whole new vocabulary derives: an 'effective curtain', a 'rich exit', 'a good stunt', etc.) but essentially this has been done only within the framework of the logical plausibility of the subject (it has been 'justified' by the play) and in the main unconsciously and in pursuit of something entirely different (something that had been enumerated at the 'start' of the proceedings). What remains to us in reorganising the system we use to structure a show is merely to shift the focus of attention to the essential (what was earlier regarded as attendant decoration but is in fact the principal messenger of the abnormal intentions of a production and is not logically connected with the run-of-the-mill reverence of literary tradition), *to establish this particular approach as a production method* (which, since the autumn of 1922, has been the work of the Proletkult Workshops).

The school for the montageur is cinema and, principally, music-hall and circus because (from the point of view of form) putting on a good show means constructing a strong music-hall/circus programme that derives from the situations found in the play that is taken as a basis.

As an example here is a list of the sections of numbers in the epilogue to *Wise Man*:[4]

1. The hero's explanatory monologue. 2. A fragment from a detective film. (A classification of 1., the theft of the diary.) 3. An Eccentric[5] music-hall entrée (the bride and her three rejected suitors – all one person in the play – in the role of best men): a melancholy scene reminiscent of the song 'Your hands smell of incense' and 'May I be punished by the grave' (we intended that the bride would have a xylophone and this would be played on six rows of bells, the officers' buttons). 4.5.6. Three parallel two-phrased clowning entrées (the theme: payment for organising the wedding). 7. An entrée with a star (the aunt) and three officers (the theme: the restraint of the rejected suitors), punning (by reference to a horse) on a triple volte number on a saddled horse (on the impossibility of bringing it into the room, traditionally, in 'triple harness'). 8. Good agit-songs ('The priest had a dog' accompanied by a rubber priest like a dog. The theme: the start of the wedding ceremony). 9. A break in the action (a paper-boy's voice announcing that the hero is leaving). 10. The villain appears in a mask. A fragment from a comedy film. (A résumé of five acts of the play. The theme: the publication of the diary.) 11. The continuation of the (interrupted) action in another grouping (a simultaneous wedding with the three rejected suitors). 12. Anti-religious songs ('Allah-Verdi'[6] – a punning theme tune on the need to bring in a mullah because of the large number of suitors that one bride is marrying) from the choir and a new character used only in this scene, a soloist dressed as a mullah. 13. General dancing. Some play with a poster inscribed: 'Religion is the opium of the people.' 14. A farcical scene. (The bride and her three suitors are packed into a box and pots are smashed against the lid.) 15. The marital trio – a parody of life. (The song: 'Who here is young?') 16. A precipice. The hero's return. 17. The hero's winged flight beneath the big top (the theme: suicide in despair.) 18. A break. The villain's return. The suicide is held up. 19. A sword fight (the theme: enmity). 20. An agit-entrée involving the hero and the villain

on the theme of NEP.[7] 21. An act on a sloping wire (crossing from the arena to the balcony over the audience's heads. The theme: 'leaving for Russia'). 22. A clowning parody of this number (with the hero). Descent from the wire. 23. A clown descends the same wire from the balcony, holding on by his teeth. 24. The final entrée with two clowns throwing water over one another (as per tradition), finishing with the announcement: 'The End'. 25. A volley of shots beneath the seats of the auditorium as a finale. The connecting features of the numbers, if there is no direct transition, are used as linking elements: they are handled with different arrangements of equipment, musical interludes, dancing, pantomime, carpet-clowns.

Translated by Richard Taylor

NOTES

1 i.e. classical speeches (Ostuzhev was an actor), nineteenth-century melodrama (Dickens' *Cricket on the Hearth* was a 1915 Moscow Art Theatre production), and twentieth-century provocation: see Eisenstein's final item.
2 Georg Grosz, German artist and occasional theatre designer, who collaborated with Piscator and Brecht.
3 Alexander Rodchenko, leading constructivist artist-photographer, and pioneer of photo-montage.
4 See note, p. 93.
5 A clown entry.
6 A Christian chant of the Georgians, not intending to refer to the Muslim Allah.
7 Lenin's New Economic Policy of 1921, re-admitting limited private enterprise.

FROM The Montage of Film Attractions: The Model Actor (1924)

THE BASIC PREMISS

1 The value lies not in the figurativeness of the actions of the model actor but in the degree of his motor and associatively infectious capabilities vis-à-vis the audience (i.e. the whole process of the actor's movement is organised with the aim of facilitating the imitative capacities of the audience).

2 Hence the first direction concerns the *selection* of versions presented to the audience: a reliance on invention, i.e. on the *combination* of the movement, required by the purpose, from the versions that are most

characteristic of real circumstances (and consequently automatically imitated by the audience) and simplest in form. . . .

3 The refinement of this version of movement: i.e. the ascertainment of the purely mechanical schema of its normal course in real life.

4 Breakdown of movement into its pseudo-primitive primary component elements for the audience – a system of shocks, rises, falls, spins, pirouettes, etc. – for the director to convey to the performer the precise arrangement of the motor version and to train these inherently neutral expressive (not in terms of plot but in terms of production) motor units.

5 Assembly (montage) and co-ordination into a temporal schema of these neutral elements of the movements in a combination that produces action. . . . The realisation of the movement does not proceed in a superficially imitative and figurative manner vis-à-vis a real action (murder, drunkenness, chopping wood, etc.) but results in an organic representation that emerges through the appropriate mechanical schema and a real achievement of the motor process of the phenomena being depicted. . . .

Expressive movements fall into three groups:

1 A set of rational directions in the direct execution of common motor intentions (all aspects of an appropriately constructed movement – of a boxer, a hammerman, etc. – and also reflex movements that have at some time been automated into conscious purposes – the leap of a tiger, etc.).

2 A set of instances with varying purpose with two or more motivations for their realisation when several purposes that resolve particular motivations build up in the body and, lastly:

3 The most interesting case in terms of its motor formation is the case of a psychologically expressive movement that represents a motor exposure of the *conflict* of motivations: an instinctively emotional desire that retards the conscious volitional principle. . . .

It would be a great error to perceive our statement as advocating in the model actor's work the affective condition that was long ago condemned in theatre and is absolutely unthinkable in cinema, given the peculiarities of its production. It is here a matter of assessing the mechanical interactions that constantly occur within us but that flow from us in cases where a similar process has to be consciously realised in front of an audience or a camera.* We must also bear in mind that both series of movements that are

---

* The majority of movements are reflex and automatic and it was Darwin who pointed out the difficulties involved in reproducing these kinds of movements. One example is the difficulty involved in reproducing a 'premeditated' swallow. It is interesting to note the immediate departure from the laws of movement that occurs when they are consciously reproduced: whereas if the hands of an actor (which, according to the general laws, are part of his body as a whole) are in real life always engaged in motor movement, on stage 'they do not know what to do' because this law is being broken.

coming into conflict are equally consciously constructed and the effect of the affective movement is achieved by the artificial mechanical setting in motion of the body as a whole and must in no way result from the emotional state of the performer.

Translated by Richard Taylor

Sergei Eisenstein (1898–1948), the leading Soviet film director, started out in theatre, initially working under Meyerhold. 'The Montage of Attractions' was written a year before he gave up the stage for film, and relates to his 1923 production of *Enough Stupidity in Every Wise Man*. This marked the centenary of its author, Ostrovsky, whose early reform of the Russian stage had enabled it to achieve a strong critical realism, and whom Meyerhold had once argued represented the true line of Russian drama in a 'theatre of life' and a 'theatre of action', before its deviation through Turgenev and Chekhov into a 'theatre of mood'.[1] Hence the call of Lunacharsky, Soviet Commissar for Culture, for a move 'Back to Ostrovsky'. But what to do with such bourgeois classics in the new proletarian era was hotly debated. In Eisenstein's hands Ostrovsky was scandalously transformed. With the text entirely rewritten by Sergei Tretyakov, Eisenstein devised a production in which the tensions in Ostrovsky's play were rendered in a series of irreverent musical, theatrical and circus effects, as he describes here. As the formalist critic Victor Shklovsky pointed out, the results were close to those of FEKS (The Factory of the Eccentric Actor – see Kozintsev's manifesto in Part III), which Eisenstein had seen: 'FEKS and Eisenstein took the classics for scrap' – unlike Meyerhold, who 'took them for resurrection'.[2] None the less, Meyerhold claimed the technique of 'attractions' originated with him, defining them as 'episodes, each with an unfailingly effective conclusion'.[3] Eisenstein had been his assistant the year before on his production of a nineteenth-century satire on the police, *Tarelkin's Death*. It was staged in vigorous eccentric style, with a trapeze, stage traps, collapsing furniture and chases.

The interest in movement and gymnastic actor-training so widespread in Russia in the 1920s also originated in Meyerhold. The actors in *Tarelkin's Death* were trained in his 'biomechanics', a system of which he left no full account. Its constructivist spirit ('1. The body is a machine. 2. The worker is a machine operator'[4]) is linked by Meyerhold to Taylor, the American pioneer of time and motion studies, concerned with efficient movement in the workplace. But the subsequent influence on Eisenstein of Rudolf Bode's *Expressive Gymnastics*,[5] is reflected in his and Tretyakov's 1923 article 'Expressive Movement'.[6] Bode, a student of Dalcroze, rejected exercise isolating or dissociating parts of the body (techniques practised by Meyerhold), in favour of organic rhythm and natural movements that engaged it as a whole. This is consonant not only with Dalcroze, but with Duncan and the modern dance movement continuing in Mary Wigman and Rudolph Laban, and diverges from the more mechanistic emphasis of Meyerhold. The extra dialectical twist Eisenstein gives to Bode here, crucial from the dramatic point of view, is to acknowledge that in human beings those forces may be working in contradiction to each other, according to splits between desires, goals, loyalties, etc. Movement can therefore express or show these things, and is to that degree re-humanised, without recourse to the 'affective' – (a probable code-word for Stanislavski's method and its cultivation of 'affective memory').

NOTES

1 See the essay from his *O teatre*, 1912, in Andrew Field's *The Complection of Russian Literature*, London, Allen Lane, 1971.
2 Victor Shklovsky, 'Birth and Life of FEKS', 1928, in *Futurism, Formalism, FEKS*, London, BFI, 1978.
3 *Meyerhold on Theatre*, ed. Edward Braun, London, Methuen, 1969, p. 318.
4 Konstantin Rudnitsky, *Meyerhold the Director*, Ann Arbor, Mich., Ardis, 1981, p. 292.
5 *Ausdruckgymnastique*, Munich, 1922. For Bode's influence, see François Albera, *Eisenstein et le constructivisme russe*, Lausanne, L'Age d'Homme, 1990.
6 *Millenium Film Journal*, no. 3, Winter–Spring 1979.

24

ERNST TOLLER

From Post-war German Drama (1928)

I have been asked by the editor of *The Nation* to write a few words on post-war German drama. We are in the habit of using the term "post-war drama" without stopping to ask ourselves if there really is such a type, distinct in presentation, treatment, kind, and form from that of the pre-war period.

Did the war really cause this decisive change in German drama? Not at all. It is strikingly confirmed today, after ten years, that the present tendencies in the drama began their development years before the war, and that since then they have simply been in more rapid eruption.

The younger dramatists felt that an unbridgeable gulf divided them from the older generation. The struggle between the generations, the father-and-son problem, the fight between compromise and directness, between bourgeois and anti-bourgeois, had stirred young intellects before the war made a reality of what they had prophetically seen coming. To be sure, the war destroyed many moral and social, many spiritual and artistic values. But the foundations of these values had become rotten. In place of the idea, there had come to the fore a realpolitik which was leading to the abrogation of all reality. Freedom had become hypocrisy – freedom for the few, spiritual and economic bondage for the many. In the first dramas of Sorge, Hasenclever, and Werfel this hatred toward our elders was already smoldering. And these were the same elders who did nothing to prevent the war but, tricking it out in romanticism, pitilessly and unfeelingly sent battalion after battalion of young German manhood out to die.

During the war very little got to the public through the strict censorship. But after the collapse, every day brought new works from the newly liberated minds. The form which this art took was called expressionism. It was just as much reaction as it was synthetic and creative action. It turned against that tendency in art which was satisfied merely to set down impressions, one after the other, without troubling to question their essential nature, justification, or the idea involved. The expressionists were not satisfied simply to photograph. They knew that environment permeates the artist and is reflected in his psychic mirror in such a way as utterly to transfigure this environment. Expressionism wanted to influence environment, to change it in giving it a brighter, more righteous appearance, to make it impossible, for example, for a catastrophe like the war ever to threaten mankind again. Reality was to be comprehended anew in the light of the ideal, was to be born again.

All activity resolves itself into outer and inner activity, both of equal importance and strength as motivating forces. In style expressionism was pregnant, almost telegraphic, always shunning the peripheral, and always probing to the centre of things. In expressionistic drama man is no accidental private person. He is a type posited for many, and ignoring the limits of superficial characterization. Man was skinned in the expectation that somewhere under his skin was his soul. The dramatic exponents of expressionism were Sorge, Göring, Balach, and Toller. Of their works may be mentioned Sorge's "Der Bettler," Kaiser's "Von Morgen bis Mitternacht," Hasenclever's "Der Sohn," Unruh's "Ein Geschlecht," "Der arme Vetter" by Balach, and Toller's "Die Wandlung" and "Masse-Mensch."[1]

During the epoch of expressionism a significant development took place. A new character appeared on the stage – proletarian man. Of course, there had already been plays whose action took place in a proletarian milieu. But something fundamental divided expressionistic proletarian drama from such a play as Hauptman's "Die Weber" or Bucher's "Wozzek." In the old dramas the proletarian was a dull creature who rebelled against his fate with strong but rash impulse. The artist who pictured him wanted to awaken sympathy. In the new drama, the proletarian is active, conscious, rebelling against his fate, and struggling for a new reality. He is driven on by feeling, by knowledge, and by the idea of a brighter future.

It is useless to talk of the fiasco of expressionism, or to ask whether expressionism produced works which will still be remembered in fifty years. Expressionism wanted to be a product of the time and to react to it. And that much it certainly succeeded in doing. Never since Schiller's "Die Räuber," since "Kabale und Liebe,"[2] has the theater been so much a rostrum for current happenings or so much upset by the strife and counter-strife of public opinion; passionate partisanship on one side, and violent one-sided reproaches on the other.

Let us examine for a moment the reproach of "tendency" leveled against expressionism. When a piece of writing portrays spiritual behavior, feelings, reactions to the phenomena of life and knowledge it does not seem tendential to the bourgeois, because these things have become traditional and because they express his conception of the world, his philosophy, his naked economic interest. He overlooks the fact that such writing also has a tendency, namely his own.

But when new observations are made in a drama, in opposition to those ideas to which the bourgeois has been accustomed, he calls such a work tendential. The atmosphere in any work of art, in so far as it transects a given social milieu, always has a definite impress that one is safe in calling partisan. There is, however, one type of partisanship which the artist must avoid, namely that partisanship of the black and white kind which depicts all persons on one side as devils of the blackest sort, and all those on the other as angels.

But since the spirit, the idea did not succeed in changing the character of the times; since the old reality with the old abominations, with the old greed, the old rapacious striving, the old danger zones, simply reappeared; since the peace which all were yearning for turned out to be a grin behind which the next war is looming; since the spiritual had again become a veneer and a mockery, younger dramatists appeared who thought that as the ideal was lacking there was no reason for it, especially in art. They set out to portray life and nothing but life. But the decisive thing in life for them was the uninhibited accord or antagonism of the sexual impulse. The chaotic, the sexual, became the focus of the new drama which tended to the epic in form. Side by side with this the struggle between the generations played a definite role. Speech became naturalistic again, but it was distinguished from the old naturalism by a dynamic impetus that gave it a distinctive rhythm. As dramatists of this type one may mention Brecht, Bronnen, and Zuckmayer.

The later German dramatists were unquestionably influenced by America, but the German brand of Americanism did not represent the great minds of America. What was taken over was the tempo, the banal optimism, the superficiality, in short that new matter-of-factness which has very little meaning and no connection whatever with the major arts.

German drama exists, as does all German art, between two worlds. The bourgeois world is spiritually and ethically convulsed and the world of the workers is visible as yet only among small or petty groups.

NOTES

1 I.e. *The Beggar*; *From Morning to Midnight*; *The Son*; *A Family*; *The Poor Cousin*; *Transfiguration*; *Masses and Man*.
2 *The Robbers*, 1782; *Intrigue and Love*, 1784.

Ernst Toller (1893–1939), of Jewish parentage, saw front-line action in the First World War, but was invalided out in 1916. He became a left-wing pacifist, took part in the 1919 communist take-over in Munich and was appointed Commissar for Education in the short-lived Bavarian Soviet Republic. In consequence he was committed to prison with a five-year sentence, where he wrote his first play, *Transfiguration* (1919). Subsequent plays include *Masses and Man* (1921), *Hinkemann* and *The Machine Wreckers* (1922), and *Hoppla! Such is Life* (1927), which was directed by Piscator. At the coming of the Nazis in 1933, he escaped from Germany to live in England and subsequently the United States, where he committed suicide.

25

VSEVOLOD MEYERHOLD

FROM The Reconstruction of the Theatre (1929)

Comrades – when we come to discuss the influence which the modern revolutionary theatre can exert upon the spectator at a time when its own organizers have still to agree on the precise form it should take, we must not overlook a single aspect of it, particularly in view of the need to take account of the demands both of our Party and of the new spectator. Once the theatre is regarded as a means of agitation, it follows that the first concern of all those concerned in the theatre is the clarity of the message conveyed from the stage; the spectator will want to know precisely why a play is being performed and what the director and actors are trying to say in it.

We can induce the spectator to join us in examining a wide range of topics presented as a debate, but employing dramatic situations and characters. We can persuade him to reason and to argue. This ability to start the spectator's brain working is just one of the theatre's properties. But it has another, quite different property: it can stimulate the spectator's feelings and steer him through a complex labyrinth of emotions. Since the theatre has the power to stimulate the emotions as well as the intellect, it follows that it is wrong for a play as a work of art to limit itself to sheer rhetoric, employing raisonneurs and indulging in dialogues borrowed from the so-called 'conversational theatre'. We reject such a theatre as a mere debating chamber. I could recite this lecture to piano or orchestral accompaniment, leaving pauses for the audience to listen to the music and digest my arguments; but it would not transform my lecture and you, the audience, into a dramatic performance.

Since a dramatic performance depends on laws peculiar to the theatre, it is not enough for it to appeal purely to the spectator's intellect. A play must do more than prompt some idea or depict events in such a way as to invite automatic conclusions. Actors do not perform simply to demonstrate the idea of the author, the director or themselves; their struggles, the whole dramatic conflict has a far higher aim than the mere exposition of thesis and antithesis. It is not for that that the public goes to the theatre.

My principal aim today is to try to resolve the confusion which to this day is troubling the theatrical front. In trying to do this, I shall refer to events abroad as well as in the Soviet Union; I must consider not only our world but the world at large. The masses, hungering for spectacle as well as bread, want entertainment which appeals to the heart as well as the intellect, which engages them totally. For this reason our theatre managers and directors must aim to make their productions sparkle with interest and variety. The aim of the theatrical powers that be is to provide as much variety as possible, and for this reason they must try whenever possible to employ every art form.

There was a time when Wagner's idea of a new theatre which would be a dramatic synthesis of words, music, lighting, rhythmical movement and all the magic of the plastic arts was regarded as purely utopian. Now we can see that this is exactly what a production should be: we should employ all the elements which the other arts have to offer and fuse them to produce a concerted effect on the audience.

The theatre which relies on the rhetoric of raisonneurs, which is purely agitatory and thus anti-artistic has long since been exposed as a harmful phenomenon. Other theatres have been successfully propagandist by actually silencing the actor at the play's climax, introducing music to heighten the tension (e.g. *Bubus, the Teacher* by my theatre and *Days in the Melting Pot* by the Leningrad Young Workers' Theatre). You must regard the dramatic theatre as a musical theatre as well. In taking advantage of every possible technical advance, the theatre cannot afford to ignore the cinematograph; the action of the actor on stage can be juxtaposed with his filmed image on a screen.

Alternatively, we might see the dramatic theatre transformed into a kind of revue in which the actor appears now as a dramatic artist, now as an opera singer, now as a dancer, now as an equilibrist, now as a gymnast, now as a clown. Thus, by employing elements of the other arts the theatre can make the performance more diverting and deepen the spectator's comprehension of it.

. . . We can see now that all those thundering broadsides of ours were just so many blank charges: all those speeches *à thèse*, those attempts at 'agitation', so often dull and sometimes just plain stupid; those schematized types, signalling their characters as though by semaphore: one signal for the virtuous 'reds', another for the evil 'whites'.

And what about all those scenes in so-called revolutionary plays depicting 'the decline of Europe'? Has it not struck you that the reason for their success is their blatant disregard for the directives of the Glavrepertkom?[1] Dramatists and directors present a picture of 'decadence' in the hope of disgusting the audience. But far from being disgusted, the spectator falls into raptures over the 'delights' before him: he enjoys watching unclothed women dancing the foxtrot, he enjoys listening to jazz. And why does he enjoy it? Surely because the so-called 'positive' scenes are full of dreary raisonneurs; there's not one single character who radiates the fervour demanded by such objects as socialist reconstruction.

The theatre is faced with a new task. The theatre must work on the spectator in order to awaken and strengthen in him a militancy strong enough to help him conquer the oblomovism, manilovism,[2] hypocrisy, erotomania and pessimism within himself. How can we acquaint the manual labourers of socialism with the full magnitude of the revolution? How can we imbue them with that 'life-giving force' (to quote Comrade Stalin) which will carry the masses forward to a world of new revolutionary creative effort?

How indeed, if not through the theatre?

And once again the actor stands out as the main transmitter of the invigorating shock. But what must we do to make this shock effective, to help the actor transmit it to the audience? Above all, we must strengthen those elements of the production which strike directly at the spectator's emotions.

In the light of present conditions we must take down that old slogan which has been so violently distorted by the more diehard of our critics. I mean: 'Down with beauty in the theatre!' When we started to build stage-constructions in place of old-style sets we thundered: 'Down with beauty!' We meant that painted designs pandered to the snob with his own peculiar conception of the function of the theatre; to such spectators painted sets seemed indispensable.

The modern spectator, who developed his own sense of style during the struggles of the Revolution and has shown himself quite ready to accept the extremes of stylized production (he has become familiar with stylization through watching productions at the Meyerhold Theatre and theatres of that type, as well as club performances at which he can experience the impact of a theatre employing the most primitive means) – the modern spectator finds constructions wholly convincing.

Now that the taste of the mass spectator has become far more sophisticated, we must think in terms of more complex musical spectacles. So surely it is time we reconsidered the slogan, 'Down with beauty'. By employing a good sound construction (as a convenient platform for acting) we do not free ourselves from the obligation to construct it beautifully. When Ford markets a good sound automobile he also tries to make it look beautiful, even if his conception of beauty is different from, say, that of the 'World of Art'. We must realize that the beauty of Ford's car is a direct outcome of its efficiency and reliability.

Today's aesthetic must take account of the new standards which have been created by new social conditions. The art of today is different from the art of a feudal or bourgeois society. We must understand clearly what we mean by beauty and reject all beauty that is not utilitarian. We need beauty today as much as we ever did in order to counteract the effects of the 'oblomovism' whose roots are spreading rapidly through our society. And now that the kulaks are putting out even stronger roots in our villages, now that the Church is ensnaring our youth, it is time we all told the so-called 'Kulturträger'[3] of the theatre to make still greater efforts to help our art flood the country with beauty.

Translated by Edward Braun

NOTES

1 Board that handled stage censorship, set up in 1923.
2 Sloth and self-satisfied blindness, from the protagonist of Goncharov's novel *Oblomov* and Manilov in Gogol's *Dead Souls*.
3 Upholders of culture. In German in the text.

Vsevolod Meyerhold (1874–1940), Russian actor, director and (briefly) film-maker, of German parentage. Though his work was not explicitly political before the Revolution, he was one of the first in theatre to side with the Bolsheviks, and his part in transforming Soviet theatre into a revolutionary cultural force open to the avant-garde movements of the time is large. In 1921 he became director of the Moscow State Higher Theatre Workshop, a school with eighty students, and developed 'biomechanics', a system of exercise publicly demonstrated in 1922, and employed in his productions. In 1937 he was attacked in *Pravda*, and a year later the Meyerhold Theatre was shut down. Stanislavski courageously invited him to direct his Opera Studio. But in 1939 he was arrested, and his wife, Zinaida Raikh, murdered. He was shot a year or so later. On biomechanics, see Robert Leach, *Vsevolod Meyerhold*, Cambridge University Press, 1989.

26

ERWIN PISCATOR

FROM Basic Principles of a Theory of Sociological Drama (1929)

1   THE FUNCTION OF MAN

The War finally buried bourgeois individualism under a hail of steel and a holocaust of fire. Man, the individual, existing as an isolated being, independent (at least seemingly) of social connections, revolving egocentrically around the concept of the self, in fact lies buried beneath a marble slab inscribed "The Unknown Soldier." Or, as Remarque[1] formulated it, "The generation of 1914 perished in the war, even if some did survive the shellfire." What came back had nothing more in common with concepts like man, mankind, and humanity, which had symbolised the eternal nature of the God-given order in the parlours of prewar days. . . .

The epoch whose social and economic conditions have in fact perhaps deprived the individual of his right to be a man, without affording him the higher humanity of a new society, has raised itself on a pedestal as the new hero. It is no longer the private, personal fate of the individual, but the times and the fate of the masses that are the heroic factors in the new drama.

Does the individual lose the attributes of his personality in the process? Does he love, hate or suffer less than the heroes of former generations? Certainly not, but all his emotional complexes are seen from a new angle. It is no longer one man alone, insulated, a world in himself, who experiences his fate; that man is inseparably bound up with the great political and economic factors of the times, as Brecht once pointedly observed: "Every Chinese coolie is forced to take part in world politics to earn his daily bread." He is bound in all his utterances to the destiny of the age, regardless of what his station in life might be.

For us, man portrayed on the stage is significant as a social function. It is not his relationship to himself, nor his relationship to God, but his relationship to society which is central. Whenever he appears, his class or social stratum appears with him. His moral, spiritual or sexual conflicts are conflicts with society. The Ancients may have focused on his relationship to the Fates, the Middle Ages on his relationship to God, Rationalism on his relationship to nature, Romanticism on his relationship to the power of the emotions –: a time in which the relationship of individuals in the community to one another, the revision of human values, the realignment of social relationships is the order of the day cannot fail to see mankind in terms of society and the social problems of the times, i.e., as a political being.

The excessive stress on the political angle – and it is not our work, but the disharmony in current social conditions which makes every sign of life political – may in a sense lead to a distorted view of human ideals, but the distorted view at least has the advantage of corresponding to reality.

We, as revolutionary Marxists, cannot consider our task complete if we produce an uncritical copy of reality, conceiving the theatre as a mirror of the times. We can no more consider this our task than we can overcome this state of affairs by theatrical means alone, nor can we conceal the disharmony with a discreet veil, nor can we present man as a creature of sublime greatness in times which in fact socially distort him – in a word, it is not our business to produce an idealistic effect. The business of revolutionary theatre is to take reality as its point of departure and to magnify the social discrepancy, making it an element of our indictment, our revolt, our new order.

2 THE SIGNIFICANCE OF THE TECHNICAL SIDE

It has probably become clear from what has already been stated that technical innovations were never an end in themselves for me. Any means I have used or am currently in the process of using were designed to elevate the events on the stage onto a historical plane and not just to enlarge the technical range of the stage machinery.

This elevation, which was inextricably bound up with the use of Marxist dialectics in the theatre, had not been achieved by the plays themselves. My technical devices had been developed to cover up the deficiencies of the dramatists' products. . . .

It is not mere chance that in an age whose technical achievements tower above its achievements in every other field the stage should become highly technical. And neither is it mere chance that this technical invasion should receive an impetus from a sector which is in conflict with the social order. Intellectual and social revolutions have always been closely bound up with technical upheavals. And a change in the function of the theatre was inconceivable without bringing the stage equipment technically up to date. In this regard it seems to me that we have just caught up with something which should have been done long ago. With the exception of the revolving stage and electric light the stage at the beginning of the twentieth century was still in the same position that Shakespeare had left it in: a square segment, a picture frame through which the spectator gets a "forbidden look" at a strange world. The insurmountable gulf between stage and auditorium has decisively shaped international drama for three centuries. It was a drama of make-believe. The theatre existed for three hundred years on the fiction that there were no spectators in the house. Even works which were revolutionary in their day deferred to this assumption, were forced to defer to it. Why? Because the theatre as an institution, as a piece of apparatus, as a house had never until 1917 been in the hands of the oppressed class, and because that class had never been in a position to liberate the theatre structurally as well as intellectually. This task was taken in hand straight away and with the utmost energy by the stage directors of Revolutionary Russia. I had no choice but to follow the same path in my conquest of the theatre, but in our context that path led neither to the end of the theatre, nor, at least to date, to a change in theatre architecture, but only to radical changes in stage machinery, which, taken all in all, amounted to the destruction of the old box form.

From the Proletarisches Theater to *Storm over Gotland*[2] I was sustained by various sources in my attempts to put an end to bourgeois forms and replace them with a form which would bring the spectator into the theatre not as a fictitious concept but as a living force. This tendency was, of course, in the beginning political, and all technical means were subordinate to it. And if these means were subordinate, still incomplete, strained, overemphatic, the reason is to be sought in the conflict with a house which was without provision for them.

NOTES

1 Author of *All Quiet on the Western Front.*
2 The Proletarisches Theater was founded by Piscator in 1920; he produced E. Welk's *Storm over Gotland* in 1926.

FROM The Documentary Play (1929)

The first production in which the text and staging were based solely on political documents was *In Spite of Everything* (Grosses Schauspielhaus, July 12, 1925)[1]. . . .

The show was a collective effort. The separate tasks of writer, director, musical director, designer and actor constantly overlapped. The scenery was built and the music composed as we wrote the script, and the script itself emerged gradually as the director worked with the group. Different scenes were put together simultaneously in different parts of the theatre, sometimes even before a definite script had been worked out. Film was to be combined organically with live action on the stage for the first time. (As planned, but not carried out in *Flags*.)

. . . What do I consider the essential point of my whole work? Not the propagation of a view of life through formal clichés and billboard slogans, but the presentation of solid proof that our philosophy and all that can be deduced from it is the one and only valid approach for our time. You can make all sorts of assertions, but repeating assertions does not make them more true or effective. Conclusive proof can be based only on scientific analysis of the material. This I can only do, in the language of the stage, if I can get beyond scenes from life, beyond the purely individual aspect of the characters and the fortuitous nature of their fates. And the way to do this is to show the link between events on the stage and the great forces active in history. It is not by chance that the factual substance becomes the main thing in each play. It is only from the facts themselves that the constraints and the constant mechanisms of life emerge, giving a deeper meaning to our private fates. For this I need some means of showing how human-superhuman factors interact with classes or individuals. One of the means was film. But it was no more than a means, and could be replaced tomorrow by some better means.

The film used in *In Spite of Everything* was documentary. From the archives of the Reich which were made available to us by one of our contacts, we used authentic shots of the war, of the demobilization, of a parade of all the crowned heads of Europe, and the like. These shots brutally demonstrated the horror of war: flame thrower attacks, piles of mutilated bodies, burning cities; war films had not yet come into "fashion," so these pictures were bound to have a more striking impact on the masses of the proletariat than a hundred lectures. I spread the film out through the whole play, and where that was not enough I projected stills.

For the basic stage I had a so-called "Praktikabel" built, a terraced structure of irregular shape with a raked platform on one side and steps and levels on the other. This structure stood on a revolving stage. I built the various acting areas into terraces, niches and corridors. In this way the overall structure of the scenes was unified and the play could flow uninterrupted, like a single current sweeping everything along with it.

The abandonment of the decorative set was taken a stage further than in *Flags*. The predominant principle was that of a purely practical acting structure to support, clarify and express the action. Freestanding structures, a self-contained world on the revolving stage, put an end to the peep-show world of the bourgeois theatre. They can also be set up in the open. The squared stage area is merely an irritating limitation.

The whole performance was a montage of authentic speeches, essays, newspaper cuttings, appeals, pamphlets, photographs, and film of the War and the Revolution, of historical persons and scenes. And all this was in the Grosses Schauspielhaus that Max Reinhardt had once used to stage classical (bourgeois) theatre. . . . In our case arena and stage were fused into one. In this there was one decisive factor: Beye had organized block bookings for the trade unions that summer. Class-conscious workers were sitting out front, and the storm broke. I had always been aware that we were not filling the house, and had wondered how we could actually reach this mass audience. Now I had them in my hand – and even today I still see that as the only real possibility for mass theatre in Berlin.

For the first time we were confronted with the absolute reality we knew from experience. And it had exactly the same moments of tension and dramatic climaxes as literary drama, and the same strong emotional impact. Provided, of course, that it was a political reality ("political" in the original sense: "being of general concern").

Translated by Hugh Rorrison

NOTE

1   *In Spite of Everything* ranged from the outbreak of the war to the assassination of Karl Liebknecht, and took its title from a proclamation of the latter following the defeat of the Spartacus rising. The *Grosses Schauspielhaus* or Great Play-house was originally a circus. It had been converted into a huge theatre seating 3,000 by Max Reinhardt.

Erwin Piscator (1893–1966), German actor and director: wounded in the First World War, his first productions were for army theatre units. In 1918 he joined the KDP (German Communist Party), and in 1920 set up an agit-prop group, but it folded under police harrassment the following year. *Flags* (1924), his first production for the Volksbuhne, about an immigrant work-ers' campaign in Chicago for an eight-hour day, was the start of his 'epic theatre' work, making use of the revolve, mechanised techniques and projections. It persuaded the Communist Party, previously dismissive of theatre, to commission a political revue from him (*The Red Revue*, 1924). After a series of productions, he was forced out of the Volksbuhne in 1927. Remaining independent of the Communist-controlled Workers' Theatre League, he mounted a series of further productions, though the 'Total Theatre' Gropius designed for him was never built and his work was dogged by financial problems. In 1931 he was invited to the USSR to film a book by Anna Seghers, so was outside Germany when the Nazis came to power. But the USSR too became dangerous for him as Stalin's purges began and fellow-artists and friends, like Tretyakov, were arrested and shot. He moved to the US, and worked and taught in New York till the postwar anti-communist witch-hunt of Senator McCarthy drove him out. He returned to Berlin in 1951, to run the new Free Volksbuhne Theatre for his last years. Unlike Brecht's theatre, it was in the western sector. For accounts of his work, see Maria Ley-Piscator, *The Piscator Experiment*, New York, J. H. Heineman, 1967; C. D. Innes, *Erwin Piscator's Political Theatre*, Cambridge University Press, 1972; and John Willett, *The Theatre of Erwin Piscator*, London, Eyre Methuen, 1978.

27

WORKERS' THEATRE
MOVEMENT

'Agit-Prop' Style (1932)

THE NATURALISTIC METHOD

The experience gained with these plays [by Shaw, Capek, Elmer Rice, etc.]
shows:

1 that the naturalistic form, namely that form which endeavours to show
   a picture on the stage as near to life as possible, is suitable for showing
   things as they appear on the surface, but does not lend itself to
   disclosing the reality which lies beneath. And it is just this reality
   existing beneath the polite surface of capitalist society that the Workers' Theatre must reveal.
2 That the unities of space and time, which are one of its main features,
   greatly hinder the portrayal of the class struggle in dramatic form
   (consider, for instance, the difficulty in bringing together in a reasonable, naturalistic way, an ordinary worker and an important capitalist).
3 That the audiences reached by such plays which demanded a well-
   equipped stage were insignificant compared to the mass of workers
   who could not be brought to the theatre or hall to witness them.

'AGIT-PROP' STYLE

So to enable the message of the Workers' Theatre to reach wide masses of
the workers, and to give a much more flexible and dynamic picture of
society than is possible on the curtained stage, a new form is being evolved.
This form, which is known in Germany as the 'Agit-Prop' style needs no
elaborate stage, but an open platform. No scenery that is not easily carried
about by hand; no make-up; and a minimum of costume. In a word, the
propertyless class is developing the 'property'-less theatre.

Wherever this form has been adopted it has led to a great expansion of
the movement. No longer does the Workers' Theatre play – as do the
amateur dramatic societies – to a circle of friends and relatives. It goes
out to the workers wherever they may be, at meetings, on the street corners,

in the parks; and now has the immediate task facing it of taking their performances to where the workers are actually waging the class struggle, at the factories, the labour exchanges, etc.

There are other advantages of the 'Agit-Prop' style:

1 Its flexible, and usually short, form is quickly adapted to meet local and topical situations. The preparation of special items dealing with events as they arise, should be a matter of days only.
2 Instead of emphasising the ability to portray characters, a difficult job for workers with very little spare time, it uses instead the class experience of the worker-player, which convinces a worker audience much more than the studied effects of the professional actor.
3 The direct approach to the audience, together with the fact that the performance is surrounded by and part of the crowd, is of great value in making the worker audience feel that the players are part of them, share their problems and their difficulties, and are pointing a direct, reasonable way out.

Nevertheless it may be that the naturalistic method should not be entirely ruled out from the workers' theatre, and this question must be thoroughly discussed at the Conference.

This piece is from a longer document presented at the British Workers' Theatre Movement's first National Conference in 1932. The English branch of the WTM was set up in 1926 by Christina Walshe during the miners' lockout after the collapse of the General Strike. It was given new impetus by Tom Thomas and the Hackney People's Players in 1928, who switched from straight plays to the agit-prop revue format already developed in Germany and by the Soviet Blue Blouse movement (see Part III). Direct contact with German groups came in 1931, when they were invited by the German Workers' Theatre Confederation to tour the Rhineland, and with the Soviets in 1933 at the International Workers' Theatre Olympiad in Moscow. By this time over thirty English groups were operating. The Movement's politics were to the left of the Labour Party and the ILP, but their critique of these clashed with the strengthening Popular Front movement set up to oppose fascism in the 1930s. As a result Tom Thomas was asked to resign, and the WTM folded. For a full study, see *Theatre as a Weapon: Workers' Theatre in the Soviet Union, Germany and Britain, 1917–34*, by Kathleen McCreary and Richard Stourac (London, Routledge & Kegan Paul, 1986), themselves leading figures in agit-prop theatre in the 1960s and 1970s (Agit-Prop Street Players, Red Ladder, Broadside Mobile Workers' Theatre). Detailed history of the English movement, including its important development in Manchester under Ewan McColl and Joan Littlewood, has been valuably rescued from impending oblivion in *Theatres of the Left 1880–1935*, by Raphael Samuel, Ewan McColl and Stuart Cosgrove (London, Routledge & Kegan Paul, 1985), and Howard Goorney's *The Theatre Workshop Story* (London, Eyre Methuen, 1981).

28

BERTOLT BRECHT

Prologue to *The Exception and the Rule* (1930)

THE PLAYERS:

> We are about to tell you
> The story of a journey. An exploiter
> And two of the exploited are the travellers.
> Examine carefully the behaviour of these people:
> Find it surprising though not unusual
> Inexplicable though normal
> Incomprehensible though it is the rule.
> Consider even the most insignificant, seemingly simple
> Action with distrust. Ask yourselves whether it is necessary
> Especially if it is usual.
> We ask you expressly to discover
> That what happens all the time is not natural.
> For to say that something is natural
> In such times of bloody confusion
> Of ordained disorder, of systematic arbitrariness
> Of inhuman humanity is to
> Regard it as unchangeable.

Translated by Ralph Manheim

FROM Notes on the Opera
Rise and Fall of the City of Mahagonny
(1930)

The modern theatre is the epic theatre. The following table shows certain changes of emphasis as between the dramatic and the epic theatre:*

DRAMATIC THEATRE	EPIC THEATRE
plot	narrative
implicates the spectator in a stage situation	turns the spectator into an observer, but
wears down his capacity for action	arouses his capacity for action
provides him with sensations	forces him to take decisions
experience	picture of the world
the spectator is involved in something	he is made to face something
suggestion	argument
instinctive feelings are preserved	brought to the point of recognition
the spectator is in the thick of it, shares the experience	the spectator stands outside, studies
the human being is taken for granted	the human being is the object of the inquiry
he is unalterable	he is alterable and able to alter
eyes on the finish	eyes on the course
one scene makes another	each scene for itself
growth	montage
linear development	in curves
evolutionary determinism	jumps
man as a fixed point	man as a process
thought determines being	social being determines thought
feeling	reason

* This table does not show absolute antitheses but mere shifts of accent. In a communication of fact, for instance, we may choose whether to stress the element of emotional suggestion or that of plain rational argument.

Translated by John Willett

FROM Theatre for Pleasure
or Theatre for Instruction (c. 1935)

THE EPIC THEATRE

Many people imagine that the term 'epic theatre' is self-contradictory, as the epic and dramatic ways of narrating a story are held, following Aristotle, to be basically distinct. The difference between the two forms was never thought simply to lie in the fact that the one is performed by living beings while the other operates via the written word; epic works such as those of Homer and the medieval singers were at the same time theatrical performances, while dramas like Goethe's *Faust* and Byron's *Manfred* are agreed to have been more effective as books. Thus even by Aristotle's definition the difference between the dramatic and epic forms was attributed to their different methods of construction, whose laws were dealt with by two different branches of aesthetics. The method of construction depended on the different way of presenting the work to the public, sometimes via the stage, sometimes through a book; and independently of that there was the 'dramatic element' in epic works and the 'epic element' in dramatic. The bourgeois novel in the last century developed much that was 'dramatic', by which was meant the strong centralization of the story, a momentum that drew the separate parts into a common relationship. A particular passion of utterance, a certain emphasis on the clash of forces are hallmarks of the 'dramatic'. The epic writer Döblin provided an excellent criterion where he said that with an epic work, as opposed to a dramatic, one can as it were take a pair of scissors and cut it into individual pieces, which remain fully capable of life.

This is no place to explain how the opposition of epic and dramatic lost its rigidity after having long been held to be irreconcilable. Let us just point out that the technical advances alone were enough to permit the stage to incorporate an element of narrative in its dramatic productions. The possibility of projections, the greater adaptability of the stage due to mechanization, the film, all completed the theatre's equipment, and did so at a point where the most important transactions between people could no longer be shown simply by personifying the motive forces or subjecting the characters to invisible metaphysical powers.

To make these transactions intelligible the environment in which the people lived had to be brought to bear in a big and 'significant' way.

This environment had of course been shown in the existing drama, but only as seen from the central figure's point of view, and not as an independent element. It was defined by the hero's reactions to it. It was seen as a storm can be seen when one sees the ships on a sheet of water unfolding their sails, and the sails filling out. In the epic theatre it was to appear standing on its own.

The stage began to tell a story. The narrator was no longer missing, along with the fourth wall. Not only did the background adopt an attitude to the events on the stage – by big screens recalling other simultaneous events elsewhere, by projecting documents which confirmed or contradicted what the characters said, by concrete and intelligible figures to accompany abstract conversations, by figures and sentences to support mimed transactions whose sense was unclear – but the actors too refrained from going over wholly into their role, remaining detached from the character they were playing and clearly inviting criticism of him.

The spectator was no longer in any way allowed to submit to an experience uncritically (and without practical consequences) by means of simple empathy with the characters in a play. The production took the subject-matter and the incidents shown and put them through a process of alienation: the alienation that is necessary to all understanding. When something seems 'the most obvious thing in the world' it means that any attempt to understand the world has been given up.

What is 'natural' must have the force of what is startling. This is the only way to expose the laws of cause and effect. People's activity must simultaneously be so and be capable of being different.

It was all a great change.

The dramatic theatre's spectator says: Yes, I have felt like that too – Just like me – It's only natural – It'll never change – The sufferings of this man appal me, because they are inescapable – That's great art; it all seems the most obvious thing in the world – I weep when they weep, I laugh when they laugh.

The epic theatre's spectator says: I'd never have thought it – That's not the way – That's extraordinary, hardly believable – It's got to stop – The sufferings of this man appal me, because they are unnecessary – That's great art: nothing obvious in it – I laugh when they weep, I weep when they laugh. . . .

CAN EPIC THEATRE BE PLAYED ANYWHERE?

Stylistically speaking, there is nothing all that new about the epic theatre. Its expository character and its emphasis on virtuosity bring it close to the old Asiatic theatre. Didactic tendencies are to be found in the medieval mystery plays and the classical Spanish theatre, and also in the theatre of the Jesuits.

These theatrical forms correspond to particular trends of their time, and vanished with them. Similarly the modern epic theatre is linked with

113

certain trends. It cannot by any means be practised universally. Most of the great nations today are not disposed to use the theatre for ventilating their problems. London, Paris, Tokyo and Rome maintain their theatres for quite different purposes. Up to now favourable circumstances for an epic and didactic theatre have only been found in a few places and for a short period of time. In Berlin Fascism put a very definite stop to the development of such a theatre.

It demands not only a certain technological level but a powerful movement in society which is interested to see vital questions freely aired with a view to their solution, and can defend this interest against every contrary trend.

The epic theatre is the broadest and most far-reaching attempt at large-scale modern theatre, and it has all those immense difficulties to overcome that always confront the vital forces in the sphere of politics, philosophy, science and art.

Translated by John Willett

FROM Alienation Effects in Chinese Acting: The A-Effect (1936)

The A-effect was achieved in the German epic theatre not only by the actor, but also by the music (choruses, songs) and the setting (placards, film etc.). It was principally designed to historicize the incidents portrayed. By this is meant the following:

The bourgeois theatre emphasized the timelessness of its objects. Its representation of people is bound by the alleged 'eternally human'. Its story is arranged in such a way as to create 'universal' situations that allow Man with a capital M to express himself: man of every period and every colour. All its incidents are just one enormous cue, and this cue is followed by the 'eternal' response: the inevitable, usual, natural, purely human response. An example: a black man falls in love in the same way as a white man; the story forces him to react with the same expression as the white man (in theory this formula works as well the other way round); and with that the sphere of art is attained. The cue can take account of what is special, different; the response is shared, there is no element of difference in it. This notion may allow that such a thing as history exists, but it is none the less unhistorical. A few circumstances vary, the environments are altered, but

114

Man remains unchanged. History applies to the environment, not to Man. The environment is remarkably unimportant, is treated simply as a pretext; it is a variable quantity and something remarkably inhuman; it exists in fact apart from Man, confronting him as a coherent whole, whereas he is a fixed quantity, eternally unchanged. The idea of man as a function of the environment and the environment as a function of man, i.e. the breaking up of the environment into relationships between men, corresponds to a new way of thinking, the historical way. Rather than be sidetracked into the philosophy of history, let us give an example. Suppose the following is to be shown on the stage: a girl leaves home in order to take a job in a fair-sized city (Piscator's *American Tragedy*). For the bourgeois theatre this is an insignificant affair, clearly the beginning of a story; it is what one has to have been told in order to understand what comes after, or to be keyed up for it. The actor's imagination will hardly be greatly fired by it. In a sense the incident is universal: girls take jobs (in the case in question one can be keyed up to see what in particular is going to happen to her). Only in one way is it particular: this girl goes away (if she had remained what comes after would not have happened). The fact that her family lets her go is not the object of the inquiry; it is understandable (the motives are understandable). But for the historicizing theatre everything is different. The theatre concentrates entirely on whatever in this perfectly everyday event is remarkable, particular and demanding inquiry. What! A family letting one of its members leave the nest to earn her future living independently and without help? Is she up to it? Will what she has learnt here as a member of the family help her to earn her living? Can't families keep a grip on their children any longer? Have they become (or remained) a burden? Is it like that with every family? Was it always like that? Is this the way of the world, something that can't be affected? The fruit falls off the tree when ripe: does this sentence apply here? Do children always make themselves independent? Did they do so in every age? If so, and if it's something biological, does it always happen in the same way, for the same reasons and with the same results? These are the questions (or a few of them) that the actors must answer if they want to show the incident as a unique, historical one: if they want to demonstrate a custom which leads to conclusions about the entire structure of a society at a particular (transient) time. But how is such an incident to be represented if its historic character is to be brought out? How can the confusion of our unfortunate epoch be striking? When the mother, in between warnings and moral injunctions, packs her daughter's case – a very small one – how is the following to be shown: So many injunctions and so few clothes? Moral injunctions for a lifetime and bread for five hours? How is the actress to speak the mother's sentence as she hands over such a very small case – 'There, I guess that ought to do you' – in such a way that it is understood as a historic dictum? This can only be achieved if the A-effect is brought out. The actress must not make the sentence her own affair, she

115

must hand it over for criticism, she must help us to understand its causes and protest. The effect can only be got by long training. In the New York Yiddish Theatre, a highly progressive theatre, I saw a play by S. Ornitz showing the rise of an East Side boy to be a big crooked attorney. The theatre could not perform the play. And yet there were scenes like this in it: the young attorney sits in the street outside his house giving cheap legal advice. A young woman arrives and complains that her leg has been hurt in a traffic accident. But the case has been bungled and her compensation has not yet been paid. In desperation she points to her leg and says: 'It's started to heal up.' Working without the A-effect, the theatre was unable to make use of this exceptional scene to show the horror of a bloody epoch. Few people in the audience noticed it; hardly anyone who reads this will remember that cry. The actress spoke the cry as if it were something perfectly natural. But it is exactly this – the fact that this poor creature finds such a complaint natural – that she should have reported to the public like a horrified messenger returning from the lowest of all hells. To that end she would of course have needed a special technique which would have allowed her to underline the historical aspect of a specific social condition. Only the A-effect makes this possible. Without it all she can do is to observe how she is not forced to go over entirely into the character on the stage.

In setting up new artistic principles and working out new methods of representation we must start with the compelling demands of a changing epoch; the necessity and the possibility of remodelling society loom ahead. All incidents between men must be noted, and everything must be seen from a social point of view. Among other effects that a new theatre will need for its social criticism and its historical reporting of completed transformations is the A-effect.

Translated by John Willett

'Theatre for Pleasure or Theatre for Instruction' was unpublished in Brecht's lifetime. John Willett surmises that it was intended for the Moscow conference of producers to which he was invited in 1935. 'Alienation Effects in Chinese Acting' was also not published for some years in German, though an English translation appeared in *Life and Letters* in 1936. His opening observations on Chinese acting can be found in Part V. A reworking of the incident discussed above occurs in *The Good Person of Szechwan*, scenes 4 and 5.

Bertolt Brecht (1898–1956), German poet, playwright and director. Following First World War service as a medical orderly, Brecht began writing for the stage, the dark nihilism of his earliest plays changing as his work moved increasingly to the left. When the Nazis came to power in 1933, he escaped into exile in Denmark, Sweden, Finland, and finally in 1941 the United States, where he attempted to work both in the theatre and in Hollywood. After the war, the attentions of Senator McCarthy's Un-American Activities Committee were turned upon him as a suspected Communist, though he was not a Party member. Returning to (East) Berlin in 1948, he set up the Berliner Ensemble with his wife, the actress Helene Weigel, and worked there until his death.

29

ATHOL FUGARD

The Coat (FROM *Notebooks 1960/1977*)

August 1966

Where to begin?

Norman found guilty and sentenced to five years.

Back to Cradock yesterday with May. He called me as a witness in mitigation.

So what is left?

A coat goes back to New Brighton.

In a stranger's shopping-bag.

The two men who preceded Norman. 'Number One accused' – aged fifty-eight with a wife and ten children. 'Number Two accused' – forty-three with wife and children. Both found guilty – similar charges to Norman. The old man grabbed May when she was talking to Norman afterwards in the cells – took off his old coat (it would be taken from him now that he was a prisoner) and gave it to May, asking her to go to his family and tell them what had happened and give them the coat to 'use'. So May carried it back to New Brighton in her shopping-bag.

To Sheila: 'The continuum of first-degree experience. What can I say, or write about today that could have even a hundredth part of the consequence of that coat going back. Even the greatest art communicates only second-degree experience. That coat is first-degree, it is life itself. That man's family will take it back, smell him again, remember him again, it will be worn by a son or, tonight, will keep one of the small children warm in her blanket on the floor – move into her dreams, put her father back into her life. That coat withers me and my words.'

The message he gave May for his family: 'Wait for me. I'll be back.' . . .

September

The Coat: Images – prickly-pear sellers at Smelly Creek.

New Brighton – stones in the roads. The wife and mother is folding the coat – behind her the actors sit and watch her –

Actor: It will get older.
Wife: Yes.
Actress: It will get mouldy.
Wife: Yes.
Actor: And crumble.
Wife: Yes, yes, yes, yes: To all your questions, yes; to all my feelings and fears, yes; to God, yes. To you, my husband, yes. To my children, yes.

Also: The informer.

Actress: (handing over the coat to the Wife) He said you must use it.
Actor: Something hard and real to hold.
Wife: I've still got the coat.

What is the coat? = our time; our poverty; our uselessness; our need; our shape.

Actress: I went up with Njikelana. We left when it was over. The van with prisoners passed us near Cookhouse, going very fast. A man was looking out of the window. It might have been him.
Wife: Tell me about the road.
Actor: The child is sick. (etc.)
Wife: Then I must sell it.

Why did he send it? What is the coat? What does it mean?

There are no victories. Memories fade, the heart forgets, whatever happens the man himself will one day die. We are here a short time; and at the end of that short time one of the few things we can have is the dignity that comes from courage and truth.

Wife: I am not here forever.
Actor: Then your children...
Wife: They are not here forever...
Actor: What are you trying to tell us?
Wife: A man wore this coat.

The Coat: three temptations – a child is cold; a child is sick; hunger.
'Give it to the child!'
'No.'
'But he said use it didn't he?'

'I am an actor. I live in New Brighton. Today, a worn old coat came back to the township in a stranger's shopping-bag. We want to tell you about it, there are certain facts. There are also questions. For some of these we have guessed at the answers. For others we have no answers.'

An actor called Mulligan...John...Humphrey. An actress called Mabel

119

. . . Nomhle. (Five chairs on an empty stage. The actors enter and sit. Mulligan comes forward and speaks to the audience.)

The Coat: moving on to foolscap paper. Notes becoming extensive – possible form also emerging. Not yet clear in my own mind as to what I am after. Encumbered by what I would *like* to believe, i.e. the woman *not* selling the coat. Maybe she does. Either is possible of course – the point is Truth and honesty in dealing with either alternative.

The point *not*: to sell or not to sell, yes or no. But *yes and no*, conflict, irresolution and finally just a posture = I am flesh and blood, bewildered, blind, desolate. I will cling stupidly to this one thing. Already a life is crystallising around it.

Last night May filled in a few details about the coat. She said it was quite a good one, worth possibly two Rand. The wife was about sixty. In front of May she went through the pockets – all she found was a little twist of brown paper containing some powder. This turned out to be medicine bought from a witch-doctor to reduce the court sentence. The old woman said it had worked. She'd heard stories about men getting life sentences and had expected the same for her husband. Instead of which he only got three years. She asked about her husband, said she would wait.

Brecht's *Messingkauf Dialogues* provoking my thinking about the coat.

First change is a shift away from the cold statement I had been working out, i.e. five actors telling an audience, etc. Better: does she sell the coat? Let's find out. (It will certainly create more of Brecht's 'ease' and a chance to talk and think about it. The audience will participate.) . . .

November

I am also working on *The Coat* with the group. We have been asked to do something for a 'Theatre Appreciation Group' here in P.E. in four weeks' time, and we've decided to spring this on them. This is a tremendous opportunity. . . .

The local Native Commissioner has given his permission for a play-reading by Serpent Players before the (white) Theatre Appreciation Group provided three conditions are observed:

1   It must not be public – members only.
2   Serpent Players may not use the toilets at the hall.
3   They must leave immediately after the reading – no social gathering or discussion.

The group expect us to be reading a comedy by Soyinka. We have been working on *The Coat*. I am a little frightened – there could be repercussions. And if there are, what were my motives? – vanity, foolhardy recklessness plus a genuine desire to shatter white complacency and its conspiracy of silence.

Serpent Players tonight – what should have been our last rehearsal for tomorrow night's reading was instead a moving, absurd, sensible and idiotic discussion – given all the pros and cons – of whether, with the possibility of the Special Branch being in our audience, we should proceed with *The Coat* as a group venture or as a reading by myself alone. . . .

The reading of *The Coat* a considerable success. Full cast was at the bus terminal at seven. I gave a few notes beforehand and the reading went off very well – my faith in the actors, in our subject, the shape and content of the audience's experience of us, completely justified.

Wrote to Mary about it and spoke of Serpent Players' moment of 'posthumous glory'. The extent to which fear shattered us at one moment means that we just aren't a 'group' with a solidarity and identity over and above that of us as a collection of individuals.

Or, I said to her, it was a resurrection. I told how in four weeks we had put together a script and our analysis by way of improvisation and discussion of the coat. With the actors using their own names. Mulligan started the ball rolling with a friendly chat to the audience (we had about 150) about the group, our approach and methods – and hence the coat. 'But just before we start let me answer any of you who might be asking, why the coat? Why not the man who wore the coat? Isn't a man a better subject for an actor's exercise? Yes, he would have been better, but, you see, it was the *coat* that came back. May brought back the coat.'

Mulligan sits down, May comes forward: 'I brought back the coat from Cradock – 160 miles away. I had gone up there for my husband's trial. The coat isn't his. It belongs to another man from New Brighton. There have been a lot of men from New Brighton in the Cradock cells. The charges are mostly the same: membership of a banned organisation; contributing to its funds: holding a meeting...distributing pamphlets...etc.'

You could have heard a pin drop. The audience's complacency shattered – they sat and watched us with the horror and fascination that freezes you a few feet away from a puff-adder.

The piece is pure Brecht. The *Messingkauf Dialogues* did it. Improvisation and discussion, improvisation and discussion – and behind an apparent easy carelessness, a logic, in our case centered on the question: 'Would she ever sell it?'

Athol Fugard (b. 1932), South African playwright. Son of an Afrikaner mother and Anglo-Irish father, Fugard grew up in the Cape, and studied philosophy and social anthropology at Cape Town University, falling under the influence of Kierkegaard and Camus before quitting without a degree to hitch-hike around Africa and work as a seaman for two years. He then turned to experimental theatre, and was soon working with black actors in Sophia-town, developing scripts on the basis of their improvisations. This inter-racial work fell foul of the *apartheid* it defied, after the Group Areas Act of 1965 decreed both mixed casts and mixed audiences illegal without special licence. The script of *The Coat* is now available, in his *The Township Plays* (1993). For comment on Fugard and the biases of inter-racial theatrical work in South Africa from the 1950s to the 1970s, see Robert Mshengu Kava-nagh, *Theatre and Cultural Struggle in South Africa*, London, Zed Books, 1985.

30

ARIANE MNOUCHKINE

FROM Meetings with the Théâtre du Soleil (1974)

In September 1973, following its productions on the French Revolution, *1789* and *1793*, the Théâtre du Soleil under its director Ariane Mnouchkine embarked on a new work about contemporary life in France, entitled *L'Age d'Or* (*The Age of Gold*). The passages below are from a series of interviews conducted a year later by Denis Bablet, when the preparatory work on it was still continuing.

ARIANE MNOUCHKINE: . . . after *1793* we had to manage to find the courage to speak of our own time, but actually we weren't ready.

DENIS BABLET: *In what way?*

In every way.

In knowing about today's reality?

Certainly. I believe no-one is ready in that area. But above all in improvisation technique, in the theatrical forms which would allow us to treat contemporary reality as we wanted, without it becoming pathetic, caricatural, psychological obviously, a parody, a tract, a placard, etc.

'Contemporary reality' — it's an extremely large phrase. What exactly do you understand by it?

If you like, you could replace the term 'contemporary reality' with present-day struggles — struggles, or for some people non-struggles; and then, and above all, the contradictions at the heart of the people.

But the problem is not the same as it was for *1789*. With *1789* we could always take sides quickly. Where immediate contemporary events are concerned, we don't think we always have the analysis to hand which would let us say: 'There! Such an event means such and such.' We know very well that it's fluctuating; something that's evident one day is contradicted the next. The reality of today is much more complex, much more elusive . . . there is really no criterion to say that one situation is more important than another. What makes the situation of a woman in a council flat expecting a child she doesn't want more important than that of a hated office boss? Given that we have unconstructed material — that's the problem

123

– unfinished, completely raw, but an enormous amount, we know we have the material for two or three shows.

Where construction's concerned, in '89 and '93 there was nevertheless a basis because of history . . .

. . . A linear construction. That's one of the problems. . . . We live in a world that's terribly fragmented, scattered. What you learn of events is everything that happened at the end, at the same time, fragments. Take an accident at work: you read, 'A worker gets killed' but you don't know what his life was like before, what state he was in when he arrived on site that day, what he had to put up with, etc. So, either you choose: 'We're going to tell the story of the worker Abdullah from his arrival in France, and what he's gone through up until his accident at work'; or you decide rather: 'Well, no, we'll try and give the vision of our epoch as it strikes us, that's to say: we learn of Abdullah's death but we see only four or five situations involving Abdullah before the accident, but perhaps we see too the situation of another worker, who could have been Abdullah, but whose death we don't see, and who'll make us understand, through the oppression he suffers at a certain moment, why someone else got killed, because he goes through the same thing.' . . .

We've chosen not to talk of great events but of people, and for that reason to try and have groups of workers from a particular factory, groups of nurses or soldiers come and tell us not what's known about them, that's to say what you read in all the left-wing papers, but what we don't know, and it's that that's difficult to get them to say.

The people we see, for an hour, at first they give us their public views. We meet works committees, so there are militants among them, and it's always them who speak at the start. Listening to them, you get the impression you're reading long passages from *Libération*, *Politique Hebdo*, *L'Huma[nité]*.[1] So after a short while we say, 'We know that, we've read all the papers. What we want to know is what underlies all that. Oppression with a big O doesn't exist. What exists is a man oppressing another man. So, how does that happen, how does that show itself, or how does it betray itself, and how do you fight against it?' . . .

These contacts with the workers, are they something you envisaged from the beginning?

No, it happened when they came to see us, a month ago, a month and a half. It was really a bad moment. We felt we needed a change. I thought that in fact the actors needed to act. I say the actors, but I had cold feet too. Our work needed confirming. We were questioning ourselves. 'Such a character comes back on the bus, and such and such happens to him. To us it's very clear. But how if people don't understand what we've been working at for six months?' Or else: 'We're agreed on using masks, but what if people say: "Why are the actors in masks?"' We needed a holiday, and at the same time we needed to work. We left for the Cevennes, because we had the chance of

a place to live there, and we said to ourselves: 'No-one knows who we are. No-one expects "wonderful shows" from us.' We performed every day, sometimes even twice a day, in villages which had had notice just the day before, through a little parade, that actors were coming to improvise. One very fine day we performed in a little square, and otherwise in little church halls or village halls. And then in two secondary schools at Ales.
And what did you perform?
What they asked for, nothing else. But obviously we introduced the characters we'd worked on here. . . . People recognised the characters perfectly. The more 'classic' a character was, the more it relied on the essential, even traditional elements of a Punch, a Harlequin or a Pantalone, the more it was taken as something real, something they knew.

They laughed at the same moment as we did, they got bored at the same time we did. . . .
In any case, the Théâtre du Soleil's new show won't be a show with a beginning, a middle and an end?
No.
It will be like a puzzle?
If you like. Like tales, stories and legends. Tales of the twentieth century.
. . .
Why not ask an author to collaborate on it?
We have authors, we are all authors. It's more and more true. I don't see why one only has the right to call oneself an author if one has a pen. *An actor who improvises is an author*, an author in the widest sense of the term. So we've got authors. But the problem is that we are very much beginners within this process. For each show we're beginners. If we don't now want authors, it's because an author never considers himself a beginner.

Why stay faithful to improvisation? Because I believe actors are more authors through their sensibility and their bodies than they would be with a blank page.

Remember the show's postulate: actors who recount in fifty years' time...[2] They are actors who have found character-types of today, like Balzac in his day when he recounted the human comedy. . . . You can say naturally that the character-type is the capitalist villain with his top hat and his big cigar. Obviously it's that, that kind of cliché, that we've wanted to avoid. The capitalist for us is the result of a lot of work on Pantalone. In commedia dell'arte, Pantalone is a fantastic emanation of the bourgeoisie. We've taken him up, a completely worked-out figure, transposed him, and we find ourselves with a capitalist equipped with all his wiles, his intelligence, his violence, etc., and who is not at all an *opinion about* the capitalist. That's what we seek, I don't say we always succeed.
Why have you chosen to speak of contemporary reality via characters borrowed from commedia dell'arte, etc.?
They are not characters borrowed. I think it's rather as if you said, 'You are

building a house; why do you use bricks when now people build houses in concrete?' In which case the answer could be: 'Because we think brick is the most economical, the least polluting, the most essential.' It's exactly that. It turns out we have a certain way of treating theatre. We haven't gone stealing a character. Where commedia dell'arte is concerned, we've set about taking up again work that it seemed to us had been interrupted, and we've undertaken to try and bring it to a conclusion. . . .

The first time I came here during your work, you were all sitting round the table in the foyer, and you were reading extracts from Jacques Copeau's Appels,[3] *which had just come out. They were about improvisation, and Copeau's desire to create an improvised comedy of our time which would take up the principles of commedia dell'arte. . . . Copeau's idea is . . . to replace Pantalone by a particular modern character, Harlequin by another, etc. That's not what you're doing, is it?*
Isn't it?
You don't have the Worker with a capital W, the Bourgeois with a capital B, as abstract entities.
Oh, no!
I think that's a wrong idea in Copeau.
I think it was a wrong idea, but that if Copeau had worked on it in practice, he would have realised it. The Arab doesn't exist, any more than The Worker or The Policeman. What is interesting is to know how a man, in such and such conditions and circumstances, finds he's a policeman and accepts it. You realise that, starting from a certain past, with certain initial difficulties, in a certain social milieu, there are a whole series of characters who could become a character-type – that a prison warder, a policeman, a works-foreman could belong to the same category. But with us this character-type has a name: he's called Max, and today we've seen him as an overseer and also as a prison guard. The police in general don't exist. Radical theatre has recently gone through this evolution. It's not about denouncing the police in general, the capitalist in general; you learn nothing from that, and that kind of theatre can only let you say, 'The police are bad' or 'Capitalism grinds workers underfoot.' But why and how?

Translated by Richard Drain and Micheline Mabille

NOTES

1   Left-wing papers.
2   To help them 'historicise' their material (in accord with Brecht's 'epic theatre' principles), the company imagined themselves looking back to the present day from the future.
3   The work of Jacques Copeau (1878–1949), director of the small Vieux Colombier theatre from 1913, deeply affected the French stage by challenging both the formalised histrionics of the Comédie-Française and the lightweight facility of the boulevard theatres. Copeau believed in a non-commercial theatre of high

quality whose bare stage was a platform for an integrated ensemble of actors trained in a range of skills including those of clowning and commedia. Through his nephew, Michel St Denis, who founded the Old Vic Theatre School, the Young Vic Company and the Stratford Studio of the RSC, his ideas have also deeply touched English theatre. *Appels*, the first volume of a series that gathers together his many writings, came out in 1974, the year of this interview. See the selection *Texts on Theatre*, London, Routledge, 1990; and *Jacques Copeau* by John Rudlin, Cambridge University Press, 1986.

Ariane Mnouchkine (b. 1934) studied in Paris and Oxford, and, after travelling to the far east, founded the Théâtre du Soleil in 1964. Their first production was of Arnold Wesker's *The Kitchen* (1967). The group's collective creations began with *The Clowns* (1969), and turned towards revolutionary history in *1789* (1970) and *1793* (1972). *The Age of Gold* was performed in 1975. Then followed the epic film *Molière*, directed by Mnouchkine. The company then moved back to classic and scripted work, including plays by Hélène Cixous, notably two epic pieces set in Cambodia and India. The latter is discussed by Cixous in Part V.

31

JUDY CHICAGO

Womanhouse – Performances (1975)

I think that the reason our performances in Fresno and at Womanhouse created so much tension, excitement, and response was that we told the truth about our feelings as women in them. Because performance can be so direct, because we were developing our performances from a primitive, gut level, we articulated feelings that had simply never been so openly expressed in artmaking. Although many women in the arts have struggled to give voice to their experiences as women, their forms, like mine, have been so transposed (into the language of sophisticated artmaking) that the content could be ignored by a culture that doesn't understand or accept the simplest facts of women's lives, much less subtle and transformed imagery. We learned a profound lesson about aesthetic perception (particularly in men) when in Fresno, the chairman of the art department, a sophisticated, liberal man, came to visit our studio. He saw an environment by Faith Wilding, a piece that dealt with the sacrifice of the female by male culture. It was a religious piece, implying crucifixion, death, and destruction, and the symbolism was very overt. Hanging around the walls were bloody Kotexes, which he perceived as "white material with red spots," so disassociated was he from the ability to perceive content or to recognize anything that did not grow out of *his* cultural experience. If a man like that, educated in art language, cannot recognize a bloody Kotex, or understand a not very subtle work of art, how can he be expected to respond to any art work that relates *in any way* to female experience or differs from male cultural references to any degree?

What this suggests is that the cultural gap between men and women at this moment in history is almost unimaginable. Women in the arts, in the professions, in the academies, blinded by the illusion of quality, are just beginning to grasp how profoundly alienated women and men really are. As we move out of the historical time when men were the primary breadwinners and women were confined to procreative and domestic functions, we are left with a heritage of social roles and attitudes that are entirely inconsistent with reality but that assert their hold on us nonetheless. The problems women face in achieving equality are primarily problems of values, values that keep us subject even if we "open doors." Our subjugation is psychological and our "otherness" the result of cultural differences between us and men so profound as to sometimes make it seem that we are members of different species. How can these differences be overcome, so that men and women can reach across the culture gap?

> The gap between male and female . . . is not a universal constant, but rather the distance between public and private that developed with the first industrial revolution. . . . Today the hemisphere of the public has been assigned to the male and the hemisphere of the private to the female. Each sex has become a symbol for its territory. The conflict between them can then be seen as a reflection of the longing of each to be part of the other's sphere, to link the public with the private in our schizoid world, to embrace the whole of life.*

When we performed, the audience was usually shocked, then fascinated by the fact that we were bringing the "private" sphere into the light, making the private public, and in so doing, taking a large step toward bridging the culture chasm between men and women. Because women have always taken responsibility for the private in life, men have been totally relieved of that responsibility. Not only do women have to move into public life, but men have to share the burdens of private life before any real change can take place. This means that men have to be educated emotionally, and the first step in that education is to be made to "see" women, to feel with us, experience our point of view.

The view from the private world is considerably different from the view from the public perspective. By bringing the private into public view, women bring the deepest level of psychic reality out of the bedroom, and in this case, onto the stage, where culture itself can be confronted, rather than a single male representative of that culture, as in heterosexual relationships where one woman struggles with one man. Some men have responded to our performances by calling them "therapy," in an effort to discredit them as art. This reflects the total schizophrenia of male culture, which has taught us all to believe that authentic feeling must be restricted to the therapist's office or to the bedroom. To express feeling is to be "womanly," and if we want to change the values of this culture, we must educate the entire society to appreciate rather than denigrate "womanliness" in art and in life.

In order for this to be accomplished, men's damage must be exposed, faced, altered. Men must be helped to feel again, and the point of greatest disjuncture in male personalities is pivoted upon their sense of "difference" from and "superiority" to women. When we brought men into *our* environment, Womanhouse, our studio, our performances, we brought them into an unfamiliar world, where their only guides were their feelings, a part of

---

* Nancy Reeves, *Womankind* (Chicago: Aldine-Atherton, Inc., 1971), p. 29.

themselves as atrophied as our muscles for assertion and independence. Too often, men are unable to comprehend the world with their "gut" and instead judge, objectify, and abstract information. In dealing with ourselves as women and making art aimed first at women, we were violating role definition and pleasing each other rather than men – that is, we were "being independent." In so doing, and in letting men be the observers to our independence, we forced them to be independent emotionally and thus to face their own damaged abilities. It was only in that kind of situation that men could make an empathetic identification with the despair we feel about *our* damage. As long as we go to men, move into their sphere without demanding that they move into ours simultaneously, we will always be at a disadvantage, we will always be the "other" in their world. What we glimpsed in our performances was the opportunity to make men feel themselves "other" and thereby force them to identify with us on a psychic level. It is not enough for us to learn to identify with men; we have done that all our lives. *Men have to learn to identify with us*, and it is this process that feminist performance and feminist art can promote, particularly if they exist on a wide scale throughout the country. Womanhouse and the performances we did there helped me clarify the possible relationship between women's art and the culture at large. I wondered if there was a way for abstract art to have the same kind of impact on values that the representational art and performances of Womanhouse had provided.

ABLUTIONS

Judy Chicago, Suzanne Lacy, Sandra Orgel, Aviva Ramani
Performed in Venice, California, in 1972

Late in the spring, some months after Womanhouse was dismantled, we presented another performance, this time a piece that was performed only once. We used a studio space for the theatre and again sat the audience on the floor. The piece was about an hour and a half long. It had grown out of several months' work in the performance workshop, after we had moved into our studio at school. In the informal performance sessions, several themes had arisen: binding, like Chinese foot-binding, brutalization, rape, immersion, body anxiety, and entrapment. We decided to do a piece that would combine all these issues. *Ablutions* began when the audience entered the room. A tape played throughout the performance of women telling about their experiences of being raped. Three bathtubs were sitting on the floor, each one filled with a different, not quite identifiable substance. Around the tubs, covering an area about fifty feet by twenty feet, were hundreds of broken egg shells, piles of rope, of kidneys, and of chain. After about twenty minutes one woman dressed in jeans and T-shirt led a nude woman to a chair in the back of the performance space, seated her, and began to slowly

130

bind her feet, first one, then the other, with a bandagelike material, and continued binding her over a period of forty minutes, until she was completely bound, her body tied to the chair, mummylike.

A few minutes after the binding had begun, another woman came out and slowly eased herself into the first bathtub, which contained one thousand eggs, with unbroken yolks. She started to wash herself, allowing the eggs to run down her body, an image of immersion in her own biology. After five minutes, she rose and moved on to the second tub, this one filled with blood, a metaphor for brutalization and at the same time a reference to menstruation. Another woman came out and got into the egg tub, and when the first woman moved on to the third tub, filled with clay, followed her into the second tub. After the first woman had been in the last tub for five minutes, she was lifted out by two other women. The image, as she rose up from the clay bath, was of some ancient female fetish figure. The remains of the blood and the eggs showing through the scaly clay covering made her seem to be an eerie, mythological figure. She was dried and wrapped in a sheet, then tied up like a corpse and left, while the two women did the same thing to the other bather. While this was going on, a fifth woman appeared and began to nail kidneys to the wall, at intervals of three feet, all in a line. The two women, after wrapping the bathers, sat down face to face, like mirror images, and began to adorn themselves, hanging ropes and chains around their heads in a strange parody of women at their toiletries.

When the woman doing the binding finished, she began to tie ropes around the silent, mummified figure in the chair. Then she started circling the room, tying the ropes to the tubs, to the prone figures, to the seated women, who were still covering their heads with ropes and chains. The other woman finished nailing kidneys to the wall, and then she began tying the kidneys together, pulling the rope tight so that the blood ran out of the meat and down the wall. Then she carried the ropes to the bathtubs, the figures, and back again to the wall. Both women moved slowly, the only action the roping and tying, the only sound the voices of women relating the facts of their rapes. Round and round the women walked, tying everying up neatly, like some obsessive housekeeping duty, until the performance area was like a spider web and all the figures caught, contained, bound by their circumstances and their own self-victimization. The voices on the tape droned on, repeating the never-ending stories of continual brutalization, from which there seemed to be no escape. Finally, one woman, then the other, left; the tape continued for a few minutes, then ended on a chilling note, the voice of a woman repeating the words: "I felt so helpless, so powerless, there was nothing I could do but lay there and cry softly."

Judy Chicago (b. 1939) takes her name from her birthplace rather than from her father. She studied painting and sculpture at UCLA, and went on to initiate women's arts programmes at Fresno State and Cal Arts. 'Womanhouse' was a house in Los Angeles she helped convert into an environment expressing women's experience and creativity. Following earlier experiments, she worked there on performances, and subsequently collaborated on *Ablutions*. She is best known abroad for *The Dinner Party*, a collaboratively-crafted work consisting of a triangular table with thirty-nine place-settings dedicated to celebrated women, each featuring a plate decorated with a vaginal flower-like form. This may possibly have suggested to Caryl Churchill the idea for the opening act of *Top Girls*.

32

HÉLÈNE CIXOUS

Aller à la mer (1977)

How, as women, can we go to the theatre without lending our complicity to the sadism directed against women, or being asked to assume, in the patriarchal family structure that the theatre reproduces *ad infinitum*, the position of victim?

Who is this victim? She is always the Father's daughter, his sacrificial object, guardian of the phallus, upholding the narcissistic fantasy which helps the Father to ward off the threat of castration. Like Electra or Antigone, she is eliminated. Or, like Ophelia, she is three times condemned to be buried alive by the three jealous father-figures – Polonius, Laertes and Hamlet – who are in agreement only in laying down the law to her: "Be thou woman, be mad about me, get thee to a nunnery." Locked up and put away. If she is Ophelia, her body banned and her soul violated, she will never have lived. And if, like Cordelia, she finds the strength to assert a femininity which refuses to be the mirror of her father's raving, she will die. For in every man there is a dethroned King Lear who requires his daughter to idealize him by her loving words and build him up, however flat he may have fallen, into the man he wishes to appear: "Tell me that I am the greatest, the me-est, the most like a king, or I'll kill you."

With even more violence than fiction, theatre, which is built according to the dictates of male fantasy, repeats and intensifies the horror of the murder scene which is at the origin of all cultural productions. It is always necessary for a woman to die in order for the play to begin. Only when she has disappeared can the curtain go up; she is relegated to repression, to the grave, the asylum, oblivion and silence. When she does make an appearance, she is doomed, ostracised or in a waiting-room. She is loved only when absent or abused, a phantom or a fascinating abyss. Outside and also beside herself. That is why I stopped going to the theatre; it was like going to my own funeral, and it does not produce a living woman or (and this is no accident) her body or even her unconscious.

This "Vieux Jeu" (Old Hat/Old Game) still involves playing the Role, maintaining the *ancien régime* of performance and mirror-gazing; it encourages the double perversion of voyeurism and exhibitionism, and the division of labour and of "jouissance" (pleasure) (who is "in" the theatre, who works, who is exploited by whom?), and it reinforces the opposition between the real and the imaginary which benefits those in whose interests the pretence exists. Appearing in all the circuses, courtrooms and other scenes of society where men are going to put themselves on display and revel in the sight, the Old Man is overdoing it these days; this is the heyday of directors indulging in ostentation, with too much reliance on elaborate sets, glitz and clever props.

If I go to the theatre now, it must be a political gesture, with a view to changing, with the help of other women, its means of production and expression. It is high time that women gave back to the theatre its fortunate position, its *raison d'être* and what makes it different – the fact that there it is possible to get across the living, breathing, speaking body, whereas the cinema screens us from reality by foisting mere images upon us.

I say "Women," not "daughters." *Le Portrait de Dora* was the first step for me in a long journey; it was a step that badly needed to be taken, so that a woman's voice could be heard for the first time, so that she could cry out, "I'm not the one who is dumb. I am silenced by your inability to hear." Again, this is a scene with the Father, but it is a scene in which the relationship is broken off; in the end Dora walks out, leaving the "Vieux Je" (Old Ego/Old Hat) behind her. This journey takes her from dependence, through suffering, until she exits onto an entirely different stage/scene.

If the stage is woman, it will mean ridding this space of theatricality. She will want to be a body-presence; it will therefore be necessary to work at exploding everything that makes for "staginess," going beyond the confines of the stage, lessening our dependency on the visual and stressing the auditory, learning to attune all our ears, especially those that are sensitive to the pulse of the unconscious, to hear the silences and what lies beyond them. "Distantiation" will not exist; on the contrary, this stage-body will not hesitate to come up close, close enough to be in danger – of life. A body in labour.

The scene takes place where a woman's life takes place, where her life story is decided: inside her body, beginning with her blood. This will be a stage/scene without event. No need for plot or action; a single gesture is enough, but one that can transform the world. Take for example this movement of women towards life, passed on from one woman to another, this outstretched hand which touches and transmits meaning, a single gesture unfolding throughout the ages, and it is a different Story. It will be a text, a body decoding and naming itself in one long, slow push; the song of women being brought into the world, of the infinite patience of a woman expecting Woman. All it requires is one woman who stays beyond the bounds of prohibition, experiencing herself as many, the totality of those she has been, could have been or wants to be, moving ever more slowly, more quickly than herself, anticipating herself. It is coming to pass, this arrival of Woman into the world; I hear it from so far away, and no other stage/scene but this space with a hundred simultaneous scenes/stages where she moves, several woman, unchecked in this place expanded by her look, her listening. And if this scene/stage is movement, if it extends to where *everything* happens and Woman is Whole, where instead of being acted out, life is lived, women will be able to go there and feel themselves loving and being loved, listening and being heard, happy as when they go to the sea, the womb of the mother.

Translated by Barbara Kerslake

Hélène Cixous (b. 1938), French writer and dramatist, well known for her essays, fiction and more recently her plays, which began with *Portrait of Dora* (1972), Freud's much discussed patient. A few of her essays have been repeatedly cited and debated by feminists in English-speaking countries for their espousal of a 'feminine writing'. In response some have charged her with 'essentialism', but this is to ignore her attempts to break down the rigid opposition of the terms masculine/feminine, and replace it with a spectrum of differences opened up by an acceptance of bisexuality. Amongst her writings on theatre, it is this essay that most clearly addresses the issue of theatre's sexual politics. Its conclusion plays on the final word of its title – 'Going to the Seaside' but also, re-spelt, 'Going to the Mother'. Its perspective on Western dramatic tradition can be supplemented by her comments on Shakespeare, Kleist and the Greeks in 'Sorties', the second part of *La Jeune Née* (1975).

33

CAROLEE SCHNEEMANN

Art in the Dark:
A Letter to *Artforum* (1983)

To the Editor:

Thomas McEvilley's recent analysis of the shamanistic origins of performance art, 'Art in the Dark,' leads me to some considerations of essential differences between the works of male and female performance artists. For all of us the violence and offensiveness of our shamanistic explorations have been in proportion to the metaphysical fractures which fuel patriarchal oppositions. But an iconographic identification of the contradictory implications and uses of related materials and actions for female versus male performers mentioned in the article would be highly instructive.

From a feminist perspective, a great deal of shamanistic male performance art has been centred on unravelling a repository of collectively unconscious guilt, and on desire for power or for contact with generally despised aspects of nature and body – the femaleness suppressed in our culture. McEvilley focuses on the critical neglect of these unconscious processes and on the sexual prohibitions which activated shamanistic performance art, but he fails to identify the denied 'femaleness' of 'areas that were previously as unmapped and mysterious as the other side of the moon'. What he notes as 'behavior deliberately contrived as the most inappropriate and offensive' (suggesting personal exorcism of social taboos and prohibitions) remains bound to the patriarchal psychosocial structures that it attempts to illuminate. In early male performance art the panoply of physical taboos, mutilations, and violations – which had its apotheosis in 'fucking female corpses' – is understood by feminine analysis as the crazed expulsion of female complementarity (which was socially annexed and denied primacy).

The erotic female archetype, creative imagination, and performance art itself are all subversive in the eyes of patriarchal culture because they themselves represent forms and forces which cannot be turned into functional commodities or entertainment (to be exchanged as property and value), remaining unpossessable while radicalizing social consciousness. The shamanistic performances of women usually relate to a historic tradition that is pre-Greek, pre-Christian in its inspiration. My mythic associations are *not* Dionysian but properly Aphroditean – Goddess of human passion and of unity of desire and will. Dionysus is the son of Aphrodite – his attributes were derived from her and eventually absorbed into the succeeding patriarchal infrastructures. Dionysus represents the ancient Indo-European bull god in transition from deifying the Goddess to annexing her powers. His potency evolves from a hermaphroditic form, to consort, to dominator. Shamanistic mythology in women's performance art must be acknowledged as what lies behind and is obscured by Greek mythology. Our performance of taboo acts is linked with an identification of our bodies with nature, with the celebration of the cosmic and the sacredness of the ordinary and the lived experience. Ordeals of endurance, physical violation – binding, shooting, puncturing, tying up – are not characteristic of the work of those women artists mentioned in the article (Mary Beth Edelson, Barbara Smith, Rachel Rosenthal, myself – Linda Montano's Christian references the exception). Our use of the body in ritual inculcates not male mysteries but female or communal ones, aligned with intuitions of ancient Goddess presence and investigating those integrations of body and spirit which masculist culture and mythos have torn asunder. The differences in male and female approaches are epitomised by a pair of performances in Holland in 1979. Hermann Nitsch's drenching of tied, shivering performers with gallons of cow's blood was assimilated by the audience, while the fabric coil of menstrual blood that I extracted in my work was considered 'obscene'.

Finally, McEvilley describes *Meat Joy* as a 'fertility rite', diverting its motivation back toward a male birth fetishization. *Meat Joy* was what I described as 'an erotic celebration to sensitize my guilty culture'. As Henry Sayre wrote recently in *The Minnesota Review* (Spring 83), 'the real distinction between most male body art and that of most women lies in the fact that, as a rule, the male's relation to his body is one of self-violation while the female's relation is one of self-exploration and definition.'

Carolee Schneemann
New York

Carolee Schneemann (b. 1939), American artist and performance artist. Since the 1960s, she has exhibited (paintings and kinetic sculptures, video and film) and performed in major cities including New York, San Francisco, London, and at the Venice Biennale (1991). She has also taught at various universities. She writes: 'I believe in the pure thrust of intuition, trust of the body. Putting my body in a central position in my art reveals contradictions in our culture. I resist social, erotic and aesthetic restraints, and have opened my energies to finding materials and forms which celebrate and transcend predicted directions of the work.' For descriptions and illustrations of her work, see for example Sally Banes, *Democracy's Body: Judson Dance Theater 1962–1964*, Ann Arbor, Michigan, UMI Research Press, 1980; Moira

Roth, ed., *The Amazing Decade: Women and Performance Art 1970–1980*, Los Angeles, Astro Artz, 1982; Henry M. Sayre, *The Object of Performance: The American Avant-Garde Since 1970*, University of Chicago Press, 1989; and *Performance Art Journal*, June 1993.

34

SUZANNE LACY AND LESLIE LABOWITZ

FROM Feminist Media Strategies for Political Performance (1985)

Ten seven-foot-tall, heavily veiled women stepped silently from a hearse. As reporters announced to cameras, "We are at City Hall to witness a dramatic commemoration for the ten victims of the Hillside Strangler," the women in black delivered an unexpected message. They did not simply grieve but attacked the sensationalized media coverage that contributes to the climate of violence against women. One at a time, the actresses broke their ominous silence to link these murders with *all* forms of sexual violence (an analysis missing from the media) and to demand concrete solutions.

City council members promised support to activists, Holly Near sang "Fight Back" (written especially for the performance), and news programs across the state carried reports of the performance and its activist message. *In Mourning and In Rage* was perhaps our most compelling example of a one-time media performance, staged as a guerrilla intervention to the conventions of sex crime reportage. Follow-up talk show appearances and activities by local rape hot line advocates created a much broader discussion of the issues than could be covered at the performance itself.

HOW TO DO A MEDIA PERFORMANCE

To create an effective media performance, you first need to ask yourselves three questions:

What is the problem? When communicating through the media, time is of the essence. The subtleties of your analysis simply won't be respected or recorded, and you must take great care to present your information in the clearest, most coherent fashion. The *art* is in making it compelling; the *politics* is in making it clear. To do this, you must first clarify your issue.

What is your goal? Simply getting people to *see* your art is not enough when you are working with serious and confrontational issues. What do you want to have happen as a result of your media campaign or event? This, perhaps the most difficult part of your analysis, needs to embody your best and most realistic projections. (Try not to fall into the self-delusive artist's stance about the "tremendous but unidentifiable impact" of your work!)

Who is your audience? Once you clarify who you want to reach, you may decide that the media form you have chosen is not appropriate to that audience. You probably won't reach children on the eleven o'clock news or working people on middle-of-the-afternoon talk shows. In a small community like Watts, California, word-of-mouth could be more effective than the *Los Angeles Times*, depending on your message. What does your audience already know about the topic at hand, and what do you want them to know? What is their attitude on the subject and how would you like to see them respond to your event?

Our media artworks fell into two categories: the media event and the public informational campaign. The first is a one-time event designed specifically for TV newscasts, choreographed to control the content as it is distributed through the media. These events cannot take the place of person-to-person contact through community organizing or long-term media education, but they serve as a very exciting and useful way to identify an issue or point of view about an issue for a large audience. A successful media event is one part of an overall strategy to influence public opinion, but it needs to be followed up with the in-depth information people will need to make knowledgeable choices.

The public informational campaign, a term used by public relations people, can do just that. Several different kinds of media coverage about a specific issue are placed over an extended period of time. More than a one-time media event, this kind of campaign can educate and organise a constituency. During such projects (*Three Weeks in May, Reverence to Rape to Respect, Making it Safe*, and *The Incest Awareness Project*) we reinforced radio interviews, talk shows, TV newscasts, and feature articles with activities that put us in direct contact with the public, such as street performances, lectures, demonstrations, and art exhibitions. Conceiving of the entire campaign as a conceptual performance, we paired art with informative events, designed talk show appearances as mini-performances, and used media opportunities to talk about performance art as well as the issues.

When you are staging a media event:

- The coordinating committee of your group should select the key images and the message. At least one member of this committee should be an artist who can design a format, create the visual images, and assist in the artistic production. Sometimes everyone's imagination will be captured by an exciting image that is evoked automatically or created by an individual in your group; other times a brainstorming session is needed. Your first images may be clichés accumulated from popular culture. Keep exploring your consciousness until strong and original ones come up. If you need a push, look at mythological images; in the case of women, for example, many images reflect positive expressions of power, even though they have accrued negative connotations in this culture. These images need to be reclaimed, and their continued existence in our collective mythology indicates a potentially strong audience response. For instance, *In Mourning and In Rage* took this culture's trivialised images of mourners as old, powerless women and transformed them into commanding seven-foot-tall figures angrily demanding an end to violence against women.

- To get the press to cover your event, establish its timeliness. Reporters come out for issues they think are current and topical; relate to news items already given airplay (if they don't feel the topic has burned out); have an element of sensationalism, high drama, or risk; and on an otherwise slow news day, have a "human interest" angle (although predicting what an assignment editor will deem to be humanly interesting is not always easy). It is important to determine whether your performance will fit preconceptions of what is newsworthy and at the same time maintain its integrity as art and as political action. For example, the media's dramatization of the Hillside Strangler murders ensured coverage of our memorial performance by major local newscasters at the time. As a result, we were asked to appear on TV talk shows to discuss our alternatives to the media's highly sensationalized coverage of the murders.

- Don't fall into the trap of creating media gimmickry. Superficial images that don't go deep into the cultural symbols of society have less impact, particularly when compared to sophisticated and high-impact commercial images. News reporters react negatively to cute tricks aimed at obtaining coverage; they may manipulate, but they don't like to be manipulated. Events designed to express gut-level feelings and real community concerns do not come across as manipulation.

- Avoid overworked images. Activists fall into their own conventions, which may have the opposite effect than desired. For example, picket lines may establish such preconceptions in the mind of viewers that your meaning would be overlooked.

- Do your best to control the media's interpretation of your information, particularly when it is counter to prevailing attitudes. The press release, which will frame the media's perception of your planned action, is an art form in itself. It must be written simply, with enticing descriptions of visual opportunities and a clear political perspective on the issue. It should also include names of participating government officials and celebrities, if there are any, and give the impression that this will be the most important event of the day. Once your event is assigned to a reporter, that person becomes the next key in making sure your message

141

remains relatively undistorted. To prepare for your contact with reporters, analyze television newscasts in your area: find out who the reporters are, how much time is allotted to your kind of issue, and, most important, how news footage is edited. How long is the average news slot? Does the newscaster stand in front of the image while describing the action? What is the ratio of visual-to-verbal information? Design your event to fit the normal newscast format in order to control its coverage as much as possible.

— Arrange the time of day, the day of the week, and the location to suit reporters' schedules. In Los Angeles, Tuesday or Wednesday morning (when news is usually slow) is considered the best time to call a press conference. Weekend news has already broken, and there is a better chance of getting on the evening news the same day. A strategic location will have effective "visuals" or provide a good background, be familiar to reporters, and have electrical outlets, parking, and other facilities. For example, Los Angeles City Hall was chosen as the site for *In Mourning and In Rage* because we were presenting demands to members of the city council, in session at that hour; we also knew the media would be likely to cover the session that day.

— Keep your event under twenty minutes and provide at least one high-impact visual image that is emblematic of your message. Both words and images should be easy to understand; anything ambiguous should be clarified by a speech during the performance or by a simply worded press release. The performance should be confined to a limited area so that the camera can frame the whole set without losing information. Sequences should be clear, logically connected, and few in number.

— Have one director for the performance and another for the reporters. Since the performers in these events are usually not professionals, an artist should supportively guide them through the piece and control the timing. The media director should greet reporters as they arrive, sign them in, hand out press kits and press statements (explaining the symbolism of each image), and give shot sheets (which break down the event's sequences) to the camera people. This director is also responsible for keeping reporters at the site for the entire event. Don't give out interviews or explicit information before the event is over, and brief everyone involved not to give out information but to direct all questions to the media director. Reporters love to "get the scoop" and leave for their next assignment.

Prior to their collaboration on this project, **Suzanne Lacy** taught performance (theatre and visual art) at the Los Angeles Woman's Building, and worked with Judy Chicago in *Ablutions*. **Leslie Labowitz** studied in Germany in the mid-1970s with Joseph Beuys. Like his, their work extends widely across the boundaries of the arts to engage with large issues. It

142

draws support from Ariadne, the 'social art network' they set up, that brings together women in the arts, media, politics and the community. Suzanne Lacy has since done a series of large-scale works in different cities, involving numerous participants in living 'tableaux'. For example, *Room for Living Room* took place in a furniture showroom, where 100 women from widely different backgrounds occupied the furniture and discussed survival; in *Whisper, the Waves, the Wind* (1984), 150 women dressed in white sat on the beach at tables covered with white cloths; the audience listened on the clifftop to their recorded voices as they discussed women's lot. For an account of these and other works, see the *Drama Review*, vol. 32, no. 1, Spring 1988. She writes elsewhere: 'Strong feminist art might or might not be *obviously* political; by virtue of its expression of a repressed cultural experience, it will always *in fact* be political, as long as women's experience is not widely acknowledged in our society.' (*Frontiers: a Journal of Woman Studies*, vol. 2, no. 1, Spring 1977).

35

EDWARD BOND

FROM Commentary on *The War Plays* (1991)

Red Black and Ignorant is part one of Bond's *War Plays* trilogy. 'TE' stands for his term 'Theatre Event'.

In *Red Black and Ignorant* the soldier returns home with his order to kill someone – anyone – in the neighbourhood. His mother represses her revulsion, dresses him in his uniform and sends him to kill her neighbour. The text gives her and her son's reasons for what they do. They may have other motives in a subtext (perhaps a writer is not always in control of the subtext). Does the son have an Oedipal relation to the father so that already he wants to kill him (as in the end he does) instead of the neighbour? Could it be unconscious guilt that makes him stand as passively as a child being dressed to run an errand?

The text (and any subtext) are written but a metatext is not. It is inferred and created by studying and rehearsing the written texts. It may contain many ideas, actions and emotions – because it is open-ended – and some of these may already be in the written text. The neighbour is a friend and the mother does not want him killed – that is text and subtext. But some things will only be in the metatext. Years ago when the mother sent her son on errands was she already training him in the obedience a soldier needs when he kills? In a way, when a soldier kills he is running an errand for his officers. That is a metatext question because it touches on the nature of society. The metatext of *Red Black and Ignorant* says that it takes a lot of culture to make us killers.

Suppose the soldier has a subtextual motive to kill – perhaps it's even why he joined the army, to be nearer to macho power. Is that the incident's meaning? If it is, why doesn't he kill the officer? The officer is far more like a father than the neighbour – the officer is strong and commanding, the neighbour weak. The soldier does not kill the officer because the officer is part of organized social power and the soldier would be punished if he did. And the order comes from society, anyway. So it is society that gives the motive its meaning. Otherwise it is like saying we drown because we breathe, when we should ask why a drowned person was in the water. Perhaps the soldier's fear of officers is repressed into the unconscious, where it could be attached to any number of motivations? The act's origin – its cause and meaning – is still social.

An Oedipal subtext would not explain what happens, any more than that we breathe tells us why we drown. What is relevant is not the motive but the cause. That is found by philosophic analysis of society. The truth is in the social world and in the metatext. Obviously that is what the acting should show – in action, gesture, texture – if it is to show the incident's truth. In this scene neither the mother nor son act on their motivations, they react to the officer as if he were Fate. The meanings provided by the subtext and the metatext are radically different. It is not a difference of artistic sensibility or taste. Apart from acts of radical innocence, the meanings of our acts are never our motivations for doing them. The reasons for our acts come from society: as good actors have always known, it is our *excuses* for our acts that come from our unconscious – that has always decided the texture of good acting. We act as we do because we are in a particular sort of society. Acts are like moves in a game: the rules of the game give the meanings of the moves and players move according to the rules.

The incident with the soldier is suitable for a TE because it contains contradictory imperatives, and their resolution increases or diminishes our humanity. Should the actress hand the actor his helmet as if it were a school cap? Or brush dirt from his knee? – reaction is obsessed with dirt because it believes that cleanliness is next to obedience. Should she hesitate to give him the jacket? If she gave it to him and then took it back, she would emphasise the mother's doubt. But she would not show us how the mother has learnt to deal with doubt. So she dresses him hurriedly and forcefully and is so intent – perhaps frantic – on getting him into his jacket that she drops it. At that moment the jacket is to her the most important thing in the world – but suddenly her hands are empty. The jacket isn't there any more! She is so surprised she doesn't know where she is. It's almost as if she's thrown the jacket away – or has someone come in and snatched it? An actress can use this moment. Then slowly she stoops to the floor to pick up the jacket. The stooping can be slightly metaphorized so that it seems as if she bows to the ground before the soldier. He stands ram-rod straight at attention. Is he awkward at being treated as a child as he prepares to 'act like a man'? At being in a killer's uniform in the family kitchen? At the sudden obeisance – which he demanded in his song but had not expected from his mother? For the audience his awkwardness is in the metatext because the mother's bow puts it there. The TE turns 'mother and child' into 'soldier and victim'. Does the mother's costume help the image? Should the costume be changed? TE turns everything on stage into a prop. There is no self-contained T-design. T-design identifies the text but establishes the structure of the metatext and makes it useful.

Usually TEs should be based on the play's philosophy. They join with it in a common language and this has a cumulative effect. But they *may* not share the play's philosophy. A reactionary interpretation of the jacket incident might base the TE on the way a medieval lady arms her knight for the crusade. This would conflict with the rest of the play, in which soldiers do not behave as knights are supposed to have behaved (they behave as they actually did). But a TE based on the play's philosophy might still use the incident in the same way. Then it would be satirical. The director should ask if satire was useful at that moment, not merely if it 'worked'. It would be useful only if it was consistent with the philosophical use of the rest of the play. Put like that, it seems obvious – yet in rehearsals such questions are often ignored.

Some TEs should be critical. When Gloucester is blinded in *King Lear*, a generous-minded 'retainer' is killed. The killing of the servant is more appalling than the blinding of the duke, though I have never seen the point made on stage. The TE should attack feudalism – perhaps guided by the way I treated the related incident in my *Lear*, when a soldier is ordered to assault Warrington.

The War Plays' philosophy is socialist, that is it is written in the understanding that there could be no reason in the subtext why the soldier must kill *anyone*. The incident's truth is in the metatext. That does not restrict the interpretation or make it doctrinaire. The subtext would be restrictive because its explanation is closed and invites pathos, which our age makes maudlin (as in Beckett's messenger boy and Cocteau's 'Poor Oedipus!'). T-theatre expands texts and ramifies their social, psychological and theatrical possibilities. . . .

TEs are not simply Brechtian alienation effects. Brecht frequently revised his understanding of theatre, I am commenting on it as it is generally understood. Brecht wanted to found a Diderot Theatre Society. Diderot was a rationalist social-philosopher but a romantic artist. He said 'Poet be dark!', Brecht wanted poets to be light. Yet alienation theory depends on a philosophy of mind held by Diderot and other eighteenth-century rationalists. It appeals to objective judgement but does not secure the means of achieving it. The mind cannot get outside itself to be objective. The structure of mind is part of the continuum of society: both are part of one reality, and our examination of particular problems repeats the general problem – if not absolutely (since the examining mind must repeat its willed incorporation into society) then with a drag of distortion. Himmler killed out of love but organized the killing objectively. Objectivity does not penetrate passion or complacency. Theatre must infiltrate the processes which make the social mind; TEs attempt to do this. . . .

The masks of *The Caucasian Chalk Circle* weight one side of the triangle. The audience see the masks but the characters do not. On stage the two social worlds are properly separated but not realistically joined. The audience is given privileged understanding of the metatext, but it does not do the audience-work – that is done for it by authority. This makes *The Caucasian Chalk Circle* a fable, which clarifies but also obscures meaning by putting product *inside* process. . . . A metatext is not alienation but a commitment that involves the psyche-social processes of real life. The audience commits itself to judgement because it questions itself.

Many of my scenes – maybe all – cannot be performed unless the performance is based on the metatext; the metatext acting cannot be parasitic on the text because the text will not function as a subtext. It records modern society and the whole of modern society is alienated: you cannot alienate alienation. If the metatext is not acted there is nothing there. Because of when they were written Brecht's plays still have strands of traditional theatre in them. Inevitably some of the revolutionary break with the past was the effort to get away from it, not to construct an alternative with its own capacity for change. Since Brecht's time capitalism has become adept at weaving alienation and empathy into one self-negating experience. Modernism tried to find a metatext in the subtext, but the social-psyche of post-modernism does not have the structural means to do that, it simply does not know them: they were paths on a mountain that has been swept away. TEs are now the only alternative to fake-theatre.

Edward Bond (b. 1934), British playwright and poet, who, like Shaw, achieved the unwanted distinction of having his early work banned from public performance (*Saved*, 1965, *Early Morning*, 1968). The passages above are drawn from an extended discussion, but may serve to introduce his recent theory concerning the metatext and the Theatre Event. His reference to the 'stage gap', and to the weighting of 'one side of the triangle' effected by the masks in *The Caucasian Chalk Circle*, pick up earlier discussion (as does the reference to Himmler). The 'triangle' consists of actor, character and audience (differing from the 'Theatre-Triangle' of Meyerhold – director/spectator, author, actor); this forms a 'gap', symbolised by the stage, 'that *only* philosophy can fill. . . . The actor's philosophy, not the character's psychology, gives the performance's meaning.' While not simply an alienation effect, the 'TE' Bond discusses here is not unrelated to Brecht's *Gestus*, 'both gist and gesture' (John Willett. And see note, p. 305). For his relation to Brecht, see 'A Note on Dramatic Method' in *The Bundle* (1978), and 'On Brecht: A Letter to Peter Holland', *Theatre Quarterly*, vol. 8, no. 30, Summer 1978.

36

CHARLES LUDLAM

Opinions

The 'opinions' offered here are drawn from essays and interview material spanning Ludlam's career, that have been assembled by Steven Samuels into a posthumous volume where they are presented undated.

Gay people have always found a refuge in the arts, and the Ridiculous theatre is notable for admitting it. The people in it – and it is a very sophisticated theatre, culturally – never dream of hiding anything about themselves that they feel is honest and true and the best part of themselves. *Nothing* is concealed in the Ridiculous. . . .

The people who wanted to show the respectable gay image – La Coste shorts and pleats – were horrified that in my plays they were always disreputable drag queens, and that monstrosities were being committed. In my plays, people exhibit terrible behavior because it's showing the ridiculous side of life.

My art is not based on showing a positive image for any one group. I think that would be a terrible cop-out. That kind of theatre, the preachy type, has less to do with the gay sensibility than with showing how gay people could be just like straight people. . . .

Also, I think it's very dangerous to create an all-gay community because there's no influence from the outside world.

Everybody but a couple of people in my company are gay, but what we do is political in a different way from gay theatre. It's just entertainment, not agit-prop. It isn't preachy and it's for everybody. . . .

I think the distinction between gay theatre and what I do, which some people call "queer theatre," is that gay theatre is really a political movement to show that gay people can be admirable, responsible members of the community. It shows their problems. I don't do that. "Queer theatre" embraces more variation, and the possibility of something being odd or peculiar rather than just simply homosexuality. . . .

I see nothing wrong with a man playing a woman's role. In the Kabuki and in the Elizabethan theatre men played women's roles and no one

148

blinked an eye. Originally, all women's roles in Shakespeare were played by men. And, in the reverse, Sarah Bernhardt played Hamlet.

Hamlet is traditionally a man's part, Marguerite is traditionally a woman's part. What ladies have been given to do in various male impersonations is just what I did in *Camille*. Women are Peter Pan and all the rest of it; I, a man, am Marguerite Gautier. . . .

I will do more female roles in the future, even though it gets more and more taboo.

A friend of mine, Christopher Scott, said he felt for men right now there is an incredible identity problem about masculinity and that drag threatens this. But I think an artist is like a shamanistic figure. It's not what everybody does, it's that the artist is a different beast.

If you have a flare for playing females, it's foolish to let anything hold you back. Artists have to be very androgynous, especially actors. They have to be capable of understanding human feelings in general. . . .

My plays let men and women step out of their traditional roles. Theatre is a way of experimenting with life – a kind of research-and-development department for the culture at large.

We're imprisoned in our gender, and the ability to get out of it is very forbidden. Tiresias was turned into a woman, revealed from his experience that women get more pleasure from sex than men, and they blinded him as punishment for the revelation.

So there is that desire to know what it is to be the opposite sex. It's one of the major curiosities, and I think it exists for everybody. For those who *can* cross that barrier, it's a magical act.

Theatre has a magical and religious basis. Many of the things we see strike us in a very primordial way, but these are mysteries. I don't think everything can be explained.

I don't think everything about female impersonation can be explained. The fact that it bothers people is its power to a large extent. The fact that it can disturb or puzzle or confuse or shock is part of its magic. . . .

I think my theatre is political, but what is political is perhaps misunderstood. Politics is about spheres of influence, and in that sense it is political.

If a man plays Camille, for instance, you begin to think it's horrible, but in the end you are either moved or won over. You believe in the character beyond the gender of the actor, and no one who has experienced that can go back.

In such cases, this theatre is political in the highest sense of influence. But as far as pushing for political upheaval goes, it's not true to the nature of art. . . . Artists are trying to make the best of the situation *now* and improve it from *within*. They are not assaulting it from the outside, trying to batter it down.

149

The more you oppose something, the more you strengthen it. If you are able to change it from inside, you can make it what you want it to be. . . .

Instead of having to wait for utopia, we can make utopia right now, right away, start working on it now.

"Utopia" is Greek for "nowhere"; that means "not possible," to begin with. What I am saying is that the impossible can be possible. The impossible is constructed of fragments of the possible — in a new arrangement.

What can be imagined is only what is experienced. Imagination is the process of taking many little things that you experience and piecing them together in a new arrangement.

I am trying to make it clear that the process of rearranging them is a practical process that everyone can immediately get involved in. Make the dream into reality by simply rearranging the pieces.

Charles Ludlam (1943–87), American actor, playwright, and director of the Ridiculous Theatrical Company of New York, made his New York acting debut and had his first play staged by John Vaccaro at the Play-House of the Ridiculous in 1966. Sacked by Vaccaro the following year, he set up his own company. A string of plays followed, and performances which included the title roles in *Camille* ('a tearjerker' based on *La Dame aux camélias*), *Hedda Gabler*, and other female roles. His numerous productions included one of *The English Cat*, the opera by Edward Bond and Hans Werner Henze. Stefan Brecht's *Queer Theatre* (Frankfurt, Suhrkamp Verlag, 1978) looks at his work in context.

Part III

THE POPULAR
DIMENSION

Popular theatre is the modern, demanding, trouble-making, tenacious form of our time; in short, the major adventure.

Jean Vilar

Are you fed up standing by your stall serving the occasional punter when the pitchers in your market have big crowds around them spending hundreds of pounds? Learn how to get a crowd, how to hold them, how to entertain them and most of all, how to get them to spend their money! Tricks of the trade from one of the best pitchers on the road.

Michael Levy, London market stall pitcher, advertising a course in 'pitching'
(reported by John Windsor, Independent, *10 July 1993)*

INTRODUCTION

1

As theatre has found itself gradually pushed from the centre of the popular arts to their periphery, a belief in 'popular theatre' has repeatedly figured in thinking about its role, and energised a series of initiatives that have radically extended its boundaries and possibilities. But at the start of the century many looked down on theatre as an all-too-popular affair. Those striving to convert it to higher purposes did not expect or look for mass support. There was a frequent call for smaller theatres, where the new techniques of naturalism could register effectively for a select audience, and for club theatres, where an oppressive censorship could be evaded. The reform of the stage was seen to depend on the support of two slim minorities: those with stomach for the new realistic problem plays, or those with a taste for advanced artistic styles. Both parties believed themselves the only hope of redeeming the stage from the brash vulgarity and sentiment into which it had sunk. It is worth remembering that when Strindberg, at the peak of his fame, for the first time took direction of his own theatre, its seats numbered a mere 150, a capacity barely viable today except on the 'profit-sharing' or unwaged fringe.

None the less, it is also true that from its very inception modern theatre has been haunted by the dream that it might be a people's theatre: a theatre for the people at large. In the symbolist period, inspired by Wagner and Nietzsche, the notion of a theatre like that of the Greeks that might once more unite people and performers in a profound or ecstatic ritual event was much aired, particularly in Germany and Russia. A quasi-religious drama was envisaged, fully involving music and movement, in a space no longer split in two by a proscenium arch. Such ideas influenced the youthful Meyerhold, and are the prelude to the 'ritual theatre' of recent years. But while the latter has been accused of primitivism, the inspiration of the former was coloured by nationalism. The hope was that the class conflicts dividing the nation might be dissolved in a moving communal event, and its people once more realise their oneness.

If we wish to compare theory with practice, and see how a national people's theatre turned out, we may look to the Abbey in Ireland. W. B. Yeats here wryly reflects on its history, and on the differences between those who wished it to speak for the people and the people it needed to speak to. The writers whose founding efforts it had sprung from were entranced by Irish folk culture. But its audience were Dubliners. Living in a city bristling with religion alongside some of the worst slums in Europe, few were rural or pagan enough to feel much affinity with the myths and faery folk that so beguiled its founders.

But another form of people's theatre also needs to be considered. In 1909, Georg Fuchs, mentor of the advanced Munich Artists' Theatre, devoted a whole chapter of his book *Revolution in the Theatre* to the variety stage (or 'vaudeville'). That this was 'of the people' in every sense he makes clear. 'All the fresh audacious boys and girls who have no money for an expensive education in the higher walks of theatre find a home in vaudeville.' This, he argues, is why variety is free of the 'nervous diseases' zealously explored on the modern stage elsewhere. Instead it manifests an 'unfailing vital impulse which maintains these artists in an enchanted world of make-believe, of joyous vitality, of dreamlike fantasy, and of a drama which has its roots in the body, in the animal instincts, and in the senses'.[1] To Fuchs the lesson was clear: it was 'these unintellectual theatre folk who really know most about the living functions of the drama'. Unlike the dramatic stage, where 'the art of acting has been so ground into the dust by the tyranny of literature' that 'an amazing neglect of physical discipline' is evident, variety performances were characterised by 'sure, clean work . . . and sound technique'. Theatre has everything to gain, Fuchs argues, from a compar-able schooling in physical skills. So begins a changed emphasis which affected theatre deeply in subsequent years.

Variety theatre grows out of music hall, as Vesta Tilley, one of its finest artistes, here explains; and is related in many ways to that other popular spectacle, the circus, with whom it shared its acts and skills. From Mr Sleary's circus troupe in Dickens' *Hard Times* to the Natcha-Kee-Tawaras of Lawrence's *The Lost Girl*, the live act has served as a potent symbol of the popular imagination and the creative energies of the underclass. Its adoption by writers and importation into the sphere of the arts registers a shift of allegiances that corresponds to significant social change. As entrepreneurial capitalism thrived, writers and artists sought to take their distance from the burgeoning bourgeoisie. The dandy and the bohemian flourished, in con-tempt of the narrow philistinism of the well-to-do. Though the latter paid the piper, artists sought a cultural compact with its class antagonists above or below: the aristocracy, peasantry or proletariat. The artistically-minded slowly transferred their scorn from the taste of the masses to the taste of the bourgeoisie; and in order to give 'a slap in the face'[2] to the latter, they re-embraced the former.

Enjoyment of popular forms was soon succeeded by attempts to fuse them with 'art' forms. The beginning of the twentieth century sees these attempts spreading rapidly, in a process which coincides and is deeply involved with the onset of modernism. In theatre it sparks off a bohemian *liaison* with variety, the circus, Punch and Judy and other forms of popular culture. Examples already on hand in this volume include Jarry's debt to *guignol* or puppet theatre (in which he is followed by Ionesco), Apollinaire's various transpositions of popular song and dance rhythms, and the cabaret leanings of Dada and the futurists.

The new-found enthusiasm of artists and writers for popular entertainment needed no scholarly backing. But in the theatre, an interest in the history of popular forms soon followed. It begins importantly in Vsevolod Meyerhold's essay of 1911–12, 'The Fairground Booth', whose title, taken from a play by Alexander Blok, indicates its theme. Meyerhold here upturns the account of the time, elaborated by Ivanov (a leading symbolist and early influence), which rooted post Graeco-Roman theatre history in religious rituals and the mystery play; and argues instead the crucial importance of the '*cabotin*' – the strolling performer, *raconteur,* juggler and mime, whose theatre is the market square or the fairground booth.

Meyerhold's concerns are not directly political, but they clearly serve to promote the common entertainer above the priestly scribe – and for that matter, those other scribes, from Shakespeare down, who later take his place. That the *cabotin* can perform without script is, for Meyerhold, part of the attraction. While Hamlet forbade the clowns to improvise, Meyerhold applauds them, reopening a power struggle long decided in favour of the author. He prepares the ground for Bakhtin, who was to trace so provocatively the history of carnival and 'the laughter of the people', finding there an enduring subversive energy.[3] But Meyerhold is not simply concerned with history. He is looking back to find a way forward: forward past the 'static drama' of Maeterlinck and the 'stylised theatre' he had himself pioneered so shortly before. Both he now views as literary theatre. Like Fuchs before him, and Artaud after, Meyerhold became intent on rescuing theatre from the *literati*, and restoring it to its own dynamism and forms of expression. With lasting consequences for Russian theatre, he roots these in the common *cabotin*.

2

The ground was thus well prepared for the futurists' espousal of the variety stage, vigorously spelt out by F. T. Marinetti in 1913. His piece, 'The Variety Theatre', follows Fuchs in being a vigorous celebration of a theatre sprung from the people, while also being a key futurist manifesto. It is unprecedented in the degree to which it embraces popular forms in the name of the avant-garde, and uses them to explode the conventions of bourgeois theatre. The avoidance of naturalism, psychology, plot, tedious sequence, trite moralisms and false drama; the preference by contrast for physical prowess, rapid change, absurdity and the marvellous: these features of variety were at the same time main planks of the futurist platform.

The chief channel whereby the variety ethos had reached the better educated till then was the cabaret. From its beginnings in the 1880s, cabaret flourished in major cities across Europe, offering its *habitués* new styles of informal performance and anti-establishment satire. It drew a specialised audience, and its venues were not large theatres but drinking establishments. But its entertainment was in variety format; and the freedom and vigour of variety was retained and cultivated, for this was very much what attracted the clientele. Cabaret was a sharp, funny, free-and-easy alternative to the formalities of theatre-going, licensed by its marginality to direct its satire far and wide.

But Marinetti's manifesto signals a further step in which theatre learns to profit from its rivals. It featured in a collection of Italian futurist writings published in Russia in 1913. As one might guess from 'The Fairground Booth', it fell on fertile ground. Futurism was already flourishing there as a literary movement. Vladimir Mayakovsky, its most conspicuous apostle, was a poet. But he was also strongly attracted to the stage, and his second full-scale play, *Mystery-Bouffe* of 1918, celebrates the Revolution of the year before in a rousing fairground spirit. In the new ethos of the soviets, the futurist critique of bourgeois drama had gained sharp relevance. Extended evocations of social inertia and pangs of frustrated love on country estates had become incongruous. In his 1922 article 'Avant-Garde Art and Variety', the director Nikolai Foregger writes: 'While the powerful waves of art reflect an already defined actuality, these "little" forms [the popular arts], like the foam on the crest of the waves, carry in their spray the smell and the taste of the new waters which must wash the world. In the theatrical field, it is variety which must play this role.'[4] This view was widely followed up. Circus skills, acrobatics, visual gags and slapstick were lavishly introduced into the world of theatre by FEKS (see the piece here by Grigori Kozintsev), Sergei Radlov and the Theatre of Popular Comedy, Foregger's MASTFOR cabaret, Eisenstein (as we have seen in Part II), and Yuri Annenkov.[5] An extraordinary flowering of innovative theatre resulted, spreading beyond its futurist origins into the new Soviet theatre at large.

It was commonly felt that this demanded new buildings. Existing theatres were not only incapable of housing the masses; in the workers' state, their all too evident division of the privileged from the less privileged, under attack since Antoine's time, could not be defended. For Kamensky and Mayakovsky, they were 'futile, good-for-nothing matchboxes'.[6] Meyerhold agreed: 'In those days they built box stages designed to foster illusion. Obviously it is our intention to build new theatres and to vacate those which we inherited from the age of imperialism, nobility and private ownership.'[7] For Meyerhold, theatre is the proper rival of the cinema for a mass audience, poised to overtake it as the shift to 'talkies' undermines the art of Chaplin, Keaton and Griffiths by abandoning the international language of silent film. Theatre could include film; but it could also, given newly designed spaces, place the audience in the midst of a live spectacle as no cinema could.

While established companies were reluctant to change their ways, the avant-garde widely believed that with the revolution its time had come. The Soviet authorities were open-minded but not so sure. Were the masses really best served by artistic practices dreamt up by a class fraction suspiciously akin to the bohemian fringe? Were 'revolutionary' techniques really needed by the Revolution, as their adherents claimed? Had not those who had stormed the Winter Palace earned the right to enter the palace of their cultural inheritance, and enjoy the great works so long reserved for their masters? Or if culture was to be transformed, shouldn't it be by rejecting the sophistications of European modernism, and handing the job over to artists springing from the nation's proletariat, who would surely meet the people's needs better?

The supposed gulf between modernism and the people was bridged in practice, not simply by spectacles designed for mass audiences, but in smaller alternative forms. A seminal instance is the Blue Blouse Troupe. This was a touring company formed in 1923 by a teacher of journalism to provide a 'living newspaper'. It created its own shows on variety principles, converting cabaret modes to agit-prop purposes. What is remarkable is that beginning as one troupe it ended as five thousand. Groups all over the country, both professional and amateur, started up in emulation, drawing on its freely disseminated material. Performances offered skits, verse, monologues and 'avant-garde oratory' among 'an uninterrupted montage of scenes, songs, music, dance, mime, acrobatics and gymnastics'.[8] Messages were punched home with bold visual effects. Blue Blouse offered a model on which countless variations have been devised by agit-prop and guerilla theatre groups ever since.

But however much evidence there is to refute it, the antithesis of modernism and the people was to be graven into state culture on the left by Stalin and on the right by Hitler, and the idea has proved even harder to dislodge than they were. One classic and still pertinent discussion of it is Bertolt Brecht's essay 'The Popular and the Realistic', written a decade later, when Hitler was in power and Brecht in exile. Brecht takes up the banner of 'realism' here without rejecting progressive experiment. He takes issue implicitly with Georg Lukács, and argues cogently that popular taste and advanced forms are not at odds. His view can be checked here against Armand Gatti's account of the response of an audience of road-sweepers to his play, *The Imaginary Life of the Roadsweeper Auguste G.*

The large-scale public provision of arts and culture, mooted so freely in the impoverished Soviet Union of the 1920s, remained the aim of the state in the eastern bloc. In the west, the case for such provision has always needed to be argued, as it is in the article here by Jean Vilar. Vilar ran France's *Théâtre National Populaire* in the years following the Second World War, when a surge of reform favoured state backing for the arts. Under his direction, the TNP's work was marked by a conviction that drama of the past had something to say to the present, and that a broad audience could discover this if the theatre-going occasion could be democratised, stripped of its formalities, and made welcoming and exciting. Brimming with an audience from the workplace as well as the university, Vilar's TNP strove to attract a new public to the theatre with a repertoire of classic and modern works, played in a vigorous and direct style.

The benefits of such a theatre for the people had been urged at the start of the century by Romain Rolland;[9] and a national popular theatre was finally established in France in 1920 under Firmin Gémier, who had established his credentials in this field by touring shows in a huge tent and mounting spectacular productions in the Winter Circus. Vilar thus inherited a strong tradition, in which a belief in mass occasions and celebrations combined with a mission of cultural enlightenment. His bold efforts to continue this tradition were denigrated by the revolutionary left as having little to do with the workers beyond offering to an upward-aspiring minority an induction into bourgeois elitist values. The TNP had offered them a feast of high culture; but what about the workers' own culture? Though its style drew on 'epic theatre' and its repertoire embraced plays by Armand Gatti, Vilar was charged with overriding it.

For a theatre venture not vulnerable to such criticism, we may turn to Dario Fo. Fo is a compatriot of Gramsci, the Italian communist activist who died following long imprisonment by the fascists in 1937. From Gramsci comes the idea that the ruling class exert control over the populace less by the state apparatus of police, law and punishment than by inducing consent through their cultural 'hegemony'. During the 1960s, as class struggle waned while the media became more and more pervasive, this view was much aired. It was argued that a mix of pacifying fictions, predictable images, stabilising concepts and dominating stereotypes breathed forth from the culture at large to infiltrate the worker's mind, sap dissidence and bolster the status quo. This modern 'popular culture' was thought by many to have nullified working people's own culture and totally colonised the space it had once occupied.

Neither Gramsci nor Fo believed the battle lost. Working in close association with the actress and feminist Franca Rame, Fo became deeply versed in the history of Italian popular culture, particularly that of the *giullare* or *jongleur*: the strolling folk-singer, mime, acrobat and comic, an Italian version of Meyerhold's *cabotin*, and embodiment of the counter-culture of the Middle Ages celebrated by Bakhtin. 'The *jongleur* was born from the people,' writes Fo, 'and from the people he took their anger in order to be able to give it back to them, mediated via the grotesque.'[10] Fo brought this figure alive in his solo piece *Mistero Buffo* (1969). He presented this as a way of inviting the people of the present 'to reappropriate *their own* culture'.[11] In a long series of plays and productions Fo re-focused popular comic techniques towards subversive satirical ends – ends they have served, he argues, throughout history.

This interest in the roots of popular culture is shared by Peter Schumann and John Fox. Schumann, a German emigré to the United States, took with him memories of Kaspar, the German Punch, and the large effigies paraded at carnival time. With the Bread and Puppet Theatre he recreated them in arresting new forms to enact stories and parables pertinent to the war in Vietnam. These were among the most striking theatre events of the 1960s. John Fox's work with Welfare State drew initially on the lively art school scene of the time, and also on a British idea of 'organic' culture that looked back to mummers' plays, maypole festivities and harvest celebrations. Updating and playing with such notions in a world of urban overspill and cross-country motorways resulted in plentiful elements of the unexpected, the maverick and the marvellous; and their immediate appeal to a wide public with no special interest in bygone customs has shown that the media's hold over people's imaginations can still be challenged.

These groups played largely in the open air, but others too were turning their back on theatres. Tired of trying to persuade 'ordinary' people to step inside such unfamiliar places, groups sallied out to meet them on their own ground. As they did so, they were obliged to become more mindful of how such people normally chose to enjoy themselves. John McGrath's careful enumeration of the elements of a popular 'good night out' registers not only a commitment to seeking out working-class audiences; but the realisation that left-wing views did not ensure a hearing from them. To win them over, it was their criteria that had to be met, rather than those of a theatre largely foreign to them. So the audience provocation of earlier groups, and even Brecht's much respected 'alienation', were dropped in favour of contact, warmth, and shows of solidarity.

Some wished to go further and involve those present not just as spectators but as active participants. Appia long before had urged this. Here Armand Gatti, Dorothy Heathcote and Kwesi Owusu describe different forms of such involvement, as do Honor Ford-Smith and Augusto Boal in Part V. Gatti describes work with 'losers' in a youth centre, Heathcote with young people in schools. Owusu discusses the Notting Hill Carnival, whose survival is not only the concern of West Indians, he suggests, but 'of all who appreciate and cherish the vitality of popular creativity'. That appreciation is essential to the work of both Gatti and Heathcote; and has been a main strand in the history of the modern stage.

NOTES

1 Passages quoted are from Georg Fuchs, *Revolution in the Theatre: Conclusions Concerning the Munich Artists' Theatre*, Ithaca, NY, Cornell University Press, 1959, condensed and adapted by Constance Connor Kuhn from *Die Revolution des Theaters*, Munich, George Muller, 1909; reissued Port Washington, NY, Kennikat Press, 1972.

2 'A Slap in the Face of Public Taste' is the title of a Russian futurist manifesto published in 1912 by the Hylaea group, which included Mayakovsky. It can be found in Vladimir Markov's *Russian Futurism: A History*, London, MacGibbon & Kee, 1969, pp. 45–6.

3 See Mikhail Bakhtin, *Rabelais and His World*, Bloomington, Indiana University Press, 1984.

4 Nikolai Foregger's article can be found in *Du cirque au théâtre*, in the 'Théâtre années vingt' series, Lausanne, La Cité, L'Age d'Homme, 1983, pp. 229–34.

5 Annenkov's essay on circus, 'Merry Sanatorium', is in the *Drama Review* vol. 19, no. 4, T68, December 1975.

6 Vassily Kamensky, cited in Wiktor Woroszylski, *The Life of Mayakovsky*, London, Gollancz, 1972, p. 233.

7 *Meyerhold on Theatre*, ed. Edward Braun, London, Methuen, 1969, p. 255.

8 *The Red Flag*, 18 December 1928, cited by Richard Stourac in unpublished dissertation (see under Blue Blouse in 'Sources and Selected Further Writings').

9 Rolland's writings on this topic first appeared in Peguy's *Cahiers de la Quinzaine* in 1903, and were published in book form under the title *Le Théâtre du Peuple* in 1904. Partially translated by Barrett H. Clark as *The People's Theatre*, New York, 1918, they can be sampled in Eric Bentley's *The Theory of the Modern Stage*, Harmondsworth, Penguin, 1968.

10 Dario Fo, *Mistero Buffo*, translated by Ed Emery, London, Methuen, 1988, p. 1.

11 Ibid., p. xvii.

37

GORDON CRAIG

From One Word about the Theatre as it was, as it is, and as it will be (1905)

To tell you what the theatre was, is to tell you the history of the theatre.

This book is too short to go into the history of the theatre, but it is possible in a few words to say that history hints the first development of the theatre as being more complete than its last.

In its first development it was self-reliant.

The first sign we have of the art of the theatre is in the religious rites. All the arts which I wish to see back again in the theatre were brought together and focussed in the religious rites.

Then the poet, being by far the most intellectual of the people engaged in these rites, and the spoken word being as powerful, the spoken word and the poet gradually usurped all else. If anyone has studied the nature of the theatre, he sees that it must have been quite different from what it pretends to be to-day.

The theatre was for the people, and always should be for the people. The poets would make the theatre for a select community of dilettanti. They would put difficult psychological thoughts before the public expressed in difficult words, and would make for this public something which is impossible for them to understand, and unnecessary for them to know; whereas the theatre must show them sights, show them life, show them beauty, and not speak in difficult sentences. And the reason why the theatre is being kept back to-day is because the poet is pulling one way, saying they should only be given words, using the theatre and all its crafts as a medium for those words; and the people are pulling the other way, saying they desire to see the sights, realistically or poetically shown, not turned into literature. So far most of the brainy people are on the side of the poets; they have got the upper hand. Still the plays in the theatres are, artistically, failures; the theatre itself is a failure artistically and commercially, and the secret of this failure is the battle between the poet and the people.

For a note on Craig see p. 18.

This piece comes from the introduction to Craig's first major statement of his views, *The Art of the Theatre* of 1905; but, unlike the rest of the volume, he did not reprint it in the subsequent collection, *On the Art of the Theatre* (1911).

38

VESTA TILLEY

Recollections (1934)

The rise of the Music Hall to Variety Theatre, from "Sing-Song" to "Palace", began with the advent of women visitors. Some of the original Music Halls were literally Pot Houses with wooden platforms for the artistes, and plain benches and tables for the patrons, sawdust floors, mugs of beer and all the usual taproom surroundings. There was little or no comfort for the audience, save heat and light and plenty of beer, an old piano or violin for the orchestra, and the performers in those days had a very hard time.

I write, of course, of the Music Hall as it was in my very early days. . . .

When I made my first acquaintance with the Music Hall a woman was rarely seen among the audience, but as the attraction of Variety increased, more suitable Halls were requisitioned for the purpose. Stages with Prosceniums were provided, gas footlights, rows of wooden seats with backs, clean sanded or sawdusted floors, with a bar always prominent at the back of the hall; women gradually came with their menfolk, more attention was paid to the performer, audiences remaining seated until the customary interval, when the bar was patronised, two or three instrumentalists occupied the orchestra, and printed programmes of the entertainment were sold at a halfpenny each. The audience was entirely working class, and the performance brightened many a dull life in working towns.

Then came the larger hall, with Pit and Gallery, the price of admission varying from one penny in the Gallery to sixpence for a seat in a "Private" Box, seating generally fifty people. As these humble places were superseded by more imposing theatres, they became known as Penny Gaffs, but the best Variety artistes of the time were schooled in them, and in many cases founded reputations which lasted a lifetime. . . .

Slowly but surely a better type of audience patronised the Music Halls, and there was real variety in the programmes they offered. The legitimate theatres were not keeping pace with the times, their seating accommodation was indifferent, ventilation was nothing like that of the modern Music Hall, and the result was that in addition to creating an audience of its own, the up-to-date Music Hall became a very strong competitor of the

163

legitimate theatre. There was a time when the actors and actresses of the legitimate theatre looked down upon the Music Hall, and scorned the idea of appearing there, but as large music halls have of late years been converted into cinema theatres, so many legitimate theatres were being at this time converted into Variety theatres. . . .

Since then I can recall very few actors and actresses who have not appeared on the Variety stage. When Sir Oswald Stoll was running high-class Variety at the London Coliseum, Madame Sarah Bernhardt and other famous actors and actresses were included in the programmes. . . .

There was a big invasion of the Variety theatre by legitimate stars, much to the indignation of the Music Hall artistes, who complained that the long sketches they presented kept many Music Hall artistes out of work. Personally, I welcomed their advent. It helped to raise the tone of the Variety stage, and attracted many theatrical patrons. At the same time, there was little fear that the intruders would oust the old-established Variety act. They were acceptable in dramatic and comedy sketches, but in the few instances in which they endeavoured to become Music Hall artistes they were not exactly successful. In fact, the only actor I can recollect who made a distinct hit, as a singer of dramatic and comedy songs, was Albert Chevalier, a very great artiste and a charming man. It is quite a different thing to attempt to entertain a huge audience of some two or three thousand people as a single turn, to having the support of a chorus of dancing girls and beautiful scenery and surroundings, when the senses are charmed by the support as much as by the individual.

Vesta Tilley (1864–1952), English male impersonator and variety singer, well exemplifies the combination of popular origins and scrupulous artistry that Georg Fuchs credited to the variety stage. Vesta Tilley had her schooling on the stage. She had no formal education. Her father worked as 'Chairman' (or compère) of a provincial music hall, and from the age of six had turned her into a regular performer. She went on to become one of the most celebrated stars of the period. She specialised in deft satiric mimicry of the bourgeois and upper-class male, adding to the 'alienation effect' by singing in her natural voice. That her subtle and refined art could win her such a huge and admiring following witnesses to an aspect of popular taste not always acknowledged. Sarah Maitland's *Vesta Tilley*, London, Virago, 1986, is an interesting consideration of her life and work. See too Laurence Senelick's 'The Evolution of the Male Impersonator on the Nineteenth-Century Popular Stage', *Essays in Theatre*, vol. I, no. 1, 1982.

39

VSEVOLOD MEYERHOLD

FROM The Fairground Booth (1911–12)

The cabotin is a strolling player; the cabotin is a kinsman to the mime, the histrion,[1] and the juggler; the cabotin can work miracles with his technical mastery; the cabotin keeps alive the tradition of the true art of acting. It was with his help that the Western theatre came to full flower in the theatres of Spain and Italy in the seventeenth century. Whilst acknowledging the mystery and welcoming its revival on the Russian stage, Benois[2] speaks disparagingly of cabotinage as some sort of evil; yet the mystery-players themselves sought the help of the cabotins. The cabotin was to be found wherever there was any sort of dramatic presentation, and the organizers of mystery-plays relied on them to perform all the most difficult tasks. From the history of the French theatre we know that the mystery-player was incapable of performing without the help of the juggler. During the reign of Philippe le Bel[3] farce suddenly made an unexpected appearance amongst the religious subjects in the form of the bawdy adventures of Renart.[4] Who but the cabotins were capable of performing this farce? With the gradual development of processional mysteries there appeared more and more new plots which demanded of the performer an ever-widening range of technical accomplishments. The solution of the complex problems posed by the mystery-plays fell on the shoulders of the cabotins. Thus we see that cabotinage was common even in the mystery-plays and the cabotin played a decisive part in their development.

Having sensed its own inadequacy, the mystery began gradually to absorb the elements of popular entertainment as personified by the mummers, and was forced to go from the ambo [pulpit], through the parvis [exterior court] into the churchyard, and thence out on to the market-place. Whenever the mystery play tried to come to terms with the theatre, it was bound to resort to the principles of mummery, and no sooner had it reached a compromise with the art of the actor than it was absorbed by this art and ceased to be a mystery-play.

Perhaps it has always been so: if there is no cabotin, there is no theatre either; and, contrariwise, as soon as the theatre rejects the basic rules of theatricality it straightway imagines that it can dispense with the cabotin.

Apparently, Benois regards the mystery as the means of arresting the decline of the Russian theatre, and cabotinage as the cause of it. I hold the opposite view: it is 'the mystery' (in Benois' sense) which is ruining the theatre and cabotinage which can bring about its revival. In order to rescue the Russian theatre from its own desire to become the servant of literature, we must spare nothing to restore to the stage the cult of cabotinage in its broadest sense.

But how can this be done? First of all, it seems to me that we should apply ourselves to the study and restoration of those theatres of the past in which the cult of cabotinage once held sway.

Our dramatists have no idea at all of the laws of true theatre. In the Russian theatre of the nineteenth century the old vaudeville was replaced by a flood of plays of brilliant dialectic, plays *à thèse*,[5] plays of manners, plays of mood. . . . *

The story-teller employs fewer and fewer descriptive passages, enlivens his narrative by allocating more and more dialogue to his characters, and eventually invites the reader into an auditorium. Has the story-teller any need of the cabotin? Of course not. The readers themselves can go up on to the stage and read the dialogue of their favourite author role-by-role out loud to the public. This is what is meant by 'an affectionate rendering of the play'. No time has been lost in finding a name for the reader turned actor, for now we have the term 'the intellectual actor'. The same deathly hush prevails in the auditorium as in the reading-room of a library and it sends the public to sleep. The reading-room of a library is the only proper place for such gravity and immobility.

In order to make a dramatist out of a story-teller who writes for the stage, it would be a good idea to make him write a few pantomimes.[6] The pantomime is a good antidote against excessive misuse of words. Only let the new author not fear that we want to deprive him altogether of the right to speak on the stage. He will be permitted to put words into the actor's mouths, but first he must produce *a scenario of movement*. How long will it be before they inscribe in the theatrical tables the following law: *words in the theatre are only embellishments on the design of movement?* . . .

Nowadays the majority of stage-directors are turning to pantomime and prefer this form to verbal drama. This strikes me as more than a coincidence. It is not just a question of taste. In their attempts to propagate pantomime, directors are not merely attracted by the peculiar fascination which the genre possesses. In order to revive the theatre of the past contemporary directors are finding it necessary to begin with pantomime, because when these silent plays are staged they reveal to directors and actors the power of

* I mention the old vaudeville not because we must necessarily revive it in the theatre; rather, I quote it as a dramatic form which is linked on the one hand with theatrical – as opposed to literary – traditions, and on the other with the tastes of the people . . . the vaudeville originated in the art of the folk song and the folk theatre.

the primordial elements of the theatre: the power of the mask, gesture, movement and plot.

However, the mask, gesture, movement and plot are ignored by the contemporary actor. He has lost sight of the traditions of the great masters of the art of acting. He no longer listens to what his elder colleagues have to say about the self-sufficiency of the actor's art.

In the contemporary theatre the comedian has been replaced by 'the educated reader'. 'The play will be read in costume and make-up' might as well be the announcement on playbills today. The new actor manages without the mask and the technique of the juggler. The mask has been replaced by make-up which facilitates the exact representation of every feature of the face as it is observed in real life. The actor has no need of the juggler's art, because he no longer 'plays' but simply 'lives' on the stage. 'Play-acting', that magic word of the theatre, means nothing to him, because as an imitator he is incapable of rising to the level of improvisation which depends on infinite combinations and variations of all the tricks at the actor's command.

The cult of cabotinage, which I am sure will reappear with the restoration of the theatre of the past, will help the modern actor to rediscover the basic laws of theatricality. Those who are restoring the old theatre by delving into long-forgotten theories of dramatic art, old theatrical records and iconography, are already forcing actors to believe in the power and the importance of the art of acting.

In the same way as the stylistic novelist resurrects the past by embellishing the works of ancient chroniclers with his own imagination, the actor is able to re-create the technique of forgotten comedians by consulting material collected by scholars.* Overjoyed at the simplicity, the refined grace, the extreme artistry of the old yet eternally new tricks of the histrions, mimi, atellanae, scurrae, joculatores and ministrelli,[7] the actor of the future should or, if he wishes to remain an actor, *must* co-ordinate his emotional responses with his technique, measuring both against the traditional precepts of the old theatre. . . .

The prologue and the ensuing parade, together with the direct address to the audience at the final curtain, so loved both by the Italians and Spaniards in the seventeenth century and by the French vaudevillistes, all force the spectator to recognize the actors' performance as pure play-acting. And every time the actor leads the spectators too far into the land of make-believe he immediately resorts to some unexpected sally or lengthy address *a parte*[8] to remind them that what is being performed is only *a play* . . . the

---

* Just consider what we can surmise from the stage direction: 'Enter Don Gutierre, as though jumping over a fence' (in Calderon's *Doctor of his own honour*). This 'as though' gives the actor a clear picture of the agility of his Spanish counterpart's entrance. . . .

new *theatre of masks* will learn from the Spaniards and the Italians of the seventeenth century and build its repertoire according to the laws of the fairground booth, where entertainment always precedes instruction and where movement is prized more highly than words.

Translated by Edward Braun

NOTES

1   Actor.
2   Benois discerned the revival of the mystery-play in an adaptation of Dostoevsky's *The Brothers Karamazov* produced at the Moscow Art Theatre by Nemirovich-Danchenko. It exemplified a theatre 'which cannot lie' as against a theatre of 'cabotinage and deception'.
3   i.e. late thirteenth, early fourteenth century.
4   Renard the Fox, who figures in a series of popular twelfth- and thirteenth-century animal tales in verse.
5   Plays expounding a thesis.
6   Mimed shows (not pantomimes as known in Britain).
7   Actors, mimes, players of farces, jesters, jongleurs and minstrels.
8   Aside.

For a biographical note on Meyerhold see p. 101.

The Fairground Booth was a dramatisation by the Russian poet Alexander Blok (1880–1921) of his poem of the same name. It marked a break with mystical symbolism, which it satirises, and a pioneering move towards overt theatricality. For an account of it, see Harold B. Segel, *Twentieth-Century Russian Drama*, Baltimore, Johns Hopkins University Press, 1993, pp. 124–7. Meyerhold produced it in 1906, 1908 and 1914. It helped turn him away from 'stylised' theatre to styles of popular performance – an interest he pursued further in *The Lady from the Box*, his adaptation of a story of circus life (1909). Popular modes fed vigorously into his work from then on.

40

W. B. YEATS

FROM A People's Theatre: A Letter to Lady Gregory (1919)

The best stories I have listened to outside the theatre have been told me by farmers or sailors when I was a boy, one or two by fellow-travellers in railway carriages, and most had some quality of romance, romance of a class and its particular capacity for adventure; and our theatre is a people's theatre in a sense which no mere educational theatre can be, because its plays are to some extent a part of that popular imagination. It is very seldom that a man or woman bred up among the propertied or professional classes knows any class but his own, and that a class which is much the same all over the world, and already written of by so many dramatists that it is nearly impossible to see its dramatic situations with our own eyes, and those dramatic situations are perhaps exhausted – as Nietzsche thought the whole universe would be some day – and nothing left but to repeat the same combinations over again.

. . . Our dramatists, and I am not speaking of your work or Synge's but of those to whom you and Synge and I gave an opportunity, have been excellent just in so far as they have become all eye and ear, their minds not smoking lamps, as at times they would have wished, but clear mirrors.

Our players, too, have been vivid and exciting because they have copied a life personally known to them. . . . One of our early players was exceedingly fine in the old woman in *Riders to the Sea*. 'She has never been to Aran, she knows nothing but Dublin, surely in that part she is not objective, surely she creates from imagination,' I thought; but when I asked her she said, 'I copied from my old grandmother.' Certainly it is this objectivity, this making of all from sympathy, from observation, never from passion, from lonely dreaming, that has made our players, at their best, great comedians, for comedy is passionless.

We have been the first to create a true 'People's Theatre', and we have succeeded because it is not an exploitation of local colour, or of a limited form of drama possessing a temporary novelty, but the first doing of something for which the world is ripe, something that will be done all over the world and done more and more perfectly: the making articulate of all the dumb classes each with its own knowledge of the world, its own dignity, but all objective with the objectivity of the office and the workshop, of the newspaper and the street, of mechanism and of politics.

Yet we did not set out to create this sort of theatre, and its success has been to me a discouragement and a defeat. . . . You and I and Synge, not understanding the clock, set out to bring again the theatre of Shakespeare or rather perhaps of Sophocles. I had told you how at Young Ireland Societies and the like, young men when I was twenty had read papers to one another about Irish legend and history, and you yourself soon discovered the Gaelic League, then but a new weak thing, and taught yourself Irish. At Spiddal or near it an inn-keeper had sung us Gaelic songs, all new village work that though not literature had *naïveté* and sincerity. The writers, caring nothing for cleverness, had tried to express emotion, tragic or humorous, and great masterpieces, *The Grief of a Girl's Heart*, for instance, had been written in the same speech and manner and were still sung. . . . We thought we could bring the old folk-life to Dublin, patriotic feeling to aid us, and with the folk-life all the life of the heart, understanding heart, according to Dante's definition, as the most interior being; but the modern world is more powerful than any propaganda or even than any special circumstance, and our success has been that we have made a Theatre of the head, and persuaded Dublin playgoers to think about their own trade or profession or class and their life within it, so long as the stage curtain is up, in relation to Ireland as a whole. For certain hours of an evening they have objective modern eyes.

W. B. Yeats (1865–1939), Irish poet and playwright, was of protestant Anglican descent, his father an attorney and painter (John Butler Yeats). He was at school in London till he was 15, and returned as a young man to live there. In 1896 he went back to Ireland, and in 1898 he, Lady Gregory and Edward Martyn set up a company to produce Irish plays, the 'Irish Literary Theatre' (oddly its initial members were English). Their project found a permanent home in 1904, in the Abbey Theatre. It was here that Yeats' tussle with the people – the uninhibited Abbey audience, as distinct from the mythologised folk – began. He writes of this essay: 'I took the title from a book by Romain Rolland on some French theatrical experiments. "A People's Theatre" is not quite the same thing as "A Popular Theatre".' Rolland's title was *The Theatre of the People*. For a substantial extract from it, see Eric Bentley (ed.), *The Theory of the Modern Stage*, London, Penguin Books, 1968.

41

F. T. MARINETTI

FROM The Variety Theatre (1913)

We are deeply disgusted with the contemporary theatre (verse, prose, and musical) because it vacillates stupidly between historical reconstruction (pastiche or plagiarism) and photographic reproduction of our daily life; a finicking, slow, analytic, and diluted theatre worthy, all in all, of the age of the oil lamp.

Futurism exalts the Variety Theatre because:

1   The Variety Theatre born as we are from electricity, is lucky in having no tradition, no masters, no dogma, and it is fed by swift actuality.

2   The Variety Theatre is absolutely practical, because it proposes to distract and amuse the public with comic effects, erotic stimulation, or imaginative astonishment.

3   The authors, actors, and technicians of the Variety Theatre have only one reason for existing and triumphing: incessantly to invent new elements of astonishment. Hence the absolute impossibility of arresting or repeating oneself, hence an excited competition of brains and muscles to conquer the various records of agility, speed, force, complication, and elegance.

4   The Variety Theatre is unique today in its use of the cinema, which enriches it with an incalculable number of visions and otherwise unrealizable spectacles (battles, riots, horse races, automobile and airplane meets, trips, voyages, depths of the city, the countryside, oceans, and skies).

5   The Variety Theatre, being a profitable show window for countless inventive forces, naturally generates what I call "the Futurist marvellous," produced by modern mechanics. Here are some of the elements of this "marvellous": (a) powerful caricatures; (b) abysses of the ridiculous; (c) delicious, impalpable ironies; (d) all-embracing, definitive symbols; (e) cascades of uncontrollable hilarity; (f) profound analogies between humanity, the animal, vegetable, and mechanical worlds; (g) flashes of revealing cynicism; (h) plots full of the wit, repartee, and conundrums that aerate the intelligence; (i) the whole gamut of laughter and smiles,

to flex the nerves; (j) the whole gamut of stupidity, imbecility, doltishness, and absurdity, insensibly pushing the intelligence to the very border of madness; (k) all the new significations of light, sound, noise, and language, with their mysterious and inexplicable extensions into the least-explored part of our sensibility; (l) a cumulus of events unfolded at great speed, of stage characters pushed from right to left in two minutes ("and now let's have a look at the Balkans": King Nicholas, Enver-Bey, Daneff, Venizelos, belly-blows and fistfights between Serbs and Bulgars, a *couplet*, and everything vanishes); (m) instructive, satirical pantomimes; (n) caricatures of suffering and nostalgia, strongly impressed on the sensibility through gestures exasperating in their spasmodic, hesitant, weary slowness; grave words made ridiculous by funny gestures, bizarre disguises, mutilated words, ugly faces, pratfalls.

6   Today the Variety Theatre is the crucible in which the elements of an emergent new sensibility are seething. Here you find an ironic decomposition of all the worn-out prototypes of the Beautiful, the Grand, the Solemn, the Religious, the Ferocious, the Seductive, and the Terrifying, and also the abstract elaboration of the new prototypes that will succeed these.

The Variety Theatre is thus the synthesis of everything that humanity has up to now refined in its nerves to divert itself by laughing at material and moral grief; it is also the bubbling fusion of all the laughter, all the smiles, all the mocking grins, all the contortions and grimaces of future humanity. Here you sample the joy that will shake men for another century, their poetry, painting, philosophy, and the leaps of their architecture.

7   The Variety Theatre offers the healthiest of all spectacles in its dynamism of form and color (simultaneous movement of jugglers, ballerinas, gymnasts, colorful riding masters, spiral cyclones of dancers spinning on the points of their feet). In its swift, overpowering dance rhythms the Variety Theatre forcibly drags the slowest souls out of their torpor and forces them to run and jump.

8   The Variety Theatre is alone in seeking the audience's collaboration. It doesn't remain static like a stupid voyeur, but joins noisily in the action, in the singing, accompanying the orchestra, communicating with the actors in surprising actions and bizarre dialogues. And the actors bicker clownishly with the musicians.

The Variety Theatre uses the smoke of cigars and cigarettes to join the atmosphere of the theatre to that of the stage. And because the audience cooperates in this way with the actors' fantasy, the action develops simultaneously on the stage, in the boxes, and in the orchestra. It continues to the end of the performance, among the battalions of fans, the honeyed dandies who crowd the stage door to fight over the *star*; double final victory: chic dinner and bed. . . .

FUTURISM WANTS TO TRANSFORM THE VARIETY THEATRE INTO A THEATRE OF AMAZEMENT, RECORD-SETTING, AND BODY-MADNESS

1   One must completely destroy all logic in Variety Theatre performances, exaggerate their luxuriousness in strange ways, multiply contrasts, and make the absurd and the unlifelike complete masters of the stage. (Example: Oblige the *chanteuses* to dye their décolletage, their arms, and especially their hair, in all the colors hitherto neglected as means of seduction. Green hair, violet arms, blue décolletage, orange chignon, etc. Interrupt a song and continue with a revolutionary speech. Spew out a *romanza* of insults and profanity, etc.)

2   Prevent a set of traditions from establishing itself in the Variety Theatre. Therefore oppose and abolish the stupid Parisian "Revues," as tedious as Greek tragedy with their *Compère* and *Commère* playing the part of the ancient chorus, their parade of political personalities and events set off by wisecracks in a most irritating logical sequence. The Variety Theatre, in fact, must not be what it unfortunately still is today, nearly always a more or less amusing newspaper.

3   Introduce surprise and the need to move among the spectators of the orchestra, boxes, and balcony. Some random suggestions: spread a powerful glue on some of the seats, so that the male or female spectator will stay glued down and make everyone laugh (the damaged frock coat or toilette will naturally be paid for at the door) – sell the same ticket to ten people: traffic jam, bickering, and wrangling – offer free tickets to gentlemen or ladies who are notoriously unbalanced, irritable, or eccentric and likely to provoke uproars with obscene gestures, pinching women, or other freakishness. Sprinkle the seats with dust to make people itch and sneeze, etc.

4   Systematically prostitute all of classic art on the stage, performing for example all the Greek, French, and Italian tragedies, condensed and comically mixed up, in a single evening – put life into the works of Beethoven, Wagner, Bach, Bellini, Chopin by inserting Neapolitan songs. – put Duse, Sarah Bernhardt, Zacconi, Mayol, and Fregoli side by side on the stage – play a Beethoven symphony backward, beginning with the last note – boil all of Shakespeare down to a single act – do the same with all the most venerated actors – have actors recite *Hernani* tied in sacks up to their necks – soap the floorboards to cause amusing tumbles at the most tragic moments.

5   In every way encourage the *type* of the eccentric American, the impression he gives of exciting grotesquerie, of frightening dynamism; his

crude jokes, his enormous brutalities, his trick weskits and pants as deep as a ship's hold out of which, with a thousand other things, will come the great Futurist hilarity that should make the world's face young again.

Translated by R. W. Flint

For a biographical note on Marinetti see p. 22.

This was the futurists' second theatre manifesto; the first, 'The Manifesto of Futurist Playwrights', apparently also by Marinetti though with a string of signatories, had appeared in January 1911. It was largely an attack on current theatre and the tastes of its audience, urging playwrights and actors to abhor immediate success and enjoy being whistled at or booed (see 'The Pleasure of being Booed' in R. W. Flint (ed.), *Marinetti: Selected Writings*, London, Secker & Warburg, 1972). 'The Variety Theatre' was thus their first manifesto to offer a positive model for the futurist stage, and was soon available in other European countries. Dated September 1913, it appeared in an edited translation two months later in the *Daily Mail* under the title 'The Meaning of the Music Hall'; and Craig printed it in *The Mask* in January 1914.

42

VLADIMIR MAYAKOVSKY

FROM Open Letter to the Workers (1917)

Comrades!

The double conflagration of war and revolution has emptied our souls and our cities. Like burned-out skeletons stand the palaces of yesterday's splendour. The smashed cities are awaiting new architects. The hurricane of the revolution has extirpated the crooked roots of slavery from our souls. The soul of the people is awaiting a new sowing.

To you, who have taken over Russia's heritage, to you, who (I believe!) tomorrow will become masters of the whole world, I direct the question: with what fantastic structures will you cover the site of yesterday's fires? What songs and music will flow from your windows? To what bibles will you open your souls?

I observe with astonishment how renowned theatres resound with *Aidas* and *Traviatas*, with their Spaniards and counts; how in the poems to which you listen the same noblemen's hothouse roses are flowering; how your eyes are opening wide in front of pictures showing the pomp of the past.

Will you, perhaps, when the elements let loose by revolution quiet down, go out on Sunday into the squares before your local Soviet buildings, with watch chains on your waistcoats, and stolidly play croquet?

You should know that for your necks, the necks of Goliaths of labor, there are no sizes in the bourgeois collar wardrobe that fit.

Only the outburst of the Spirit of Revolution will rid us of the rags of old art.

Translated by Boleslaw Taborski

VLADIMIR MAYAKOVSKY

FROM Prologue to *Mystery-Bouffe* (2nd version, 1922)

(*Spoken by one of* THE UNCLEAN)

In just a minute
we'll present to your view
our *Mystery-Bouffe.*
But first I must say a few words.
This play
is something new.
Without help, nobody has yet succeeded
in jumping higher than his head.
Likewise, a new play must be preceded
by a prologue, or else it's dead.
First, let me ask you:
Why is this playhouse in such a mess?
To right-thinking people
it's a scandal, no less!
But then what makes you go to see a show?
You do it for pleasure –
isn't that so?
But is the pleasure really so great, after all,
if you're looking just at the stage?
The stage, you know,
is only one-third of the hall.
Therefore,
at an interesting show,
if things are set up properly,
your pleasure is multiplied by three.
But if the play isn't interesting,
then you're wasting your time
looking at even one-third of what's happening.
For other theatrical companies
the spectacle doesn't matter:
for them
the stage
is a keyhole without a key.
"Just sit there quietly," they say to you,
"either straight or sidewise,

and look at a slice of other folks' lives."
You look – and what do you see?
Uncle Vanya
and Auntie Manya
parked on a sofa as they chatter.
But we don't care
about uncles and aunts:
you can find them at home – or anywhere!
We, too, will show you life that's real –
very!
But life transformed by the theatre into a spectacle most
    extraordinary!

In the future, all persons performing, presenting, reading, or publishing *Mystery-Bouffe* should change the content, making it contemporary, immediate, up-to-the-minute. – *Mayakovsky*

Translated by Guy Daniels

Vladimir Mayakovsky (1893–1930), Soviet poet, playwright, propagandist, screen-writer, born in Georgia, joined the Bolshevik Party at 14, leaving school to engage in political activities, for which he spent a month in prison. He went on to art studies, and in the 1910s became a leading futurist poet. *Mystery-Bouffe*, his second play, was written for the anniversary celebrations of the revolution in 1918. He and his friend Kamensky had grandiose dreams of staging it in a gigantic arena before thousands of spectators, but this was not to be. It went on in the Music Drama Theatre in Petrograd, and, although directed by Meyerhold, was largely shunned by professional actors and had only a short run. It was not put on in Moscow till four years later (when the 'second version' was prepared). He finally succeeded in getting it published, but only in a theatre magazine, and was not paid for it until he applied pressure through the Moscow TUC legal department. All this suggests some wariness towards his work – akin to the wariness expressed by Trotsky towards futurism in his *Literature and Revolution*. Subsequently, the sharp satire on bureaucrats in his play *The Bathhouse* (1929) aroused the ire of the authorities, and gave his critics their opportunity; increasingly isolated in the darkening atmosphere of that time, Mayakovsky shot himself.

43

GRIGORI KOZINTSEV

FROM AB: Parade of the Eccentric (1922)

Eccentric: clown; also a term for any ludicrous and irrational novelty turn with surprise effects.

1   THE KEY TO THE EVENTS

1   YESTERDAY – comfortable offices. Bald foreheads. People pondered, made decisions, thought things over.
TODAY – a signal. To the machines: Driving bolts, chains, wheels, hands, legs, electricity. The rhythm of production.
YESTERDAY – museums, temples, libraries.
TODAY – factories, works, dockyards.
2   YESTERDAY – the culture of Europe.
TODAY – the technology of America.
Industry, production under the Stars and Stripes. Either Americanisation or the undertaker.
3   YESTERDAY – sitting rooms. Bows. Barons.
TODAY – the shouts of newspaper-sellers, scandals, policemen's truncheons, noise, shouting, stamping, running.

The pace today:

The rhythm of the machine, concentrated by *America*, realised on the *street*.

2   ART WITHOUT A CAPITAL LETTER, A PEDESTAL OR A FIG-LEAF

Life requires art that is
hyperbolically crude, dumbfounding, nerve-wracking, openly utilitarian, mechanically exact, momentary, rapid.

otherwise no-one will hear, see or stop. Everything adds up to this: the art of the 20th century, the art of 1922, the art of this very moment is

Eccentrism

178

3 OUR PARENTS

Parade allez:

In literature – the cabaret singer, the cry of the auctioneer, street language.
In painting – the circus poster, the jacket of a cheap novel.
In music – the jazzband (the commotion of a Negro orchestra), circus marches.
In ballet – American song and dance routines.
In theatre – the music-hall, cinema, circus, cabaret, boxing.

4 WE ARE ECCENTRISM IN ACTION

1   Presentation – rhythmic wracking of the nerves
2   The high-point – the trick
3   The author – an inventor–discoverer
4   The actor – mechanised movement, not buskins but roller-skates, not a mark but a nose on fire. Acting – not movement but a wriggle, not mimicry but a grimace, not speech but shouts.
     We prefer Charlie's backside to Eleanora Duse's[1] hands:
5   The play – an accumulation of tricks. The speed of 1000 horse power. Chase, persecution, flight. Form – a divertissement.
6   Humped backs, distended stomachs, wigs of stiff red hair – the beginning of a new style of stage costume. The foundation – continuous transformation.
7   Horns, shots, typewriters, whistles, sirens – Eccentric music. The tap-dance – start of a new rhythm.
     We prefer the twin soles of an American dancer to the five hundred instruments of the Marynsky Theatre.
8   The synthesis of movements: acrobatic, gymnastic, balletic, constructive-mechanical.
9   A can-can on the tightrope of logic and commonsense. Through the 'unthinkable' and the 'impossible' to the Eccentric. . . .

Only *our* methods are indivisible and inevitable:

THE AMERICANISATION OF THE THEATRE
in Russian means
ECCentriSM

Translated by Richard Sherwood

NOTE

1   Eleanora Duse, the renowned Italian actress, toured internationally in the early years of the century.

Grigori Kozintsev (1905–73), Soviet theatre and film director. Kozintsev, Trauberg and Kryzhitsky 'patented' Eccentrism in 1921; and together with Sergei Yutkevich, opened FEKS, the Factory of the Eccentric Actor, in 1922. Their first production, of Gogol's *The Wedding*, 'engineered' by Kozintsev and Trauberg, took place the same year, and Cocteau's *The Wedding on the Eiffel Tower* followed in 1923. Like Eisenstein, who was working in a similar spirit, they then turned to film-making, though Kozintsev returned to some stage work after 1948. He is now best known in the West for his impressive film versions of *Hamlet* (1964) and *King Lear* (1971), where his earlier irreverence towards the classics is no longer visible. For more on Eccentrism, see Mel Gordon, 'Russian Eccentric Theatre: The Rhythm of America on the early Soviet Stage', in Nancy van Norman Baer, *Theatre in Revolution: Russian Avant-Garde Stage Design 1913–1935*, London, Thames & Hudson, 1991. For the influence of Italian futurism on Eccentrism, see Frantisek Deak in the *Drama Review*, vol. 19, no. 4 (T68), December 1975, pp. 88–94.

44

BLUE BLOUSE

Simple Advice to Participants (1925)

The Collective: Should be made up of twelve to twenty, two to three times as many men as women, with various skills: in voice, physical culture, speaking and playing.

Costume: All need a blue blouse, black trousers or skirts, black stockings and shoes. Down with naturalistic costumes, peasant shoes, blankets and birch [footwear] – folksy stuff, wigs – down with them. We use blue blouses and trousers to which things can be attached: stripes, leggings, cuffs, belts, bibs, etc.; head-gear: hats, top hats, peaked caps – to differentiate the characters.

The Stage: We are against bright beauty and realistic sets and decoration (no little birch trees and rivers), no clumsy props and set. On the stage there should only be a piano and a simple bough of a tree, only things necessary for demonstration.

Props: Tables, stools and other objects should only be put on stage if they can be used in the play and in movement. If they are not useful, they slow down the tempo of movement and obstruct access to the stage. Things on stage must play with the actor.

Placards/Posters: must be clear, letters and drawings visible from the last row.

Director/Producer: The organising centre of the collective, the theatrical master of the new formation which builds the action on the development of physical culture, mechanised movement, and on clear gestures and control of body and language.

Actor/BB Member: must in accordance with the above possess all the skills of the new BB training and act without emotion, typical for BB members.

Souffleur [Prompter] Does not exist – all texts must be learned by heart.

Stock Characters: 'Old Lovers', 'Slavonic Rag Wearers' don't exist in the BB any more – instead of these old-fashioned terms we have:

Masks: In the middle ages the comedy-masks presented a number of social

181

types. BB uses masks for positive and negative types as defined by the new world and soviet economy: Capitalist, Banker, Premier, NEP-man, Kulak, Menshevik and Social Revolutionary, General, Lady, Female Worker, Female Komsomol, Red Army Man, the Peasant and Worker and many others not yet entirely defined.

Musical Illustration: Musicians must definitely be familiar with classical music, be able to read scores, and have good technique.

Music: The music featured in BB issues must be used all the time, must be applied to the appropriate texts in accordance with their sense so that little by little, the tunes boring everybody can be squeezed out.

Harmonica and Balalaika: In the mass scenes of the village type, i.e. *New Way of Life*, and in the accompaniment of *Chastushki* it is desirable to use harmonica and balalaika.

Tempo/Speed: The BB members must learn to work with industrial tempo, the march-parade, a definite beat. The leading role belongs to the accompanist. All little numbers, the satirical pieces and sketches (feuilleton) use medium speed, and at the finale the speed increases again, ending on a high note.

Text: On international and All-Soviet Union questions material must be taken from BB issues and needs to be conveniently divided among the members. Also material on local themes must definitely be used. If you have material on local themes it must be explained to those unfamiliar with it.

Literary Montage: (or the assembling of material). Should be used as developed by the centre first, but also performed and adapted in the provinces. Material for montage: Pathos – poems by proletarian and LEF poets, for humour – texts from humorous soviet journals and magazines can be used.

Organisation of Everyday Life: Not a photograph but a construction – BB not only shows our way of life like a mirror but influences the brain of the spectator with all scenic means and prepares him for the perception of the new social conditions.

Content and Form: Words in BB are everything, movement, music and acting add to them, make them more expressive, more meaningful, able quickly to organise the feelings and will of the audience – content and form are equally necessary.

Programme: a BB evening is made up of one and a half to two hours – this is the right length. Three quarters of the success depends on the following: 1) Parade, 2) *Oratoria*, 3) International survey, 4) Feuilleton, 5) Satirical sketch – village type, 6) *Lubok*-scene (living poster) – 3–4 people, 7) Dialogue–Duet, 8) *Rayok* – quick-fire speech/tongue-twister/story,

9) *Chastushki*: two or four line folk verse, topical, humorous, satirical – sung in a lively manner. 10) A local theme, 11) Finale-march.

The lead articles/MC/Narrator: in two to three crisp phrases they should explain the content of the sequence of numbers and after a whistle and without any pause the pianist plays a chord and the action begins.

Blue Blouse was originally a Soviet group started by Boris Yuzhanin in 1923. Solidarity with the workers was shown by their costume – the factory worker's loose blue smock from which they took their name. Based at the Moscow Institute of Journalism, Yuzhanin aimed to offer the group's audiences, many of whom could not read, a 'living newspaper' – a concept which spread to left-wing groups internationally. Yuzhanin refused to use professional writers, but practised 'lit-montage', i.e. the scripts were cut-ups, principally of material from papers and magazines. He staged them in revue style, performing in factories, workers' clubs and in the open air. The words ('the basic principal material') were backed with 'gesture and move-ment, sound and music'. Other groups started up on the same pattern, and were freely supplied with material. Eventually more than five thousand Blue Blouse groups were active, with a membership of 100,000. In 1927 Blue Blouse visited Germany, where the workers' theatre movement was already practising similar techniques, but later the same year they were brought to a halt, obliged to merge with the more orthodox TRAM.

45

VSEVOLOD MEYERHOLD

From The Reconstruction of the Theatre (1929)

Up to now we have been in no position to finance cultural projects, but obviously it is our intention to build new theatres and to vacate those which we inherited from the age of imperialism, nobility and private ownership. In those days they built box-stages designed to foster illusion, stages for plays during which the spectator could relax, take a nap, flirt with the ladies, or exchange gossip.

We who are building a theatre which must compete with the cinema say: let us carry through the 'cinefication' of the theatre to its logical conclusion, let us equip the theatre with all the technical refinements of the cinema (by that I don't mean simply the erection of a cinema screen on stage). Give us the chance to work in a theatre incorporating modern techniques and capable of meeting the demands which our conception of the theatrical spectacle will create, and we shall stage productions which will attract just as many spectators as the cinema.

The revolution in the form and content of the modern theatre is being delayed only by the lack of funds to re-equip our stage and auditorium.

We must consider the demands of the contemporary spectator and think in terms of audiences not of three to five hundred (the proletariat is not interested in so-called 'intimate' or 'chamber' theatres) but of tens of thousands. Consider the packed crowds at football, volley-ball and ice-hockey matches: soon we shall be presenting dramatized sporting events in the same stadia. The modern spectator demands the kind of thrill which only the tension generated by an audience of thousands can give.

Nowadays, every production is designed to induce audience participation: modern dramatists and directors rely not only on the efforts of the actors and the facilities afforded by the stage machinery but on the efforts of the audience as well. We produce every play on the assumption that it will be still unfinished when it appears on the stage. We do this consciously because we realise that the crucial revision of a production is that which is made by the spectator.

The author and the director regard all the work which they carry out on a production simply as preparation of the ground on which those two vital theatrical forces, the actor and the spectator, will work daily in the course of the performance. The author and the director provide no more than the framework, and it must not cramp or hinder the actor and the spectator, but encourage them to work harmoniously together. We directors and dramatists know that what we prescribe during rehearsals is only an approximation: the final realization and consolidation of the production is carried out by the audience in co-operation with the actor. Hence the number of 'revisers' must be huge; the revision must be carried out by a mass audience.

Translated by Edward Braun

For a biographical note on Meyerhold see p. 101.

Meyerhold writes here three years after Lissitzky had designed a revolutionary constructivist remodelling of his theatre, for a proposed production of Tretyakov's *I Want a Child*, with a stage in the form of a spiral ramp and tiered seating behind the proscenium. Its aim was to abolish the division of stage from spectator and allow audience intervention in the play's arguments. Meyerhold's ideas are paralleled in Germany by those of Piscator, for whom Walter Gropius, architect and director of the Bauhaus, designed a new 'Total Theatre' oval in plan, with three possible stages plus a walkway encircling the audience. Neither project was realised, though accounts by Gropius can be read in Piscator's *The Political Theatre* (London, Eyre Methuen, 1980, pp. 181–3) and in his collection *The Theatre of the Bauhaus* (London, Eyre Methuen, 1979).

46

KARL VALENTIN

FROM Compulsory Theatre

Why all these empty theatres? It's simply because the public stays away. And who's responsible? The State, no-one else. Why don't they introduce compulsory theatre? If every one *had* to go to the theatre, things would be totally different. Why did they bring in compulsory schooling? If he wasn't obliged to, no schoolkid would go to school. Where theatre's concerned, even if it's not easy, you could still perhaps set up the same thing without any trouble. Goodwill and a sense of duty can bring about anything.

Isn't theatre also a school, question mark!

Compulsory theatre could start from childhood. The programme for children would certainly be based entirely on fairy tales like 'Hansel and Gretel' and 'The Wolf and the Seven Snow-Whites'.

There's a hundred schools in the city, each school has a thousand children a day, that's a hundred thousand children. These hundred thousand children, every day, school in the morning, theatre in the afternoon, admission per child 50 pfennigs, at the State's expense naturally, that's a hundred theatres, a thousand seats each. So 500 marks a theatre – with a hundred theatres that's 50,000 marks.

Think how many actors would get the chance of a job! Compulsory theatre, introduced district by district – it would put new life in the whole economy. To say: should I go to the theatre today? isn't the same thing as saying: I've got to go to the theatre today. With an obligation to go to the theatre like that, the citizen concerned gives up of his own free will all those other stupid evening pastimes, like skittles, cards, pub politics, romantic rendezvous, not forgetting ridiculous party games that just waste your time, like Who's afraid of the black man, Tailor lend me your wife, and so on.

The citizen knows he's got to go to the theatre – he doesn't have to choose the play, there's no uncertainty – 'Now should I go and see Tristan and Isolde today' – no, he's *got* to go and see it – because it's his duty to.

He's forced to go to the theatre 365 times a year, whether he hates the theatre or not. A schoolkid hates going too, but he's content to, because he has to. Compulsion! Today it's only compulsion that'll get our audiences into the theatre. Kind words have got us nowhere for years. . . .

But what an amazing atmosphere there'd be in a packed house with an audience of say fifty thousand – only an actor could know about that. It's only with such eminently forceful measures that we can help get these empty houses back on their feet – not with free tickets, no – solely by making it compulsory – and the citizen can't be compelled except by the state.

Translated by Anna Millan and Richard Drain

Karl Valentin (1882–1948), German clown and satirist. Valentin's career in Germany as a cabaret performer of his own sketches stretched from 1907 to 1942. Brecht wrote that while influenced by Büchner and Wedekind, 'the man he learnt most from was the clown *Valentin*, who performed in a beer hall. He did short sketches, in which he played refractory employees, orchestral musicians or photographers, who hated their employer and made him look ridiculous.' (*The Messingkauf Dialogues*, London, Methuen, 1965, p. 69). He survived the Nazi regime, for unlike many of the best cabaret performers, he was not Jewish and was liked by Goebbels (see Peter Jelavich, *Berlin Cabaret*, Cambridge, Mass., Harvard University Press, 1993, p. 230). But in this undated sketch he skates on thin ice. Despite Brecht's accolade, his sketches remain largely unpublished in Britain, though two are included in Laurence Senelick's *Cabaret Performance, Vol. 2: Europe 1920–1940*, Baltimore, Johns Hopkins University Press, 1993.

47

BERTOLT BRECHT

FROM The Popular and the Realistic (1938)

The ruling strata are using lies more openly than before, the lies are bigger. Telling the truth seems increasingly urgent. The sufferings are greater and the number of sufferers has grown. Compared with the vast sufferings of the masses it seems trivial and even despicable to worry about petty difficulties and the difficulties of petty groups.

There is only one ally against the growth of barbarism: the people on whom it imposes these sufferings. Only the people offer any prospects. Thus it is natural to turn to them, and more necessary than ever to speak their language.

The words *Popularity* and *Realism* therefore are natural companions. It is in the interest of the people, the broad working masses, that literature should give them truthful representations of life; and truthful representations of life are in fact only of use to the broad working masses, the people; so that they have to be suggestive and intelligible to them, i.e. popular. None the less these conceptions need a thorough clean-up before being thrown into sentences where they will get smelted and put to use. It would be a mistake to treat them as fully explained, unsullied, unambiguous and without a past. ('We all know what's meant by that, no need for hair-splitting.') The German word for 'popular', *Volkstümlich*, is itself none too popular.[1] It is unrealistic to imagine that it is. A whole series of words ending in *tum* need handling with care. One has only to think of *Brauchtum*, *Königstum*, *Heiligtum*,[2] and it is well known that *Volkstum*[3] too has a quite specific ceremonious, sacramental and dubious ring which we cannot by any means overlook. We cannot overlook it, because we definitely need the conception of popularity or *Volkstümlichkeit*.

It is part of that supposedly poetic way of wording, by which the 'Volk' – more folk than people – is presented as particularly superstitious, or rather as an object of superstition. In this the folk or people appears with its immutable characteristics, its time-honoured traditions, forms of art, customs and habits, its religiosity, its hereditary enemies, its unconquerable strength and all the rest. A peculiar unity is conjured up of tormentor and tormented, exploiter and exploited, liar and victim; nor is it by any means a simple matter of the many, 'little' working people as against those on top.

The history of all the falsifications that have been operated with this conception of *Volkstum* is a long and complex story which is part of the history of the class war. We shall not embark on it but shall simply keep in mind the fact of such forgery whenever we speak of our need for popular art, meaning art for the broad masses of the people, for the many oppressed by the few, 'the people proper', the mass of producers that has so long been the object of politics and now has to become its subject. We shall remind ourselves that powerful institutions have long prevented this 'folk' from developing fully, that it has been artificially or forcibly tied down by conventions, and that the conception *Volkstümlich* has been stamped as a static one, without background or development. With this version of the conception we shall have no dealings, or rather we shall have to fight it. Our conception of 'popular' refers to the people who are not only fully involved in the process of development but are actually taking it over, forcing it, deciding it. We have in mind a people that is making history and altering the world and itself. We have in mind a fighting people and also a fighting conception of 'popularity'.

'Popular' means intelligible to the broad masses, taking over their own forms of expression and enriching them / adopting and consolidating their standpoint / representing the most progressive section of the people in such a way that it can take over the leadership: thus intelligible to other sections too / linking with tradition and carrying it further / handing on the achievements of the section now leading to the section of the people that is struggling for the lead.

We now come to the concept of 'Realism'. It is an old concept which has been much used by many men and for many purposes, and before it can be applied we must spring-clean it too. This is necessary because when the people takes over its inheritance there has to be a process of expropriation. Literary works cannot be taken over like factories, or literary forms of expression like industrial methods. Realist writing, of which history offers many widely varying examples, is likewise conditioned by the question of how, when and for what class it is made use of: conditioned down to the last small detail. As we have in mind a fighting people that is changing the real world we must not cling to 'well-tried' rules for telling a story, worthy models set up by literary history, eternal aesthetic laws. We must not abstract the one and only realism from certain given works, but shall make a lively use of all means, old and new, tried and untried, deriving from art and deriving from other sources, in order to put living reality in the hands of living people in such a way that it can be mastered. We shall take care not to ascribe realism to a particular historical form of novel belonging to a particular period, Balzac's or Tolstoy's, for instance, so as to set up purely formal and literary criteria of realism. We shall not restrict ourselves to speaking of realism in cases where one can (e.g.) smell, look, feel whatever is depicted, where 'atmosphere' is created and stories develop in such a way that the characters are psychologically stripped down. Our conception of *realism* needs to be broad and political, free from aesthetic restrictions and independent of convention. *Realist* means: laying bare society's causal network / showing up the dominant viewpoint as the viewpoint of the dominators / writing from the standpoint of the class which has prepared the broadest solutions for the most pressing problems afflicting human society / emphasizing the dynamics of development / concrete and so as to encourage abstraction.[4]

It is a tall order, and it can be made taller. And we shall let the artist apply all his imagination, all his originality, his sense of humour and power of invention to its fulfilment. We will not stick to unduly detailed literary models or force the artist to follow over-precise rules for telling a story. . . .

Anybody who is not bound by formal prejudices knows that there are many ways of suppressing truth and many ways of stating it: that indignation at inhuman conditions can be stimulated in many ways, by direct description of a pathetic or matter-of-fact kind, by narrating stories and parables, by jokes, by over- and understatement. In the theatre reality can be represented in a factual or a fantastic form. The actors can do without (or with the minimum of) makeup, appearing 'natural', and the whole thing can be a fake; they can wear grotesque masks and represent the truth. There is not much to argue about here: the means must be asked what the end is. The people know how to ask this. Piscator's great experiments in the theatre (and my own), which repeatedly involved the exploding of conventional forms, found their chief support in the most progressive cadres of the working class. The workers judged everything by the amount of truth contained in it; they welcomed any innovation which helped the representation of truth, of the real mechanism of society; they rejected whatever seemed like playing, like machinery working for its own sake, i.e. no longer, or not yet, fulfilling a purpose. The workers' arguments were never literary or purely theatrical. 'You can't mix theatre and film': that sort of thing was never said. If the film was not properly used the most one heard was: 'that bit of film is unnecessary, it's distracting'. Workers' choruses spoke intricate rhythmical verse parts ('if it rhymed it'd all slip down like butter, and nothing would stick') and sang difficult (unaccustomed) compositions by Eisler ('it's got some guts in it'). But we had to alter particular lines whose sense was wrong or hard to arrive at. When there were certain subtleties (irregularities, complexities) in marching songs which had rhymes to make them easier and simple rhythms to 'put them across' better, then they said: 'that's amusing, there was a sort of twist in that'. They had no use for anything played out, trivial, so ordinary that one doesn't need to think ('there's nothing in it'). If an aesthetic was needed, here it was. I shall never forget how one worker looked at me when I answered his request to include something extra in a song about the USSR

190

('It must go in – what's the point otherwise?') by saying that it would wreck the artistic form: he put his head on one side and smiled. At this polite smile a whole section of aesthetic collapsed. The workers were not afraid to teach us, nor were they afraid to learn.

I speak from experience when I say that one need never be frightened of putting bold and unaccustomed things before the proletariat, so long as they have to do with reality. There will always be educated persons, connoisseurs of the arts, who will step in with a 'The people won't understand that'. But the people impatiently shoves them aside and comes to terms directly with the artist. There is highly cultured stuff made for minorities, designed to form minorities: the two thousandth transformation of some old hat, the spicing-up of a venerable and now decomposing piece of meat. The proletariat rejects it ('they've got something to worry about') with an incredulous, somewhat reflective shake of the head. It is not the spice that is being rejected, but the meat; not the two thousandth form, but the old hat. When they themselves took to writing and acting they were compellingly original. What was known as 'agit-prop' art, which a number of second-rate noses were turned up at, was a mine of novel artistic techniques and ways of expression. Magnificent and long-forgotten elements from periods of truly popular art cropped up there, boldly adapted to the new social ends. Daring cuts and compositions, beautiful simplifications (alongside misconceived ones): in all this there was often an astonishing economy and elegance and a fearless eye for complexity. A lot of it may have been primitive, but it was never primitive with the kind of primitivity that affected the supposedly varied psychological portrayals of bourgeois art. It is very wrong to make a few misconceived stylizations a pretext for rejecting a style of representation which attempts (so often successfully) to bring out the essential and to encourage abstraction. The sharp eyes of the workers saw through naturalism's superficial representation of reality. When they said in *Fuhrmann Henschel*,[5] 'that's more than we want to know about it' they were in fact wishing they could get a more exact representation of the real social forces operating under the immediately visible surface. To quote from my own experience: they were not put off by the fantastic costumes and the apparently unreal setting of *The Threepenny Opera*. They were not narrow; they hated narrowness (their living quarters were narrow). They were generous; their employers were stingy. They thought it possible to dispense with some things that the artists felt to be essential, but they were amiable enough about it; they were not against superfluity: they were against certain superfluous people. They did not muzzle the threshing ox, though they saw to it that he threshed. 'The universally-applicable creative method': they didn't believe in that sort of thing. They knew that they needed many different methods in order to reach their objective. If you want an aesthetic, there you are.

Translated by John Willett

NOTES

1 *Volkstümlich* can mean national as well as popular, and was tarnished by association with Nazi rhetoric.
2 Custom, sovereignty, sanctity.
3 National traits, nationality.
4 'Making possible the concrete, and making possible abstraction from it', Stuart Hood's translation in *Aesthetics and Politics* (see below).
5 Naturalist play by Gerhart Hauptmann.

For a biographical note on Brecht see p. 116.

Written after five years in exile from Hitler's Germany, Brecht's article was not published until after the end of the war, in 1958. But for an interesting account of its original context, see John Willett's note in *Brecht on Theatre: The Development of an Aesthetic,* London, Methuen, 1964, pp. 112–15. For the larger debate that occasioned it, involving in particular Georg Lukács, see Ernst Bloch *et al.*, *Aesthetics and Politics*, London, New Left Books, 1977, where it appears in another translation. Brecht's reference to Balzac and Tolstoi is implicitly a critical reference to Lukács, who upheld these two realist writers as models.

48

JEAN VILAR

The T.N.P. – Public Service (1953)

Thankfully, there are still some people for whom the theatre is nourishment as indispensable to life as bread and wine. It is to them first of all that the *Théâtre National Populaire* addresses itself.

The T.N.P. is thus, in the first place, a public service. Exactly like gas, water and electricity. Furthermore: if you deprive the public of Molière, Corneille and Shakespeare – that public we call 'the public at large', the only one that counts: then without doubt a certain quality of spirit within it will be weakened. Now the theatre, if it is not at the same time popular and moving, is nothing. Our ambition then is evident: to share with the greatest number that which up until now had to be reserved, or so it was thought, for an elite. After all, the dramatic ceremony too draws its efficacy from the number of its participants.

But what a difficult equilibrium! And how delicate to maintain. An equilibrium between the poet, the poet's work, the general public, the actors and the technicians. However, that instability perhaps creates a style, a style that is alive. And because this style is threatened daily, that same instability breaks down tics, trickery and sclerosis. That dangerous instability also preserves it from all theory.

The art of 'popular theatre' is thus a permanent revolution.

Translated by Richard Drain and Micheline Mabille

Jean Vilar (1912–71), French actor and director, trained as an actor with Dullin, and began directing during the occupation. In 1947 he founded a major annual theatre festival at Avignon, and in 1951 was made director of the Théâtre National Populaire, Paris. At both he carried Copeau's taste for a flat uncluttered stage and simplicity of setting into large spaces, succeeding with a company trained in bold attack, and attracting a wide audience. In 1963 he left the TNP, but continued to direct the Avignon Festival till 1970.

49

ARMAND GATTI

Response of the Road-Sweepers (1962)

This discussion took place following the invited visit of a large group of road-sweepers to Gatti's play *The Imaginary Life of the Roadsweeper Auguste G.* in 1962.

And the discussion started.

'We should like to know what you think of the play. Do you have criticisms?'

Silence. One of them gets up.

'Criticisms?' And then abruptly: 'What do you take us for? You invited us, and now you want us to spit in the soup. That's not our way.'

I tried to explain. A criticism was not necessarily to spit in the soup. I had so often read about myself that I was an anarchist, and right-wing on top of it, writing plays inaccessible to the people, and other crap of that sort...Perhaps they hadn't understood it all, the different time-scales for example, the Auguste of no particular age who will be the retired Auguste and who speaks to the six-year-old Auguste and to the dying Auguste.

'What are time-scales?' one of them asked me. And then I explained once more the different times, Auguste as he is in the war, in the trenches, who later becomes a road-sweeper, talks with Auguste the road-sweeper; so the Auguste who's twenty converses with the one who's thirty, while the dying Auguste when he sees the seven-year-old Auguste, tiny, trembling with cold, gets up from his bed to hold him: 'Here, don't stay there, you'll freeze to death if you stay there, you know'; all these Augustes then are one and the same person at different times of his life. I asked them if all these different times hadn't stymied them. 'Ah, we see what you're getting at,' said one. 'But what do you want to know?' I went through it again. 'Well, I can't answer you like that. We need to...' Then, a halt in the proceedings. A quarter of an hour later they return. 'Well. There were times when we didn't understand. But we understood something even so, in our own way. We understood that your play was like the news on the radio or the telly. You see things which have happened in Paris or New York, today or some other day, the scenes follow each other, they're not about the same thing, but put together they make the news. For us, your play was the news, the news about a road-sweeper.'

Translated by Richard Drain and Micheline Mabille

Armand Gatti, French playwright, was born in Monaco of Italian parents in 1924. There his father, an anarchist, was killed in an incident with the police. Gatti left school at eleven. During the occupation he was sentenced to death for working with the resistance, escaped abroad from a German labour camp, and was parachuted back into France at Arnhem. After the war he turned to playwriting. His admiration for Piscator showed itself in his preference for an 'exploded theatre' that could explore social and political realities from numerous angles. *The Imaginary Life of the Roadsweeper Auguste G.* is not imaginary in the sense of fictitious. It draws on memories of Auguste Gatti, his father, and of Gatti's birthplace, an immigrant workers' shanty-town. It was first staged in 1962 at the Théâtre de la Cité, set up in Villeurbanne, a working-class suburb of Lyon, under Roger Planchon, shortly to succeed Vilar as director of the Théâtre National Populaire. It transferred to the Odéon in Paris, where 300 members of the road-sweepers' union were invited to a performance. They left without comment. A week later, Gatti and company were asked back to the Trades' Union Centre and given a presentation set of miniature implements. They pressed their hosts to say what they thought of the play. Gatti's recollections date from 1987.

50

PETER SCHUMANN

From Problems Concerning Puppetry and Folk Music and Folk Art in the Light of God and McNamara[1] (1966)

Puppet theater is theater of tiny dolls, theatre of huge masks which a dancer operates from inside, theater of men on sticks or men hanging from strings. It ranges from half minute nightclub acts and five minute sidewalk shows to the 365 nights that it takes to perform the "Legend of Roland" in Sicily. It seems to have been everything from funmaking, slap-stick, social criticism to the terrible reenactment of a hari-kiri on Japan's Bunraku stage. Masks are older than actors, faces of wood and stone are older than mimes. Masked dancers and the effigies they carry are certainly at the origin of theater.

The communion of all, the shape of that communion of all, that which was theater, is no more. Theater is in the present an outlet of spirit, or a check-point of soul of modern society, or, as understood in the USA: show business. In this modern theater puppetry is nothing but an unimportant branch, a low-ranking form of entertainment, which seems to have a comeback right now because some smart people found out how well that little stuff fits the little television screen.

What is left of the great old forms of puppet theater, besides obscure Indian or Persian marionettes and shadow puppets, which very few of us will be lucky enough to see, is the great Bunraku theater of Japan and the Sicilian puppet theater of medieval legends. Both forms are dying out.

I figure the same can be said of the more familiar Western world Punch-, Kasper-, Guignol-, Petrushka-, Pulcinello- theaters. They still happen to be alive some place, they are sometimes brought back to life with artificial respiration, but their social conditions are no more; you need too many licenses and you are not allowed to play for money in the street, etc., etc. Throwing a baby out of the window is fun, as Punch does even in the days of Batman, but the distinct social and political criticism that went along with many of these wild shows needs a different street, a different audience and different cops than what we have here. . . .

In Bunraku you have to study for years to be allowed to move a hand. In a

Kasper show you play twelve voices, seven puppets, thunder, daylight, devil and dragon all at the same time. Liszt locked himself up with his piano for more than ten years. Pan plays the flute without Conservatorium. Both those holy ghosts, the ghost of Pan and the ghost of the intensely concentrating hermit are altogether missing in modern puppetry, as well as in moder theater.

I don't want to lament about that but I want to ask: how are gods brought back to life? The fact is, they are dead, nobody brings them back to life; our life, the life that we lead, buries them. . . .

I was always under the impression that puppeteers and circus people are closest to God and mankind because they don't deal with false gold, because they carry their gifts in their hands, they make fun, they point out some things and not much more, and I think that God likes that attitude better than the ordinarily pretty messed up human ambitions, the complicated ways of heartbreaking compositions, or the withholding and condensing intellect.

But that kind of holy simpleton and ruffian puppetry is dying out and is not likely to come back, as I have pointed out. At the present it is obviously replaced by the Union of the Professional-Puppet and Gag Institutes and these institutes have money behind them and the simpletons don't have money behind them and so they are going to lose. On the big commercial and *Life*-magazine surface the simpletons will lose. For the recording of time and for the coming revolution the simpletons are the avant-garde. And this is my prophecy: new simpletons are going to grow up all over the world; puppeteers with more puppets than tears and puppeteers with more tears than puppets; – folksingers who don't necessarily have voices or guitars but maybe just clap-hands or some kind of rattles; – painters who don't care so much how their pictures look on the wall; – and theater directors who give up Broadway and Off-Broadway and Off-Off-Broadway and train cows to balance baseballs on their tails. Nowadays, they find that out in every business, among the shoemakers as well as among the Presbyterian churches: we have neglected the stuff that life is made of so long and the whole cart is on the wrong track so much, that we simply have to get out and start walking.

NOTE

1   McNamara: not he of the celebrated band, but Robert Strange McNamara, Ford Motor Company Executive and Secretary of 'Defence' 1961–8, during the US invasion of South Vietnam and subsequent Vietnam War, and author of *The Essence of Security* (1968). His middle name acquired fame through Stanley Kubrick's *Dr Strangelove* (1963).

Peter Schumann (b. 1934), American theatre artist and puppeteer. Schumann grew up in Germany, studied sculpture there, and started a New Dance group. A John Cage concert helped attract him to New York, where, after working with Yvonne Rainier in Merce Cunningham's dance workshop, he founded the Bread and Puppet Theatre (1961), named after its practice of handing out bread to the audience at the beginning of the show in a form of homely communion. Working as a loose association of performers, Bread and Puppet were one of the seminal groups of the time, contributing powerfully to the peace movement during the Vietnam War with remarkable shows like *Fire* (1965), and *Johnny Comes Marching Home*, performed by small puppets on a 15-foot table. Masked actors mingle in their work with puppets that range from the gigantic to the doll-like, and that hold their own in any setting. Much of their work has been presented out of doors. It is characterised by an extreme simplicity of story-telling and presentation, made powerful by striking imagery and ceremony. A two-volume book has been devoted to their work by Stefan Brecht: *The Bread and Puppet Theatre*, London, Methuen, 1988. Both Peter Schumann and the Bread and Puppet Theatre are still active; touring shows, giving workshops and producing illustrated publications from their home-base in Glover, northern Vermont.

51

DOROTHY HEATHCOTE

FROM Drama as a Process for Change (1976)

This week I had to teach a high school class. I wanted them to come to some understanding of loyalty within a feudal situation. I had been given a 'history brief', you see: loyalty within a feudal situation – this is an 'English' class. I did not, therefore start thinking about how the place was going to look. I did not start thinking, 'Right, we need a Tudor mansion'. Instead I said to myself, 'How do I introduce the whole idea of loyalty? What strategy will I use whereby there shall be a slow realization that the choices between loyalty and disloyalty become available to the class? And, how do I do this within a Tudor framework? And what shall be the dilemma? What will make it possible for them to make that choice?' They were fifteen years old.

I call this 'classic form', the careful looking at the internal structure of how you bridge between one part of the learning and the next development. . . . The internal meanings are so important, for example, when I say in the *Tudor Mansion* work, 'Good morrow. Have you walked from your homes today?' I am trying to establish, 'You had a life before you came into this room, and that is the attitude you will bring to my Tudor house'. I am changing my language slightly to limit the view and distort the world.

A child says, 'Yes, I walked all the way', and I reply, 'Is your hovel far from here?' If the onlookers look at the outside, they might say, 'There she is insulting him again, calling his home a hovel'. If they look at the inside, they see how I am upgrading whilst I am using the word hovel because in the act of saying hovel, I am actually starting to draw the house on the board to begin imagery with the class. The boy says, 'Yes, and it isn't a hovel, it's my home.' 'Forgive me. I had assumed you had all lived in rather poor circumstances.' I am slowly establishing in my class the ability to fight my own role attitude. The internal form is going to grow a strength in that class that will tell me where I am overstepping my rights because I am trying to build a group of people who are proud of their origins. . . .

Drama is such a normal thing. It has been made into an abnormal thing by all the fussy leotards, hairdos and stagecraft that is associated with it. All it demands is that children shall think from within a dilemma instead of talking about the dilemma. That's all it is; you bring them to a point where they think from within the framework of choices instead of talking coolly about the framework of choices. You can train people to do this in two minutes, once they are prepared to accept it.

Do you think this thing called drama offers you anything? Can it help you to extend the understanding about something by thinking from within a framework? Do you believe it might help you to help your classes bring about any behavioural change? It might be the behavioural change of 'stop chucking the books about', or it might be the behavioural change of 'notice the archaeology or the architecture of it more'. These are all different aspects of behavioural change, for they are the beginning of perceptive changes. Do you think it is valuable to help you extend with your classes the range of attitudes they are capable of examining, and do you think it would help them to develop ordinary gumption?

The children in the Tudor mansion met their final moment when they had to make the choice of being loyal or not. They were raided by three men sent from her majesty, Elizabeth I, to look for hidden Catholic priests. They could betray me as Lady Norris, or they could keep me safe. I had done nothing to win their loyalty. We had only grown into a feeling for this building, this house, this responsibility for the Norris family. There had been no proselytizing. There had been no religious teaching. There had only been the furnishing of a mansion, ready for Lady Norris and her family to occupy. And, in the course of the furnishing, they discovered that there were certain spaces in the house that seemed unnecessary. As soon as the three soldiers arrived, with their pikes, seeking for evidence of popery, every child jumped to the conclusion that they were searching for the great Bible which I carried, and would not be separated from. Slowly, they had realized I valued the Bible. Children had kept coming up and saying, 'M'Lady, uh, do you want me to do anything with your book?' And I would say, 'Not yet. I think I would rather keep it with me until I have seen all of the house that you have created.' I do not think they ever realized it was a Bible I was carrying, but as soon as those troopers came, every one of those children realized that Lady Norris's book would give the whole game away if they were to find it. And from then on they hid it. It disappeared. I never saw where it went. They did not know they were going to have to choose whether to be loyal or disloyal. They just were caught in 'a moment of authenticity', of real choice and real concern. Drama gives us the opportunity as teachers to allow our classes to stumble upon authenticity.

What mattered then to me was that suddenly they were in a very real situation with their capacity to understand it being employed in the process of change. It is not for me as a teacher to dictate how they should go about choosing. I have set it up. It has a form. But how they choose is for them to decide. We can then all reflect together upon the choices they made. So a choice becomes consciously understood and pondered on. . . . What I want is the reflective energy that comes out of the experience – an examination of that condition we are now in, as people, because of how we handled the Tudor situation.

What I am always saying in the drama situation is, 'From where you are, how does this problem seem to you? And when it's been dealt with, let's look at where you now are.' Because what I am really saying is, 'It's where you are that makes you deal with your life. It's how you understand that makes you deal with your way of life so that all the time the growth you bring about is the reality of the class you've got.'

FROM Material for Significance (1980)

When children dramatize what do they have to be able to do? Once teachers understand this they should be able to make the work more successful in school. Children should not be required to perform the tasks of actors, which is to convince other people who are called watchers or onlookers, that what they see is authentic as to action and spontaneity. The supreme skill of the actor is to appear spontaneous while being very deliberate in everything he does. Is this skill ever appropriate to the schooling of children? And if so, when? It is a waste of public money to spend time learning to be deliberate while appearing to be spontaneous, especially if you are quite a young child.

On the other hand, is there any point in letting children play at social affairs? And for what ends? And at what ages? Both actors and children in dramatic play are playing at life. One group is choosing a companion and creating a depiction of experience, and the other is submitting an experience of life to making a rigorous demonstration of events so that onlookers of the event feel that they are experiencing spontaneity. Both kinds of drama depict life. Both kinds of people know they are not actually living through the events they have activated. That is, they both share in art. They know it is a depiction.

. . . Quite a large number of teachers will say that depicted worlds are 'not what we want to be doing in schools'. But all the curriculum of schools is based upon depictions. All teachers talk. Language depicts real experiences; geographers use maps-depictions for places; pictures are used by most teachers in one form or another; writing is a depiction, so are engineering drawings; depictions are in. They have always been respectable because when you can't be in direct contact with the actual event, or place, or person, you must use depictions. The whole school's curriculum is founded on the idea that depictions are respectable. Drama is also a depiction; of living in social situations. Why is it that the other depictions mentioned above are seen as work and drama depictions are seen as 'only' play? I suppose we can't get away from the fact that a good map looks 'like it will be serious'. After all, you can really get lost without a good map. And the same might be said about pictures of Henry VIII. After all, 'the fellow really did live, didn't he?' So it is with engineering drawings, chemical formulas, or symbols in physics. They are all serious business. Some of us believe that drama can assist that serious business.

It is in the nature of schools that depictions are used, because they are a good way of representing the world about which the children are expected to learn. The serious depictions are deemed to be those which actually take on a solid existence of their own. Books, with their written depictions and taped languages, make you feel that they're a substance to be reckoned with. 'In the bank' as you might say. And you can see that their contents are 'for real' too. However, it is my contention that most of the very real and existing depictions are employed in schools as part of a huge 'con'. These real-looking things are employed for 'dummy runs' (I owe this beautiful terminology to a student of mine). The reason schools are dedicated to the 'dummy-runs' is not that they do not mean to be serious, but that almost everything they ask of children makes it impossible for the children to believe they are serious in asking it. What is serious about a situation which prevents the children having any influences on outcomes?

What I'm trying to do here is to shake the reader out of the conventional view of the curriculum, by using the principle of 'ostranenie' defined by Viktor Shklovsky[1] as being 'that of making strange'. We very readily cease to 'see' the world we live in and become anaesthetized to its distinctive features. The arts permit us 'to reverse that process and to creatively deform the usual, the normal, and so to inculcate a new, childlike, non-jaded vision in us'.

Dramatic work is undervalued because in the present age the conventionally acceptable view of situations seems more stable and less disturbing. Art experiences insist upon a restructuring of ordinary perceptions of reality so that we end by seeing the world instead of numbly recognizing it. We cannot say that drama is just 'acting stories' in the light of those poles of playing and acting.

NOTE

1 Russian formalist critic. On 'ostranenie' or estrangement see the Introduction to Part II, p. 80.

Dorothy Heathcote (b. 1926), has revolutionised the concept of drama in education in Britain in a number of ways, shifting it away from scripts or prescribed story-lines towards a 'drama of discovery' where the outcomes are in the balance, but decided finally by those involved. She has enlarged its concentration on individual development to take in a collective engagement with issues by the whole group; and, following the distant precedent of Harriet Finlay-Johnson, she has ignored subject divisions and demonstrated the uses of drama in bringing alive subjects across the whole curriculum, sciences as well as the arts. She is also famous for her practice of providing stimulus by working in role herself, but denies that this method is essential. She has discussed her work in a series of papers, which form her invaluable *Collected Writings on Education and Drama*, eds Liz Johnson and Cecily O'Neill, London, Hutchinson, 1984.

52

DARIO FO

FROM Retrieving the Past, Exposing the Present (1978)

We should begin by studying peasant culture and its relevance to us: to deny it is to perpetuate Croce's attitude,[1] which relegates it to 'folklore'. It's also a mistake to deny it because capitalism has taken advantage of it and made it commercial: what goes unnoticed is that the bourgeoisie has 'picked up' only its surface aspects. Without plumbing the depths of this culture, or even when it does, it talks about an archaic peasant 'pre-culture', a mythical culture of the people's religious spirit, seen as an object of archaeological research.

We need to get right to the bottom of it to find out what it's based on – to find out, for example, that even today workers express themselves in their original language, their dialect, in the structural form of the words they use, and in proverbs which are a plastic form of figurative expression. This is the 'origin', because peasant culture has remained in the worker, even though today he couldn't give a damn about singing an *osteria*[2] song and sings songs from the juke-box and dresses and behaves with a city mentality.

There's no willingness to see (or else it's misinterpreted) the extraordinary significance of the worker's communication within the context of class struggle: how he makes a 'spectacle', in the original sense of the word, out of class struggle, and makes it a means of cultural expression; the use of particular expressions, slogans, noises, sounds, that are expressed in forms of the grotesque and sarcasm; whistling, dancing to a particular rhythm, breaking up words, inventing rhyming shouts, thumbing his nose at the boss or 'demolishing' him.

On the one hand the proletariat is inventive and has an enormously imaginative range of expression, and this expression and imagination are part of their culture; on the other hand they need to 'retrieve' and acquire a culture. These are the needs the intellectual has to start from.

This poses the problem of what has to be done, of how to express particular things – how to communicate in a basic language. Language is a way of 'arriving' at saying certain things: the same sentences and words used in a particular way, are part of the language of the proletariat. Why?

The language is characterized by the conditions of the relationship of the demonstration (or the representation) of things. Language is the 'figurative' dimension which tends to express the proletariat through its rhythm, its sound (which is almost always spoken rather than written), its tempo, its vocalization, its timbres, and in its chromatic vocal dimension.

These are much more important aspects of popular tradition than lexical items. Our experience has caused us to realize that popular theatre has to be so-called 'epic' theatre, which can be compared to the Brechtian one, but must use as its starting point the tradition of epic form originated by the people: a slogan used during a demonstration is an epic statement.

In this context, the radical difference between bourgeois theatre and popular theatre needs to be analyzed. In the bourgeois theatre we have the two walls of the wings, the backdrop, and then the magic wall that divides the actor from the audience. The audience in the aristocratic and bourgeois theatre is in the position of an accidental spectator, in that it is unseen: the light is over there and the spectator is in the dark, while the actor's voice reaches the audience amplified, giving the illusion of always being just a short distance away.

The actors tend to speak to one another, and thus the spectator eavesdrops on a story which doesn't involve him, but he empathizes with it, and the actor takes pains to make it his (the story), to live it out: as the bourgeois theatre says, 'live your character, become your character'. This means putting yourself into the character, finding a way to invest all your own inhibitions, lapses, or redeeming features in the character, and naturally all the actor does is replay himself, re-present himself. In this way he becomes the centre of the play, and the audience tries to see itself in the character he represents. Stanislavski's theatre lays down similar guidelines.

Popular theatre is the complete opposite: no mention is made of the individual, the isolated character above and beyond: it's about togetherness. There is a community dimension in performing theatre, and the characters are a pretext to make the people 'speak'. This means that the characters aren't acted but represented, and, since they are familiar, the actor can't talk about himself, but to others about particular situations which the character indicates.

In order to do this he needs to act in the epic style in the third person, as Brecht said, to be like a 'call boy' who represents the character to the audience, props it up or humiliates it, reports it or condemns it, hates it or loves it, as the case requires.

Vocal mannerisms or poses or rhythms are not sufficient to do this: this kind of theatre needs to be 'written', to contain moments, interruptions which grab the audience's attention, destroying the fourth wall, and using intermediary characters (as in medieval times the madman, the 'joker' or *giullare* was used as a continuous commentator on what was happening on stage). Other ways of involving the audience by provoking a reaction are pretences (for example, a fly irritating the actor, a baby crying), stage accidents (the curtain or the scenery catching fire), or rumours or false alarms circulating in the stalls. All these things destroy the 'fixity of place', creating conditions for the stage action to spill over into the audience, and vice versa.

Accidents and provocations are not, of course, enough to create an epic theatre. The most important thing is the language – which doesn't merely mean using particular adverbs or grammatical structures, but employing the totality of theatre in the sense of gestures, sounds, song, words, colours, and dance, bearing in mind that every element has a meaning determined by its rhythm, tonality, and onomatopoeia. This means that a particular sentence can have a dramatic or a grotesque meaning depending on the rhythm agreed upon among the actors, between the actor and the character, and between the actor and the audience.

Brecht used cabaret-theatre as a structure because it was linked to the great German popular tradition. In Italy we are fortunate in having a much vaster popular tradition, such as theatre in the piazzas, the *fabulatori* (storytellers), puppet shows, marionettes, acrobats, etc. All these are kinds of epic theatre, using the rhythms of the sonnet form, iambic pentameters or alternate rhyme, octosyllabic lines, assonance and concomitance.

It is also important to stress that the epic (and therefore popular) theatre is realistic, not naturalistic or visceral. This raises another problem, that of rationality in the theatre. An actor is acclaimed for using reason rather than emotion. In the eighteenth century Diderot explained in *The Paradox of the Actor* that the actor who lives out his character's drama, and doesn't act in a rational way, is the worst type of actor. A pitfall in this argument is in thinking that the epic theatre is a totally rational theatre which doesn't involve feeling, but only reason. This is a misconception about Brechtian theatre: Brecht requires an emotional dimension – feelings such as anger, which arise from the analysis of the reality presented at a given moment (as in *The Mother* or *The Threepenny Opera*).

The human factor, and passion, is fundamental to popular theatre, so much so that in the Chinese popular theatre all the elements that can involve one on an emotional level are brought into play, with the proviso that the emotional response must be balanced by the critical and analytical response.

The type of theatre which I would like to propose has two directions. First, theatre as a retrieval of medieval peasant culture, linked to the important moments of our history, and tied up with class struggle, religious conflicts and so on. Second, theatre as counter-information about the events which occur in our social reality: exposing the violence of the system, police repression, and using the grotesque and satire in such a way that the comedian's distorting lens enables the public to experience a synthesizing, didactic vision, which means giving them alternatives or moments of critical reflection, etc.

Another fundamental aspect of this type of theatre is that it is the result of a debate: it doesn't rain down vertically on people's heads, but when it is performed it has already been digested and debated, and has even created conflicts and arguments. This means that the audience is directly involved in the play, modifying it and suggesting changes – the play is part of the audience's reality.

This was the case with *Accidental Death of an Anarchist*, which has gone through three different versions, and with *Knock Knock! Who's There? Police!*[3] The same is true of *Mistero Buffo*, which consists of some thirty texts, which may be interchanged according to the social fabric and the political needs of a particular situation.

Only in this way can the theatre 'be part of' reality, of class struggle, and within this context take on the role or the function of urging and providing an impetus. Thus, the workers at RASA, a refinery between Augusta and Siracusa, wanted to put on one of our plays inside the factory, and stopped work so they could build an improvised stage on a lorry, get loudspeakers, etc., and as a result there was a long debate, which was sparked off by our work, in which the workers asserted themselves and discussed their problems and their struggles.

One final but important point which needs to be stressed: talking about popular theatre, theatre for the masses, means refusing to have our plays organized by public institutions or by the various state-subsidized structures. We believe it is essential to 'transplant' our plays to political spaces run by comrades of the rank and file.

Translated by Tony Mitchell

NOTES

1 Benedetto Croce, 1866–1952, Italian philosopher, historian of ideas and literary critic. In opposition to the disruptive challenges of much modernism, Croce upheld aesthetic and ethical views which favoured art that aspired to ideals of classical harmony and balance. Highly influential, he became a target of Marxist criticism following the fall of Mussolini in 1945.
2 Inn.
3 Sequel (1972), closed down under police pressure, to his *Accidental Death of an Anarchist* (1970), Fo's response to the death in police custody of a 'suspect' against whom there was no evidence following a bomb explosion in Milan.

Dario Fo (b. 1926), Italian performer, writer, director, activist. Son of a socialist railway worker, Fo listened to travelling story-tellers when he was young, and started improvising stories and performing sketches in variety shows. In 1951 he met Franca Rame, whose family ran a travelling theatre troupe, and in 1958 formed with her the Fo-Rame Company. This ran successfully till 1967, when, 'fed up with being court jesters of the bourgeoisie', they disbanded it to set up Nuova Scena (New Stage) under the aegis of the Communist Party, to perform to the proletariat in community centres and workers' clubs. They split with the Party in 1969 to form the theatre collective, La Commune. Fo has written, performed and directed a long succession of plays, farces, monologues, pantomimes and puppet shows.

53

JOHN McGRATH

FROM A Good Night Out (1981)

I'd like to conclude now by discussing some fairly generalized differences between the demands and tastes of bourgeois and of working-class audiences. . . .

The first difference is in the area of *directness*. A working-class audience likes to know exactly what you are trying to do or say to it. A middle-class audience prefers obliqueness and innuendo. It likes to feel the superiority of exercising its perceptions which have been so expensively acquired, thus opening up areas of ambiguity and avoiding any stark choice of attitude. In *Lay Off*, for example, a show with the English 7:84, we spoke straight to the audiences about what we thought of the multinationals. In a factory occupation where we played the show at Swinton, just outside Manchester, there was no problem whatsoever. It was appreciated that we said what we thought. Equally in Murray Hall in East Kilbride there was no problem. But after a performance in London in Unity Theatre, a socialist publisher came up to me and said, 'I don't like to be told what to think, I preferred *Fish in the Sea*.' Now the national press who saw the show felt patronized, but not the working class of Manchester because they knew we were saying what we thought and they were prepared to weigh it up. Some critics even said they thought we were patronizing the working class; but in fact, they were, because the working-class audiences have minds of their own and they like to hear what your mind is.

Second, *comedy*. Working-class audiences like laughs; middle-class audiences in the theatre tend to think laughter makes the play less serious. On comedy working-class audiences are rather more sophisticated. Many working-class people spend a lot of their lives making jokes about themselves and their bosses and their world as it changes.

So the jokes that a working-class audience likes have to be good ones, not old ones; they require a higher level of comic skill. Comedy has to be sharper, more perceptive, and more deeply related to their lives. The Royal Court audience, for example, doesn't laugh very much, and most comedy in the West End is mechanical or weak; in a club, it is vital to have good jokes and sharp comedy. The nature of much working-class comedy is sexist, racist, even anti-working class. We all know the jokes about big tits and pakis and paddies and the dockers and the strikers – there are millions of jokes current in these areas. Therefore, without being pompous about it, comedy has to be critically assessed. The bourgeois comedy, largely of manners, or of intellect, tends to assume there is a correct way of doing things and that that is the way of the average broadminded commuter or well-fed white, etc. Working-class comedy is more anarchic and more fantastical, the difference between the wit and wisdom of the Duke of Edinburgh and Ken Dodd.

Third, *music*. Working-class audiences like music in shows, live and lively, popular, tuneful and well-played. They like beat sometimes, more than the sound of banks of violins, and they like melody above all. There's a long submerged folk tradition which is still there. It emerged recently as a two million sale for a song called 'Mull of Kintyre'; but standards of performance are demanded in music and many individuals in working-class audiences are highly critical and have high standards about the music in shows. But the music is enjoyable for itself, for emotional release, and for the neatness of expression of a good lyric, or a good tune. Middle-class theatre-goers see the presence of music generally as a threat to the serious-ness again, unless of course it is opera, when it's different. Big musicals, lush sounds and cute tunes are O.K. in their place, but to convey the emotional heart of a genuine situation in a pop song is alien to most National Theatre goers. Music is there for a bit of a romp to make it a jolly evening.

Fourth, *emotion*. In my experience a working-class audience is more open to emotion on the stage than a middle-class audience who get embarrassed by it. The critics label emotion on stage mawkish, sentimental, etc. Of course, the working-class audiences can also love sentimentality; – in fact, I quite enjoy a dose of it myself, at the right moment, as does everybody – but emotion is more likely to be apologized for in Bromley than in the Rhondda Valley.

Fifth, *variety*. Most of the traditional forms of working-class entertain-ment that have grown up seem to possess this element. They seem to be able to switch from a singer to a comedian, to a juggler, to a band, to a chorus number, to a conjurer, to a sing-along, to bingo, to wrestling, to strip-tease, and then back again to a singer, and a comedian and a grand 'Altogether' finale, with great ease. If we look at music-hall, variety theatre, club entertainment, the *ceilidh* in Scotland, the *noson llawen* in Wales, panto, and through to the Morecambe and Wise show on television, you can see what I'm talking about.

The middle-class theatre seems to have lost this tradition of variety round about 1630, when it lost the working class and it has never rediscovered it. The now-dominant strain in British middle-class theatre can be traced back to Ibsen by way of Shaw and Rattigan, and so on. The tradition is one of two or three long acts of concentrated spoken drama, usually with no more than five or six main characters. The actors communicate the plot by total immersion in the character they are playing, and move around on a set or sets made to look as much like the real thing as possible. The variety within this kind of theatre is more a question of variation of pace and intensity while doing essentially the same thing throughout. I make no value judgements on these formal elements, merely note that the bourgeois is no less bizarre in its essence than the popular, and one might be forgiven for seeing more creative possibilities in the latter. However, the received opinion is that the former is more serious, and is more capable of high art.

Six, *effect*. Working-class audiences demand more moment-by-moment effect from their entertainers. If an act is not good enough they let it be known, and if it's boring they chat amongst themselves until it gets less boring, or they leave, or they throw things. They like clear, worked-for results: laughs, respectful silence, rapt attention to a song, tears, thunderous applause. Middle-class audiences have been trained to sit still in the theatre for long periods, without talking, and bear with a slow build-up to great dramatic moments, or slow build-ups to nothing at all, as the case may be. Through TV, radio and records, working-class audiences have come to expect a high standard of success in achieving effects. They know it comes from skill and hard work, and they expect hard work and skill.

Seven, *immediacy*. This is more open to argument, even more so than what I have stated so far. But my experience of working-class entertainment is that it is in subject matter much closer to the audience's lives and experiences than, say, plays at the Royal Shakespeare Company are to their middle-class audiences. Of course there is a vast corpus of escapist art provided for the working class; but the meat of a good comic is the audience's life and experience, from Will Fyffe to Billy Connolly, or from Tommy Handley to Ken Dodd. Certainly in clubs, pantos and variety shows this is the material that goes down best. A middle-class audience can be more speculative, metaphysical, often preferring the subject to be at arm's length from their daily experience. It prefers paradigms or elaborate images to immediacy, an interesting parallel from *Timon of Athens* to, for example, a comedy directly about the decline of the private sector.

Eight, *localism*. Of course, through television, working-class audiences have come to expect stuff about Cockneys, or Geordies, or Liver birds, and have become polyglot in a way not very likely some years ago. But the best response among working-class audiences comes from characters and events with a local feel. Middle-class audiences have a great claim to cosmopolitanism, the bourgeoisie does have a certain internationality, interchangeability. I can't imagine Liverpool Playhouse crowds reacting very differently from, say, Leeds Playhouse, or Royal Lyceum, Edinburgh, audiences to the latest Alan Ayckbourn comedy. They all receive it, anyway. Just as they all get imitations of the National Theatre and the Royal Shakespeare's 'Aldwych's greatest hits'. Yet this bourgeois internationality must be distinguished from internationalism, which is an ideological attribute that ebbs and flows in the working class alarmingly, but which can be there.

Nine, *localism*, not only of material, but also a *sense of identity* with the performer, as mentioned before. Even if coming from outside the locality, there is a sense not of knowing his or her soul, but a sense that he or she cares enough about being in that place with that audience and actually knows something about them. Hence the huge success of Billy Connolly in Glasgow, of Max Boyce in South Wales. Working-men's clubs in the north of England depend on this sense of locality, of identity, of cultural identity with the audience. There are few middle-class audiences who know or care where John Gielgud, for example, came from. They don't mind if he is a bit disdainful when he's in Bradford, because he's a great man, an artist, and he exists on another planet.

There are many other broad general differences but these are enough to indicate that if a socialist theatre company is interested in contacting working-class audiences with some entertainment, they can't simply walk in with a critical production of Schiller, or even a play written and performed in a style designed to appeal to the bourgeoisie of Bromley, or even the intelligentsia of NW1. A masterpiece might survive, of course. I'm not saying that the working class are incapable of appreciating great art in the bourgeois tradition. They may well be, but if a theatre company wants to speak to the working class, it would do well to learn something of its language, and not assume that the language of bourgeois theatre of the twentieth century is all that is worthy of being expressed.

There is a danger that in schematically drawing up a list of some features of working-class entertainment I am indulging in what is called 'tailism', i.e. trailing along behind the tastes of the working class, debased as they are by capitalism; and merely translating an otherwise bourgeois message into this inferior language. It is a real danger and I have seen people with the best intentions falling into it. But this is not the present case for two important reasons. One is, as I have already said, that these features of working-class entertainment must be handled critically. To enumerate once more: directness can lead to simplification; comedy can be racist, sexist, even anti-working class; music can become mindlessness; emotion can become manipulative and can obscure judgement; variety can lead to disintegration of meaning and pettiness; effect for effect's sake can lead to trivialization; immediacy and localism can close the mind to the rest of the world, lead to chauvinism, and 'Here's tae-us-wha's-like-us'-ism; and a sense of identity with the performer can lead to nauseating, ingratiating performances with neither dignity nor perspective.

The second reason is this. Given a critical attitude to these features of working-class entertainment, they contain within them the seeds of a revitalized, new kind of theatre, capable of expressing the richness and complexity of working-class life today, and not only working-class life. In terms of theatre they are some of the first sounds in a new language of theatre that can never be fully articulate until socialism is created in this country. But before then we can work to extend those first sounds into something like speech by making more and more demands of them, by attempting bolder projects with them, and above all, by learning from our audiences whether we are doing it right or not.

John McGrath (b. 1935), British playwright, screen-writer, director, had written plays, film and television scripts (*The Reckoning*, 1969, and *Z Cars*), and worked for the Liverpool Everyman, before forming his company 7:84 (7 per cent of the population holds 84 per cent of its wealth) in 1971. In 1973 some of its members went off to form Belt and Braces with Gavin Richards, extending the musical side of their work. Meanwhile 7:84 developed a second branch in Scotland. A series of plays and shows for them followed, which were widely toured to community centres and halls, until the English company was forced out of business by withdrawal of its subsidy, and under pressure McGrath left the Scottish company. For the story of this, see his book, *The Bone Won't Break*, London, Methuen, 1990.

54

ARMAND GATTI

The Workshop of Popular Creation
(1983–5)

For me, Toulouse has never been a city but more an English present infinitive: to lose. And it's in this present infinitive that I spent three years . . . years carried through under the name: 'The Workshop of Popular Creation'.

This experiment was made in the present infinitive, with, as follow-on, the more fundamental experiments that we have made in the theatre. Perhaps the fact of acting in this infinitive comes from my metaphysical need to be always on the side of the losers. . . . And as with the ancients, who once a year let into the city those who were shut out of it, that's to say, the slaves – it is those who are the bearers of expression, the bearers of the city's different realities, which obviously they were much closer to than any of the culturally privileged – (there obviously you see the dialogue between the work and the city, that I get from Vilar). . . .

All these people coming from different backgrounds – from prison (some are still doing time, others are barely released), from psychiatry, from illiteracy – we try to inculcate in them the idea that their dignity – that dignity which during their whole existence up till then they've been deprived of – comes with the mastery of writing. The experiment is carried out in the following way: we start with sheets and sheets of writing, followed by public readings on one and only one theme: Who am I? It's not always easy, especially when at the start writing, spelling, is most frequently phonetic. . . .

The second question that's put, after Who am I, is Who am I addressing? . . . correlating that with reading and writing. What were the illiterates doing during all this time given over to writing? since in principle they were excluded from it by definition. They handed in their sheets at the same time as the others but it was the rejects or the psychiatric cases who were doing the writing for them. They paired up. The group of illiterates split up according to friendships, they got together with people they felt affinities with. The one taught the other the writing they needed for the experiment.

So there were two topics: who am I, and who am I addressing, and these

214

two topics were to become the ground of the theatrical writing. All the plays that were made – that I wrote – following that, were always made on those two foundations.

The third stage is the choice of subject. Any subject is good in principle. The whole thing is that the people who participate need to recognise themselves in it. This path towards recognition of oneself through the subject becomes the pivot of the writing. In general, they're always topics of their own time. It's a contemporary topic, but a topic they can identify with. . . .

It's obvious that all these experiments need to be continued. It's theatrical expression by those who have been denied a voice. It's their need to express themselves that becomes the driving force of the play. The point isn't to make a stage career or to have a long run. It's to be taken in charge by the forces of the imaginary – an imaginary which is there, but reduced to zero by social conventions and the way they insert themselves into society – when meanwhile those forces are asking only to express themselves, to exist – and above all in these people whose expression is restricted, which is not to say completely non-existent. . . .

As far as theatrical expression is concerned, these are absolutely exceptional moments, which bring fantastic inspiration and a joy in being that's quite special, and I think that if there's theatre writing tomorrow, it will start from what the city expresses, from its own adventures, the city must invent itelf, the imagination must be present, and the poets must be supporting it. An arts centre should not be some kind of garage, some kind of attic displaying the best museum pieces. Out there is indigence, poverty, non-contact with the other. Commercial society puts its stamp on everything and, more seriously, puts its stamp on words as well.

Translated by Richard Drain and Micheline Mabille

For a biographical note on Gatti see p. 195.

Having written and directed numerous plays, Gatti began experiments in collective creation in the 1970s. They included a film made with a theatre workshop group in Derry, *Nous étions tous les noms d'arbres*, 1981. He opened the Workshop of Popular Creation in 1983 under the name 'The Archaeopteryx' – the name of the earliest known bird whose fossilised remains date from the Jurassic period: 'that fabulous bird which had within it all the possibilities of life and of creation'. It closed when its grant ran out in 1985. These verbal recollections date from 1987.

55

JOHN FOX

FROM How Welfare State's Events are Commissioned, Conceived and Carried Out (1983)

I find I am increasingly out of joint with the 19th century concept of the romantic specialist super-creator. I would like to believe this is only a historic hiccup – that in an ideal culture the 'artist' merely serves (not leads) the community in a functional capacity and that necessary images and archetypes naturally and inevitably reveal themselves. It is only because we allow so few people to Dream profoundly in our society that we set up the specialist ARTIST. Hopefully this will change but for the meantime we have to live with it.

Boris[1] and I certainly are the primary creators. We write the scenarios. But this needs qualifying. We pick a team that can work together and that is ideal for the gig – but we often write the work round the needs of the people we choose. It's like a good band. We provide the tunes but the soloists explore harmonies and we love to write work to incorporate imaginative engineers, or wonderful sculptors, people we can enjoy creating with. Then in practice we all learn from each other through observation and consultation and helping each other. As the work grows, in practice, on the best occasions it feels like being inside a great rolling planet of creative fission.

Eds: *What do you mean by Dreaming?*

JF: You have to get a foot in the door as it were, find an angle that seems to be the right one. If you're working for Hallowe'en and November 5th, as we were at Bracknell, then we've got our own track record of bonfires (12 in all). There is some literature about traditional customs. So we've got a pattern of the way things have been done in certain traditions to draw upon. The reading we store in our heads, then we visit the place and just by talking to people in pubs, and reading local papers, looking at the place, you find what the local preoccupations are. For instance, we found at Bracknell that the local electronics industry is important. Then you think, it's Hallowe'en, you've got scarecrows – you pick scarecrows because it's a simple image that anyone could get hold of, and anyone could make. You start to talk about black crows and you think perhaps the black crows should be missiles, because Ferranti and others make missile control gear. And you say 'How do we update Hallowe'en, do we update it at all, or do we chuck it out of the window?' But if it still means something about externalised fear and getting rid of demons that are going to terrify you over the long winter, then why aren't the demons of today black missiles up the road at Greenham Common, where the women are clambering over bulldozers trying to act out everyone else's soul by saying 'Let's stop this, these are the black crows of modern technological society.' So that gets mixed up with traditional imagery, but you have to be wary . . . if you make it too agitprop, you only preach to the converted, or you alienate. If you make it too sweet, all you come up with is a jolly spectacle which probably makes things worse in the long run by stopping people thinking. So you've got your own traditions, you've got the country's traditions, you've got the specific preoccupations of the place, like the electronics; you've also got the pattern of the season and the specific geography of the place you're in. They all start to go together in a sort of cauldron – a cauldron in my head, and hopefully in company members' heads, and then it starts to simmer and distil, and you start to conjure a few key images in the steam.* . . .

Eds: *Dreaming can be a very obscure, private process, can't it?*

JF: For me the process *is* personal and private – like water divining. But the discoveries, the images I find should be clear and common archetypes. I think at some point, whether you use Jungian phraseology or not, at some point you're looking down into the Collective Unconscious through your own subconscious. Like a glass-bottomed boat, and the artist is floating around letting people see down into the images. The job of the artist is to have antennae to pick it up and reveal it, articulate it for other people to read. It is to objectify his subjective experience in a form that's accessible to the majority. Our job, or the job of any artist, I would submit, who works publicly, is to find the images that are the pegs a lot of other people connect with. A good example of the way this imagery grows and changes was at Haverhill. I was thinking about rats, which was a spillover from an earlier gig for scientists at Babraham where they were all cutting up rats. I was going to create an event which I thought was relevant because everybody had been moved out from the GLC to this town

---

* The form of the communication becomes part of the problem. Didactic and literal illustration can be counter to a more poetic, intuitive and sensual approach. False polarisations can be induced by the method of simply demonstrating.

which was, at that time, nowhere. I wanted a piece called The Great Rat Race. I knew there were a lot of punks and motorbike boys, and I wanted to have people riding round the streets as packs of rats, with all these psychedelic jesters trying to catch them. It would actually be the Rat Race, but it would also be the Pied Piper comes to town. Then Kevin West, who was our recce man on the ground, rang and said whatever you do, *don't* do the rat race.* So I said give me another idea then. So he said 'Windmills'. Now the Ministry of Defence blew up the last windmill there in the war, because it was supposed to help German bombers to navigate. And everyone resented it because it was apparently one of the best working windmills left in the country. So this image happened to be, for whatever reason, at the back of people's heads. People could identify with it, They love making windmills. I'd no idea about doing windmills, but having done windmills, you naturally think of Don Quixote and start to invent a character called Donald Quixotty, a development of a kind of lunatic angel Andy Burton's been developing for years. And he went into the Bracknell gig too, left over from Haverhill. There were some bike boys in the bar at Bracknell who told me about seeing the Peter O'Toole Don Quixote film, and they immediately knew the story. Half the time your stories might be culled from 'Tradition', but they may also come from a James Bond movie. It's what people know about, and what dreams they themselves put into these images. If you have, as we did, a procession of bike boys with Donald Quixotty, you're dealing with young men with dreams, but you're also dealing with all the films that've been around, be it 'Easy Rider' or 'Mad Max II'. It doesn't matter, so long as you can use the imagery in a positive way to release energy for good. . . .

Eds. *Size and scale are important aspects of your work. Is that for the audience's sake?*

JF: Objects or images in the street need to be seen, need to be above people's heads. So if you're talking about a puppet, you're talking about something at least ten or twelve feet high for a start. Once you start to make that, all the other scale tends to follow. I think we also do *enjoy* the spectacle. We're a bit wary of the spectacle being purely an opium, though. But if it can also release the image, then the power of it, the scale of it, is all right. I think Breton's right about the poet of the future making dreams concrete. People have seen our Houses of Parliament structure and actually thought that a building had gone up in the town. They couldn't believe that it had gone up virtually overnight. There's something about the power of that. It's there in

---

* It was too close to the truth for comfort. The inhabitants felt they were victims of the Rat Race – being moved out of London at the behest of politicians.

front of you, you can't deny it, which affects everybody. If nothing else, it affects policemen and politicians to know you won't go away.

NOTE

1   Boris Howarth, Associate Director of Welfare State.

Initially based in an art school rather than a theatre, **John Fox** founded Welfare State in 1968, a collective of artists and performers, to create large-scale ceremonies and enactments outdoors for a wide, non-theatre-going public. Art schools in that era were still independent, and a base for independent performance activities. Welfare State were not alone in wishing to redirect such work away from a limited artistic audience towards people at large, but they succeeded particularly well thanks to their grasp of popular mythology, and the large scale and visual audacity of their events. Planting themselves at a deliberate distance from metropolitan culture (in Bradford, then moving to Burnley in 1972), and evolving forms of parade and performance with spectacular props, Welfare State has sought to revive a sense of theatre as live communal event, drawing on whatever myths or rituals might still have a purchase on the popular imagination. They have equally created small private ceremonies for members and friends to mark betrothals, weddings, births and deaths.

56

KWESI OWUSU

FROM Notting Hill Carnival: 'De Road is de Stage de Stage is de Road' (1986)

The procession had already started. It meandered through the valleys, shallow waters of the Niger and dizzy heights of Adamawa. Ages passed in a cyclic dance of time. The cradle song soon faded behind the Kilimanjaro as the winds hurried Sir John Hawkins' mast towards the Caribbean. Clouds gathered, crickets stayed the night and squirrels hid in trees. Then a whip struck a thunderbolt which spun in the sky and exploded. A tear dropped, the procession lingered on 'til morn. When dawn broke the sun lit the skies again. The breeze had a new chant and a new song bellowed again from the horns. Old instruments held the rhythm. The majestic colours grew brighter. The procession turned into a Notting Hill street. . . .

In Trinidad, carnival emerged as a cultural symbol of the emancipation of black people from slavery. It was born out of the experiences of the African working classes and their particular socio-political and religious conditions. The end of slavery marked a qualitative step in the struggle for the holistic culture being formulated by one's own history. The masses welcomed the challenge. They had come out of bondage owning nothing but the power and creativity of their labour. The state tried to put constraints on its expression; but the harder they tried the more it surfaced. . . .

The Trinidadians who responded to post-war mass unemployment and came to England brought with them this tradition of celebration and creativity. Some, like Russell Henderson, Sterling Betancourt and Vernon Fellows, were in fact former steel bandsmen and band leaders in their home towns. The first Notting Hill Carnival was held on August Bank Holiday in 1965. It was a small but significant affair which was barely given national media coverage. Before then, cultural events reflecting the search for a popular Caribbean expression were taking place in London's pubs and clubs, basement blues sessions, and shabeens.

That these events should develop into an open street celebration in Notting Hill was no accident. Notting Hill had a large black community. More significantly, 'it was the closest to being liberated territory'. In the now famous riots of 1958, the black community successfully defeated a major wave of extreme right-wing attacks after the murder of Kelso Cochrane. Carnival built on this victory, and drew confidence from its significance. When people converged on Notting Hill they did not come merely to enjoy themselves. They came to meet old friends and make new ones, to visit family and relatives, and chat freely on the streets as they did back home in the Caribbean. It was an annual mecca, and the revellers came to re-enact a powerful cultural and political symbolism which was essential to daily black existence, survival and struggle.

From 1965 to 1975 carnival developed an infrastructure which it slowly consolidated, as more steel bands and revellers joined the celebrations. For half of the year local projects, advisory centres and clubs were transformed into Mas camps where bands met to chat about carnival themes, ideas, and make costumes. During this crucial period the realization that carnival could happen here despite the meagre resources of the community gained in popularity. . . .

State attempts at controlling the Notting Hill Carnival and containing its social and political impact reached their climax in the period between 1975 and 1977. Although this in itself is a brief slice of history, its significance is considerable because it echoes both the cultural repression of Caribbean colonial history, and the history of repression of popular culture and events of mass jollification in England.

Before the industrial revolution of the late eighteenth and nineteenth centuries, working people in Britain celebrated several open festivals and recreations which mirrored their life experiences, their hopes and joys, as well as extending their social milieu and breaking the routine boredom of daily existence. Such festivity, with its exhilarating human warmth and friendship, is well portrayed in 'The Collier's Wedding', by the eighteenth-century poet Edward Chicken or in the nineteenth-century writer Thomas Hardy's 'Under the Greenwood Tree'.

Several of these events were organised around such public occasions as Christmas, the annual parish feast and Whitsun, described by one observer as 'a universal festival in the humble ranks of life throughout the kingdom'. Of the Christmas ritual in Northumberland in 1769 John Walis wrote:

> Young men march from village to village, and from house to house, with music before them, dressed in an antic attire, and before the . . . , entrance of every house entertain the family with . . . , the antic dance . . . with swords or spears in their hands, erect, and shining. This they call, the sword-dance. For their pains they are presented with a small gratuity in money, more or less, according to every house-holder's ability. Their gratitude is expressed by firing a gun.

Mass jollifications are well illustrated in English painting, especially by artists interested in depicting the lives of the lower ranks of society. Examples can be found in the work of William Hogarth, whose 'A View from Cheapside' depicts a revelling group of Londoners in 1761, including a Black horn-player. Thomas Rowlandson, similarly, offers us a glimpse of a hectic English fair in 'Brooke Green Fair'. In the English life of the time there were numerous popular sports and pastimes, including football, wrestling, cudgels, ninepins, lying at alehouses and throwing at cocks. They sometimes attracted large crowds of working men and women. Inevitably such festive occasions also provided a platform for social and political satire, such as the 'mock mayor ceremonies' observed during the Easter holidays. In Randwick, Gloucestershire, for example, a mock mayor was elected each year from what one commentator uncharitably referred to as 'the meanest of people'.

With the onset of the industrial revolution these popular cultural events were systematically suppressed by the state through a series of labour laws which imposed a rigid work schedule on the workers. Open air activities were curtailed. But the process of stopping fairs started even before this period: in 1761–2 alone, two standing orders from the Court of Quarter Sessions prohibited twenty-four fairs. More standing orders were subsequently published, until the number of fairs had declined significantly by the end of the century.

Open air events were particularly affected by land enclosure acts. Once the open fields used for such events had been removed by laws which imposed absolute rights of private property on land, it was often difficult to find alternative playing places:

> By the middle of the nineteenth century, any kind of open space for recreation was very much at a premium. The custom of playing games on public thoroughfares was no longer tolerated; enclosure usually eliminated any public use of agricultural land; and the rapid growth of cities involved the appropriation of much open space, some of which had served as customary playgrounds, for commercial building.

. . . Much of the official hostility to popular culture and working class jollification was underlined by a concern for effective labour discipline. As industry came to be seen as the lynch-pin of English progress, frugality, prudence and 'slogging' became the ideological images appropriate to its effective establishment. To the gentlemen riding on the tide of the industrial miracle, and transforming the world in its wake, traditional recreations came to be seen as self-indulgent diversions, wasteful of time, money and energy. One such gentleman, Richard Baxter, advised that 'all sports are unlawful which take up any part of the time, which we should spend in greater works'.

The historian Christopher Hill suggests that this emphasis on labour discipline derived particularly from the puritanism which held sway before the Restoration. In the morally charged debates of the time, the new industrial ethic came to flirt, quite curiously, with religious dogma that equated enjoyment with immoral behaviour and sin. Popular festivals came to be increasingly regarded by officialdom as occasions legitimising moral degeneration and debauchery. The views of Josiah Tucker, though strong, were not unrepresentative:

> The lower class of people are at this day so far degenerated from what they were in former times, as to become a matter of astonishment and a proverb of reproach . . . we shall find them all agreed . . . to be the most abandoned and licentious wretches on earth. Such brutality, and insolence, such debauchery and extravagance, such idleness, irreligion, cursing and swearing and contempt of all rule and authority, human and divine, do not reign so triumphantly among the poor in any other country, as in ours.

Attacks on popular culture were greatly helped by fanatical evangelical movements, among them the so-called primitive Methodists, who demonstrated at popular celebrations to 'undermine the influence of profane festivity'. By the end of the first industrial revolution, most popular festivities had disappeared or become 'domesticated'.

For the present, the Notting Hill Carnival and other offshoots across the country stand as significant symbols, crucial antitheses to this history of state repression. Their survival and development are therefore not the concern of the Black community alone, but of all who appreciate and cherish the vitality of popular creativity.

Note: Several footnotes to the text are here omitted.

Kwesi Owusu, British writer, performer and independent film-maker. As well as his involvement with carnival, Kwesi Owusu has worked in 'black orature', the African and West Indian tradition of expressive performance in language and song, whose thrust has historically been anti-colonial, and which remains 'a bastion of resistance'. (See his chapter 'The Tradition of Orature' in *The Struggle for Black Arts in Britain*, London, Comedia, 1986.) Owusu includes in this tradition others in this volume – Ntozake Shange and Augusto Boal – as well as Ngugi Wa Thiong'o, Linton Kwesi Johnson, Miriam Makeba and Gil Scott Heron. His own involvement has been with the African Dawn collective, for whom he has written poetry (see *Apples and Snakes*, London, Pluto Press, 1984) and whose work can be heard on an album, *Besiege the Night*.

Part IV

THE INNER DIMENSION

The work of living art . . . can result only from a radiation from inside to outside.

Adolphe Appia

Admire this indiscreet intrusion of the spectacle into intimate zones of the sensibility,
the spectacle acting not only as a reflection but as a force.

Antonin Artaud on Balinese theatre

INTRODUCTION

1

'The nineteenth century marks itself out as an era very distant from inner creation. The concentration on material phenomena and the material side of phenomena logically brought about in the inner sphere the decline of creative power, which appears to have sunk to the lowest ebb.' So writes Wassily Kandinsky in the early 1910s. It is a common theme from the beginning of the century. 'The new drama rejects the external in favour of the internal', announced Vsevolod Meyerhold in 1907. The affirmation of an 'inner sphere' at odds with external 'phenomena' reflected the sharp opposition that was thought to exist between the materialistic civilisation of modern times and aesthetic and spiritual insights. This underlay the attack on realism, which, it was argued, clogs the spirit and withers the imagination by devoting itself so laboriously to material appearances. 'To train a company of actors to show upon the stage the actions which are seen in every drawing room, club, public house or garret must seem to every one nothing less than tomfoolery', wrote Gordon Craig in 1907.[1] It might seem absurd to argue that realism in the hands of, say, Ibsen, had failed to address the inner life. But the probings of realism were suspect to its successors, who shared Edward Bond's view that 'The famous stage as a room with the fourth wall missing is really a coffin with the lid off.'[2] They argued that realism gave access only to psychological mechanisms, predetermined by heredity and social environment, and not to the inner spirit.

That playwrights were very ready to explore the latter had been shown by Maeterlinck and Strindberg. August Strindberg, who opens this part, began as a naturalist. But impressed by Maeterlinck, he moved on, and began writing plays where 'time and space do not exist' and the action takes on 'the disconnected but seemingly logical form of a dream'. Such a venture raises no innate problem for the writer: words are not bound to the solid physical world – nor to the planks of a stage. But could theatres materialise such dreams, such inner states? Many believed the great obstacle blocking their expression was the existing stage. This came with a battery of standard fixtures: footlights, cumbersome sets and painted backdrops, false perspectives and laborious scene changes. These were now under challenge on two counts. Not only was their depiction of things crude; the importance of the material things they depicted was now denied.

If 'the material side of phenomena' was a mere distraction, why should it be so slavishly represented on stage? Did a forest really require ten thousand leaves? Adolphe Appia suggests it might need none at all. Craig ponders how to stage a scene depicting a man in a snowstorm, and in a few brief comments questions the whole nature of theatrical representation. An actor may be superfluous; perhaps 'movements of some intangible material' would be more expressive. Or perhaps an actor could acquire such expressiveness, not by merely imitating someone in a snowstorm, but by seeking 'symbolic gestures which should suggest a man fighting the elements'.

Craig expressed strong belief in 'the supreme force – movement', to which the actor might 'minister'. 'In the beginning with you it was Impersonation', he writes to his hypothetical artist-apprentice; 'you passed on to Representation, and now you advance into Revelation. . . . You now will reveal by means of movement the invisible things.'[3] This belief may well have been stimulated by Isadora Duncan, with whom he was involved at the time. Duncan's dance was revelatory for many. As theatre sought to express the inner sphere, dance pointed the way.

Not only Duncan but another dancer too was a crucial influence in these years. Loïe Fuller, whose standing in the history of dance is blurred by the swirling draperies that virtually concealed her person, entranced those who saw her with a new, near-abstract vision of beauty, in which rhythmically changing forms under varying light seemed to offer the most radical challenge to theatrical realism yet seen. She was surely a technical innovator, fully exploiting the system of lighting via reflectors that so appealed to Appia.[4] Catching the play of light on a continuously changing flow of draperies, she anticipated him by '*painting in time and space*' – his phrase describing how the artist would use the 'new art material' theatre could become.[5] The play of abstract forms and colours she created opened the way towards the experiments of the futurists,[6] Kandinsky and the Bauhaus.

As for her dancing, contemporary accounts of her and Isadora Duncan make much of the matter in which they most differ: Fuller danced amidst yards of drapery, while Duncan danced with very little drapery at all. But their ideas on dance were similar. Like Duncan, Fuller found most current dance depressingly unnatural: 'motions of the arms and legs . . . regulated by the time rather than by the spirit of the music'. She abhorred ballet and the endless grind of mechanical discipline it called for. There needed to be an inner reason for dancing: the dancer should feel moved to dance.

Duncan agreed. The first time Craig watched her perform (in 1904), he was struck by the fact that she entered, walked to the piano, and stood 'quite still' while the pianist concluded a Chopin piece, and then played another. Only then, as the playing began a third time, did she begin to move.[7] Such stillness itself was enough to impress an audience with her difference. Other dancers set to work regardless; here was one who waited for an inner impulse. This signalled clearly to her audience that she was not just a dancer, but a creative artist. Her dance, free of pirouettes and strained poses, full of fleeting suggestions of figures from Greek art, confirmed this.

This was a double breakthrough, for performers and for women. To announce, and then demonstrate, that the performer may be an artist – not just an *artiste* – was to establish a claim to full creative autonomy. Henceforth the performer might be neither the servant of a text, nor of a director, nor of a ballet master. She might practise what Appia called not 'the static fine arts' but 'living art'.[8] To demonstrate at the same time that artists may be women was even more audacious. For the belief was widespread that creative artists were male by definition. The realisation that they were not had consequences for theatre that are still, almost a hundred years later, gathering force.

Duncan recalls in her autobiography standing still in her studio for hours when she was young 'as if in a trance – but I was seeking and finally discovered the central spring of all movement . . . the unity from which all diversities of movement are born'.[9] The inner sphere for Duncan is the body. This crucially expands the meaning of the inner sphere for theatre, and the scope of this part. 'If the stage is woman . . . she will want to be a body-presence', affirms Hélène Cixous.[10] Duncan was that seventy years before, and her writings are about that. But the holistic spirit of her thought dissolves distinctions between body and mind. Both, where she was concerned, rejected narrow ideals of precision, completeness and containment in favour of openness, process, impulse and feeling. It is not to argue that such things are forever female to say that at that time only a woman could have embodied them so strongly, and opened up theatre to their possibilities so unequivocally.

2

They surface later, though transformed by a different culture as well as gender, in Lorca's panegyric on the *duende* – that mysterious power which 'surges up from the soul of the feet' in artist-performers to bring what they do alive. Once more we are in the world of nature; as in Duncan's writings, the breeze and ocean waves are guiding metaphors. Not harmony though, but tempest, struggle, injury and death are the dark elements invoked here. At the moment of creation all art is a form of performance, in which the artist, shaman-like, wrestles with a daimon or makes daring passes with a dangerous bull. We are already approaching the Theatre of Cruelty proposed by Artaud. But here the performer is primary, the dancer, singer or musician serving as the model for all artists.

How does this development affect the actor? Meyerhold noted Bryusov's pronouncement of 1902: 'The theatre's sole obligation is to assist the actor to reveal his soul to the audience.'[11] But in the new ensembles, the actor took second place to the director. At first, under naturalism, actors had been told to renounce their old ways, and impersonate more closely the behaviour of real people. This demanded observation and imitative talent, but did not necessarily engage the depths of their being. But neither did the new stylised theatre. To assume a series of pictorial poses, and intone one's lines with no concern for natural delivery, required even less inward involvement. It could hardly be that all actors would rest satisfied with this, and one in particular did not: Constantin Stanislavski.

Stanislavki's most important teachings start from the conviction that, like other artists, actors too must cultivate an inner life. Only then can they incorporate the intuited inner life of their characters – that life from which their words and gestures should flow. 'External action on the stage', he writes, 'when not inspired, not justified, not called forth by inner activity . . . does not penetrate the heart.'

Though his key works were not published until the late 1930s and 1940s, the spirit of his teaching was born at the start of the century. The paradox his writings partly disguise via their labours towards coherence and 'system', is that it sprang from both the major currents of that era, though they flowed in opposite directions. Stanislavski belonged with those upholding the 'inner sphere'; but became deeply involved with a version of the naturalism they were attacking. He made efforts to free himself from this entanglement; but failed to convince his most talented students – Meyerhold and Evgeny Vakhtangov in particular – that he had succeeded. His teachings have continued to serve naturalism above all else to this day.

His ideas are placed in a different context here. His emphasis on the inward life of the actor leads as much towards Jerzy Grotowski as towards 'method' acting and its renowned Hollywood subscribers. These have encouraged the view that he called for the total submergence of the actor within the character. But this is to put the cart before the horse. He teaches that the character can come alive only if the actor does. This involves getting fully in touch with one's deeper memories and emotions, one's inner self; for it is only from this centre that the genuine can be generated. It is here, and in their search for a method to tap such resources, that Stanislavski and Grotowski find common ground.

3

Stanislavski's remains the most searching attempt to equip the actor to explore what Paul Kornfeld called 'the psychological human being'. But for Kornfeld and other German expressionists, the psychological human being fell far short of true human potentiality. Artists needed to concern themselves with that, and with its deep emotional sources. Kornfeld elaborates this in the passage included here from his long essay of 1918. To render such things in performance, they will need to 'act out themselves', their own felt emotions, in a fashion even more radical than Stanislavski proposes, for they must work from a core of their being which has nothing to do with everyday behaviour. Consonant with these notions an expressionist style developed in which acting became 'speaking with the body'. Actors sought through movement 'the expression of a psyche, the illustration of an inner state'[12] rather than imitation of behaviour.

Kornfeld's essay reflects the change undergone by the elevated aesthetic aspirations common at the turn of the century. After four years of war, human reason, which had failed to prevent the slaughter of so many, is cast aside, along with other discredited human pretensions. Kornfeld's exhortation to actors to 'break open their envelope' anticipates Grotowski; and his insistence on the 'seed of madness' which that will reveal opens the way to Artaud. The expressionists believed that such a process was in some way redemptive, the necessary prelude to a transformation of society. Artaud shed their idealism, but he too sought a cure, at once for the psyche and for our civilisation. His concern with theatre is a concern with its role in that cure. In this the affinities between him and the expressionists are often considerable, even if direct influence was slight.

As a founding member in Paris of the surrealist group, Artaud sought a theatre that might 'succeed in making all that is obscure, buried and unrevealed in the mind show itself in a sort of real, material projection'.[13] In this quest, there is a tension between his insistence on the 'real, material' nature of theatre and the pressure of inner purposes that he summons its material elements to carry though. This is compounded by Artaud's growing concern in the writings that followed this statement (of 1926) to find means not simply of 'showing' something to an audience, but of touching their nerves, and reaching their consciousness through the body, as the piping of the snake charmer (to use one of his images) reaches the snake. In this way, his theatre aims to be a 'kind of *magical operation*'.[14]

With such objectives it is not surprising that in Artaud's theatre words as vehicles of rational meaning had no automatic primacy, but were demoted in favour of sensory experience. More worth remarking is Artaud's insistence that theatre, while not dependent on verbal language, must itself be treated and used as a language. He is not just concerned with striking sensory effects. Though the project remained largely unrealised, he is concerned to develop and utilise a calculated theatre semiotics.

In assembling its elements, Artaud was more and more drawn to the accoutrements of ritual – the masks, 'puppets many metres high', incantation, and rhythmic movements proposed in his 'Theatre of Cruelty' manifesto. But the usual function of ritual, to effect stabilising and reassuring continuities, he discards, intending instead a cathartic upturning of his audience's rational Western consciousness. Though hailed as the father of 'ritual theatre', the role of Artaud's theatre is closer to the shamanic. It acts out a battle with dark forces and aims to harrow hell in the marrow of our bones.

Artaud's views came into their own after his death. In the 1960s he was widely regarded as a prophet before his time. This was an era of rising wages when a fully employed work-force was settling down contentedly on its new sofas in front of its first television sets. The left lamented that this was the 'society of the spectacle',[15] wholly populated with passive and pacified onlookers. What better than Artaud's proposed theatre, with its 'cries, moans, sudden appearances, surprises', and its cruelty 'in the gnostic sense of a whirlwind of life that devours the dark',[16] to shake audiences from their lethargy? The possibility that such effects might turn into yet another spectacle did not deter theatre groups. The spirit of Artaud haunted a thousand productions in a thousand shapes, from the naked challenge of the Living Theatre[17] to the 'panic' fantasies of Arrabal[18] and the outrageous travesties of Ludlam and the Ridiculous.

And what of Grotowski? When in 1966 his Theatre Laboratory was first seen outside Poland, their production (*The Constant Prince*) was 'immediately catalogued as an authentic example of Artaudian theatre'.[19] It was true that it wholly dispensed with the lavish theatrical means Artaud had propounded – masks, giant puppets, music, advanced lighting. Grotowski proposed a 'poor theatre' which did not try to compete with the technology of its rivals, but stripped itself down to its essential element: the human actor. Given the austerity of Polish conditions, this was perhaps to make a virtue of a necessity. But be that as it may, to the lucky few who gained entry – for audiences were restricted to around a hundred – it was self-evident that scenery was needless, and that the two lights used served to illuminate more than two hundred might do elsewhere. The acting they threw into relief, physically testing, springing from a total engagement of consciousness and riveting in its graphic vividness, was for most a revelation. Grotowski's actors, as Kornfeld had urged, offered a vision of humans opened up to the core of their being. It was here that the affinity with Artaud was felt. They seemed indeed, to recall Artaud's phrase, to be 'gesturing through the flames'. But the techniques of the Laboratorium were their own, as they had to be. For as Grotowski points out in the course of a measured assessment, Artaud 'left no concrete technique behind him'.[20]

Grotowski's closest heir is Eugenio Barba, the founder of Odin Theatre (represented in Part V). It has been suggested by Iben Nagel Rasmussen, one of its most remarkable performers, that in both companies the unprecedented sense of emotional opening and inner exposure achieved owes considerably to the women who worked in them.[21] Certainly the broad direction of such work has been followed up by women since in a range of independent ways. 'To cross our frontiers, exceed our limitations, fill our emptiness – fulfil ourselves':[22] Grotowski's description of his aims reverberates with unconscious feminist meanings. Women are pursuing them in the theatre with the creative energy that comes with the exploration of new territory.

The expression of inner emotions this has entailed at first met with a mixed reaction from feminists. Too long had women found themselves credited with feeling as distinct from thinking, and regarded as under the sway of 'Mother' Nature. Some feared the reinforcement of this stereotype, and were uneasy that physical modes of expression made yet once more the bodies of women the focus of the (male) spectator's gaze. But these doubts were largely overcome by the evident ability of such work to 'confront the myth' (in Grotowski's phrase) rather than endorse it, and to move or delight women with striking images of their shared experience.

Such work has already featured in the commentaries by Judy Chicago and Carolee Schneemann in Part II. It is illustrated further here by Louise Steinman. In so far as it is centred in the body of the performer, such work picks up part of the heritage of Isadora Duncan. It only remains to remember the most essential bodily organ of all, of which Rachel Rosenthal reminds us in *Rachel's Brain*. The history traced here thus completes its trajectory. The early desire to express the mind's spiritual intuitions or dream-haunted presentiments had to contend with the physicality of the stage. As the inner life began to achieve embodiment, its focus widened to include the body: the living body of the performer. The inner dimension began to be seen not only as that of the mind, but of the body's inward energies. As these two elements joined forces, new modes of theatre were born. These continue to strike home to us and enlarge our sense of what we are and might be.

NOTES

1 Gordon Craig, *On the Art of the Theatre*, London, Heinemann, 1911, p. 36.
2 Edward Bond, *The War Plays*, London, Methuen, 1991, p. 296.
3 Craig, op. cit., p. 46.
4 Adolphe Appia, *Œuvres Complètes*, vol. 2, Lausanne, L'Age d'Homme, 1986, p. 349.
5 Ibid., p. 358.
6 Without Fuller, Depero would never have included in his futurist agenda for the theatre 'decompositions of the figure and the deformation of it, even until its absolute transformation; e.g., a dancing ballerina who continually accelerates, transforming herself into a floral vortex, etc.' ('Notes on the Theatre', 1916, in Michael Kirby, *Futurist Performance*, New York, E. P. Dutton, 1971, p. 207).
7 Francis Steegmuller, '*Your Isadora*', New York, Random House, 1974, p. 23.
8 *Adolphie Appia: Essays, Scenarios and Designs*, eds W. R. Volbach and R. C. Beacham, Ann Arbor, Mich., and London, UMI Research Press, 1989, p. 69.
9 *My Life*, New York, Liveright, 1927, p. 75.
10 'Aller à la mer'. See p. 133.

11 *Meyerhold on Theatre*, ed. Edward Braun, London, Methuen, 1969, p. 38.
12 Felix Emmel, *Das Ekstatische Theater*, 1924, and Josef Kainz, *Josef-Kainz-Gedenkbuch*, 1924. Both cited in Michael Patterson, *The Revolution in German Theatre 1900–1933*, London, Routledge & Kegan Paul, 1981, pp. 81–2.
13 Antonin Artaud, *Œuvres Complètes*, vol. 2, Paris, Gallimard, 1961, p. 29.
14 Ibid., p. 35.
15 See Guy Debord, *Society of the Spectacle*, Detroit, Black & Red, 1970.
16 Antonin Artaud, Letter of 12 September 1932, *Œuvres Complètes*, vol. 5, Paris, Gallimard, 1964, p. 155.
17 See note p. 276.
18 See Fernando Arrabal, *Le Panique*, Paris, Union Générale d'Éditions, 1973.
19 Ferdinando Taviani in Eugenio Barba, *The Floating Islands*, Holstebro, Denmark, Odin Teatret, 1979, p. 14.
20 See Jerzy Grotowski, 'He Wasn't Entirely Himself' in *Towards a Poor Theatre*, Holsebro, Denmark, Odin Teatrets Forlag, 1968, reprinted London, Methuen, 1969.
21 Iben Nagel Rasmussen, 'Les Muettes de Passe', *Buffoneries*, no. 8, Cazilhac, France, 1983, pp. 5–20.
22 Grotowski, *Towards a Poor Theatre*, op. cit., p. 21.

57

AUGUST STRINDBERG

A Reminder:
Prefatory Note to *A Dream Play* (1902)

As he did in his previous dream play,[1] so in this one the author has tried to imitate the disconnected but seemingly logical form of the dream. Anything may happen; everything is possible and probable. Time and space do not exist. On an insignificant background of reality, imagination designs and embroiders novel patterns: a medley of memories, experiences, free fancies, absurdities and improvisations.

The characters split, double, multiply, vanish, solidify, blur, clarify. But one consciousness reigns above them all – that of the dreamer; and before it there are no secrets, no incongruities, no scruples, no laws. There is neither judgment nor exoneration, but merely narration. And as the dream is mostly painful, rarely pleasant, a note of melancholy and of pity with all living things runs right through the wabbly[2] tale. Sleep, the liberator, plays often a dismal part, but when the pain is at its worst, the awakening comes and reconciles the sufferer with reality, which, however distressing it may be, nevertheless seems happy in comparison with the torments of the dream.

Translated by Edwin Bjorkman

NOTES

1 The trilogy *To Damascus*.
2 Moving to and fro (variant of wobbly).

August Strindberg (1849–1912), Swedish writer of plays, fiction and autobiographical works, made his theatrical mark indelibly with his disturbing studies of male–female conflict, *The Father* (1887) and *Miss Julie* (1888); but moved far from the naturalistic orientation of these in later work, as this prefatory note suggests. His readiness to treat 'the stage as a dream picture' (the title of a 1903 essay by Hugo van Hofmannsthal), and to replace plot with symbolic incidents that mark the protagonist's journey through life via a series of 'stations', was a crucial influence on the expressionists. Artaud too discerned a kindred spirit in Strindberg, and one of his few achieved productions was of *A Dream Play*, in 1928, its Paris première. His early readers in Britain (where it was not staged till 1930) are likely to have read the translation above, authorised by Strindberg himself, which came out in a first selection from his plays in the year he died.

58

ADOLPHE APPIA

FROM How to Reform Our Staging Practices (1904)

Now comes the critical point: the plasticity of scenery necessary to the beauty of the actor's attitudes and movements. Painting has gained the upper hand on our stages, replacing everything that could not be realised plastically; and has done so to the sole end of creating the illusion of reality.

Are the images it thus accumulates on its vertical canvases indispensable? Not at all; not a single play calls for a hundredth part of them; for let us take note: these images are not living, they are *indicated* on the canvases like a sort of hieroglyphic language; they simply *signify* the things they wish to represent, and all the more so because they cannot enter into real organic contact with the actor. The plasticity demanded by the actor aims at a completely different effect, for the human body does not seek to create the illusion of reality *since it is itself reality!* What it demands of the scenery is simply that it bring out that reality; which has the natural consequence of completely changing the whole object of the scenery: in one case the desire is to achieve the real appearance of objects; in the other, to give the highest possible degree of reality to the human body.

Between these two principles there is a technical antagonism. So it is a question of choosing one or the other. Shall it be the accumulation of dead images and decorative opulence on vertical canvases, or rather the spectacle of the human being in all its plasticity and mobility? . . .

In the theatre, we are there to be present at a dramatic *action*: that action is due to the presence of the characters on stage; without the characters there is no action. Thus the actor is the essential factor in the staging of the scenes; it is him we come to see, it is him we look to for emotion, and it is this emotion we have come in search of. It is therefore a matter of basing the staging of the scenes on the presence of the actor at all costs, and to do that, of getting rid of everything that is in contradiction with his presence. . . .

Let us take as an example the second act of *Siegfried*. How should we present a forest on stage? First let us be clear on this point: is it a *forest* with characters, or rather *characters* in a forest? We are in the theatre to be present at a dramatic action; so something happens in this forest which obviously cannot be expressed by painting. Here then is our starting point: certain people do such and such, say such and such, in a forest. To create our scenery, we do not have to try and see a forest; we should be picturing to ourselves in detail and in sequence all the acts that take place in that forest. So a perfect knowledge of the score is indispensable, and the vision which inspires the director thus completely changes its nature; his eyes must stay riveted *on the characters*; if he then thinks of the forest, it will be of a special atmosphere around and above the actors, an atmosphere which he cannot grasp other than *in its relations with* the living and moving beings from whom his eyes must not turn. So no longer at any stage of his vision will his picture be an arrangement of inanimate painting; instead it will always be animated. The staging of the scene thus becomes the composing of a picture in time; instead of starting out from a painting commissioned by whoever from whoever, and then afterwards leaving the actor the paltry installations we know about, we start from the actor: it is acting and its artistry we wish to highlight; we are ready to sacrifice everything for that. It will be Siegfried here, Siegfried there; and never, the tree for Siegfried, the path for Siegfried. I repeat, we no longer seek to create the illusion of *a forest*, but rather the illusion of *a man* in the atmosphere of a forest; the reality here is *the* man, besides which no other illusion counts. Everything must be destined for him, the whole text must join to create around him the atmosphere indicated, and if we let Siegfried out of sight for an instant and lift our gaze, the scenic picture necessarily has no more illusion to give us. Its arrangement has no other end but Siegfried; and when the forest, softly stirred by the breeze, attracts Siegfried's gaze, we, the spectators, *watch Siegfried* bathed in moving light and shadow, and not cut-out scraps set in motion by strings.

Translated by Richard Drain and Micheline Mabille

For a biographical note on Appia see p. 16.

Craig writes of stage forests in similar terms four years after this piece was published in 'Some Evil Tendencies of the Modern Theatre' (*On the Art of the Theatre*, London, Heinemann, 1911, p. 107); and it is Craig whom Peter Brook credits for such thinking in 'How Many Leaves Make a Forest?' in *The Shifting Point*, London, Methuen, 1988. But Appia preceded him, and the Wagnerian context of his discussion is significant. He had studied music extensively and Wagner was deeply important to him, from his two first publications, *Staging Wagnerian Drama* (1895) and *Music and the Art of Theatre* (1899), on through his various designs for Wagner's works, which continued until his last years. Wagner's proposed *Gesamtkunstwerk*, the composite yet totally unified artwork that 'music-drama' ideally might be, dissolved the boundaries between the arts: 'so may each of the individual arts find its own self again in the perfect, thoroughly liberated artwork' (*Wagner on Music and Drama*, New York, E. P. Dutton, 1964, p. 121). For Appia this challenged the stage to become a visual equivalent of music, thus exposing its usual practices as crassly misconceived. Later he became deeply interested in the development of music into movement explored in Dalcroze eurhythmics. His emphasis on the performer widened into a belief that 'art should be lived and not merely contemplated'; and that all might participate in the 'living art' or 'living theatre' which eurhythmics exemplified (*The Essays of Adolphe Appia*, ed. R. Beacham, Ann Arbor, Mich. and London, UMI Research Press, 1989, p. 367). Subsequently, Appia's idealistic communalism fostered a powerfully unruly offspring when his phrase 'living theatre' was resurrected in the Living Theatre of Judith Malina and Julian Beck.

59

GORDON CRAIG

Study for Movement (1906–13)

Here we see a man battling through a snowstorm, the movements of both snow and man being made actual. Now I wonder whether it would be better if we should have no snowstorm visualised, but only the man, making his symbolical gestures which should suggest to us a man fighting against the elements. In a way I suppose this would be better. Still I have some doubts; for, following that line of argument in its logical sequence, then, would it not be still more near to art if we had no man, but only movements of some intangible material which would suggest the movements which the soul of man makes battling against the soul of nature? Perhaps it would be even

better to have nothing at all. If this is to be, then art, being almost at its last gasp, today we seem to be nearer perfection than we were even in the days of the great symbolical designers of India. But if we are to have the actual man going through actual gestures, why not have the actual scene going through its actual pantomine?

I don't know if anybody is really interested in such questions; no one seems to be making any efforts to answer them one way or another. Let us turn over the page.

FROM The Artists of the Theatre of the Future (1907)

By means of suggestion you may bring on the stage a sense of all things – the rain, the sun, the wind, the snow, the hail, the intense heat – but you will never bring them there by attempting to wrestle and close with Nature, in order so that you may seize some of her treasure and lay it before the eyes of the multitude. By means of suggestion in movement you may translate all the passions and the thoughts of vast numbers of people, or by means of the same you can assist your actor to convey the thoughts and the emotions of the particular character he impersonates. Actuality, accuracy of detail, is useless upon the stage. . . .

In preparing a play, while your mind is thinking of scene, let it instantly leap round and consider the acting, movement and voice. Decide nothing yet, instantly leap back to another thought about another part of this unit. Consider the movement robbed of all scene, all costume, merely as movement. Somehow mix the movement of the person with the movement which you see in your mind's eye in the scene. Now pour all your colour upon this. Now wash away all the colour. Now begin over again. Consider only the words. Wind them in and out of some vast and impossible picture, and now make that picture possible through the words. Do you see at all what I mean? Look at the thing from every standpoint and through every medium, and do not hasten to begin your work until one medium *force* you to commence. You can far sooner trust other influences to move your will and even your hand than you can trust your own little human brain . . . do not trouble about the costume books. When in a great difficulty refer to one in order to see how little it will help you out of your difficulty, but your best plan is never to let yourself become complicated with these things . . . the main strength of this branch of the work lies in the costume as mass. It is the mistake of all theatrical producers that they consider the costumes of the mass individually.

It is the same when they come to consider movements, the movements of masses on the stage. You must be careful not to follow the custom. We often hear it said that each member of the Meiningen Company composing the great crowd in *Julius Caesar* was acting a special part of his own. This may be very exciting as a curiosity, and attractive to a rather foolish audience, who would naturally say: "Oh, how interesting to go and look at one particular man in a corner who is acting a little part of his own! How wonderful! It is exactly like life!" And if that is the standard and if that is our aim, well and good.

But we know that it is not. Masses must be treated as masses, as Rembrandt treats a mass, as Bach and Beethoven treat a mass, and detail has nothing to do with the mass. Avoid the so-called "naturalistic" in movement as well as in scene and costume. . . .

This tendency towards the natural has nothing to do with art, and is abhorrent when it shows in art, even as artificiality is abhorrent when we meet it in everyday life. We must understand that the two things are divided, and we must keep each thing in its place . . . we must not get into our heads that every haphazard natural action is right. In fact, there is hardly any action which is right, there is hardly any which is natural. Action is a way of spoiling something, says Rimbaud.

For a biographical note on Craig see p. 18.

The essay from which these passages are drawn is headed with a first dedication to 'the young race of athletic workers in all the theatres'; but as this race does not exist (Craig tells us), he re-dedicates it to a single individual who will 'some day master and remould' the theatre. It is this notional 'young man' whom Craig then instructs at length in the true principles of his craft, and whom he addresses here. It is evident in the complete essay that he is to command every aspect of theatre and not just one. The 'Study for Movement' was made in 1906; the comment on it is likely to have been written later, for its publication with other designs in *Towards a New Theatre* (1913).

60

VSEVOLOD MEYERHOLD

FROM The Stylised Theatre (1907)

The stage has become estranged from its communal-religious origins; it has alienated the spectator by its objectivity. The stage is no longer *infectious*, it no longer has the power of *transfiguration.*

But thanks to such dramatists as Ibsen, Maeterlinck, Verhaeren and Wagner, the theatre is moving back towards its dynamic origins. We are rediscovering the precepts of antiquity. Just as the sacred ritual of Greek tragedy was a form of Dionysian *catharsis*, so today we demand of the artist that he heal and purify us.

In the New Drama external action, the revelation of character, is becoming incidental. 'We are striving to penetrate *behind* the mask, *beyond* the action into the character as perceived by the mind; we want to penetrate to the *inner mask.*'

The New Drama rejects the external in favour of the internal, not in order to penetrate man's soul and thus renounce this earth and ascend to the heavens (*théâtre ésotérique*), but to intoxicate the spectator with the Dionysian cup of eternal sacrifice.

'If the New Theatre is once again dynamic, then let it be totally dynamic.' If the theatre is finally to rediscover its dynamic essence, it must cease to be 'theatre' in the sense of mere 'spectacle'. We intend the audience not merely to observe, but to participate in a *corporate* creative act. . . .

The stylized theatre liberates the actor from all scenery, creating a three-dimensional area in which he can employ natural, sculptural plasticity. . . . By freeing the actor from the haphazard conglomeration of irrelevant stage properties, and by reducing technical devices to the minimum, the stylized theatre restores prominence to the creative powers of the actor. Concentrating on the restoration of tragedy and comedy (as manifestations of Fate and Satire), the stylized theatre avoids the 'mood' of Chekhovian theatre, which transforms acting into the passive experiencing of emotions and reduces the actor's creative intensity.

Having removed the footlights, the stylized theatre aims to place the stage on a level with the auditorium. By giving diction and movement a rhythmical basis, it hopes to bring about the revival of the *dance*. In such a theatre, dialogue can easily merge into melodic declamation and melodic silence.

The task of the director in the stylized theatre is to direct the actor rather than control him (unlike the Meiningen director). He serves purely as a bridge, linking the soul of the author with the soul of the actor. Having assimilated the author's creation, the actor is left *alone*, face to face with the spectator, and from the friction between these two unadulterated elements, the actor's creativity and the spectator's imagination, a clear flame is kindled.

Translated by Edward Braun

For a biographical note on Meyerhold see p. 101.

After working with the Moscow Art Theatre for four years, and running his own company in the Ukraine and Georgia, Meyerhold was invited back by Stanislavski to run the Art Theatre's new experimental studio. There he began to explore the stylisation he is concerned with here – experiments he pushed further after the closing of the studio following the 1905 Moscow rising, when he was invited by the actress Vera Komissarzhevskaya to join her theatre in Petersburg to promote the 'new' drama. Meyerhold's methods, however, proved too much for her, and in the year this essay was written, Meyerhold was dismissed to pursue his work elsewhere.

61

LOÏE FULLER

FROM Light and the Dance (1908)

Since it is generally agreed that I have created something new, something composed of light, colour, music, and the dance, more especially of light and the dance, it seems to me that it would perhaps be appropriate, after having considered my creation from the anecdotal and picturesque stand-point, to explain, in more serious terms, just what my ideas are relative to my art, and how I conceive it both independently and in its relationship to other arts. If I appear to be too serious I apologise in advance. . . .

Colour is disintegrated light. The rays of light, disintegrated by vibra-tions, touch one object and another, and this disintegration, photographed in the retina, is always chemically the result of changes in matter and in beams of light. Each one of these effects is designated under the name of colour.

Our acquaintance with the production and variations of these effects is precisely at the point where music was when there was no music.

In its earliest stage music was only natural harmony; the noise of the waterfall, the rumbling of the storm, the gentle whisper of the west wind, the murmur of the watercourses, the rattling of rain on dry leaves, all the sounds of still water and of the raging sea, the sleeping of lakes, the tumult of the hurricane, the soughing of the wind, the dreadful roar of the cyclone, the crashing of the thunder, the crackling of branches.

Afterwards the singing birds and then all the animals emitted their various sounds. Harmony was there; man, classifying and arranging the sounds, created music.

We all know what man has been able to get from it since then.

Man, past master of the musical realm, is to-day still in the infancy of art, from the standpoint of control of light. . . . Yet, notwithstanding, colour so pervades everything that the whole universe is busy producing it, every-where and in everything. It is a continued recurrence, caused by processes of chemical composition and decomposition. The day will come when man will know how to employ them so delightfully that it will be hard to conceive how he could have lived so long in the darkness in which he dwells to-day.

. . . A clear sparkling day produces upon us quite a different effect from a dull sad day, and by pushing these observations further we should begin to comprehend some more delicate effects which influence our organism.

In the quiet atmosphere of a conservatory with green glass, our actions are different from those in a compartment with red or blue glass. But usually we pay no attention to this relationship of actions and their causes. These are, however, things that must be observed when one dances to an accompaniment of light and music properly harmonised.

Light, colour, motion and music.

Observation, intuition, and finally comprehension. . . .

Our knowledge of motion is nearly as primitive as our knowledge of colour. We say "prostrated by grief," but, in reality, we pay attention only to the grief; "transported with joy," but we observe only the joy; "weighed down by chagrin," but we consider only the chagrin. Throughout we place no value on the movement that expresses the thought. We are not taught to do so, and we never think of it.

Who of us has not been pained by a movement of impatience, a lifting of the eyebrows, a shaking of the head, the sudden withdrawal of a hand?

We are far from knowing that there is as much harmony in motion as in music and colour. We do not grasp the facts of motion. . . .

At present dancing signifies motions of the arms and legs. It means a conventional motion, at first with one arm and one leg, then a repetition of the same figure with the other arm and the other leg. It is accompanied by music, each note calls for a corresponding motion, and the motion, it is unnecessary to say, is regulated rather by the time than by the spirit of the music. So much the worse for the poor mortal who cannot do with his left leg what he does with his right leg. So much worse for the dancer who cannot keep in time, or, to express it better, who cannot make as many motions as there are notes. It is terrifying to consider the strength and ability that are needed for proficiency. . . .

Music, however, ought to indicate a form of harmony or an idea with instinctive passion, and this instinct ought to incite the dancer to follow the harmony without special preparation. This is the true dance.

To lead us to grasp the real and most extensive connotation of the word dance, let us try to forget what is implied by the choregraphic art of our day.

What is the dance? It is motion.

What is motion? The expression of a sensation.

What is a sensation? The reaction in the human body produced by an impression or an idea perceived by the mind.

A sensation is the reverberation that the body receives when an impression strikes the mind. When the tree bends and resumes its balance it has received an impression from the wind or the storm. When an animal is frightened its body receives an impression of fear, and it flees and trembles or else stands at bay. If it be wounded, it falls. So it is when matter responds to immaterial causes. Man, civilised and sophisticated, is alone best able to inhibit his own impulses.

In the dance, and there ought to be a word better adapted to the thing, the human body should, despite conventional limitations, express all the sensations or emotions that it experiences. The human body is ready to express, and it would express if it were at liberty to do so, all sensations just as the body of an animal.

Ignoring conventions, following only my own instinct, I am able to translate the sensations we have all felt without suspecting that they could be expressed. . . .

To impress an idea I endeavour, by my motions, to cause its birth in the spectator's mind, to awaken his imagination, that it may be prepared to receive the image.

Thus we are able, I do not say to understand, but to feel within ourselves as an impulse an indefinable and wavering force, which urges and dominates us. Well, I can express this force which is indefinable but certain in its impact. I have motion. That means that all the elements of nature may be expressed.

Loïe Fuller (1869–1928), American dancer, was originally a singer and actor. Her career as a dancer began fortuitously, following her success in a part where, supposedly hypnotised, she made play with the long full Indian dress she was wearing. From this she developed the idea of dancing under changing light whilst swirling the voluminous materials of her costume on sticks. Her European fame dates from her first appearance in Paris (at the Folies Bergère) in 1893. Her system of using reflected rather than direct light had been first developed in Paris by Mariano Fortuny, praised by Appia for his 'brilliant invention', (*Œuvres Complètes*, vol. 2, Lausanne, L'Age d'Homme, 1986, p. 99), who also devised projections of clouds, using glass slides. For an account of Fuller's technical innovations in lighting and costume, see Sally Sommer, 'Loïe Fuller', *Drama Review*, vol. 19, no. 1 (T65) March 1975, pp. 53–67.

62

ISADORA DUNCAN

Depth

The true dance is an expression of serenity; it is controlled by the profound rhythm of inner emotion. Emotion does not reach the moment of frenzy out of a spurt of action; it broods first, it sleeps like the life in the seed, and it unfolds with a gentle slowness. The Greeks understood the continuing beauty of a movement that mounted, that spread, that ended with a promise of re-birth. The Dance – it is the rhythm of all that dies in order to live again; it is the eternal rising of the sun.

It is not for us to arrive at knowledge; we know, as we love, by instinct, faith, emotion.

Emotion works like a motor. It must be warmed up to run well, and the heat does not develop immediately; it is progressive. The dance follows the same law of development, of progression. The true dancer, like every true artist, stands before Beauty in a state of complete suspense; he opens the way to his soul and his "genius", and he lets himself be swayed by them as the trees abandon themselves to the winds. He starts with one slow movement and mounts from that gradually, following the rising curve of his inspiration, up to those gestures that exteriorize his fullness of feeling, spreading ever wider the impulse that has swayed him, fixing it in another expression.

The movements should follow the rhythm of the waves: the rhythm that rises, penetrates, holding in itself the impulse and the after-movement; call and response, bound endlessly in one cadence.

Our modern dances know nothing of this first law of harmony. Their movements are choppy, end-stopped, abrupt. They lack the continuing beauty of the curve. They are satisfied with being the points of angles which spur on the nerves. The music of today, too, only makes the nerves dance. Deep emotion, spiritual gravity, are entirely lacking. We dance with the jerky gestures of puppets. We do not know how to get down to the depths, to lose ourselves in an inner self, how to develop our visions into the harmonies that attend our dreams.

We are always in paroxysms. We walk angularly. We strain ourselves always to hold a balance between points. We are ignorant of the repose of a descent, and the comfort of breathing, of mounting again, skimming, returning, like a bird, to rest. The bird never struggles. The dancer ought to be light as a flame. Even violence is the greater when it is restrained: one gesture that has grown slowly out of that reserve is worth many thousands that struggle and cut each other off.

Isadora Duncan (1877–1927), American dancer. This essay, found in a French version among her papers after her death, is undated, though a letter of 1905 – 'I've been writing about dance waves soundwaves light waves – all the *same*' (Francis Steegmuller, '*Your Isadora*', New York, Random House, 1974, p. 91), suggests it may have been written then. Duncan's insistence that dance must have 'depth' and spring from within affected the whole modern dance movement that followed. Compare Laban on the need to 'penetrate to the hidden recesses of man's inner effort. We need an authentic symbol of the inner vision to effect contact with the audience . . .' (*The Mastery of Movement on the Stage*, London, Macdonald & Evans, 1950, revised edn 1971, p. 20).

Duncan came to London in 1899, and was inspired by the flowing movement of the Greek sculpture she found there, the spirit of which she sought to recapture in her dance. She first toured Europe 1900–02, disdaining second-rate ballet music and dancing to Beethoven, Schubert and Chopin. An involvement with Gordon Craig led to a prolific interchange of letters and a child. Her dance school for children, which she had set up in 1904, continued until 1919, when she lost its premises. In 1921 she was invited to the Soviet Union to set up another. This did her no good in her homeland, where she was accused on a subsequent fund-raising tour of Bolshevism and flagrant immorality.

63

WASSILY KANDINSKY

FROM On Stage Composition (1911–12)

The nineteenth century marks itself out as an era very distant from inner creation. The concentration on material phenomena and the material side of phenomena logically brought about in the inner sphere the decline of creative power, which appears to have sunk to the lowest ebb.

Out of this one-sidedness, naturally, other kinds of one-sidedness inevitably developed.

So too on the stage . . . there developed and petrified stage works of three kinds, divided one from the other by high walls.

a   Drama
b   Opera
c   Ballet

a   The drama of the nineteenth century is generally a more or less clever and probing narrative of events of a more or less personal nature. It is usually a depiction of outward life, where the life of the human soul plays a part only in so far as it has dealings with outward life. *The cosmic element is completely missing.*

    Outward events and the outward linking of the action is the form of today's drama.

b   Opera is a drama to which music is added as a main element, with the result that the cleverness and penetration of the dramatic parts suffer badly. Both its elements are connected to one another in an entirely external fashion; i.e. either the music illustrates (or intensifies) the dramatic action, or else the dramatic action is drawn into helping explain the music. . . .

    Outward events, the outward linking of its separate parts and the two modes (drama and music) is the form of today's opera.

c   Ballet is a drama with all the features already described and the same content. But here the seriousness of the drama loses even more than in opera. In opera, as well as love themes, there are also others: religious, political and social conditions are the ground on which grow rapture, despair, honesty, hatred and suchlike other feelings. Ballet contents itself with love in a childish fairytale form. Apart from music, solo and group movement come to its aid. Everything remains in a naive form of external linkage. In practice it even happens that solo dances are inserted or cut out as convenient. The 'whole' is so problematic that such surgical measures remain totally unnoticed.

Outward events, the outward linking of its separate parts and the three modes (drama, music and dance) is the form of today's ballet.

Let us take the inner standpoint. The whole situation changes.

1 The outward appearance of each element suddenly disappears. And its inner value takes on fullness of sound.
2 It becomes clear that in using the inner sound, outward action can be not only subsidiary, but also, as an obscuring element, damaging.
3 The worth of outward links is shown in the right light, i.e. as needlessly limiting, and weakening of the inner effect.
4 There comes of its own accord the feeling that an *inner unity* is necessary; this is sustained and amplified by outward disunity.
5 The possibility is laid bare that each of the elements can retain its own outward life which outwardly is in conflict with the outward life of other elements.

Further, if we put these abstract discoveries into practice, we see that it is possible –

with regard to 1: to take only the inner sound of an element as medium
with regard to 2: to strike out the outward event (= the action)
with regard to 3: – whereby outward links fall apart of themselves, just like –
with regard to 4: – the outward unity – and –
with regard to 5: the inner unity puts in our hands a countless series of resources which before could not have existed.

Here inner necessity becomes the sole source.

Translated by Richard Drain and Anna Millan

Wassily Kandinsky (1866–1944), Russian artist; also an accomplished musician. The larger article from which these passages are taken served as an introduction to his stage piece, *The Yellow Sound*. The idea of inner values taking on 'sound', which it attempts to realise, may seem odd, but would probably not if the milder word 'resonance' were substituted. Kandinsky's word underlines his interest in synesthesia, that interdependence of the senses from which some gather the impression of 'seeing' sounds in terms of colour, or 'hearing' colours as sounds. Our more normal dividing of the senses is analogous to the 'outward disunity' which only brings home the need for an inner unity. While insisting on the latter, Kandinsky licenses any combination of outward elements in a work of art, thus propounding a crucial modernist principle (see for example its radical application by Robert Wilson, p. 9). Such ideas relate closely to those developed in his important *Concerning the Spiritual in Art* (written 1910, published 1912). For Kandinsky, the function of a work of art was to produce a 'spiritual vibration' in the spectator, and it could do so only if its outward appearance was given depth by an inner resonance and internal meanings. For this, art needed to be autonomous, freed from its requirement to represent the outside world and free (in the case of painting) to explore the intrinsic qualities of pigment and artistic materials. The relation of such ideas to the theatre aesthetic of Witkiewicz and Kantor is worth noting.

Kandinsky moved to Munich to study art in 1896. There the abstract tendencies of *Jugendstil* (*art nouveau*), and the advanced theatre reform movement which found expression in the Munich Artists' Theatre, set up in 1908, arguably did much to stimulate his interest in artistic synthesis and his move to abstract painting (see Peg Weiss, *Kandinsky in Munich: The Formative Jugendstil Years*, Princeton University Press, 1979). Kandinsky knew Peter Behrens, who proposed the idea of theatre as a synthesis of the arts (*Festivals of Life and Art*, 1900), and who, as architect, worked with Georg Fuchs to devise a new 'total' theatre. He knew too Alexander Salzmann who designed lighting and sets for Dalcroze's 'light-theatre' at Hellerau which was designed in collaboration with Appia and opened in 1910. Kandinsky's artistic experiments took theatrical form in the four 'colour-tone dramas' that he composed between 1909 and 1914, of which *The Yellow Sound* was one. The outbreak of war brought to an end plans for a production at the Munich Artists' Theatre, and finally none of the four was staged.

64

CONSTANTIN STANISLAVSKI

FROM Inner Impulses and Inner Action; Creative Objectives (1916–20)

In most theatres action on the stage is taken incorrectly to mean external action. It is commonly thought that plays are rich in action if people are arriving or departing, getting married or being separated, killing or saving one another; in brief, that a play rich in action is one with a cleverly woven and interesting external plot. But this is an error.

Scenic action does not mean walking, moving about, gesticulating on the stage. The point does not lie in the movement of arms, legs, or body but in inner movements and impulses. So let us learn once and for all that the word "action" is not the same as "miming", it is not anything the actor is pretending to present, not something external, but rather something internal, nonphysical, a *spiritual activity*. It derives from an unbroken succession of independent processes; and each of these in turn is compounded of desires or impulses aimed at the accomplishment of some objective.

Scenic action is the movement from the soul to the body, from the center to the periphery, from the internal to the external, from the thing an actor feels to its physical form. External action on the stage when not inspired, not justified, not called forth by inner activity, is entertaining only for the eyes and ears; it does not penetrate the heart, it has no significance in the life of a human spirit in a role.

Thus inner impulses – the urge to action and the inner actions themselves – acquire an exceptional meaning in our work. They are our motive power in moments of creation, and only that creativeness which is predicated on inner action is scenic. By "scenic" in the theatre we mean action in the spiritual sense of the word.

By contrast, a passive state kills all scenic action, it produces feelings for the sake of feelings, technique for the sake of technique. That kind of feeling is not scenic.

Sometimes an actor practically luxuriates in inaction, wallows in his own emotions. Blinded by the feeling that he is at home in his part, he thinks that he is creating something, that he is truly living the part. But no matter how sincere that passive feeling may be, it is not creative, and it cannot reach the heart of the spectator, so long as it lacks activity and does not promote the inner life of the play. When an actor feels his part passively his emotion remains inside him, there is no challenge to either inner or outer action.

Even in order to project a passive state in theatrical terms one must do it actively. Escaping from active participation (in any matter or event) is in itself action. Indolent, sluggish action is still action, typical of a passive state. . . .

Real life, like life on the stage, is made up of continuously arising desires, aspirations, inner challenges to action and their consummation in internal and external actions. Just as the separate, constantly repeated explosions of a motor result in the smooth motion of an automobile, so this unbroken series of outbursts of human desires develops the continuous movement of our creative will, it establishes the flow of inner life, it helps an actor to experience the living organism of his part.

In order to invoke this creative experience on the stage an actor must keep up a continuous fire of artistic desires all through his part so that they in turn will arouse the corresponding inner aspirations, which then will engender corresponding inner challenges to act, and finally these inner calls to action will find their outlet in corresponding external, physical action.

Need one point out that while the actor is on the stage all these desires, aspirations, and actions must belong to him as the creative artist, and not the inert paper words printed in the text of his part; not to the playwright, who is absent from the performance; nor yet to the director of the play, who remains in the wings? Need one emphasize that an actor can experience or live his part only with his own, genuine feelings? Can one live in ordinary life or on the stage with the feelings of others unless one has been absorbed by them body and spirit as an actor and human being? Can one borrow the feelings or the sensations, the body and soul, of another person and use them as one would one's own?

An actor can subject himself to the wishes and indications of a playwright or a director and execute them mechanically, but to experience his role he must use his own living desires, engendered and worked over by himself, and he must exercise his own will, not that of another. The director and the playwright can suggest their wishes to the actor, but these wishes must then be reincarnated in the actor's own nature so that he becomes completely possessed by them. For these desires to become living, creative desires on the stage, embodied in the actions of the actor, they must have become a part of his very self.

CREATIVE OBJECTIVES

How does one evoke the desires of one's creative will on the stage? One cannot simply say: "Desire! Create! Act!" Our creative emotions are not subject to command and do not tolerate force. They can only be coaxed. Once coaxed, they begin to wish, and wishing they begin to yearn for action.

There is only one thing that can lure our creative will and draw it to us and that is an attractive aim, a creative objective. *The objective is the whetter of creativeness, its motive force. The objective is the lure for our emotions*: This objective engenders outbursts of desires for the purpose of creative aspiration. It sends inner messages which naturally and logically are expressed in action. The objective gives a pulse to the living being of a role.

Life on the stage, as well as off it, consists of an uninterrupted series of objectives and their attainment. They are signals set all along the way of an actor's creative aspirations; they show him the true direction. Objectives are like the notes in music, they form the measures, which in turn produce the melody, or rather the emotions – a state of sorrow, joy, and so forth. The melody goes on to form an opera or a symphony, that is to say the life of a human spirit in a role, and that is what the soul of the actor sings.

Such objectives may be reasoned, conscious, pointed out by our mind, or they may be emotional, unconscious, arising of their own free will, intuitively.

A conscious objective can be carried out on the stage with almost no feeling or will; but it will be dry, unattractive, lacking in scenic quality and therefore unadaptable to creative purposes. An objective which is not warmed or infused with life by emotions or will cannot put any living quality into the inert concepts of words. It can do no more than recite dry thoughts. If an actor achieves his objective purely through his mind he cannot live or experience his part, he can only give a report on it. Therefore he will not be a creator but a reporter of his role. A conscious objective can be good and scenically effective only when it is attractive to the living feelings and will of the actor and sets them to working.

The best creative objective is the unconscious one which immediately, emotionally, takes possession of an actor's feelings, and carries him intuitively along to the basic goal of the play. The power of this type of objective lies in its immediacy (the Hindus call such objectives the highest kind of superconsciousness), which acts as a magnet to creative will and arouses irresistible aspirations. In such cases all the mind does is to note and evaluate the results. Often such objectives are destined to remain, if not entirely, then at least half in the realm of the unconscious. All we can do is to learn how not to interfere with the creativeness of nature, or work to prepare the ground, seek out motives and means whereby even obliquely we can catch hold of these emotional, superconscious objectives.

Unconscious objectives are engendered by the emotion and will of the actors themselves. They come into being intuitively; they are then weighed and determined consciously. Thus the emotions, will, and mind of the actor all participate in creativeness.

255

The ability to find or create such objectives as will arouse the activity of an actor, and the ability to handle such objectives, are the crucial concerns of our whole inner technique. . . .

Conscious or unconscious objectives are carried out both inwardly and outwardly, by both body and soul. Therefore they can be both *physical* and *psychological.*

For example, going back to the imaginary scene when I made my morning call on Famusov, I recall an infinite number of physical objectives which I had to execute in my imagination. I had to go along a corridor, knock at a door, take hold of and turn the doorknob, open the door, enter, greet the master of the house and anyone else present, and so forth. In order to preserve the truthfulness of the occasion I could not simply fly into his room in one movement.

All these necessary physical objectives are so habitual that we execute them mechanically, with our muscles. In our inner realm, too, we find an infinite number of necessary, simple psychological objectives.

I recall now, as an example, another imaginary scene in the life of the Famusov household — the interrupted meeting between Sophia and Molchalin. How many simple psychological objectives Sophia had to execute with her emotions in order to soften her father's anger and escape punishment. She had to mask her embarrassment, she had to throw her father off balance by her calm, embarrass and move him to pity by the angelic expression on her face, disarm him with her humility, undermine his position, and so forth. She could not, without destroying the truthfulness and living quality of her action, by one sweep of emotions, one inner movement, one psychological objective have brought about the miraculous transformation in the heart of the angry man.

Physical and simple psychological objectives are to some degree necessary to all human beings. When a person has been drowned, for example, he is forced to breathe by mechanical means. As a result, his other organs begin to function; his heart begins to beat, his blood begins to circulate, and finally by the sheer momentum of living organisms his spirit is revived. This is the inborn habitual and mutual bond among the physical organs.

It is this sort of organic habit, a part of our nature, this sort of consecutiveness and logic in our actions and feelings, that we make use of in our art when we give birth to the process of living a part. This common necessity of the actor-human-being and the human-being-part is what brings the actor and his part close together for the first time.

Constantin Stanislavski (1863–1938), Russian actor, director and teacher, founded the Moscow Art Theatre with Nemirovich-Danchenko in 1898, working as both actor and director. His search for a method of inducing in the actor a wholly engaged creative state of mind, both in the rehearsal process and on stage, began in 1906. It led finally to his celebrated 'method', and to his books written from the point of view of an acting class led by their teacher, a wise and dedicated *alter ego* by the name of Tortsov. But the passages here were written before the invention of that appealing fiction. They arise from the remarkable discussion to which he here alludes of Griboyedov's classic comedy *Woe from Wit* which depicts the Famusov household. Sophia is Famusov's daughter, responsive to the warm attentions of his secretary, Molchalin. As the play starts, they have been together all night, and their 'meeting' is interrupted by her angry father (played by Stanislavski in both the 1905 and 1914 productions). As a director, his concern not only with the inner life of the characters, but with their deep integration into their social milieu, repays study, and helps account for Brecht's interest (under-represented in *Brecht on Theatre*). This volume was in preparation at too early a date to draw on the forthcoming *Collected Works*. On the Stanislavski 'myth' promoted around prior translations, see Sharon Marie Carnicke, 'Stanislavsky, Uncensored and Unabridged', *Drama Review*, vol. 37, no. 1, Spring 1993.

65

PAUL KORNFELD

From The Inspired and the Psychological Being (1918)

If the human being is the centre of drama, the artist still has the choice of placing at that centre the human soul, or the human character. The playwrights of the previous generation – whose influence still makes itself felt in the present generation and in all the arts – chose the second way, and found their satisfaction in wandering through the winding mazes of a character, and imprisoning humanity, victim of its labyrinthine complexities, in the simplicity of an aphorism. The human being became a mechanism whose reactions in given circumstances it was diverting to observe and examine. Audiences were quite satisfied, because they found themselves confirmed in their notions about themselves, and about human beings – seeing them as a sum of aptitudes and capacities, dominated and directed by a psychological causality similar to material causality, whose laws, once explored, allowed the essence of man to be lost. Those conforming to the spirit of the times became all too willingly the victims of this error, because on the one hand it spared them a deep knowledge of themselves, while on the other it flattered their penchant for self-analysis; because it tried to raise their daily existence, their life, their 'psyche', into the sphere of art, and so persuaded them that their daily living represented true life, their psyche the human spirit, their little embarrassments great problems. Confronting this error, which robs man of his spirit, one is tempted to speak of a criminal art. For man is not a mechanism, conscious subjectivism is a bad sign, and psychological causality is of as little importance as material causality. . . .

A generation of actors should be formed who are as far from purely exterior naturalness, as from stiff bathos – that lack of the natural, that substitute, that imitation of feeling which employs a certain number of conventional movements and stereotyped looks and mimicries, drawn on according to need, as if from a bank book; – a generation of actors who, free of all convention, free too of the cult of reality, follow the practice of all avowed art in acting out themselves; – more, present that within humanity which an intellectual analysis cannot reveal, create a new reality closer to the true human being, where their acting is capable of stirring emotions by virtue of emotions they have themselves lived; – a generation of young actors that should be brought together before their humanity has been wasted by routine, and before they are unable to do anything because they have ceased to be anything; a generation that in all likelihood, when its own acting too will have gone stiff with convention, should itself be renewed and revived again by a new youth, so that theatre may never cease to fulfil its role.

Each day and each hour, still and for ever in turmoil, shaken to their roots, people should break open their shell, tear themselves free of their daily existence, so that even the most reasonable among them reveal and recall that at the core of their being there lies that seed of madness that is not the overthrow of reason but its surpassing; the surpassing of that reason which, led by logic and dominated by the characteristics of its accidental individuality, fills up their days.

Translated by Richard Drain and Anna Millan

Paul Kornfeld (1889–1942), Czechoslovakian-born writer and playwright, of Jewish parentage, moved to Frankfurt 1916, and later to Berlin. This is part of a long essay that appeared in 1918, and it is by this essay that Kornfeld has been chiefly remembered, although he also wrote seven plays. It incorporates the best part of a short piece he appended to the first of them (*Die Verführung* (*The Seduction*) 1917), under the title 'Afterword to the Actor'; this is included in Toby Cole and Helen Krich Chinoy (eds), *Actors on Acting*, New York, Crown, 1949. From 1922 he disengaged himself from expressionism. In 1928 he was appointed dramaturg at a theatre in Darmstadt. With the rise of the Nazis he retreated back to Prague, but did not escape them. He died in the Lodz concentration camp.

66

EVGENY VAKHTANGOV

FROM Stenogramme of Two Discussions between Vakhtangov and His Students (1922)

Stylised theatre was necessary in order to break down and do away with theatrical vulgarity. Using stylised means to do away with theatrical vulgarity, Meyerhold arrived at an understanding of genuine theatre.

Carried away by real truth, Stanislavsky brought naturalist truth to the stage. He sought for theatrical truth in life's truth. Meyerhold arrived at genuine theatre through stylised theatre, which he now rejects. But in his enthusiasm for theatrical truth, Meyerhold did away with emotional truth. . . .

Emotion in theatre and in life is the same thing, although the means for conveying this emotion are different. A partridge is exactly the same whether it is cooked in a restaurant or at home. But in a restaurant it is cooked and served so that there is a theatrical flair about it, while at home it is something ordinary and domestic, not theatrical. Stanislavsky served up truth by means of truth, water by means of water, and a partridge was simply a partridge, while Meyerhold did away with truth altogether, that is, he retained the dish and the way of cooking it, but he served up paper, not a partridge. And the feeling was cardboard, too. Meyerhold was a master and knew how to serve things up in a masterful way, as in a restaurant, but you couldn't eat it. However, by breaking down theatrical vulgarity through stylised theatrical means, Meyerhold arrived at genuine theatricality, summed up in the following formula: the audience should not forget that they are in the theatre for a single instant. Through this approach, Stanislavsky arrived at the formula: the audience should forget they are in the theatre.

A perfect work of art is eternal. A work of art is one in which there is harmony of form, content, and material. Stanislavsky created something which harmonised only with the mood of Russian society during that era. Not everything contemporary is eternal but whatever is eternal is contemporary. Meyerhold never felt "today", but he felt "tomorrow". Stanislavsky never felt "tomorrow", he only felt "today". We need to feel, however, "today" in tomorrow and "tomorrow" in today.

When the Revolution began, we felt that art should not be the same as before. We had not yet found the real form that was needed, and that is why *St. Anthony*[1] had a transitory form. The next stage will be the quest for the eternal. In Chekhov's plays life's means coincided with theatrical means. The theatrical means we are using now in *St Anthony* – "exposing the bourgeoisie" – coincide with life's demands, today's demands. But this time will pass. The need to expose people will no longer exist, because socialism is not a society of the proletariat, but a society of equal, satisfied, well-fed people. When need ceases to exist, along with any concept of need, there will not be any necessity to expose the bourgeoisie. Thus, the means we have chosen will cease to be theatrical. We shall have to find genuine theatrical means. We shall have to find the eternal mask.

Translated by Doris Bradbury

NOTE

1   Maeterlinck's *The Miracle of St. Anthony* had been produced by Meyerhold in 1906 as a marionette show. Lengthy work on the play by Vakhtangov's Studio (1916–18) resulted in a very different production, which aimed for simplicity, a spiritual warmth and 'something amusing' in each role. Vakhtangov returned to the play in 1920 and restaged it in 1921, turning it sharply towards the grotesque. (See Nick Worrall, *Modernism to Realism on the Soviet Stage*, Cambridge University Press, 1989, pp. 106–12.)

Evgeny Vakhtangov (1883–1922), Soviet director. Vakhtangov was a student at the Moscow Art Theatre; and his most accessible pronouncements, in *Acting: a Handbook of the Stanislavsky Method*, compiled by Toby Cole (New York, Lear, 1947), leave the impression that he was wholly dedicated to Stanislavski's ideas. But he writes in 1921, 'Stanislavski's theatre is already dead and will never be resurrected. I am happy about this'; and 'May naturalism in the theatre die!' He believed that 'the time has come to bring theatricality back to the theatre' (*Evgeny Vakhtangov*, compiled by Lyubov Vendrovskaya and Galina Kaptereva, Progress Publishers, Moscow, 1982, pp. 141–2, 154), and to this degree sided with Meyerhold. But Meyerhold 'knows nothing about the actor' (p. 141), and his work is here equally criticised. For Vakhtangov, theatricality involved self-consciousness on the part of the actor (which commended him to Brecht) and physical expressivity in equal measure. Indeed, it could be argued that, like Alexander Granowski's Moscow Yiddish Theatre, the Goset, Vakhtangov's work introduced what were virtually expressionist techniques into Russian theatre.

This distinguished it from Meyerhold's, which in the Soviet period took on a strong constructivist and mechanistic aspect. Naturally the young Vakhtangov learnt from both his great predecessors, but he is not simply some kind of cross between the two, as he is sometimes presented. For a valuable account of his work, see the book by Nick Worrall referred to in note 1 above.

67

FEDERICO GARCÍA LORCA

FROM Play and Theory of the Duende (1930)

All over Andalusia, from the rock of Jaén to the whorled shell of Cádiz, the people speak constantly of the "duende", and identify it accurately and instinctively whenever it appears. The marvelous singer El Lebrijano, creator of the debla, used to say, "On days when I sing with duende, no one can touch me." The old Gypsy dancer La Malena once heard Brailowsky play a fragment of Bach and exclaimed, "Olé! That has duende!" but was bored by Gluck, Brahms, and Darius Milhaud. Manuel Torre, who had more culture in the blood than any man I have ever known, pronounced this splendid sentence on hearing Falla[1] play his own *Nocturno del Generalife*: "All that has black sounds has duende." And there is no greater truth.

These black sounds are the mystery, the roots fastened in the mire that we all know and all ignore, the mire that gives us the very substance of art. . . .

The duende, then, is a power, not a work; it is a struggle, not a thought. I have heard an old maestro of the guitar say, "The duende is not in the throat; the duende climbs up inside you, from the soles of the feet." Meaning this: it is not a question of ability, but of true, living style, of blood, of the most ancient culture, of spontaneous creation.

This "mysterious power which everyone senses and no philosopher explains"[2] is, in sum, the spirit of the earth, the same duende that scorched the heart of Nietzsche, who looked for its external forms on the Rialto Bridge and in the music of Bizet, without ever finding it and without knowing that the duende he was pursuing had leaped straight from the Greek mysteries to the dancers of Cádiz or the beheaded, Dionysian scream of Silverio's siguiriya.[3] . . .

The muse and angel come from without; the angel gives lights, and the muse gives forms (Hesiod learned from her). Loaf of gold or tunic fold: the poet receives norms in his bosk of laurels. But one must awaken the duende in the remotest mansions of the blood. . . .

But there are neither maps nor disciplines to help us find the duende. We only know that he burns the blood like a poultice of broken glass, that he exhausts, that he rejects all the sweet geometry we have learned, that he smashes styles and makes Goya (master of the grays, silvers, and pinks of the best English painting) work with his fists and knees in horrible bitumins. . . .

Every art and in fact every country is capable of duende, angel, and muse. And just as Germany has, with few exceptions, muse, and Italy shall always have angel, so in all ages Spain is moved by the duende, for it is a country of ancient music and dance where the duende squeezes the lemons of dawn – a country of death. A country open to death. . . . The duende does not come at all unless he sees that death is possible. The duende must know beforehand that he can serenade death's house and rock those branches we all wear, branches that do not have, will never have, any consolation.

With idea, sound, or gesture, the duende enjoys fighting the creator on the very rim of the well. Angel and muse escape with violin and compass; the duende wounds. In the healing of that wound, which never closes, lies the invented, strange qualities of a man's work. . . .

In Spain, as among the peoples of the Orient, where the dance is religious expression, the duende has unlimited range over the bodies of the dancers of Cádiz, praised by Martial, over the breasts of singers, praised by Juvenal, and in the liturgy of the bulls, an authentic religious drama where, as in the Mass, a God is sacrificed to and adored.

It seems as if all the duende of the classical world has crowded into this perfect festival, expounding the culture, the sensitivity of a people who discover man's best anger, bile, and weeping. Neither in Spanish dance nor in the bullfight does anyone enjoy himself. The duende takes it upon himself to make us suffer by means of a drama of living forms, and clears the stairways for an evasion of the surrounding reality.

The duende works on the body of the dancer as the wind works on sand. With magical power he changes a girl into a lunar paralytic, or fills with adolescent blushes the broken old man begging in the wineshop, or make's a woman's hair smell like a nocturnal port, and he works continuously on the arms with expressions that are the mothers of the dances of every age.

But he can never repeat himself. This is interesting to emphasize: the duende does not repeat himself, any more than do the forms of the sea during a squall.

Translated by Christopher Maurer

NOTES

1 Lorca's mother was an accomplished pianist, and the composer Manuel de Falla his godfather.
2 Goethe on the playing of Paganini, the celebrated pianist.
3 A form of *cante jondo* (the 'deep song' of Andalusia) developed by Silverio Franconetti.

Federico García Lorca (1899–1936), Spanish poet and playwright. The talk given in Latin America from which these brief excerpts are taken includes few references to theatre, but makes clear that *duende* is essential to all the arts. Lorca's keen interest in the flamenco singing and dance of his birth-place Andalusia was one side of a warm regard for popular expression, which influenced both his poetry and his theatre work, nourishing the imagery of his incandescent writing, and attracting him to write and present puppet plays as well as dramas. Meanwhile his tours in rural areas with *La Barraca*, the student theatre group he set up under the new republic to take plays out from Granada to the villages around (1931–2), may have helped inspire his three tragedies of rural life, *Blood Wedding* (1933), *Yerma* (1934), and *The House of Bernarda Alba* (1936). Murdered by the Falangists (fascists) in the civil war at the age of 38, his books were burnt and his work banned.

68

ANTONIN ARTAUD

Letter to *Comœdia* (1932)

Dear Sir,

Would you be good enough to let me enlarge here on some of the principles that have guided me in the project I am undertaking.

I conceive theatre as a magical operation or ceremony, and I shall strive to restore to it its primitive ritual character, by contemporary modern means, and as comprehensibly as possible to everyone. There are two sides, two aspects, to everything.

1   The physical, active, exterior aspect, expressed by gestures, sounds, images and precious harmonies. This physical side addresses itself directly to the sensibility of the spectator, that is, to his nerves. It has hypnotic powers. Through the nerves it prepares the spirit to receive the mystical or metaphysical ideas which comprise the interior aspect of a rite, and whose harmonies or gestures are only what envelops it.
2   The interior aspect, philosophical or religious, giving the last word its widest sense, that is, of communication with the Universal.

But let the spectator be reassured because every rite has three levels. And following the physical side, designed to enfold and charm after the fashion of any dance or piece of music, there appears the magical and poetic aspect of the rite where the mind may dwell without going deeper. At this level the rite tells tales and offers wondrous well-known images, just as in reading *The Iliad* one can dwell on the matrimonial mishaps of Menelaus without worrying over the deep or terrible ideas they contain and are charged to mask. . . .

But as theatre rediscovers powers of direct action on the nerves and sensibility, and through the sensibility on the spirit, it abandons the ways of spoken theatre, whose clarity and excessive logic are a hindrance to the sensibility. It is not a matter of suppressing words however, but of considerably reducing their use, or of using them in an incantatory way that is forgotten or disregarded. Above all it is a matter of suppressing a certain purely psychological and naturalistic aspect of theatre, and allowing poetry and imagination to regain their rights.

But, and this is what is new, there is a virulent and I would even say dangerous side of poetry and the imagination to rediscover. Poetry is a dissociative and anarchic force, which, through analogy, associations and images, lives only through an upheaval of known relationships. And what is new will be the upheaval of these relationships not only in the exterior realm, the realm of nature, but in the interior realm, that is, of psychology.

Now if I am asked how, I shall reply, that is my secret. I can say, at any rate, that in this new theatre, the objective, exterior side, that is to say, the scenic element, the art of the stage, will have a primordial importance, that everything will be based not on the text, but on the staging, and that the text will become once more slave of the spectacle. A new language which will have its own laws and its own means of writing will develop beside spoken language, and however physical and concrete it may be, it will have as much intellectual importance and suggestive power as that other language.

For I believe it is urgent, for the theatre, to become aware once and for all of what distinguishes it from written literature. However transient it is, theatrical art is based on the use of space, on expression in space, and, speaking strictly, the fixed arts, inscribed in stone, on canvas or on paper, are not necessarily the most valid, nor the most efficacious *magically*.

In this new language, gestures have the value of words, attitudes have a profound symbolic sense, are grasped as hieroglyphs, and the whole spectacle, instead of aiming at effect and charm, will be a means of recognition, awe and revelation for the spirit.

This is to say that poetry will inhabit exterior objects, and draw from their selection and disposition strange consonances and images; everything in the production will aim at expression through physical means that will *engage* the spirit as much as the sensibility.

In this way a certain *alchemical idea* of theatre emerges, in which contrary to the theatre we are used to, where the analytic dispersal of feelings corresponds to the crude state of scientific chemistry (which is only a degenerated branch of alchemy) — contrary to that, the forms, the emotions, the words, make up the image of a sort of living whirlpool, a synthesis in the midst of which the performance assumes the nature of a veritable transformation.

As for the works, we shall not perform written plays. The shows will be created directly on the stage, and with all the means that the stage offers, but these means will be used as a language in the same way as the dialogues and words of written theatre. This does not mean that the productions will not be rigorously shaped and *fixed* once and for all before being performed.

So much for principles. As for the material means of their realisation, you will allow me to reveal these only a little later.

Antonin Artaud

Translated by Richard Drain & Micheline Mabille

This letter to the magazine *Comœdia*, complete save for one paragraph, is an attempt to encapsulate and win favour for the main principles Artaud was seeking to realise in his projected 'Theatre of Cruelty', and which he was to extend in his book *The Theatre and Its Double* (1938). The 'material means of their realisation' that he postpones specifying, he details in the manifesto below, which appeared only a week later.

FROM The Theatre of Cruelty (First Manifesto) (1932)

The Show: Every show will contain physical, objective elements perceptible to all. Shouts, groans, apparitions, surprise, dramatic moments of all kinds, the magic beauty of the costumes modelled on certain ritualistic patterns, brilliant lighting, vocal, incantational beauty, attractive harmonies, rare musical notes, object colours,[1] the physical rhythm of the moves whose build and fall will be wedded to the beat of moves familiar to all, the tangible appearance of new, surprising objects, masks, puppets many feet high, abrupt lighting changes, the physical action of lighting stimulating heat and cold, and so on.

Staging: This archetypal theatre language will be formed around staging not simply viewed as one degree of refraction of the script on stage, but as the starting point for theatrical creation. And the old duality between author and producer will disappear, to be replaced by a kind of single Creator using and handling this language, responsible both for the play and the action.

Stage Language: We do not intend to do away with dialogue, but to give words something of the significance they have in dreams.

Moreover we must find new ways of recording this language, whether these ways are similar to musical notation or to some kind of code.

As to ordinary objects, or even the human body, raised to the dignity of signs, we can obviously take our inspiration from hieroglyphic characters not only to transcribe these signs legibly so they can be reproduced at will, but to compose exact symbols on stage that are immediately legible.

Then again, this coding and musical notation will be valuable as a means of vocal transcription.

Since the basis of this language is to initiate a special use of inflexions, these must take up a kind of balanced harmony, a subsidary exaggeration of speech able to be reproduced at will.

Similarly the thousand and one facial expressions caught in the form of masks, can be listed and labelled so they may directly and symbolically participate in this tangible stage language, independently of their particular psychological use.

Furthermore, these symbolic gestures, masks, postures, individual or group moves, whose countless meanings constitute an important part of the tangible stage language of evocative gestures, emotive arbitrary postures, the wild pounding of rhythms and sound, will be multiplied, added to by a kind of mirroring of the gestures and postures, consisting of the accumulation of all the impulsive gestures, all the abortive postures, all the lapses in the mind and of the tongue by which speech's incapabilities are revealed,[2] and on occasion we will not fail to turn to this stupendous existing wealth of expression.

Besides, there is a tangible idea of music where sound enters like a character, where harmonies are cut in two and become lost precisely as words break in.

Connections, levels, are established between one means of expression and another; even lighting can have a predetermined intellectual meaning.

Musical Instruments: These will be used as objects, as part of the set.

Moreover they need to act deeply and directly on our sensibility through the senses, and from the point of view of cruelty they invite research into utterly unusual sound properties and vibrations which present-day musical instruments do not possess, urging us to use ancient or forgotten instruments or to invent new ones. Apart from music, research is also needed into instruments and appliances based on special refining and new alloys which can reach a new scale in the octave and produce an unbearably piercing sound or noise.[3]

Lights – Lighting: The lighting equipment currently in use in the theatre is no longer adequate. The particular action of light on the mind comes into play, we must discover oscillating light effects, new ways of diffusing lighting in waves, sheet lighting like a flight of fire-arrows. The colour scale of the equipment currently in use must be revised from start to finish. Fineness, density and opacity factors must be reintroduced into lighting, so as to produce special tonal properties, sensations of heat, cold, anger, fear and so on.

Costume: As to costume, without believing there can be any uniform stage costume that would be the same for all plays, modern dress will be avoided as much as possible not because of a fetishistic superstition for the past, but because it is perfectly obvious certain age-old costumes of ritual intent, although they were once fashionable, retain a revealing beauty and appearance because of their closeness to the traditions which gave rise to them.

269

ANTONIN ARTAUD

The Stage – The Auditorium: We intend to do away with stage and auditorium, replacing them by a kind of single, undivided locale without any partitions of any kind and this will become the very scene of the action. Direct contact will be established between the audience and the show, between actors and audience, from the very fact that the audience is seated in the centre of the action, is encircled and furrowed by it. This encirclement comes from the shape of the house itself.

Abandoning the architecture of present-day theatres, we will rent some kind of barn or hangar along lines culminating in the architecture of some churches, holy places, or certain Tibetan temples.

This building will have special interior height and depth dimensions. The auditorium will be enclosed within four walls stripped of any ornament, with the audience seated below, in the middle, on swivelling chairs[4] allowing them to follow the show taking place around them. In effect, the lack of a stage in the normal sense of the word will permit the action to extend itself to the four corners of the auditorium. Special places will be set aside for the actors and action in the four cardinal points of the hall. Scenes will be acted in front of washed walls designed to absorb light. In addition, overhead galleries run right around the circumference of the room as in some Primitive paintings. These galleries will enable actors to pursue one another from one corner of the hall to the other as needed, and the action can extend in all directions at all perspective levels of height and depth. A shout could be transmitted by word of mouth from one end to the other with a succession of amplifications and inflexions. The action will unfold, extending its trajectory from floor to floor, from place to place, with sudden outbursts flaring up in different spots like conflagrations. And the show's truly illusive nature will not be empty words any more than the action's direct, immediate hold on the spectators. For the action, diffused over a vast area, will require the lighting for one scene and the varied lighting for a performance to hold the audience as well as the characters – and physical lighting methods, the thunder and wind whose repercussions will be experienced by the spectators, will correspond with several actions at once, several phases in one action with the characters clinging together like swarms, will endure all the onslaughts of the situations and the external assaults of weather and storms.

However, a central site will be retained which, without acting as a stage properly speaking, enables the body of the action to be concentrated and brought to a climax whenever necessary.

Objects – Masks – Props: Puppets, huge masks, objects of strange proportions appear by the same right as verbal imagery, stressing the physical aspect of all imagery and expression – with the corollary that all objects requiring a stereotyped physical representation will be discarded or disguised.

Decor: No decor. Hieroglyphic characters, ritual costume, thirty foot high effigies of King Lear's beard in the storm, musical instruments as tall as men, objects of unknown form and purpose are enough to fulfill this function.

Topicality: But, you may say, theatre so removed from life, facts or present-day activities . . . news and events, yes! Anxieties, whatever is profound about them, the prerogative of the few, no! In the *Zohar*, the story of the Rabbi Simeon is as inflammatory as fire, as topical as fire.

Works: We will not act written plays but will attempt to stage productions straight from subjects, facts or known works. The type and lay-out of the auditorium itself governs the show as no theme, however vast, is precluded to us.

Show: We must revive the concept of an integral show. The problem is to express it, spatially nourish and furnish it like tap-holes drilled into a flat wall of rock, suddenly generating geysers and bouquets of stone.

The Actor: The actor is both a prime factor, since the show's success depends on the effectiveness of his acting, as well as a kind of neutral, pliant factor since he is rigorously denied any individual initiative. Besides, this is a field where there are no exact rules. And there is a wide margin dividing a man from an instrument, between an actor required to give nothing more than a certain number of sobs and one who has to deliver a speech, using his own powers of persuasion.

Interpretation: The show will be coded from start to finish, like a language. Thus no moves will be wasted, all obeying a rhythm, every character being typified to the limit, each gesture, feature and costume to appear as so many shafts of light.

Cinema: Through poetry, theatre contrasts pictures of the unformulated with the crude visualisation of what exists. Besides, from an action viewpoint, one cannot compare a cinema image, however poetic it may be, since it is restricted by the film, with a theatre image which obeys all life's requirements.

Cruelty: There can be no spectacle without an element of cruelty as the basis of every show. In our present degenerative state, metaphysics must be made to enter the mind through the body.

The Audience: First, this theatre must exist.

Translated by Victor Corti

NOTES

1 Colours of objects (*couleurs des objets*).
2 While the Surrealists tended to avoid mention of Freud, Artaud's phrasing, *toutes les attitudes manquées . . . tous les lapsus de l'esprit et de la langue*, distinctly brings him to mind.
3 Artaud's word *lancinants* means monotonous, insistent and repetitive, rather than piercing. It is likely that the tolling of the great bell of Chartres Cathedral that he recorded for his production of *The Cenci* is an example of the kind of sound he had in mind. He said in an interview: 'The Tibetan Book of the Dead insists on the power of sound caught by the human ear . . . and everyone knows that the repetition of sound acts in a hypnotic way' (*Œuvres Complètes*, vol. 5, Paris, Gallimard, 1964, p. 299).
4 The idea of swivel chairs is beguiling if cost is no object, and has been tried out in Victor Garcia's Paris production of Arrabal's *Car Cemetery*. But Artaud's phrase *chaises mobiles* means moveable chairs, i.e. unlike the fixed variety normally required in theatres. It is this that would allow the action (and actors) to 'furrow' or plough through the audience.

From An Affective Athleticism (1935)

One must grant the actor a kind of affective musculature matching the bodily localisation of our feelings.

An actor is like a physical athlete, with this astonishing corollary; his affective organism is similar to the athlete's, being parallel to it like a double,[1] although they do not act on the same level.

The actor is a heart athlete.

In his case the whole man is also separated into three worlds; the affective area is his own.

It belongs to him organically.

The muscular movements of physical exertion are a likeness, a double of another exertion, located in the same points as stage acting movements.

The actor relies on the same pressure points an athlete relies on to run, in order to hurl a convulsive curse whose course is driven inward.

Similar anatomical bases can be found in all the feints in boxing, all-in-wrestling, the hundred metres, the high jump and the movements of the emotions, since they all have the same physical support points.

With this further rider that the moves are reversed and in anything to do with breathing, for instance, an actor's body relies on breathing while with a wrestler, a physical athlete, the breathing relies on his body.

The question of breathing is of prime importance; it is inversely proportional to external expression.

The more inward and restrained the expression, the more ample, concentrated and substantial breathing becomes, full of resonances.

Whereas breathing is compressed in short waves for ample, fiery externalised acting.

We can be sure that every mental movement, every feeling, every leap in human affectivity has an appropriate breath.

These breathing *tempi* have a name taught us by the Cabala, for they form the human heart and the gender of our emotional activity.

An actor is merely a crude empiricist, a practitioner guided by vague instinct.

Yet on no consideration does this mean we should teach him to rave.

What is at stake is to end this kind of wild ignorance in the midst of which all present theatre moves, as if through a haze, constantly faltering. A gifted actor instinctively knows how to tap and radiate certain powers. But he would be astonished if he were told those powers which make their own substantial journey *through the senses* existed, for he never realised they could actually exist.

To use his emotions in the same way as a boxer uses his muscles, he must consider a human being as a Double, like the Kha[2] of the Egyptian mummies, like an eternal ghost radiating affective powers.

As a supple, never-ending apparition, a form aped by the true actor, imposing the forms and picture of his own sensibility on it.

Theatre has an effect on this Double, this ghostly effigy it moulds, and like all ghosts this apparition has a long memory. The heart's memory endures and an actor certainly thinks with his heart, for his heart holds sway. . . .

To reforge the links, the chain of a rhythm when audiences saw their own real lives in a show, we must allow audiences to identify with the show breath by breath and beat by beat.

It is not enough for the audience to be riveted by the show's magic and this will never happen unless we know where *to affect them*. We have had enough of chance magic or poetry which has no skill underlying it.

In theatre, poetry and skill must be associated as one from now on.

Every emotion has an organic basis and an actor charges his emotional voltage by developing his emotions within him.

The key to throwing the audience into a magical trance is to know in advance what pressure points must be affected in the body. But theatre poetry has long become unaccustomed to this invaluable kind of skill.

To be familiar with the points of localisation in the body is to reforge the magic links.

Using breathing's hieroglyphics, I can rediscover a concept of divine theatre. . . .

N.B. – In Europe no one knows how to scream any more, particularly actors in a trance no longer know how to cry out, since they do nothing but talk, having forgotten they have a body on stage, they have also lost the use of their throats. Abnormally shrunk, these throats are no longer organs but monstrous, talking abstractions. French actors now only know how to talk.

Translated by Victor Corti

NOTES

1 Artaud chose to use this term in the title of the book where his article appears, *The Theatre and its Double*. He explains it briefly in a letter: 'if theatre is the double of life, life is the double of true theatre . . . . This title will reflect all the doubles of theatre that I believe I have found for so many years: metaphysics, plague, cruelty.'
2 The soul, which could dwell either in the body or an image, and which continued after death.

Antonin Artaud (1896–1948), French actor, director, writer, and poet, acted in productions by Dullin, Lugné-Poe and Pitoëff, and in films of Abel Gance and Carl Dreyer. A founding member of the surrealist group in 1924 and director of its 'Bureau of Surrealist Research', he prepared the third number of their journal, *The Surrealist Revolution*, in 1925. His first production was in 1926 for his newly formed Alfred Jarry Theatre. He was ejected from the surrealist group the following year, when Breton (its main spokesman), Aragon and Eluard joined the Communist Party. Breton's criticism was of Artaud's '*isolated* pursuit of the stupid literary venture', which is odd in the context of Artaud's onslaught on literary theatre. It was Breton who held (in his second surrealist manifesto) that surrealism is 'situated first of all almost exclusively on the plane of language' (i.e. verbal language), while Artaud's theatre refused to be so situated. The Theatre of Cruelty itself achieved only one production, based on Shelley's *Cenci*. For Artaud's understanding of the word 'cruelty' see his letter to Jean Paulhan of 12 September 1932: 'I use the word cruelty in the cosmic sense of rigour, of implacable necessity, in the gnostic sense of a whirlwind of life which devours the dark, in the sense of that pain without whose implacable necessity life would not know how to function' (*Œuvres Complètes*, vol. 5, Paris, Gallimard, 1964, p. 155). Another kind of cruelty took charge of his life when he was committed to a mental institution for ten years. Though finally released thanks to the playwright Adamov and friends, its wartime regime of malnutrition and electroshock left its mark, and he never resumed theatre work. 'An Affective Athleticism' remained his main statement about acting. While it may not rebut Grotowski's criticism that he left no concrete technique behind him, it opens a path towards one, which influenced notably the Living Theatre.

69

JUDITH MALINA

Notes on a Ritual Tragedy (1952)

How shall I convey the emergence of power out of what has in itself no power? To underline the passion of the playwright and the priestess when they say (in holy concord):

"It's a lot of shit, but that's how we do it."

That is how we do it. Because the play is a ritual. Any play is a ritual, but in this play the ritual is overt and we speak out about it with real brazenness, saying over and over: we haven't the strength and yet we can give the strength.

Here is the eastern ritual called the Taurobolium in which the initiate is bathed in blood of the sacrificial bull and emerges from the pit reborn. This story places us again in the pit and calls us again to partake of the rites that our sophistication long discarded, and then . . .

The arrogance to require the audience to partake! That is, to admit the *presence* of these hundreds of people.

We are the creators in an art where every night hundreds of people are ignored, a pretense is made that they do not exist; and then we wonder that the actor has grown apart from society; and *then* we wonder that the art itself staggers lamely behind its hope of being part of life.

How shall I convey my belief in what the playwright says? The *I Ching* says, "It is the Creative that begets things but they are brought to birth by the receptive." And it says of me further, "The person in question is not in an independent position, but is acting as an assistant. This means that he must achieve something." I consulted this book of ancient Chinese oracle not only for myself but for my audience. To allow ourselves to be led, all of us assistants in the ritual, which hasn't any power, but from which power is derived. The play does not take place in pagan Rome. Believe me, believe me that it takes place in the theatre. In this theatre and *tonight*. How shall we (in concord) derive power from the action? When the priestess says: "Where is the power to come from? I haven't got it," – say that it comes from the art of the play, and that it comes out *to* us, and now we have got it.

That's how we do it.

This piece is a programme note for 'The best new play that I know', Paul Goodman's *Faustina* (1948), a parable about the wife of Marcus Aurelius.

Judith Malina (b. 1926), American actor and director, was born in Germany, the daughter of a Rabbi. Escaping the Nazis, the family came to New York. There she studied acting and directing under another German exile, Piscator, and formed the Living Theatre with Julian Beck in 1951. Her *Diaries 1947–1957* give a vivid picture of these years. In 1963 they were evicted from their theatre for non-payment of taxes, and moved to Europe, where they toured four productions. The group's physicality, tribal image, challenge of the audience, anarchist messages and demand for 'paradise now' made considerable impact on the younger generation of Europe's capital cities, for whom they provided a free-wheeling dramatic rehearsal for the protests and student risings of 1968.

70

JERZY GROTOWSKI

Methodical Exploration (1967)

I

What is the Bohr Institute?

Bohr and his team founded an institution of a quite extraordinary nature. It is a meeting place where physicists from different countries experiment and take their first steps into the "no man's land" of their profession. Here they compare their theories and draw from the "collective memory" of the Institute.

This "memory" keeps a detailed inventory of all the research done, including even the most audacious, and is continually enriched with new hypotheses and results obtained by the physicists.

The late Niels Bohr and his collaborators tried to discover in this ocean of common research certain guiding trends. They provided an instigation and inspiration in the sphere of their discipline. Thanks to the work of the men to whom they gave both a welcome and a stimulation, they were able to compile essential data and profit from the industrial potentialities of the most developed countries throughout the world.

The Bohr Institute has fascinated me for a long time as a model illustrating a certain type of activity. Of course the theatre is not a scientific discipline, and even less so the art of the actor on whom my attention is centred. However, the theatre, and in particular the technique of the actor, cannot – as Stanislavski maintained – be based solely on inspiration or on other such unpredictable factors as talent explosion, the sudden and surprising growth of creative possibilities, etc. Why? Because unlike the other artistic disciplines, the actor's creation is imperative: i.e. situated within a determined lapse of time and even at a precise moment. An actor cannot wait for a surge of talent nor for a moment of inspiration.

How, then, can these factors be made to appear when they are needed? By obliging the actor who wishes to be creative to master a method.

II

In our opinion, the conditions essential to the art of acting are the following, and should be made the object of a methodical investigation:

a   To stimulate a process of self-revelation, going back as far as the subconscious, yet canalizing this stimulus in order to obtain the required reaction.
b   To be able to articulate this process, discipline it and convert it into signs. In concrete terms, this means to construct a score whose notes are tiny elements of contact, reactions to the stimuli of the outside world: what we call "give and take".
c   To eliminate from the creative process the resistances and obstacles caused by one's own organism, both physical and psychic (the two forming a whole).

How can the laws which govern such personal and individual processes be expounded objectively? How can one merely define objective laws without giving a "recipe" (for all "recipes" only end in banality)?

We believe that in order to fulfil this individuality, it is not a matter of learning new things, but rather of ridding oneself of old habits. For each individual actor it must be clearly established what it is that blocks his intimate associations, thus causing his lack of decision, the chaos of his expression and his lack of discipline; what prevents him from experiencing the feeling of his own freedom, that his organism is completely free and powerful, and that nothing is beyond his capabilities. In other words, how can the obstacles be eliminated?

We take away from the actor that which shuts him off, but we do not teach him how to create – for example how to play Hamlet, in what consists the tragic gesture, how to act a farce – for it is precisely in this "how" that the seeds of banality and of the clichés that defy creation are planted.

To do research such as this is to place oneself already on the borders of scientific disciplines such as phonology, psychology, cultural anthropology, semiology, etc.

An institute which devotes itself to research of this kind should, like the Bohr Institute, be a place for meetings, observations and the distillation of experiments collected by the most fruitful individuals in this field from different theatres in every country. Taking into account the fact that the domain on which our attention is focussed is not a scientific one and not everything in it can be defined (indeed, many things must not be), we nevertheless try to determine our aims with all the precision and consequence proper to scientific research.

The actor who works here is already a professional for, not only his creative act but also the laws which govern it, become the object of his preoccupations. An institute for methodical research is not to be confused with a school that trains actors and whose job it is to "launch" them. Nor should this activity be confused with theatre (in the normal sense of the word) although the very essence of the research demands the elaboration of a performance and its confrontation with an audience. One cannot establish a method yet remain aloof from the creative act.

III

I am interested in the actor because he is a human being. This involves two principal points: firstly, my meeting with another person, the contact, the mutual feeling of comprehension and the impression created by the fact that we open ourselves to another being, that we try to understand him: in short, the surmounting of our solitude. Secondly, the attempt to understand oneself through the behaviour of another man, finding oneself in him. If the actor reproduces an act that I have taught him, this is a sort of "dressage". The result is a banal action from a methodical point of view, and in my heart of hearts I find it sterile for nothing has opened up before me. But if, in close collaboration, we reach the point where the actor, released from his daily resistances, profoundly reveals himself through a gesture, then I consider that from a methodical point of view the work has been effective. I shall then be personally enriched, for in that gesture a kind of human experience will have been revealed, something rather special that might be defined as a destiny, a human condition.

This applies to the relationship between the producer and a single actor, but if this concept is extended to the whole troupe, a new perspective opens up onto the limits of this collective life, onto the common ground of our convictions, our beliefs, our superstitions and the conditions of contemporary life.

If such a common ground exists, we will, in all sincerity, inevitably arrive at the confrontation between tradition and contemporaneity, myth and disbelief, the subconscious and the collective imagination.

I do not put on a play in order to teach others what I already know. It is after the production is completed and not before that I am wiser. Any method which does not itself reach out into the unknown is a bad method.

When I say that the action must engage the whole personality of the actor if his reaction is not to be lifeless, I am not talking of something "external" such as exaggerated gestures or tricks. What, then, do I mean? It is a question of the very essence of the actor's calling, of a reaction on his part allowing him to reveal one after the other the different layers of his personality, from the biological-instinctive source via the channel of consciousness and thought, to that summit which is so difficult to define and in which all becomes unity. This act of the total unveiling of one's being becomes a gift of the self which borders on the transgression of barriers and love. I call this a total act. If the actor performs in such a way, he becomes a kind of provocation for the spectator.

From a methodical point of view this is effective for it gives him a maximum of suggestive power on condition, of course, that he avoids chaos, hysteria, exaltation. It must be an objective act: that is to say articulated, disciplined. But above and beyond methodical efficacity, a new perspective also opens up for the spectator. The actor's accomplishment constitutes a transcendence of the half measures of daily life, of the internal conflict between body and soul, intellect and feelings, physiological pleasures and spiritual aspirations. For a moment the actor finds himself outside the semi-engagement and conflict which characterize us in our daily life. Did he do this for the spectator? The expression "for the spectator" implies a certain coquetry, a certain falseness, a bargaining with oneself. One should rather say "in relation to" the spectator or, perhaps, instead of him. It is precisely here that the provocation lies.

I am talking of the method, I am speaking of the surpassing of limits, of a confrontation, of a process of self-knowledge and, in a certain sense, of a therapy. Such a method must remain open – its very life depends on this condition – and is different for each individual. This is how it should be, for its intrinsic nature demands that it be individual.

Translated by Amanda Pasquier and Judy Barba

Jerzy Grotowski (b. 1933), Polish director, founded his Theatre Laboratory in 1959. From research of the kind suggested here, a small number of productions issued, and it was these, first taken outside Poland in 1966, which electrified the theatre world, and established Grotowski in the eyes of many as its new prophet and teacher. The rigorous training and performance disciplines of his actors contrasted decisively with the other major challenge of the time – that of the Living Theatre, who, arriving in Europe in 1964, were attempting to de-inhibit large audiences. Grotowski's group always played to tiny audiences, and eventually he lost interest in playing to audiences at all. From the early 1970s he began increasingly to pursue his interest in human encounter in other ways, via paratheatrical projects, and has worked since to develop a transcultural 'Theatre of Sources'. For a full account, see Jennifer Kumiega's, *The Theatre of Grotowski*, London, Methuen, 1985. The Theatre Laboratory finally disbanded in 1984.

71

LOUISE STEINMAN

FROM *The Knowing Body* (1986)

Learning to be receptive means recognizing one's ability to see both the inner and the outer worlds. The Bushmen of southern Africa refer to their receptivity as "tapping in," a way of being quiet so as to hear "that which is thinking through us." Laurens van der Post has a wonderful description of a Bushman describing this ability to him. The tribesman likens it to seeing van der Post using the telegraph:

> "Wire?" I exclaimed.
> "Yes. A wire, Master. I have seen my own master go many times to the D.C. at Gemsbok Pan and get him to send a wire to the buyers telling them when he is going to trek out to them with his cattle. We Bushman have a wire here," he tapped his chest, "that brings us news."[1]

When Meredith Monk created her opera "Vessel," she used the role of Joan of Arc as a metaphor for the artist who listens to her own voices. Such listening is a challenging thing to do in our culture. Monk wrote of Joan as

> *the receiver of secret information. The belief in the receiving and then the acting on it. The archetypal sybil. If you are lucky, it comes to you. If you force it, you become empty.*[2]

If we learn to "tap in" then we can hear the thinking through, we can remember the dream, we might see the vision. Many artists learn to cultivate those moments just upon waking or just before sleep when images drift by with special intensity. Sometimes they rouse themselves to catch a phrase or to draw a sketch as the dream fades and new light comes in. . . .

As I pointed out earlier, memory is embedded in our very act of seeing and movement seems to be a particularly potent force in unlocking memory's vivid detail. Trisha Brown has an exercise where she asks students to remember the layout of their grandmother's house and then create a movement path within that house of memory. Doing the exercise I found my movement infused with new interest, new meaning, as I sidled around the large bed where my grandparents slept, crawled on my belly under the dining room table where my grandfather played interminable late-night casino games. Brown has commented:

> *Sometimes my dancing is metaphoric, using memory as a resource. Yet what may have been traumatic in, say 1941 makes hardly a ripple today when it is put through the mind and out the body. Still, memory gives a phrase a reality for me and modulates its quality and texture. . . . However, the image, the memory, must occur in performance at precisely the same moment as the action derived from it. Without thinking, there are just physical feats . . .*[3]

Memory is an activation of the mind's eye. In the Memory Theatres of classical times, we stroll through rooms of the imagination, coming upon the objects of value we had deliberately placed there. Our memories are sometimes as vivid as the images of our dreams, sometimes more so. I can still feel the fog of night walks in Edinburgh, see my grandfather carried out the door on a stretcher, breathe the dust of a road in the Cretan hills, and remember the sighting of whales from cliffs in Cornwall and Oregon. Sometimes, as French novelist Marguerite Yourcenar writes,

> These fragments of real fact have the magical intensity of vision glimpsed in my dreams, and on the other hand, certain visions from my dreams have all the weight of lived events . . . Only my reason prevents me from mixing up the two orders of phenomena, but this same reason counsels me to perhaps reconcile them, to put them all together on a plane which is certainly one of unique reality.[4]

Performance offers one of those planes of "unique reality" where memory and dreams, past and present, the everyday and the once-in-a-lifetime are reconciled and woven together upon a single loom of time. . . .

It's not surprising either, that many performers of visual theatre and image performance/dance have explored the imaging of their own anatomy. Dancers and creators of performance are once again like citizens of primal cultures, cultivating the ability to *see with the whole body. Our whole body remembers. Our whole self dreams.*

Not all dreams are healing dreams or contain signs of a cure. We can learn to distinguish between the big dreams and the little dreams, the significant visions and the banal ones. Working with the material of the dream world in performance, one accepts the challenge to be responsible to the depth of the dream and its images.

Other cultures than ours, particularly the ones that thrived in our country before ours, had techniques and rituals for harvesting the information of dreams, and they had a vocabulary for talking about them. For instance, Sarah Greys, a Swampy Cree elder who has lived in northern Manitoba for over ninety years, has stated in an interview:

When I was younger I did not feel comfortable listening to people's dreams. I could not find the right way to hold myself, standing, or with my hands on my face. I grew worry about this. Because of this I went to the marshes, and it was then I believe I went into . . . into my heron. I was my heron then, probably for some years, and I have no human things I remember from that time. But I can tell you that when I came out of that, when I walked from my heron into my own walking again, I felt much better about listening to dreams. I stood my own walking again. I could remember the water around my legs, which was good for dream-listening. From then on I was known as a person you could talk dreams with.[5]

Though my own ancestral culture has within its literature a wealth of recorded dreams and visions (Daniel's, Ezekiel's, Joseph's interpretation of Pharoah's dream), it was not until I began to study performance that I became a "person you could talk dreams with." It was in Meredith Monk's classes at Naropa Institute that I began to keep a dream journal with regularity, and where I learned physical dream-remembering techniques. In one, for example, you find a gesture or a posture from a dream and then intensify it until the tension brings the dream back to the body. How does a dream character occupy space? What does dream dialogue, spoken out loud, sound like? How does it make you feel?

Another dream-sharing technique is the Dream Circle. The dreamer sits in the middle of a circle of the assembled. In his or her hands are rattles or noise makers of some kind. She begins to recite her dream, eyes closed, clacking the rattles whenever she wishes to emphasize a word, an image. The others walk around the dreamer in a circle. They attempt to feel the dreamer's vision in their own bodies. They receive the dream from the dreamer, take it on themselves. Among Native Americans, from whom we borrow this ritual, it was used for its curative value (to dissipate the power a vision may have held on the dreamer). For performers it is an important technique for entering the world of dream and vision. For if one is to actualize an image from a dream, integrate dream imagery into a performance, and if the performance is to be realized in collaboration with others, then they too must feel the weight and texture of the dream. The dreamer repeats the dream over and over and the repetition of the words and images helps the participants absorb the meaning of them, empathize with them. In the rehearsal space, a ritual is created which takes the dream out of the totally personal, away from the purely intellectual, and allows it to permeate the body.

When Susan Banyas and I began to collaborate on a performance dealing with two women's friendship and its significance in a troubled world ("Trails to Treasures (it could be you)"), I dreamed we were dancing in the full moon in a beet field in Roumania. We leapt from beet hollow to beet hollow in the red rich dirt. Finally we were interrupted by men

283

carrying heavy stones. In the dream, I asked Susan why we were dancing in the beet field. She replied it was because she was "half-Roumanian, and half midwife."

The beet is a root crop. Its etymology connects it to the word for *bed*, that which is under the ground, the foundation, the place for memory. We are, through performance, reaching down to the bedrock of memory through the root systems of dream, whose juices course through nerve, muscle, and skin.

It is in the studio that we try to bring the dreamwork to the light of day where we live. Susan and I created beet dances, we spoke and danced as the beets, as the heavy stones. We became midwives to the birth of the essence of the dream which we would use in the staged work. Sometimes it may be the opening night of performance when the information gleaned from the presence of witnesses (the audience) brings the full realization of the dream image into one's body/mind. It is a very powerful feeling, to form this bridge between night and day. It may be in the quality of the movement, the intensity and hue of the lighting, the manner of the character's speech, the relationship of these elements to each other, the positioning of objects and people with a peculiarity that has its own logic as the dream does – any or all of this may allow the dream image to radiate its essence. Each dreamer dreams with a chemistry, as Yourcenar says, "that is his alone." But by sharing my dreams with my collaborators and hearing theirs, we create a pool of dream images from which we may all draw in common. Hopefully the result is insight into the world we all share and whose problems we collectively face. To create performance of the inner eye, of the Foreseen, the performer brings back from the dreamworld visions of variously colored intensity, helps his or her co-creators to feel the weight of these visions within their own beings. Then together they enter that vision to communicate it to the audience. The performers are "available" to the audience, and their performance is the mirror in which the audience may read its own meaning in the image. . . .

NOTES

1   Laurens van der Post, *Lost World of the Kalahari* (New York: William Morrow, 1958), 260.

2   Meredith Monk, unpublished notes for "Vessel." Courtesy of Meredith Monk.

3   Trisha Brown and Yvonne Rainer, "A Conversation about Glacial Decoy," *October* 10 (Fall 1979): 31.

4   Marguerite Yourcenar, "Recurring Landscapes: the varieties of oneiric experience" in *Parabola* 7, no. 2:91.

5   Sarah Greys, "Autobiography of a Cree Woman", trans. by Howard Norman, excerpted in *New Wilderness Letter: Special Dream-Work Issue* 10 (September 1981): 2–3.

Louise Steinman, American dancer and performance artist, co-founder of performance company SO&SO&SO&SO, guest artist and lecturer at the Center for Experimental and Interdisciplinary Arts at San Francisco State University. She has toured North America and Europe with Ping Chong and his Fuji Theatre Company. Her book, *The Knowing Body*, from which the above is taken, quotes and describes work by a number of other dancers and performance artists, including Meredith Monk, Trisha Brown, Spalding Gray, Wendy Perron and Whoopi Goldberg.

72

RACHEL ROSENTHAL

From *Rachel's Brain* (1991)

The pieces that have happened since '81 have been more concerned with what I call the big picture. At first it was "just" nuclear power, which was a big issue and still is one. But nuclear power is only part of a larger picture. . . .

Rachel's Brain (1987) is an overview of concerns I have. I realized when I decided to do it that most of the problems that I have with the way we are and the way things are and the way the Earth is, stem from the human brain and what it has wrought. That's why I wanted to do a piece about the brain. I started to do my usual research and became totally overwhelmed because the amount of knowledge is tremendous, but the amount of mystery is even greater. There is much that is unknown and hasn't been understood about the way the mind works and its relationship to the brain. Even though I wasn't able, in a short time, to render the state of science on the subject, I could at least look at my own brain and my own mind and try to understand where I am and in what way I am "Every-Woman." I could use myself as a persona that exemplifies where the human species is now. That's what the piece is about. I tried to pull in different extreme personae to express that. I bring in Marie Antoinette. She's got a wig and on top of that is a high three-master ship. She enters and does an operatic *sprechtstimme*[1] delivery of an aria. She epitomizes the Age of Enlightenment, the age of rationality, of logical thinking, of the cerebral cortex. She at first brings in this tremendous haughtiness and hubris of being human and of having this higher apparatus up there. She's completely cut off from her body. It's a metaphor I work on both the mind and body level and also on the social level. She looks at people and says: "The others are below. The others foraging in the dirt for grubs are beasts." She is the "higher" human. She ends up having to be beheaded; it's the only way out.

At the other end of the spectrum I have Koko the gorilla; Koko has been taught American Sign Language. I play Koko and Koko's trainer, Penny, the scientist who is teaching her. Koko is completely at ease in her body and with nature and she just loves the Great Mother. She has no problems with the food chain or with her body, no problems with anything; she's rooted in nature, in beauty and in love. She has trouble, however, with language. I try to show that language is what splits us in little pieces. During that scene you see her trying to sign, trying to actually do what she's being taught, to communicate with *us*. *We* are not communicating with *her*. She's been taught that the only way she can do that is by learning these little pieces of language, words, the way we speak. She's trying hard to do that. Penny teaches her to sign "To be or not to be" and "I think, therefore I am." At first Koko doesn't get it right, and goes into flights of ecstatic talk which Penny can't hear, but which the audience hears. She communicates to the audience her ecstasy about life. Then she suddenly remembers what she is supposed to do, and she tries to sign "To be or not to be"!

The piece is structured, as many of my pieces are, in scenes, a deconstruction of the theme. It's approached in different ways so that new aspects of the concept can be presented in each scene.

I work with a cauliflower. The cauliflower is the human brain, right? At one point I do a thing about the hunger of the mind. The human brain has evolved into empty spaces which are not yet programmed, so I do a metaphor between the hunger for filling these empty spaces and the hunger for food, for nourishment, and the greed of acquisition. It is both a funny and horrendous scene where I attack the brain. I call for brains and say, "Kill me another." And then a cauliflower drops down from the rafters like a dead duck and I attack it with cleavers and knives and I put pieces of it in a blender and puree it. It shows savagery existing side by side with our higher intellect, and how fundamentally split we are.

At the end of this piece, right after Koko, I come back as myself and I do a ritual with earth and plant the brain (a cauliflower) in the earth, and water it with a little watering can. I talk about the wonder and miracle of this organ and its relationship to consciousness of the Mother. I didn't want to end the piece on a comfortable note of oneness and warmth and redemption because that's not where we're at right now; I didn't want to let the audience off the hook. So I give a glimpse of wholeness but then I pull back and get scared, and I say that going down inside myself is too frightening. I don't want to do that. I take on the personae of those who seek redemption outside themselves.

I say, "Why mud pies when Higher Consciousness beckons?" So I leave the Earth and start up (I rise up in an hydraulic lift that has been rented for the purpose). I look for spirituality, salvation, being "the chosen one," somewhere up there. I keep going up higher and higher until I'm almost out of sight, and there is nobody there. No *deus ex machina*. I say, "Hello, anybody there?" Then I look down and it's a drop of thirty feet. There's a moment of panic and I ask, "The water is rising, the air is thinning, the deserts are growing, the missiles are coming, so where the fuck are you?" Then a slide of the Earth comes on and I say, "Now you see it," and then it disappears, and I continue "now you don't." The lights go out and I yell, "What the hell am I doing up here? Put me down!" and my voice echoes in the darkness. The idea is that so long as we look outside ourselves and outside the planet and hope to be hoisted up and saved while the holocaust rages below (really and figuratively), we're just not going to make it.

This persona that I'm using at the end is part society, but it's also part me because everything that I do has personal components. I notice how in my personal life and in my existence I know these things, all the right answers, I know what should be done, how I should be, all the right moves, but I don't do it. I escape, I avoid, I procrastinate. I'm scared and I don't fulfill, I don't actualize, I don't do what I should do, the same as everyone else. At the end of this piece, I join in this way all of human kind. There's a great deal of identification that happens at the end that I hope an audience can empathize with, see where I am at that point and also see the mirror, see who *they* are. It places responsibility with each individual. There is a choice and we have to see that choice, we have to decide how to choose.

NOTE

1 Speaking voice.

Rachel Rosenthal (b. 1926) studied theatre with Piscator and Barrault, dance with Merce Cunningham and art with Hans Hoffman. In 1956 she founded an improvisation group in Los Angeles, Instant Theatre. In the late 1960s she turned to sculpture, and became involved with Womanspace, a group that opened up women's art galleries. She exhibited in the Los Angeles Women's Building (set up by Judy Chicago and others), and was prominent in the Women's Art Movement. Her move into performance art dates from 1975. Her performances are characterised by striking visual images and involve elements of autobiography, ritual, healing and exorcism, as well as humour. She writes: 'In theatre you mostly work from or with a text, in performance you squeeze out yourself, you dredge it up from your unconscious. It is a process of giving it a form from the inner to the outer' (*Drama Review*, vol. 32, no. 1, Spring 1988, p. 170). The piece here is drawn from an extensive account of her development and work. See too: Eelka Lampe, 'Rachel Rosenthal Creating her Selves' (ibid., pp. 170–90).

Part V

THE GLOBAL DIMENSION

We have an Africa and Asia inside us and the complete truth is global.
Peter Brook

INTRODUCTION

1

For European theatre the century began with the discovery of the Japanese. In 1900 at the World Exhibition in Paris, and later in major cities across the continent, audiences were initiated into an exotic theatrical world as they watched the visiting kabuki company of twenty actors and musicians led by Sada Yacco and her husband Kawakami.

Ignorant of the Japanese language and of the meanings conveyed by their stage conventions, Adolphe Appia judged their performance 'exterior, almost exclusively designed for the eye'. But he acclaimed its aesthetic taste and 'painted plasticity', using them to attack 'the grotesque decorative overcharge of Western productions'.[1] By contrast, Georg Fuchs stressed its deep emotional impact: 'Japanese theatre reaches heights of intensity of which we have no idea and does so simply by stylistic means.' Its supremacy of style has a 'vital connection with fundamental principles, that is, with the elementary physical sources of mimic art', and with dance, acrobatics, wrestling and fencing, the skills he was keen to promote.[2] Meanwhile Gordon Craig, ignoring or ignorant of the origin of kabuki in all-women shows, deplored the intrusion of a woman into the male preserve of Japanese theatre, and drew a different lesson. 'Before the art of the stage can revive', he propounds, 'women must have passed off the boards'.[3] They had in fact been banned from the boards in 1630; and Craig may have been right in imputing to western influence the final slackening of this ban in the late nineteenth century; when Sada Yacco eventually returned to Japan she became the first person to present western plays there. But whatever the biases that reveal themselves, one thing is evident: in theatre an age of global dialogue had begun.

From then on the influence of non-western theatre upon our own has been deep and often crucial to new developments. But the global perspectives of the west often differ from those of the rest of the globe. The west seeks what it believes it lacks, and converts what it sees to its own uses, as the responses to Sada Yacco's company illustrate. Slanted readings are unavoidable. For a number of years interest continued to focus on

291

Japanese theatre, with little attention to other Asian forms, yet contradictory lessons continued to be drawn from it. W. B. Yeats, for example, made large use of Japanese conventions in his later plays as part of his attempt to initiate an 'unpopular' theatre, and to create a form of drama that was 'distinguished, indirect and symbolic . . . an aristocratic form'. He praised his models, 'certain noble plays of Japan', for holding their distance 'against a pushing world' and allowing us entry into a 'deep of the mind'.[4] Sergei Eisenstein, however, equally impressed, compares Japanese theatre to a football match. Its team of autonomous elements create a play of startling effects close to that recommended in his 'Montage of Attractions'. At the same time its conventions are 'profoundly logical', designed to convey clear meanings via traditional semiotic codes.[5] Yeats had been reading Noh, while Eisenstein had seen Kabuki. If they had each come across the other form, their accounts might have been different. But how different it is hard to say. They would certainly have been gazing with different eyes, and may well have continued to discover something that meshed with their own vision.

As attention widened to other Asian theatre, the scope for contradictory impressions increased. Both Bertolt Brecht and Antonin Artaud looked east, and both drew significantly on what they believed they found there. Brecht was deeply impressed by a Beijing Opera performance by Mei Lan-fang and his troupe, which he saw in 1935 on a visit to Moscow. This experience, plus the assumed encounter there with the Russian formalist concept of 'estrangement' already discussed (p. 80), resulted the following year in his essay 'Alienation Effects in Chinese Acting'. The effects he notes amount to a blueprint for the Brechtian actor. He discovers in Chinese performance both an attitude and a set of corresponding techniques. A range of emotions are represented, but the actor depicts or signals them rather than pretends he is feeling them. Brecht's appreciation of this leads directly into the briefing on the 'A-effect . . . that a new theatre will need', already included in Part II.

Brecht's ideas on acting were well advanced before he saw Mei Lan-fang. But they were not articulated in one place as a series of clear principles. At the least, Mei Lan-fang and his troupe had strongly confirmed the theatrical effectiveness of such principles. Further influence of Chinese theatre is apparent in works like The Good Person of Szechuan and The Caucasian Chalk Circle, where Brecht availed himself freely of its narrative methods, particularly the quoting and story-telling techniques that he expounded three years after seeing Mei Lan-fang in his article 'The Street Scene'.

This is not to say the Chinese would have agreed with him. 'The first thing to do,' advises Mei Lan-fang, 'is to forget you are acting and make yourself one with the part'.[6] And Mao himself so was carried away by a Beijing Opera performance that he began weeping noisily at the victim's plight, until finally, unable to restrain himself, he rose to his feet to urge the audience that revolution was the only answer to such oppression, regardless that his

belt was loosened and his trousers had fallen down.[7] This argues considerably more emotional involvement, on stage and off, than Brecht envisages.

Artaud's encounter with Asian theatre took place at a critical time for him
in 1931 when he saw a Balinese dance-theatre troupe near Paris. His 'Alfred
Jarry Theatre' had collapsed two years earlier, and it may have been the
Balinese who reinspired him with the idea of a new project – the one he is
chiefly remembered by, the 'Theatre of Cruelty'. As with Brecht, the performance provided him with an important model, and in relation to his own
ideas, much to ponder. Given the setbacks he had experienced in his
attempts to put those ideas into practice, it was doubly important for
Artaud to witness what he believed to be their realisation. Though not
conversant with Balinese conventions, he was none the less persuaded
that he was seeing and hearing just such a theatre 'language' as he was
dreaming of: a language which could speak to the mind below and above
the level of verbal concepts, and touch those nodal points of consciousness
that the eloquent speeches of French drama could never reach.

2

Whatever the misreadings involved, western theatre has clearly gained
much from these encounters. But the benefit has not always been reciprocal. In the rest of the world the first step towards a healthy theatrical culture
has often meant developing a resistance to western material and western
modes.

Wole Soyinka pokes fun at the busy succession of movements these
reflect, likening western theatre to a locomotive picking up loads of fuel,
and progressing in 'a series of intellectual spasms'. This is alien, he argues,
to the African world view, which involves 'a cohesive understanding of
irreducible truths' concerning the space people inhabit, where the community, the earth and the cosmos are presences continually sensed. But
western cultural domination does not decrease because it is alien. Enrique
Buenaventura recounts how he, as director of a company in Columbia, 'felt it
was necessary to be up on plays currently produced in Europe and the US'.[8]
Such plays largely formed their repertory, however thin their relation to the
country they worked in and the people who lived there. For Buenaventura,
as for many after him, to take a stand in the space one lived in eventually
became imperative; and the first step towards it meant stepping out of the
Palace Hotel of western culture onto the ground outside.

Across that ground two paths have been much travelled. One runs
through territory newly decolonised, and heads for a theatre which may
help forge and celebrate a national identity and popular unity. The other
skirts rich estates to run between the shacks of the poor, seeking a theatre
that might aid their empowerment. The writer and director Errol Hill has
trodden the first path, and here argues eloquently for a theatre based on

Caribbean culture and traditions. Looking back to the 1950s, when his efforts towards this goal began, he has said of himself: 'He preached that a national drama meant West Indian plays by West Indian writers about West Indian affairs presented by West Indians primarily for West Indian audiences'; and 'he urged theatre artists to seek inspiration from the indigenous theatre of the folk':[9] the various verbal and performance arts of the Caribbean, whose forms he went on to study extensively. These principles remained central to his campaign for a national theatre, and gave substance to his belief that such a theatre had a role to play in helping to heal the 'wound' effected by colonialism, and to forge an independent cultural identity.

His fellow West Indian, Honor Ford-Smith, has drawn on such arts for a different purpose. Sistren, whose work she outlines, is a Jamaican women's group, originally all street cleaners. Its object is to 'provide a forum for the voices of poor women'. Accordingly Sistren does not confine its activities to drama, nor do its drama workshops necessarily lead to theatre productions: 'The drama can be used for consciousness-raising and skill training in any field.' The spirit of her account may bring to mind the work of Paolo Freire, whose ideas exerted a significant influence throughout the Third World. Freire was concerned to rethink how millions of the impoverished in Latin America might acquire the knowledge and gain the autonomy to begin the process of revolutionary change. Freire stressed the need for mass education, but denied that this meant the imparting of instruction from above. At the root of his work is the idea of dialogue. Through dialogue the learner is involved in an exchange of experience and understanding, can set the agenda of learning, and discover rather than imbibe.

The most direct application of Freire's ideas to theatre is found in the work of the Brazilian Augusto Boal, the title of whose book, *The Theatre of the Oppressed*, echoes Freire's *The Pedagogy of the Oppressed*. Boal worked on a campaign inspired by Freire's ideas to eradicate illiteracy in Peru. For Freire, illiteracy is part of a larger 'culture of silence', in which the plight of the oppressed goes unheard. 'The dependent society is by definition a silent society.'[10] By convention a theatre audience is equally silent; as Appia had long before objected, theatre is 'a school of passivity for the spectators'.[11] To impose such a theatre on peasant spectators is to endorse the condition of their oppression. Boal's methods were developed to allow them a voice. They seek to involve those present actively, either in debate about what they have seen, or in steering the course of the action, or in performing, thus turning them from spectators into what he calls 'spect-actors'. It is often assumed there is less call for such techniques in the western democracies. Boal was unimpressed by this view. Since beginning to work in Europe in the 1970s, he has repeatedly demonstrated their effectiveness, as in the example he describes here.

Boal's recent work largely dispenses with the folk and ethnic forms so emphasised by Errol Hill, though they figure certainly in his long earlier account of popular theatre in Latin America.[12] They figure too in Sistren's work, which draws on 'oral and ritual traditions' and uses 'stories, songs for all occasions, riddles, rhymes and proverbs'. But in a changing world, old forms cannot provide an infallible recipe in any country. Buenaventura maintains that under the impact of American capitalism, the poor in Columbia have lost their folk culture in a process of 'traumatic cross-assimilation'. Errol Hill argues that 'the accretions of an imported culture' should be cast off; but to do this in the confines of theatre when people's lives outside are shaped by such accretions is to set up a safe area at a remove from those lives. Buenaventura believes his company's task is to begin to synthesise what he calls 'the two Columbian cultures'. This move towards synthesis is widely relevant in the world today, and seems likely to be a powerful creative impetus in all the arts in years to come.

3

Whether to work to fortify one's own traditions and resist cross-assimilation; or whether to seek new syntheses which may put them at risk: such choices must be made in the west too, the home now of a multitude of cultures. The remainder of this part speaks for some of them, and is concerned with these choices.

The example of the Teatro Campesino suggests there can be ways of profitably assimilating western modes while renewing one's own. Luis Valdez, its founder, worked initially with the San Francisco Mime Troupe, until the 1965 Grape Strike in Central California moved him to set up a Chicano group with some of the farm workers. The Mime Troupe's lively recipe of clowning, slapstick and broad social satire[13] was carried over and used in a series of punchy, vernacular skits that Valdez calls *actos*. These involved, rather like Commedia dell'Arte, figures standing for group arche-types: Don Coyote the farm labour contractor; Johnny Pachuco, a Chicano-cum-American hoodlum; and Juan Raza, representing the Chicano race. This Chicano focus did not hinder 'considerable cross feeding' between the Campesino, the San Francisco Mime Troupe and the Bread and Puppet Theatre.[14] But Valdez also invokes the theatre of the Mayas and Aztecs, and as time went on, *mitos*, myths, were introduced into the *actos* material, with Quetzalcoatl and Jesus appearing alongside Uncle Sam as reminders of shared roots in a long history.

Such icons may also be reminders of what Ntozake Shange calls, in the title of her piece here, 'unrecovered losses': of 'cut-off lives n limbs.' Like Valdez, Shange is, as she says, 'not an Anglo-Western civilisation person'.[15] The Afro-American culture she comes from draws vitality from being aware of those losses but determined to make them good in new terms. Her own multifarious activities as poet, playwright, novelist, creator of installations and performance artist, are inspired by this spirit, and also by her commitment to explore and affirm the lives of women. To do this, she has said, necessarily involves 'cultural aggression'.[16] In her work she uses 'combat breath'[17] – a phrase from Frantz Fanon's *A Dying Colonialism*, that describes the breathing of those in occupied territory.

Elsewhere, at the California Institute of the Arts, a number of non-Anglo-Western-civilisation persons joined together in 1980 with a different programme. They planned to see just how far they could push the 'traumatic cross-assimilation' of cultures that for Buenaventura had crippled his country's history. Their aim was to 'fuse, hybridise and juxtapose' their various artistic and performing traditions. They offered a mixture of traditional urban Mexican popular theatre, magical realism, kabuki and US multimedia. This apparently surrealist amalgam was a way of embracing reality as they had experienced it since emigrating, and even before that. Guillermo Gómez-Peña, who founded the group, was born in the Spanish Hospital of a Jewish quarter in Mexico City. Walking from district to district there he compares to travelling from continent to continent and from one epoch to another. The aim of the performances was 'the dismantling of a mono-cultural order'.[18] Such an aim is continued in different forms in the work of the Border Arts Workshop that he describes here.

4

A considerable distance separates all this work from that of the remaining Europeans included here: Peter Brook, Eugenio Barba and Hélène Cixous. The theatre they practise steers away from direct participation in day-to-day struggles. Yet 'the dismantling of a mono-cultural order' is central to the work of all three.

Hélène Cixous has written the scripts for two productions of epic scope by the Théâtre du Soleil, one surveying the modern history of Vietnam, the other of India. In the piece concerning the latter included here, she highlights the problem that faced her: 'How could I, a woman of letters, ever offer an illiterate peasant woman her turn to speak without taking that speech back from her, at one stroke of the word, and interring it beneath one of my fine phrases?' Implicitly she points here to a dilemma that haunts all western attempts to reach out to other cultures: that the voice we hear as theirs may be our own. Cixous confronts it as one who has shown herself highly conscious of a parallel problem: of male writers putting their words in women's mouths, to the point where women must struggle to rediscover what their own language is.

For Cixous it is only by rediscovering the ground of our nature that we can begin to sense what we share. A similar view is expressed by Peter Brook: 'Man is more than what his culture defines. Cultural habits go far deeper than the clothes he wears, but they are still only garments to which an unknown life gives body.' That under these garments pulses a shared humanity may be a liberal delusion. But Brook is spelling out here the basis on which much of his work has been founded, and which the nature of that work has put to the test. His group is made up of actors from different continents 'with nothing in common'. The ensemble work they have achieved without damage to their culturally distinctive styles is an impressive demonstration in support of Brook's view. The company's sorties to other continents have been a further test, undertaken to learn how to shed the cultural garments Brook speaks of, and emerge, in Cixous' term, 'naked'; and thus relate to any audience anywhere, whether on a patch of ground in an African village, or in a park before Chicano farm-workers. What is notable is not that they sometimes failed, but that they so often succeeded.

The same is true of Eugenio Barba's group, Odin Theatre, who pursued such work more fully. Barba initially spent three years with Grotowski's Laboratorium and then transferred its methods and aims to Scandinavia. Odin's first shows followed Grotowskian precedent in being designed for studio performance before an audience of sixty. But as Barba has said, 'One can work for years in a recognisable place, behind a door with "theatre" written on it. What happens when the door and its sign are knocked down?'[19] From 1972, the year of Brook's journey through Africa, Odin began performing to 'spectators who don't possess the Culture of Theatre or of Books'.[20] They travelled to poor villages in southern Italy and Sardinia, to a tribe living along the Venezuelan Amazon, and to the Peruvian Andes. Barba's early theatrical grounding in the monastic methods of the Laboratorium might seem a poor preparation for such work. In fact the continuity is deep. Grotowski's study of non-European acting styles, his concentration on the performer, his stripping away of the surrounding theatrical setting, light rigs and sound systems, and his belief in the need for an 'utter opening to another person' and 'a total acceptance of one human being by another'[21] have all remained central to Odin's work.

Odin has shifted though from Peter Brook's search for 'something which makes the same impression anywhere in the world without reference to language'.[22] Odin 'does not look for a "code" that permits communication, but a situation that permits contact between actors and spectators despite their differences and which fascinates precisely because of those differences that separate them'.[23] In Barba's view, the situation that best allows this is one of 'barter'. Odin agreed to perform if the villagers would do so too, in whatever way they chose. 'We wanted them to answer us with their own voice, their own language, that which still binds them together and makes them strong.'[24] This does not solve the dilemma of Hélène Cixous; but it finds a way round it. Odin remained, as Barba admits, a foreign body in remote communities, but one that was involved on equal terms in 'give and take'.[25]

We move here quite far from the institution we normally think of as theatre. 'But what is it that counts?' Barba has asked. 'A preconceived form of theatre, or the attitude one has towards one's surroundings, the manner in which one tries to turn one's "yes" and one's "no" into action when confronted with what one hears and sees?' Those surroundings today cannot be circumscribed: they are as immediate as our neighbours, as large as the world. Those in the pages that follow are aware of this. 'Who are you?' Barba asks himself. 'A loner who vanishes into the desert, or one who, advancing, even losing himself, finishes by making a path?' The paths of the past can be mapped, while those of the future cannot. But in these pages they are surely in the making.

NOTES

1 Adolphe Appia, *Œuvres Complètes*, vol. 2, Lausanne, L'Age d'Homme, 1986, p. 333.
2 Georg Fuchs, *Revolution in the Theatre: Conclusions Concerning the Munich Artists' Theatre*, Ithaca, NY, Cornell University Press, 1959, condensed and adapted by Constance Connor Kuhn from *Die Revolution des Theaters*, Munich, George Muller, 1909; reissued Port Washington, NY, Kennikat Press, 1972, pp. 59–60.
3 Gordon Craig, 'Sada Yacco' in *The Theatre Advancing*, 1919, reprinted New York, Benjamin Blom, 1963, p. 264.
4 W. B. Yeats, 'Introduction to Certain Noble Plays of Japan', in *Essays and Introductions*, London, Macmillan, 1961, p. 154.
5 Sergei Eisenstein, 'An Unexpected Juncture', in *Selected Works, Vol. 1: Writings 1922–34*, ed. Richard Taylor, London, BFI, 1988, p. 116.
6 Mei Lan-fang 'Reflections on My Stage Life', in Wu Zuguang, Huang Zuolin and Mei Shaowu, *Peking Opera and Mei Lin Fan*, Beijing, New World Press, 1980.
7 See Quan Yan Chi, *Mao Tse Dong: Man Not God*, ed. Gale Hadfield, Beijing, Foreign Languages Press, 1992.
8 Enrique Buenaventura, 'Theatre and Culture', *Drama Review*, vol. 14, no. 2 (T46), Winter 1970, p. 151.
9 Errol Hill, 'The Emergence of a National Drama in the West Indies', *Caribbean Quarterly*, vol. 18, no. 4, December 1972, p. 34.
10 Paolo Freire, *Cultural Action for Freedom*, Penguin Books, 1972, p. 59.
11 'Monumentality', 1922, in *Adolphe Appia: Essays, Scenarios and Designs*, eds W. R. Volbach and R. C. Beacham, Ann Arbor, Mich., and London, UMI Research Press, 1989, p. 230.
12 Augusto Boal, *Categorias de Teatro Popular*, Buenos Aires, Ediciones CEPE, 1972.
13 See R. G. Davis, *The San Francisco Mime Troupe: The First Ten Years*, Palo Alto, Ramparts Press, 1975.
14 Ibid., p. 196.
15 Kathleen Betsko and Rachel Koenig, *Interview with Contemporary Women Playwrights*, New York, Beech Tree Books, 1986, p. 366.
16 Ibid., p. 375.
17 Ntozake Shange, *Three Pieces*, New York, Penguin Books, 1982, p. xii.
18 Ibid., p. 56.
19 'Letter from the South of Italy' in Eugenio Barba, *The Floating Islands*, Holstebro, Denmark, Odin Teatret, 1979, p. 120.

20 Fernando Taviani, ibid., p. 2.
21 Jerzy Grotowski, *Towards a Poor Theatre*, Holstebro, Denmark, Odin Teatrets Forlag, 1968, reprinted London, Methuen, 1969, p. 25.
22 Cited in Barba, *The Floating Islands*, op. cit., p. 103.
23 Taviani, ibid., p. 103.
24 Barba, ibid., p. 117.
25 Ibid., p. 116.

For further discussion of the issues broached in this section, a good place to start is *Interculturalism and Performance: Writings from PAJ*, ed. Bonnie Marranca and Gautam Dasgupta, New York, PAJ Publications, 1991; and Patrice Pavis, *Theatre at the Crossroads of Culture*, London, Routledge, 1992.

73

ANTONIN ARTAUD

FROM On the Balinese Theatre (1931)

The Balinese, with gestures and a variety of mime to suit all occasions in life, reinstate the superior value of theatre conventions, demonstrate the effectiveness and greater active value of a certain number of well-learnt and above all masterfully applied conventions. One of the reasons for our delight in this faultless show lies precisely in the use these actors make of an exact amount of assured gesture, tried and tested mime coming in at an appointed place, but particularly in the mental clothing, in the deep shaded study which governs the formulation of the expressive interplay of these effective signs, giving us the impression their effectiveness has not become weakened over the centuries. That mechanical eye-rolling, those pouting lips, the use of twitching muscles producing studiously calculated effects which prevent any resorting to spontaneous improvisation, those heads moving horizontally seeming to slide from one shoulder to the other as if on rollers, all that corresponds to direct psychological needs as well as to a kind of mental construction made up of gestures, mime, the evocative power of rhythm, the musical quality of physical movement, the comparable, wonderfully fused harmony of a note. This may shock our European sense of stage freedom and spontaneous inspiration, but let no one say their precision makes for sterility or monotony. We get a marvellous feeling of richness, fantasy and bounteous lavishness emanating from this show regulated with a maddeningly conscious attention to detail. And the most impulsive correlations constantly fuse sight with sound, intellect with sensibility, a character's gestures with the evocation of a plant's movements through the aid of an instrumental cry. The sighs of a wind instrument prolong the vibrations of vocal cords so identically we do not know whether the voice itself is held, or the senses which first assimilated that voice. Those rippling joints, the musical angle the arm makes with a forearm, a falling foot, an arching knee, fingers that seem to come loose from the hand, all this is like a constant play of mirrors where human limbs seem to echo one another, harmonious orchestral notes and the whisper of wind instruments conjure up the idea of a passionate aviary where the actors themselves are the fluttering wings. Our theatre has never grasped this gestured metaphysics nor known how to make use of music for direct, concrete, dramatic

300

purposes, our purely verbal theatre unaware of the sum total of theatre, of everything that exists spatially on the boards or is measured and circumscribed in space, having spatial density (moves, forms, colours, vibrations, postures, shouts) could learn a lesson in spirituality from the Balinese theatre with regard to the indeterminable, to dependence on the mind's suggestive power. This purely popular, non-religious theatre gives us an extraordinary idea of a nation's intellectual level, which takes the struggle of a soul as prey to the spectres and phantoms of the Other World to be the basis for its civic festivals. For the last part of the show certainly deals with purely inner conflicts. And in passing we ought to note the extent of theatrical magnificence the Balinese have been able to impart to it. The sense of the stage's plastic requirements are seen to be equalled only by their knowledge of physical fear and how to unleash it. And there is a striking similarity between the truly terrifying look of their devil, probably of Tibetan origin, and a certain puppet with leafy green nails, its hands distended with white gelatine, the finest ornament of one of the first plays of the Alfred Jarry Theatre.[1]

This show is more than we can approach head on, bombarding us as it does with an overabundance of impressions each one more splendid than the last, but in a language to which we no longer seem to hold the key, and a kind of annoyance is caused by being unable to run it to earth or rediscover the thread, to turn one's ear closer to the instrument to hear it better, just one more charm to add to the show's credit. And by language I do not mean an idiom we fail to catch at first hearing, but precisely that kind of theatrical language foreign to every *spoken language*, where it seems a tremendous stage experience is recaptured, beside which our exclusively dialogue productions seem like so much stammering.

NOTE

1   His own venture, preceding the Theatre of Cruelty (both without theatres of their own). Artaud's intention to stage plays of Jarry was never realised. The play with the puppet was probably Roger Vitrac's *Les Mystères de l'amour*, the company's first production, staged in 1927.

For a biographical note on Artaud see p. 274.

It was a celebration of empire rather than Bali which enabled Artaud to encounter Balinese theatre, for the dance troupe he saw was performing at the huge Colonial Exhibition held on the outskirts of Paris in 1931. Artaud's long piece on it in *The Theatre and Its Double* assembles an article published in *La Nouvelle Revue Française* shortly afterwards (of which the opening paragraph here forms the second half), plus passages copied from letters and other notes. The abundance of these testify not just to the impact of the performance upon him, but to the importance he ascribed to it.

74

BERTOLT BRECHT

FROM Alienation Effects in Chinese Acting (1936)

The alienation effect is achieved in the Chinese theatre in the following way.

Above all, the Chinese artist never acts as if there were a fourth wall besides the three surrounding him. He expresses his awareness of being watched. This immediately removes one of the European stage's characteristic illusions. The audience can no longer have the illusion of being the unseen spectator at an event which is really taking place. A whole elaborate European stage technique, which helps to conceal the fact that the scenes are so arranged that the audience can view them in the easiest way, is thereby made unnecessary. The actors openly choose those positions which will best show them off to the audience, just as if they were *acrobats*. A further means is that the artist observes himself. Thus if he is representing a cloud, perhaps, showing its unexpected appearance, its soft and strong growth, its rapid yet gradual transformation, he will occasionally look at the audience as if to say: isn't it just like that? At the same time he also observes his own arms and legs, adducing them, testing them and perhaps finally approving them. An obvious glance at the floor, so as to judge the space available to him for his act, does not strike him as liable to break the illusion. In this way the artist separates mime (showing observation) from gesture (showing a cloud), but without detracting from the latter, since the body's attitude is reflected in the face and is wholly responsible for its expression. At one moment the expression is of well-managed restraint; at another, of utter triumph. The artist has been using his countenance as a blank sheet, to be inscribed by the gest[1] of the body.

The artist's object is to appear strange and even surprising to the audience. He achieves this by looking strangely at himself and his work. As a result everything put forward by him has a touch of the amazing. Everyday things are thereby raised above the level of the obvious and automatic. A young woman, a fisherman's wife, is shown paddling a boat. She stands steering a non-existent boat with a paddle that barely reaches to her knees. Now the current is swifter, and she is finding it harder to keep her balance; now she is in a pool and paddling more easily. Right:

303

that is how one manages a boat. But this journey in the boat is apparently historic, celebrated in many songs, an exceptional journey about which everybody knows. Each of this famous girl's movements has probably been recorded in pictures; each bend in the river was a well-known adventure story, it is even known which particular bend it was. This feeling on the audience's part is induced by the artist's attitude; it is this that makes the journey famous. The scene reminded us of the march to Budejovice in Piscator's production of *The Good Soldier Schweik*. Schweik's three-day-and-night march to a front which he oddly enough never gets to was seen from a completely historic point of view, as no less noteworthy a phenomenon than, for instance, Napoleon's Russian expedition of 1812. The performer's self-observation, an artful and artistic act of self-alienation, stopped the spectator from losing himself in the character completely, i.e. to the point of giving up his own identity, and lent a splendid remoteness to the events. Yet the spectator's empathy was not entirely rejected. The audience identifies itself with the actor as being an observer, and accordingly develops his attitude of observing or looking on.

The Chinese artist's performance often strikes the Western actor as cold. That does not mean that the Chinese theatre rejects all representation of feelings. The performer portrays incidents of utmost passion, but without his delivery becoming heated. At those points where the character portrayed is deeply excited the performer takes a lock of hair between his lips and chews it. But this is like a ritual, there is nothing eruptive about it. It is quite clearly somebody else's repetition of the incident: a representation, even though an artistic one. The performer shows that this man is not in control of himself, and he points to the outward signs. . . .

The Western actor does all he can to bring his spectator into the closest proximity to the events and the character he has to portray. To this end he persuades him to identify himself with him (the actor) and uses every energy to convert himself as completely as possible into a different type, that of the character in question. If this complete conversion succeeds then his art has been more or less expended. Once he has become the bank-clerk, doctor or general concerned he will need no more art than any of these people need 'in real life'. . . .

. . . The Chinese performer . . . rejects complete conversion. He limits himself from the start to simply quoting the character played. But with what art he does this! He only needs a minimum of illusion. What he has to show is worth seeing even for a man in his right mind. What Western actor of the old sort (apart from one or two comedians) could demonstrate the elements of his art like the Chinese actor Mei Lan-fang, without special lighting and wearing a dinner jacket in an ordinary room full of specialists? It would be like the magician at a fair giving away his tricks, so that nobody ever wanted to see the act again.

NOTE

1 A word used to translate Brecht's *Gestus*, an important term in his thinking from 1930 on, which embraces three things: the core of the action in a particular incident or scene; the attitude (social or otherwise) of the writer, speaker, performer, etc. who gives it body; and the specific means (language, delivery, depictions, gestures or actions) by which this is carried through in an effective way. For further clarification of this sometimes tricky term, see especially, 'A Short Organum' paragraphs 61–6, 'On Rhymeless Verse with Irregular Rhythms' and 'On Gestic Music', all included in *Brecht on Theatre*.

For a biographical note on Brecht see pp. 116–17.

The performances from which these passages arise, of Mei Lan-fang and his Beijing Opera troupe in Moscow, 1935, were a major event in the Soviet theatre world, but different accounts of them had different emphases. Stanislavski found Mei Lan-fang's acting 'a free movement guided by the laws of art'. Eisenstein, having seized the chance to film one of the plays presented, distinguished Beijing Opera sharply from the Japanese Kabuki he had extolled earlier, finding that paradoxically it had 'all the advantages of the principles of realism'. Meyerhold agreed, though pointed to the performances' 'scenic hieroglyphics'; like Brecht he held up Mei Lan-fang as a model, but it was the plastic qualities and plastic meanings of Chinese acting that interested him. (Wu Zuguang, Huang Zuolin and Mei Shaowu, *Peking Opera and Mei Lanfang*, Beijing, New World Press, 1980, pp. 62–3; and *Meyerhold on Theatre*, ed. Edward Braun, London, Methuen, 1969, pp. 235 and 323.)

75

ENRIQUE BUENAVENTURA

FROM Theatre and Culture (1970)

TEC, referred to below, is the Experimental Theatre of Cali, in Colombia, that Buenaventura continues to direct.

A director-actor-playwright, a "comedian" as one says too aptly in Spanish, does his job with his whole organism, and transmits experience through a form that is direct, alive – and ephemeral. He cannot pack up his way of life and memories and go off to set them down in a tranquil place without soldiers, without guerrillas, without starving proletarian masses, without students. I confess that I regret very much that I am unable to escape, that every day I have to make an almost mystical effort not to run away. My commitment, fortunately, is not just a personal attitude nor has it been an individual decision. It encompasses the story of TEC.

We have been an official theatre, pampered by the government and the press, invited to the Theatre of Nations. We have sold the cultural product like more or less honest merchants. Yet without really knowing how, without anyone suggesting it to us, the need to develop our own work with our own raw materials and to show it here led us to confront the system structurally. The challenge inherent in the kind of independence that is not proclamation, not manifesto, not folklore nor nationalism, willy-nilly ends up questioning the system. This challenge cannot be absorbed, it is not culture, it uses art for subversive ends. The system doesn't accept it. The trouble is that we don't accept it totally either. To believe that we are outside the system when we only have serious differences with it is self-deception. To shake loose entirely from established institutions requires a solidarity and experience that we do not have. Many Latin American theatre people find themselves in a similar trap. In our country, however, especially in university groups, there are ways out of the dilemma. The most common has been to do "political" theatre, to use the theatre as a form of political agitation. That way you can kick and scream, you can scratch the skin of the system – but you continue to be its prisoner, you remain in its power.

To let yourself be forced to either the pole of commercialism or that of agitprop only leads to eliminating any possibility of true artistic subversion, of undermining the system in its essentials: the consciences and conduct of its victims.

The only possibility is to become the owners of our own means of production, to develop our product and communicate among ourselves directly, even to exchange the product directly – in large zones of our community – for other things that we do not produce. Such exchange at the margin of the system is extremely difficult, not only because the system attacks us from the outside, but because its mechanisms within us, the mechanisms of moral and psychological "order," paralyze us constantly.

TEC is being thrown out of the system. What we are trying to learn is where we are landing and what we can do there. Can we continue doing theatre? And so I have returned to the question that was asked me in Montreal. There are other groups – the Living Theatre and the Bread & Puppet Theatre among them – who share our situation. What differentiates us from them is the society in which we work, the audiences to whom we direct ourselves. I think that the insistence on "giving" and "giving of oneself," on giving love, on reaching the audience, on hurting them, shaking them up, even frightening them, is imposed on those groups by an audience from big cities, obliged to consume everything. The fear of being consumed, being directed, obliges these groups in turn to produce something so irritating – or so pure – that it cannot easily and harmlessly be digested by the consumer.

Our people in Colombia do not consume. They are consumed and they are avid, in great need of something to consume. Of course, with things presented in such a simplistic way, our work seems cut out for us. Those who don't consume are apathetic because immediate and primary needs do not give them rest; they barely have time for anything else. Besides, they are on the margins of society. They are used by the system, but the system keeps them separated. They are a "reserve army"; they are the only ones who need to destroy the system to survive. Many of them don't even have the timid and secret "folk" culture I spoke of before, which still flows – like underground rivers – beneath certain isolated rural zones. The language of these outcasts needs deciphering, and we must learn it in order to establish communication. For a long time TEC has been involved in the language of books and magazines, in the language of "culture," in the problems of theatre as an institution. And it isn't easy – unless we cease to be theatre people, unless we stop doing our work in theatre as well as we can so that it will be more effective – for us to succeed in this new form of communication. Yet each day the system obliges us more to be what we have to be. We can only thank it for pushing us by its total opposition to men, opposition to life.

Now, we *could* have deduced from all this that we had to dedicate ourselves to what is usually called "popular theatre" or "theatre of the masses," a theatre for a fixed audience and about a specific set of problems. Yet this is just another trick of the system, as elementary as nationalism, folklore, or agitprop. Because the system has cast out the exploited, should you create a product for them that is no more nutritious than the food surpluses it leaves them? Some maintain that the exploited don't want anything else, that they don't have the capacity to participate in the full and complex diversion of a real theatrical production. These people have degraded the notion of "popular art" and have put it on the farcical level of our democratic vote. To accept that we must do low quality theatre at the outset in order to be able to "elevate" the level of the people, is to enter wholly into the system. It is to say that the people are not yet mature enough for freedom and that the system, through its artists and technicians, will have to prepare them little by little for it.

Then there are the demagogues who maintain that *all* true art is popular, that art has always come from the people and that it is necessary to dispense with "decadent forms" and use "popular forms." But "decadent forms" are nothing more than attempts at self-expression made by the outcast artist, the artist isolated by the system but condemned to sell his work in the market of the system itself. His only resort is to use a personal code, to perfect and refine his technique, or, as a lone witness, to make a pop-inventory of the reasons for fighting against dehumanization. In Latin American countries the avalanche of imperialism, the great colonial adventure, has caused and continues to cause cultural genocide. Destroying the indigenous cultures (which, in the original great American empires, were not "popular," but as refined and aristocratic as were those of China and India), it created a mestizo people that had barely begun to crystallize its way of life, when it was destroyed by the second and third imperialist avalanches – by capitalism and the United States, which with the help of the gentle poets of the agrarian idyll (generally landowners, in reality or nostalgia) killed mestizo art and converted folklore into archeology.

(What we need for the revolution is to be able to use freely the colonizers' conquests in science and art in developing our peoples' buried tradition, their experiences as outcasts and workers – exactly as Vietnam uses modern arms, engineers, doctors, heavy industry, planes to defend its right to live in accord with its cultural tradition.)

There is an even worse demagogy: to make the exploited believe that through their marginal position they automatically acquire an aware proletarian mentality. Such populism is fascist at root.

TEC doesn't do theatre for the masses. We do not consider theatre an adequate means of information nor do we want to propagandize anyone. We direct ourselves to the men and women whom exploitation wants to reduce to an amorphous mass, to the lowest common denominator. We believe that theatre's objective is not to jell the masses around a few minimal aims, but to present maximal aims, of great complexity, so that the condition and conscience of class is a transitory means of accomplishing those aims. We are looking for communication basically in the relationship between play and audience. That is why our work and style are not directed solely to workers or peasants, but also to the bourgeoisie and students: colonial deformation concerns us all in different ways. By making different classes aware of their role, we can divide the public, confront it with a demystified, unroutinized reality. But we need to go still further. The colonized man must be divided within himself, to show him how, at the level of habit, conditioning, morality, he continues to carry with him the exploiter against whom he is fighting. And the exploiter must be shown that all charitable ways of soothing his conscience or of calming the wrath of the exploited will not last long, because they are resting on a radically false foundation.

In this period of "impersonal", mechanized power, of neo-capitalism "without proprietors," theatres should create plays not about machines but about dehumanized beings with concrete privileges and interests, with ridiculous little stories – and also about the hands which operate that gigantic backdrop, the mass media. That is why communication in the theatre is for us not a problem only of emoting, of creativeness, of empathy. It is not a problem of "objective research," not a demonstration of ideology. It is an action which is taken apart, piece by piece, impinging on all our means of perception, touching the experiences of the actor and the spectator, and finally, is put back together for us to criticize. . . .

Our task in the theatre is to begin to synthesize the two Colombian cultures. And we must begin now, because in this period of acute and increasing contradictions we can weigh the life of imported art against the resistance from our buried cultural elements, we can see and show their traumatic cross-assimilation. If we do not work now to discover a truly artistic *and* truly revolutionary style, the problem of art in a future, different society will be reduced to vulgarizing the synthesis at the level of shallow "popular art."

In TEC's work we have prepared for a profound attack on our basic situation. We have dispensed almost entirely with scenery, lighting effects, and other purely technical resources, for two reasons. First, we live in an underdeveloped environment and are, in the true meaning of the word, a poor theatre. Second, we think that the theatre should be one means of avoiding enslavement by the mechanical and to mass media. That doesn't mean doing away with the media, but setting down a clear boundary line between the direct oral and gestural communication of man to man, and propaganda. The forms of direct communication, man to man, exist among our people and they must be studied and used.

Translated by Joanne Pottlitzer

Enrique Buenaventura (b. 1928), Colombian director and playwright, was one of a new generation of writers and directors who emerged in the 1950s concerned to forge an engaged and activist theatre – the 'new theatre' – in place of the old. Initially their guiding light was Brecht. Following Buenaventura and the Colombian example, radical theatre in Latin America widely adopted Brechtian techniques and approaches, but began to apply these to collectively devised work, *creación coletiva*. Buenaventura remains based at the TEC, which he helped to found as a theatre school in 1955. His plays range from *On the Right Hand of God the Father* (1958), which involves folklore elements, to protest pieces like *Story of a Silver Bullet* (1980).

76

ERROL HILL

From The Emergence of a National Drama in the West Indies (1972)

In 1962 on the occasion of independence celebrations in Trinidad and Tobago, Slade Hopkinson, poet, actor, teacher, in his capacity of drama critic for the government party newspaper, wrote as follows:

> Until there is a theatre based on a drama rooted in Trinidad, the theatre and drama in Trinidad will remain essentially artificial, colonial things, interesting chiefly as symptoms of the psychological sickness of a fragmented, confused people – a people who contain the possibility of a unique cultural synthesis and inventiveness, but who prevent the fulfilment of this possibility by not having the courage or the intelligence to become what they in fact are.

Taking my cue from this statement I wish to close this over-long address by stating my credo for the establishment of a West Indian national drama:

1   I believe that drama is a public art, worthy of support from the public purse; that it belongs primarily on a stage before an audience and only incidentally in the classroom and library.

2   I believe that as a public art West Indian drama has a duty to knit together what Mr Hopkinson called our fragmented, confused society. Vertically it will bring together our large peasant and working-class elements with the better educated middle and upper middle-class segments of our population; the poor and the powerful; laterally, drama can help to integrate our people of different races and different cultures by making them participants in the forging of a recognizable West Indian culture. "We begin with a wound", wrote Clifford Sealy. And until that wound is healed by uniting the disparate elements of our society, to talk of a West Indian drama is simply academic speculation.

3   I believe that a powerful means to promote social integration is for drama to turn to our indigenous culture for its inspiration. West Indian drama must consciously slough off the accretions of an imported culture which remain alien to the large majority of West Indian peoples. By

indigenous culture I refer to the folk culture developed by the largest sections of our society who, torn from their roots, had no place but the West Indies to turn for a cultural heritage and who therefore built their culture out of the memory of their past and the experience of present physical and economic slavery.

4 I believe that drama belongs to all the people and that a national drama of the kind advocated would unleash tremendous creativity from both the trained theatre artist, who will find a rich mine of folk material on which to draw, and from the folk theatre practitioner who repeatedly is found to rise to heights of performance skill when challenged to appear on the formal theatre stage. My experience in directing national pageants in Trinidad, Jamaica, and Grenada justifies this belief.

5 I believe that a national drama and theatre of the kind proposed would draw massive public support and make the national theatre economically viable. It would take time to achieve this. At the beginning the theatre must go to the people; it must travel to outlying areas in towns and villages and involve the masses in its productions by inviting them to perform as part of the programme. Continuous interaction with the mass culture is indispensable for a national drama and will prevent the theatre from once more becoming the plaything of a social or educated coterie.

6 I believe the national theatre has a duty to protect indigenous art forms facing corruption or extinction under the bombardment of alien cultural forms and values as well as a galloping commercialism. The limbo, a Trinidad dance believed to represent the physical circumstances of slaves during the "Middle Passage," used to be one of the purest expressions of bodily equilibrium and muscular control. The performer, with arms and legs spread-eagled, danced under a horizontal bar which was gradually lowered to within inches of the ground. Commercialized in night clubs and for audiences abroad, the dance became, first, the human bridge limbo with the clean line of the bar replaced by writhing bodies. Next it became the flaming limbo where admiration of human skill is turned into concern for human safety. Finally, at a recent exhibition in Madison Square Garden I was treated to the psychedelic limbo where the dancer's body disappeared altogether and all we saw were some gaudily coloured frills of costume phosphorescing under black lights. Such is the corruption our folk art faces if we do not consciously strive to preserve it in a purer and more permanent form in the national theatre.

7 Finally, I believe that intimate knowledge of the folk theatre will help our artists to devise styles and forms most appropriate for a national drama. For instance, the old fashioned proscenium arch stage may not be the type of playhouse most suited to a West Indian national theatre, yet it is the only kind available in the West Indies, with the single

exception of a thrust stage in Guyana. I feel a pervasive and predominant rhythm in the life of our people – in the drums, in music, in dance and movement, in vocal sounds including speech; but too many theatre productions are devoid of this beat. I listen to the speech of our folk and I find it sturdy and fresh, full of imagery, above all, full of hope. But I find too many of our dramatists either tied to a traditional literary form of expression or else easily content with a journalistic vernacular jargon, and the more intellectual they are the more despairing their message. I see as inseparable in folk theatre music, dance, song, speech, mime, choral response; but we have become metropolitan specialists and compartmentalise these integral theatre modes following alien practice. I see the procession as a basic choreographic form in all aspects of indigenous culture – the calypsonian Lord Kitchener leading a carnival band over the hallowed grounds of Lord's Cricket Club to celebrate our 1950 Test Cricket victory; but our audiences sit in the theatre as in an old classroom waiting to be instructed and chided by their cultured masters. I see drama primarily for all the people, not merely for the exhibition of the skills of dramatists and other artists of the theatre. I see drama as a festival of celebration, not cerebration; as ceremony not science; as acceptance of life, not as escape from life or rejection of life.

Jose Marti, Cuban patriot and revolutionary, believed in the power of drama and theatre. He urged Latin American nations at the end of the last century to build their own theatre, breaking away from outmoded European models. His words have meaning for the West Indies today:

> The theatre is copy and outgrowth of a people. A people who would be new must produce an original theatre . . . It is irritating to see a new people rich in fecund creative intelligences cling servilely to a worn and dingy theatre . . . Youth is a period of creation. Not of adaptation, but of innovation. Mediocrity copies, originality dares . . . A new people requires a new literature. This exuberant life should reveal itself in a manner of its own. These new traits call for a special theatre.

I stand with Marti.

Errol Hill (b. 1921), West Indian playwright, director and scholar, was appointed by the University of the West Indies to be its first extra-mural drama teacher in 1953. The piece reprinted here is the conclusion of a long address given at the University of the West Indies in Jamaica, and follows an account of West Indian drama from the nineteenth century to Derek Walcott. It contains too an account of the 'indigenous art forms' mentioned here, a range of popular performance traditions including the carnival and calypso, John Canoe and dead-wake ceremonies, Shango and Pocomania, Tea

Meetings, La Rose and Vieux Croix festivals, the Hosein and other Indian customs, and musical and linguistic forms. Hill's familiarity with and respect for such traditions was central to his concept of a national theatre – a theatre of, for and concerned with the people of the West Indies. Stressing the prior need for serious training, Hill undertook an energetic part of this himself, from Honduras to Guiana, working with a wide range of groups from university troupes to women's social welfare groups. For more on masquerade and carnival and their significance for theatre, see his 'Towards a National Theatre' in Douglas Kahn and Diane Neumaier (eds), *Cultures in Contention*, Seattle, Real Comet Press, 1985, pp. 114–19.

77

LUIS VALDEZ

Notes on Chicano Theater (1972)

What is Chicano theater? It is theater as beautiful, rasquachi, human, cosmic, broad, deep, tragic, comic, as the life of the Raza[1] itself. At its high point Chicano theater is religion – the huelguistas de Delano praying at the shrine of the Virgin de Guadelupe, located in the rear of an old station wagon parked across the road from DiGiorgio's camp No. 4; at its low point, it is a cuento or a chiste told somewhere in the recesses of the barrio, puro pedo.

Chicano theater then is first a reaffirmation of *life*. That is what all theater is supposed to do, of course; but the limp, superficial gringo seco productions in the "professional" American theater (and the college and university drama departments that serve it) are so antiseptic, they are anti-biotic (anti-life). The characters and life situations emerging from our little teatros are too real, too full of sudor, sangre, and body smells to be boxed in. Audience participation is no cute trick with us; it is a pre-established, pre-assumed privilege. "Qué le suene la campanita!"

Defining Chicano theater is a little like defining a Chicano car. We can start with a low-rider's cool Merc, or a campesino's banged-up Chevy, and describe the various paint jobs, hub caps, dents, taped windows, Virgin on the dashboard, etc., that define the car as particularly Raza. Underneath all the trimmings, however, is an unmistakable Detroit production, an extension of General Motors. Consider now a theater that uses the basic form, the vehicle, created by Broadway or Hollywood: that is, the "realistic" play. Actually, this type of play was created in Europe, but where French, German, and Scandinavian playwrights went beyond realism and naturalism long ago, commercial gabacho theater refuses to let go.

It reflects a characteristic "American" hangup on the material aspect of human existence. European theater, by contrast, has been influenced since around 1900 by the unrealistic, formal rituals of Oriental theater.

What do Oriental and European theater have to do with teatros Chicanos? Nothing, except we are talking about a theater that is particularly our own, not another imitation of the gabacho. If we consider our origins, say the theater of the Mayans or the Aztecs, we are talking about something totally unlike the realistic play, and something more Chinese or Japanese in spirit. Kabuki, as a matter of fact, started some time ago as something like our actos and evolved over the centuries into the highly exciting art form it is today; but it still contains pleberias. It evolved from and still belongs to el pueblo japonés.

In Mexico, before the coming of the white man, the greatest examples of total theater were, of course, the human sacrifices. *El Rabinal Achi*,[2] one of the few surviving pieces of indigenous theater, describes the sacrifice of a courageous guerrillero who, rather than dying passively on the block, is granted the right to fight until he is killed. It is a tragedy, naturally, but it is all the more transcendent because of the guerrillero's identification, through sacrifice, with God. The only "set" such a drama-ritual needed was a stone block. Nature took care of the rest.

But since the Conquest, Mexico's theater, like its society, has had to imitate Europe and, in recent times, the United States. In this same vein, Chicanos in Spanish classes are frequently involved in productions of plays by Lope de Vega, Calderón de la Barca, Tirso de Molina, and other classic playwrights. Nothing is wrong with this, but it does obscure the Indio fountains of Chicano culture. Is Chicano theater, in turn, to be nothing but an imitation of gabacho playwrights, with barrio productions of racist works by Eugene O'Neill and Tennessee Williams? Will Broadway produce a Chicano version of *Hello Dolly* now that it has produced a black one?

The nature of Chicanismo calls for a revolutionary turn in the arts as well as in society. Chicano theater must be revolutionary in technique as well as content. It must be popular, subject to no other critics except the pueblo itself; but it must also educate the pueblo toward an appreciation of *social change*, on and off the stage.

It is particularly important for teatro Chicano to draw a distinction between what is theater and what is reality. A demonstration with a thousand Chicanos, all carrying flags and picket signs, shouting CHICANO POWER! is not the revolution. It is theater about the revolution. The people must act in *reality*, not on stage (which could be anywhere, even on a sidewalk) in order to achieve real change. The Raza gets excited, but unless the demonstration evolves into a street battle (which has not happened yet but is possible), it is basically a lot of emotion with very little political power, as Chicanos have discovered by picketing, demonstrating, and shouting before school boards, police departments, and stores to no avail.

Such guerrilla theater passing as a demonstration has its uses, of course. It is agitprop theater, as the gabachos used to call it in the thirties: agitation and propaganda. It helps stimulate and sustain the mass strength of a crowd. Hitler was very effective with this kind of theater, from the swastika (卐) to the Wagneresque stadium at Nuremburg. On the other end of the political spectrum, the huelga march to Sacramento in 1966 was pure guerrilla theater. The red-and-black thunderbird flags of the UFWOC[3] (then NFWA) and the standards of the Virgin de Guadelupe challenged the bleak sterility of Highway 99. Its emotional impact was irrefutable. Its actual political impact was somewhat less. Governor Brown was not at the state Capitol, and only one grower, Schenley Industries, signed a contract. Later contracts have been won through a brilliant balance between highly publicized events that gained public support (marches, Cesar's fast, visits by Reuther, Robert and Ted Kennedy, etc.) and actual hard-ass door-to-door, worker-to-worker, organizing. Like Delano, other aspects of the Chicano movement must remember what is teatro and what is reality.

But beyond the mass struggle of La Raza in the fields and barrios of America, there is an internal struggle in the very corazón of our people. That struggle, too, calls for revolutionary change. Our belief in God, the Church, the social role of women – these must be subject to examination and redefinition on some kind of public forum. And that again means teatro. Not a teatro composed of actos or agitprop but a teatro of ritual, of music, of beauty, and of spiritual sensitivity. A teatro of legends and myths. A teatro of religious strength. This type of theater will require real dedication; it may, indeed, require a couple of generations of Chicanos devoted to the use of the theater as an instrument in the evolution of our people.

The teatros in existence today reflect the most intimate understanding of everyday events in the barrios from which they have emerged. But, if Aztlan is to become reality, then we as Chicanos must not be reluctant to act nationally – to think in national terms, politically, economically, spiritually. We must destroy the deadly regionalism that keeps us apart. The concept of a national theater for La Raza is intimately related to our evolving nationalism in Aztlan.

Consider a Teatro Nacional de Aztlan that performs with the same skill and prestige as the Ballet Folklórico de México (not for gabachos, however, but for the Raza). Such a teatro could carry the message of La Raza into Latin America, Europe, Japan, Africa – in short, all over the world. It would draw its strength from all the small teatros in the barrios, in terms of people and their plays, songs, designs; and it would give back funds, training, and augmenting strength of national unity. One season the teatro members would be on tour with the Teatro Nacional; the next season they would be back in the barrio sharing their skills and experience. It would accommodate about 150 people altogether, with 20 to 25 in the Nacional and the rest spread out in various parts of Aztlan, working with the campesino, the urbano, the mestizo, the piojo, etc.

Above all, the national organization of teatros would be self-supporting and independent, meaning no government grants. The corazón de la Raza cannot be revolutionized on a grant from Uncle Sam. Though many of the teatros, including El Campesino, have been born out of pre-established political groups – thus making them harbingers of that particular group's

317

viewpoint, news, and political prejudices – there is yet a need for independence for the following reasons: objectivity, artistic competence, survival. El Teatro Campesino was born in the huelga, but the very huelga would have killed it if we had not moved sixty miles to the north of Delano. A struggle like the huelga needs every person it can get to serve its immediate goals in order to survive; the Teatro, as well as the clinic, service center, and newspaper being less important at the moment than the survival of the union, were always losing people to the grape boycott. When it became clear to us that the UFWOC would succeed and continue to grow, we felt it was time for us to move and begin speaking about things beyond the huelga: Vietnam, the barrio, racial discrimination, etc.

The teatros must never get away from the Raza. Without the palomia sitting there, laughing, crying, and sharing whatever is onstage, the teatros will dry up and die. If the Raza will not come to theater, then the theater must go to the Raza. This, in the long run, will determine the shape, style, content, spirit, and form of el teatro Chicano.

Pachucos, campesinos, low-riders, pintos, chavalonas, familias, cuñados, tíos, primos, Mexican-Americans, all the human essence of the barrio is starting to appear in the mirror of our theater. With them come the joys, sufferings, disappointments, and aspirations of our gente. We challenge Chicanos to become involved in the art, the lifestyle, the political and religious act of doing teatro.

NOTES

1 The 'race' or Mexican people. Other Spanish or Mexican words: *Chicano*, Mexican (in US); *rasquachi*, of the underdog; *huelgistas*, strikers; *cuento* or *chiste*, tale or joke; *puro pedo*, unadulterated fart; *gringo seco*, dried-up (white) foreigner; *teatros*, theatres; *sudor*, sweat; *sangre*, blood; *Qué le suene la campanita!* May the bell ring for him; *campesino*, peasant, fieldworker; *gabacho*, yankee; *pleberias*, plebs; *el pueblo japonés*, the Japanese people; *guerrillero*, guerrilla; *barrio*, neighbourhood; *corazón*, heart; *actos*, acts; *Aztlan*, greater Mexico (including US-annexed territory); *the campesino, the urbano, the mestizo, the piojo*, the farm-worker, city dweller, person of mixed race, the louse or dregs; *huelga*, strike; *carpa*, itinerant tent show, form of Mexican popular theatre, employing oral performance and improvisation; *pachucos, pintos, chavalonas, familias, cuñados, tíos, primos*, snazzy dressers, sharp lads, guttersnipes, families, brothers-in-law, uncles, cousins; *gente*, people.

2 For an account of this work, see Richard E. Leinaweaver, '*El Rabinal Achi*, a Pre-Columbian Play: A Commentary', *Latin American Theatre Review* 1, no. 2 (1968), pp. 3–53.

3 UFWOC: United Farm Workers of California, formerly National Farm Workers Association.

Luis Valdez (b. 1940) founded El Teatro Campesino (Fieldworkers' Theatre) in California, 1965, as an arm of the United Farm Workers' movement. This was just then beginning to organise its fight against huge agri-business firms to win better conditions for the badly exploited rural workers, largely immigrants, of the south-west. The troupe split from union control in 1967. Made up of farmworkers it played on trucks in the fields and barrios, performing in a bilingual mix. It set off a widespread Chicano theatre movement throughout the whole south-west. The Campesino also played on college campuses, and became known in Europe through their invited appearances in theatre festivals. The group changed in the course of the 1970s into a mainly student group; and largely broke up after 1980, when Valdez moved off into mainstream productions elsewhere. For examples of the Campesino's *actos*, see John Weisman, *Guerrilla Theatre: Scenarios for Revolution*, New York, Doubleday, 1973. For a critique of male bias in the Campesino's work, see Yolanda Broyles Gonzalez, 'Toward a Re-Vision of Chicano Theatre History: the Women of El Teatro Campesino', in *Making a Spectacle: Feminist Essays on Contemporary Women's Theatre*, ed. Lynda Hart, Ann Arbor, University of Michigan Press, 1989.

78

PETER BROOK

FROM The World as a Can Opener (1973)

In the middle of Africa, I scandalized an anthropologist by suggesting that we all have an Africa inside us. I explained that this was based on my conviction that we are each only parts of a complete man: that the fully developed human being would contain what today is labelled African, Persian or English.

Everyone can respond to the music and dances of many races other than his own. Equally one can discover in oneself the impulses behind these unfamiliar movements and sounds and so make them one's own. Man is more than what his culture defines; cultural habits go far deeper than the clothes he wears, but they are still only garments to which an unknown life gives body. Each culture expresses a different portion of the inner atlas: the complete human truth. is global, and the theatre is the place in which the jigsaw can be pieced together.

In the last few years, I have tried to use the world as a can opener. I have tried to let the sounds, shapes and attitudes of different parts of the world play on the actor's organism, in the way that a great role enables him to go beyond his apparent possibilities.

In the fragmented theatre that we know, theatre companies tend to be composed of people who share the same class, the same views, the same aspirations. The International Centre of Theatre Research was formed on the opposite principle: we brought together actors with nothing in common – no shared language, no shared signs, no common jokes.

We worked from a series of stimuli, all coming from without, which provided challenges. The first challenge came from the very nature of language. We found that the sound fabric of a language is a code, an emotional code that bears witness to the passions that forged it. For instance, it is because the ancient Greeks had the capacity to experience certain emotions intensely that their language grew into the vehicle it was. If they had had other feelings, they would have evolved other syllables. The arrangement of vowels in Greek produced sounds that vibrate more intensely than in modern English – and it is sufficient for an actor to speak these syllables to be lifted out of the emotional constriction of the twentieth-century city life into a fullness of passion which he never knew he possessed.

With Avesta, the two-thousand-year-old language of Zoroaster, we encountered sound patterns that are hieroglyphs of spiritual experience. Zoroaster's poems, which on the printed page in English seem vague and pious platitudes, turn into tremendous statements when certain movements of larynx and breath become an inseparable part of their sense. Ted Hughes's study of this led to *Orghast* – a text which we played in collaboration with a Persian group. Though the actors had no common language they found the possibility of a common expression.

The second challenge, which also came to the actors from the outside, was the power of myths. In playing out existing myths, from myths of fire to myths of birds, the group was stretched beyond its everyday perceptions and enabled to discover the reality behind the fairytale trappings of mythology. Then it could approach the simplest everyday action, the gesture, the relation with familiar objects in the knowledge that if a myth is true it cannot belong to the past. If we know where to look we can find it at once, in a stick, a cardboard box, in a broom or a pack of cards.

The third challenge came from allowing the outside world – people, places, seasons, times of day or night – to act directly on the performers. From the start, we studied what an audience means, and deliberately opened ourselves to receive its influence. Reversing the principle on which theatre tours are based, where finished work remains constant although circumstances change, we tried, in our travels, to make our work fit the moment of playing. Sometimes this came from pure improvisation, such as arriving in an African village with no fixed plans at all and letting circumstances create a chain reaction out of which a theme would arise as naturally as in a conversation. Sometimes we let the audience dominate the actors completely – as in Lamont, California, where, one Sunday morning under a tree, a crowd of strikers who had been listening to César Chávez stimulated our actors into creating the images and characters that they needed passionately to cheer or hiss, so that the performance became a direct projection of what the audience had uppermost on its mind.

In Persia, we took *Orghast* away from its serious-minded audience and its setting of royal tombs and did a performance in a village, to see whether we could bring it down to earth. But the task was too difficult – we had not acquired the necessary experience. Two years later, in California, however, together with the Teatro Campesino, we played *The Conference of the Birds* to an audience of farmworkers in a park and it all fell into place: a Sufi poem translated from Persian to French, from French to English, from English to Spanish, played by actors of seven nationalities, had made its way across the centuries and across the world. Here it was no alien classic; it found a new and urgent meaning in the context of the Chicano struggle.

This was possible because we had learned many lessons on the way. From a shanty town near Paris to the villages of Africa, in front of deaf children, asylum inmates, psychiatrists, business trainees, young delinquents; on cliffs, in pits, in camel markets, at street corners, in community centres, museums, even a zoo – and also in carefully prepared and organized spaces – the question: What is theatre? had become for us a proposition that had to be faced and answered immediately. The constant lesson taught and retaught was respecting audiences and learning from them. Whether throbbing with excitement (I think of three hundred black teenagers in Brooklyn); or menacing, stoned on glue in the Bronx; or grave, immobile and attentive (in a Saharan oasis), the audience is always "the other person": as vital as the other person in speech or love.

And it is clear that just pleasing the other is not enough. The relationship implies an extraordinary responsibility: something has to take place. What? Here we touched the basic questions: What do we need from the event? What do we bring to the event? What in the theatre process needs to be prepared, what needs to be left free? What is narrative, what is character? Does the theatre event tell something, or does it work through a sort of intoxication? What belongs to physical energy, what belongs to emotion, what belongs to thought? What can be taken from an audience, what must be given? What responsibilities must we take for what we leave behind? What change can a performance bring about? What can be transformed?

The answers are difficult and ever-changing, but the conclusion is simple. To learn about theatre one needs more than schools or rehearsal rooms: it is in attempting to live up to the expectations of other human beings that everything can be found. Provided, of course, one trusts these expectations. This is why the search for audiences was so vital.

Peter Brook (b. 1925), English theatre and film director based in Paris, received early recognition for his work and was directing at Stratford by the age of 21. Later productions in England included the controversial *US* on the war in Vietnam, and *The Marat-Sade* of Peter Weiss. To gain freedom to do explorative work with actors from other parts of the world, he moved to Paris in 1970 and set up the International Centre for Theatre Research, soon complemented by a Centre of Creation. The experience of performing in African villages that he mentions above took place in 1972, when he and his group journeyed from Algiers across the Sahara to Nigeria and Mali. Since then, he and his actors have staged regular productions of plays, adaptations and occasionally operas, whose simple means and subtle imaginative resonance has placed him in a class of his own. For an account of the two productions mentioned, see A. C. H. Smith, *Orghast at Persepolis*, London, Eyre Methuen, 1972; and John Heilpern, *Conference of Birds*, London, Faber & Faber, 1977. For discussion by one of his actors, see Yoshi Oida, *An Actor Adrift*, London, Methuen, 1992.

79

WOLE SOYINKA

FROM Drama and the African World View (1976)

First, let us dispose of some red herrings. The serious divergences between a traditional African approach to drama and the European will not be found in lines of opposition between creative individualism and communal creativity, nor in the level of noise from the auditorium – this being the supposed gauge of audience-participation – at any given performance. They will be found more accurately in what is a recognisable Western cast of mind, a compartmentalising habit of thought which periodically selects aspects of human emotion, phenomenal observations, metaphysical intuitions and even scientific deductions and turns them into separatist myths (or 'truths') sustained by a proliferating super-structure of presentation idioms, analogies and analytical modes. I have evolved a rather elaborate metaphor to describe it; appropriately it is not only mechanistic but represents a period technology which marked yet another phase of Western man's comprehensive world-view.

You must picture a steam-engine which shunts itself between rather closely-spaced suburban stations. At the first station it picks up a ballast of allegory, puffs into the next emitting a smokescreen on the eternal landscape of nature truths. At the next it loads up with a different species of logs which we shall call naturalist timber, puffs into a half-way stop where it fills up with the synthetic fuel of surrealism, from which point yet another holistic world-view is glimpsed and asserted through psychedelic smoke. A new consignment of absurdist coke lures it into the next station from which it departs giving off no smoke at all, and no fire, until it derails briefly along constructivist tracks and is towed back to the starting-point by a neo-classic engine.

This, for us, is the occidental creative rhythm, a series of intellectual spasms which, especially today, appears susceptible even to commercial manipulation. And the difference which we are seeking to define between European and African drama as one of man's formal representation of experience is not simply a difference of style or form, nor is it confined to drama alone. It is representative of the essential differences between two

323

world-views, a difference between one culture whose very artifacts are evidence of a cohesive understanding of irreducible truths and another, whose creative impulses are directed by period dialectics. So, to begin with, we must jettison that fashionable distinction which tends to encapsulate Western drama as a form of esoteric enterprise spied upon by fee-paying strangers, as contrasted with a communal evolution of the dramatic mode of expression, this latter being the African. Of far greater importance is the fact that Western dramatic criticism habitually reflects the abandonment of a belief in culture as defined within man's knowledge of fundamental, unchanging relationships between himself and society and within the larger context of the observable universe.

Let us, by way of a paradigmatic example, take a common theme in traditional mask-drama: a symbolic struggle with chthonic presences, the goal of the conflict being a harmonious resolution for plenitude and the well-being of the community.* Any individual within the 'audience' knows better than to add his voice *arbitrarily* even to the most seductive passages of an invocatory song, or to contribute a refrain to the familiar sequence of liturgical exchanges among the protagonists. The moment for choric participation is well-defined, but this does not imply that until such a moment, participation ceases. The so-called audience is itself an integral part of that arena of conflict; it contributes spiritual strength to the protagonist through its choric reality which must first be conjured up and established, defining and investing the arena through offerings and incantations. The drama would be non-existent except within and against this symbolic representation of earth and cosmos, except within this communal compact whose choric essence supplies the collective energy for the challenger of chthonic realms. Overt participation when it comes is channelled through a formalised repertoire of gestures and liturgical responses. The 'spontaneous' participant from within the audience does not permit himself to give vent to a bare impulse or a euphoria which might bring him out as a dissociated entity from within the choric mass. If it does happen, as of course it can, the event is an aberration which may imperil the eudaemonic goals of that representation. The interjector – whose balance of mind is regarded as being temporarily disturbed – is quietly led out and the appropriate (usually unobtrusive) spells are cast to counter the risks of the abnormal event.

I would like to go a little deeper into this ritualistic sense of space since it is so intimately linked with the comprehensive world-view of the society that

---

* The remarks which follow are based on plays observed *in situ*, that is, on the spot where the performance originates and ends, and at its appropriate time of the year, not itinerant variations on the same theme. The specific play referred to here was a harvest play which took place on a farm-clearing some three miles south of Ihiala in the then Eastern Region of Nigeria, 1961.

gave it birth. We shall treat it first as a medium in the communicative sense and, like any other medium, it is one that is best defined through the process of interruption. In theatrical terms, this interruption is effected principally by the human apparatus. Sound, light, motion, even smell, can all be used just as validly to define space, and ritual theatre uses all these instruments of definition to control and render concrete, to parallel (this is perhaps the best description of the process) the experiences or intuitions of man in that far more disturbing environment which he defines variously as void, emptiness or infinity. The concern of ritual theatre in this process of spatial definition which precedes, as we shall discover, the actual enactment must therefore be seen as an integral part of man's constant efforts to master the immensity of the cosmos with his minuscule self. The actual events which make up the enactment are themselves, in ritual theatre, a materialisation of this basic adventure of man's metaphysical self.

Theatre then is one arena, one of the earliest that we know of, in which man has attempted to come to terms with the spatial phenomenon of his being. Again, in speaking of space, let us recognise first of all that with the advancement of technology and the evolution – some would prefer to call it a counter-evolution – of the technical sensibility, the spatial vision of theatre has become steadily contracted into purely physical acting areas on a stage as opposed to a symbolic arena for metaphysical contests. The pagan beginnings of Greek theatre retained their symbolic validity to dramaturgists for centuries after the event, so that the relative positions of suppliant, tyrant or *deus ex machina*, as well as the offertory or altar, were constantly impressed on their audience and created immediate emotional overtones both when they were used and by their very act of being. (I do not, for the purpose of this essay, wish to debate whether the fixity of these positions did not, contrasted with the fluid approach of African ritual space, detract from the audience's experience of cosmic relations.) Medieval European theatre in its turn, corresponding to the religious mythology of its period, created a constant *microcosmos* by its spatial correspondences of good and evil, angels and demons, paradise, purgatory and hell. The protagonists of earth, heaven and hell enacted their various trials and conflicts in relation to these traditional positions, and the automatic recognition of these hierarchical situations of man created spiritual anxieties and hopes in the breasts of the audience. But observe, the apprehended territory of man has already begun to contract! Cosmic representation has shrunk into a purely moral one, a summation in terms of penalties and rewards. The process continued through successive periods of European partial explorations of what was once a medium of totality, achieving such analytical aberrations as in this sample of compartmentalisation which claims that the right (actor's) wing of the stage is 'stronger' than the left. We shall not encounter any proofs of this ludicrous assertion in the beginnings of theatre, Greek or African.

Ritual theatre, let it be recalled, establishes the spatial medium not merely as a physical area for simulated events but as a manageable contraction of the cosmic envelope within which man – no matter how deeply buried such a consciousness has latterly become – fearfully exists. And this attempt to manage the immensity of his spatial awareness makes every manifestation in ritual theatre a paradigm for the cosmic human condition. There are transient parallels, brief visual moments of this experience in modern European theatre. The spectacle of a lone human figure under a spotlight on a darkened stage is, unlike a painting, a breathing, living, pulsating, threateningly fragile example of this paradigm. It is threatening because, unlike a similar parable on canvas, its fragility is experienced both at the level of its symbolism and in terms of sympathetic concern for the well-being of that immediate human medium. Let us say he is a tragic character: at the first sign of a check in the momentum of a tragic declamation, his audience becomes nervous for him, wondering – has he forgotten his line? has he blacked out? Or in the case of opera – will she make that upper register? Well, ritual theatre has an additional, far more fundamental anxiety. Indeed, it is correct to say that the technical anxiety even where it exists – after all it does exist; the element of creative form is never absent even in the most so-called primitive consciousness – so, where it does exist, it is never so profoundly engaged as with a modern manifestation. The real unvoiced fear is: will this protagonist survive confrontation with forces that exist within the dangerous area of transformation? Entering that *microcosmos* involves a loss of individuation, a self-submergence in universal essence. It is an act undertaken on behalf of the community, and the welfare of that protagonist is inseparable from that of the total community.

Wole Soyinka (b. 1934), Nigerian playwright, poet and novelist. Son of an Anglican canon, he studied at Ibadan and at Leeds, and was then involved with the Royal Court writers' group. Returning to Nigeria, he founded the 1960 Masks. Since then, he has been a prolific author of a long series of plays and adaptations which confront the cultural complexity of Nigerian life and the abuse of power. He was imprisoned without trial in 1967 during the civil war. Fellowships at English universities followed, during which this essay was written. In 1976 he returned to Nigeria and set up the Guerilla Theatre Unit. He was awarded the Nobel Prize in 1986; but was once more forced into exile in 1994.

80

NTOZAKE SHANGE

unrecovered losses/black theatre traditions (1979)

as a poet in american theater/ i find most activity that takes place on our stages overwhelmingly shallow/ stilted & imitative. that is probably one of the reasons i insist on calling myself a poet or writer/ rather than a play-wright/ i am interested solely in the poetry of a moment/ the emotional & aesthetic impact of a character or a line. for too long now afro-americans in theater have been duped by the same artificial aesthetics that plague our white counterparts/ "the perfect play," as we know it to be/ a truly european framework for european psychology/ cannot function efficiently for those of us from this hemisphere.

furthermore/ with the advent of at least 6 musicals about the lives of black musicians & singers/ (EUBIE, BUBBLING BROWN SUGAR, AIN'T MISBEHAVIN', MAHALIA, etc.)/ the lives of millions of black people who don't sing & dance for a living/ are left unattended to in our theatrical literature. not that the lives of Eubie Blake or Fats Waller are well served in productions lacking any significant book/ but if the lives of our geniuses aren't artfully rendered/ & the lives of our regular & precious are ignored/ we have a double loss to reckon with.

if we are drawn for a number of reasons/ to the lives & times of black people who conquered their environments/ or at least their pain with their art, & if these people are mostly musicians & singers & dancers/ then what is a writer to do to draw the most human & revealing moments from lives spent in nonverbal activity. first of all we should reconsider our choices/ we are centering ourselves around these artists for what reasons/ because their lives were richer than ours/ because they did something white people are still having a hard time duplicating/ because they proved something to the world like Jesse Owens did/ like Billie Holiday did. i think/ all the above contributes to the proliferation of musicals abt our musicians/ without forcing us to confront the real implications of the dynamic itself. we are compelled to examine these giants in order to give ourselves what we think they gave the worlds they lived in/ which is an independently created afro-american aesthetic. but we are going abt this process backwards/ by isolating the art forms & assuming a very narrow perspective vis-à-vis our own history.

if Fats Waller & Eubie Blake & Charlie Parker & Savilla Fort & Katherine Dunham moved the world outta their way/ how did they do it/ certainly not by mimicking the weakest area in american art/ the american theater. we must move our theater into the drama of our lives/ which appeals to us because it is directly related to lives of those then living & the lives of the art forms.

in other words/ we are selling ourselves & our legacy quite cheaply/ since we are trying to make our primary statements with somebody else's life/ and somebody else's idea of what theater is. i wd suggest that: we demolish the notion of straight theater for a decade or so, refuse to allow playwrights to work without dancers & musicians. "coon shows" were somebody else's idea. we have integrated the notion that a drama must be words/ with no music & no dance/ cuz that wd take away the seriousness of the event/ cuz we all remember too well/ the chuckles & scoffs at the notion that all niggers cd sing & dance/ & most of us can sing & dance/ & the reason that so many plays written to silence & stasis fail/ is cuz most black people have some music & movement in our lives. we do sing & dance. this is a cultural reality. this is why i find the most inspiring theater among us to be in the realms of music & dance.

i think of my collaboration with David Murray on A PHOTOGRAPH/ & on WHERE THE MISSISSIPPI MEETS THE AMAZON/ & on SPELL #7/ in which music functions as another character. Teddy & his Sizzling Romancers (David Murray, sax.; Anthony Davis, piano; Fred Hopkins, bass; Paul Maddox, drums; Michael Gregory Jackson, guitar, harmonica & vocals) were as important as The Satin Sisters/ though the thirties motif served as a vehicle to introduce the dilemmas of our times. in A PHOTOGRAPH the cello (Abdul Wadud) & synthesizer (Michael Gregory Jackson) solos/ allowed Sean to break into parts of himself that wd have been unavailable had he been unable to "hear". one of the bounties of black culture is our ability to "hear"/ if we were to throw this away in search of less (just language) we wd be damning ourselves. in slave narratives there are numerous references to instruments/ specifically violins, fifes & flutes/ "talking" to the folks. when working with Oliver Lake (sax.) or Baikida Carroll (tr.) in FROM OKRA TO GREENS/ or Jay Hoggard (vibes) in FIVE NOSE RINGS & SOWETO SUITE/ i am terribly aware of a conversation. in the company of Dianne McIntyre/ or Dyanne Harvey's work with the Eleo Pomare Dance Company/ one is continually aroused by the immediacy of their movements/ "do this movement like yr life depends on it"/ as McIntyre says.

the fact that we are an interdisciplinary culture/ that we understand more than verbal communication/ lays a weight on afro-american writers that few others are lucky enough to have been born into. we can use with some skill virtually all our physical senses/ as writers committed to bringing the world as we remember it/imagine it/ & know it to be to the stage/ we must use everything we've got. i suggest that everyone shd cue from Julius Hemphill's wonderful persona, Roi Boye/ who ruminates & dances/sings & plays a saxophone/ shd cue from Cecil Taylor & Dianne McIntyre's collaboration on SHADOWS/ shd cue from Joseph Jarman & Don Moye (of The Art Ensemble of Chicago) who are able to move/ to speak/ to sing & dance & play a myriad of instruments in EGWU-ANWU. look at Malinke who is an actor/ look at Amina Myers/ Paula Moss/ Aku Kadogo/ Michele Shay/ Laurie Carlos/ Ifa Iyaun Baeza & myself in NEGRESS/ a collective piece which allowed singers, dancers, musicians & writers to pass through the barriers & do more than 1 thing. dance to Hemphill or the B.A.G. (Black Artist Group)/ violinist Ramsey Amin lets his instrument make his body dance & my poems shout. i find that our contemporaries who are musicians are exhibiting more courage than we as writers might like to admit.

in the first version of BOOGIE WOOGIE LANDSCAPES i presented myself with the problem of having my person/ body, voice & language/ address the space as if i were a band/ a dance company & a theater group all at once. cuz a poet shd do that/ create an emotional environment/ felt architecture.

to paraphrase Lester Bowie/ on the night of the World Saxophone Quartet's (David Murray, Julius Hemphill, Hamiett Bluiett & Oliver Lake) performance at the Public Theater/ "those guys are the greatest comedy team since the Marx Brothers." in other words/ they are theater. theater which is an all encompassing moment/ a moment of poetry/ the opportunity to make something happen. We shd think of George Clinton/ a.k.a. Dr. Funkenstein/ as he sings/ "here's a chance to dance our way out of our constrictions." as writers we might think more often of the implications of an Ayler solo/ the meaning of a contraction in anybody's body. we are responsible for saying how we feel. we "ourselves" are high art. our world is honesty & primal response.

Ntozake Shange (b. 1948), African-American poet, playwright, novelist and performance artist. She prefers alternative spaces for her performance pieces, which characteristically involve art work, poetry and dance. She was catapulted to unwanted fame by the Broadway success of *for coloured girls who have considered suicide/when the rainbow is enuf . . .* and has since come to regard her theatre work as 'an anomaly'. (See Kathleen Betsko and Rachel Koenig, *Interviews with Contemporary Women Playwrights*, New York, Beech Tree Books, 1986, p. 366). She has spent much time in Latin America (see *See No Evil: Prefaces, Essays and Accounts 1976–1983*, San Francisco, Momo's Press, 1984), and expressed admiration for the rapport between the vernacular Teatro Popular and their working class audience. Her chosen Zulu name means 'she who comes with her own things/she who walks like a lion'. Of the pieces mentioned in her article, *a Photograph*, *spell #7* and *boogie woogie landscapes* are in *Three Pieces*, New York, St Martin's Press, 1981. *From okra to greens* has also been published (New York, French, 1983).

81

HONOR FORD-SMITH

FROM Sistren: Jamaican Women's Theatre (1981)

There exists among the women of the Caribbean a need for naming of experience and a need for communal support of that process. In the past, silence has surrounded our experience. We have not been named in literature or in history. The discovery through dialogue, through encounter with others, of the possibilities of our power can help us to shape the forces which, at present, still shape us.

. . . Jamaica is still defining its cultural identity – overcoming a legacy of self-doubt and insecurity which was part of the colonial heritage. Building confidence in traditions is an important process, one in which women have played an important part. The preserving of African tradition through the last 300 years has, to a great extent, been facilitated by women. It is they who have kept alive and communicated the customs of an uprooted people – much of this legacy has been denied by the wider society and has been submerged beneath the official character of the country. Its emergence into the open requires different methods of communication than those that survived in the past. It demands a reexamination of the past, with all its taboos and restrictions, in the language of the *present*. It requires that women, hitherto the preservers, become the authors. . . .

Sistren is a collective/cooperative structure within which its members educate themselves through drama, and later, through drama and theater, share their experiences with others. It is a small group of women exploring their understanding through drama, naming it, and presenting that naming in a product – theater. The core collective also works to organize other groups of women in Jamaica. The active relationship between the investigative base (drama workshops) and the more objective completed statement (theater) gives the educational process a tangible goal. The drama workshops aim at a constant process of consciousness-raising. The production of plays necessitates the training of the women in a particular professional skill (acting). A group like Sistren need not choose theater as the end product of its educational process. The drama can be used for consciousness-raising and skill training in any field, because it offers a way of approaching and investigating problems.

The educational process in Sistren addresses itself to the problems of the women with whom we work, as they are articulated by women from the laboring poor. It introduces these problems back into the wider society for discussion, for analysis, for solution. It suggests alternatives. Both drama and theater provide a public forum for the voices of poor women. This is a part of the process of awakening which must take place if changes in the system that create these problems are to occur.

Sistren's program consists of workshops taken and performances given. Workshops include both research work and special skill workshops in movement, silk-screen printing, and current affairs. Performances include both workshops in Drama for Problem-Solving, which are presented to community organizations and women's groups around the country, and major productions, which are presented commercially, usually composed from group experience, research and improvisation. . . .

Sistren's first two major productions were created from forms suggested by the oral and ritual traditions of the country. This tradition, African in origin, is by its nature far more participatory than that of a literary tradition. It evokes a communal response from both audience and actor. The images and symbols contained within the ritual tradition evoke immediate responses from the audience, because they come loaded with overtones from past and present. They echo in the subconscious of the viewer. Dramatic forms originating from ritual demand a supportive relationship between audience and actor. In ritual, the viewer must help the possessed in his or her journey through a reality of the spirit. In workshop the passive participator must be prepared to be drawn in to support the actress who is making discoveries through the medium of drama.

Oral literature and music are a particularly important part of the cultural experience of the women in Sistren. Stories, songs for all occasions, riddles, rhymes and proverbs are among some of the forms that are still used very actively. Oral literature, as Ruth Finnegan has pointed out, has certain techniques built into its structure that demand the attention of the listeners. These devices include onomatopaeia, repetition of a phrase or expression, questions, and songs. Proverbs and riddles depend on metaphors from daily life and the listener's knowledge of folk heroes and heroines to make subtle comments on the life around us.

Bellywoman Bangarang, the group's first major production, was developed using a method almost completely based on folk traditions. In the beginning, each member of the group was asked to go into the center of a circle and sing a folk song from her childhood. She was asked to keep singing until the song evoked either an action or an incident in her memory. When this happened she was to tell the story or act it out. Observers were required to look for ways in which they could identify with her story. If anyone felt that the experience being described aroused a memory of a similar experience in her own life she joined in by telling her story or by linking, through action, her experience to the one that had been acted out. From these simple exercises, the theme of teenage pregnancy and the rites of passage from girlhood to adulthood emerged.

The wealth of information that emerged demanded to be structured around dramatic images suitable to the theme. We chose to use folk games. The entire narrative structure of *Bellywoman Bangarang* finally rested on the structure of the games and on the resolution of the conflict in the games structure. Most games have a metaphorical content and often suggest a line of narrative action based on the game's objective. An example of this is the game "Bull in the Pen." Here the main player stands in the center of a circle of people whose arms are linked. She asks, by touching each arm, what the pen is made of. She then has to try and break out of it. Dramatically, this game can be used in several ways. In *Bellywoman* it functioned as a means of commenting on a scene that had gone before. The pen became the situation itself and the arms of the players symbolized the problems of the situation. The players then try to improvise a means of breaking out of the pen.

Riddles and proverbs were another form of oral literature used in *Bellywoman*. They were used as a means of stimulating the audience to think about taboo areas of experience. The riddles introduced themes that the audience was afraid to deal with openly, or unused to dealing with at all. Menstruation and illness during pregnancy were dealt with like this. The riddles were presented to the audience as choreopoems. The audience had to figure out the answers.

The structures of riddles and proverbs also help to evoke and suggest structures for group poems, which, if they have enough emphasis on word play and rhythm, communicate with great immediacy to an audience. These kinds of poems connect to the audience's background in ritual chanting and rhythmic bible reading. The content of the poem, or choral statement, juxtaposed with the anticipated content of the familiar form, arouses a questioning interest on the part of the viewer. Poetry like this does not have the connotations of abstraction that it carries in many other societies. It is an extremely direct way of reaching an audience through conscious use of rhythm. The use of other forms of oral and ritual tradition such as choruses and storytelling has informed our work in a continuous way. The use of craftwork is also beginning to be an important part of the group's total program. . . .

The process of working in drama for women involves the creating of a community in which some of the hidden or taboo subjects about women can be exposed and the audience confronted with them. As such, drama is not a reflection of life but a demystification of it, by the full exploration of these realities. Sistren brings to the public the voices of women from the laboring poor and in so doing helps to pressure for change. By confronting what has been considered indecent, irrelevant or accepted, we have begun to make a recorded refusal of ways in which our lives have been thwarted and restricted. We have begun to refuse the forces behind those ways.

Methods and techniques are not very important. It's where they take you that matters. What becomes of the work is determined by the content and the consciousness one brings to the theme. Work of this kind can perpetuate oppressive structures as well as it can help to change them. The form is only important in so far as it structures and analyzes the content and in so far as it leads to new understandings, new knowledge and new collective action.

Honor Ford-Smith. Sistren, the Jamaican all-women group first came together on a job-creation programme (set up by the Democratic Socialist government of 1972–80) where they were working as street-cleaners. They first performed in 1977 at a Kingston Workers' Week Concert. Full productions are supplemented by informal workshop performances with discussions. Honor Ford-Smith worked with the group as theatre director and helped it become a full-time theatre collective in 1981. The group also runs a silk-screen textile project.

82

AUGUSTO BOAL

FROM The Theatre of the Oppressed in Europe: Forum Theatre (1983)

The performance is an artistic and intellectual game played between actor and spect-actor.

1   To start off with, the show is performed as if it were a conventional play. A certain image of the world is presented.

2   The spect-actors are asked if they agree with the solutions advanced by the protagonist; they will probably say no. The audience is then told that the play is going to be done a second time, exactly as it was done the first time. The actors will try to bring the piece to the same end as before, and the spect-actors are to try to change it, showing that new solutions are possible and valid. In other words, the actors stand for a particular *vision of the world* and consequently will try to maintain that world as it is and ensure that things go exactly the same way . . . . at least until a spect-actor intervenes and changes the vision of the world *as it is* into a world *as it could be.* It is vital to generate a degree of tension among the spect-actors – if no one changes the world it will stay as it is, if no one changes the play it will come to the same end as before.

3   The audience is informed that the first step is to take the protagonist's place whenever he or she is making a mistake, in order to try to bring about a better solution. All they have to do is approach the playing area and shout 'Stop!' Then, immediately, the actors must stop where they are without changing position. With the minimum delay, the spect-actor must say where he or she wants the scene taken from, indicating the relevant phrase, moment, or movement (whichever is easiest). The actors then start the scene again from the prescribed point, with the spect-actor as protagonist. . . . The spect-actors, by acting out their ideas, train for 'real life' action; and actors and audience alike, by playing, learn the possible consequences of their actions. They learn the arsenal of the oppressors and the possible tactics and strategies of the oppressed. . . .

THE GODRANO EXPERIENCE

Two Palermo newspapers published interviews with me. Immediately, the head of the *carabinieri* at Palermo telephoned the 'brigadier' at Godrano[1] to ask why he had not detected the presence of a 'foreigner'. The *carabinieri* then showed great vigilance in tracking our every movement. And when they became aware that we were planning to do a show in the main square, they decided to ban it. There were lots of comings and goings, one step forward, two steps backward, many discussions. Finally they decided to allow the show if an authorisation came from Palermo – which would entail at least three days' worth of bureaucratic transactions. And there was a further difficulty; the show we were doing had no script on which we could be judged.

The chief of the *carabinieri* repeated his objections: 'When all is said and done, this man is a foreigner; and let's face it, foreigners can cause social unrest. Who knows what sort of ideas they have over there – and who can tell whether or not this foreigner might harm the citizens of Godrano by showing them these ideas?'

My hosts explained in detail the theory of the Theatre of the Oppressed and the policemen listened attentively. It was explained to them that I was not in the least interested in the importation of ideas; all I brought with me was a new way of working. As for ideas, it was the inhabitants of Godrano who would be supplying them, not me.

> You mean to say it's the actual people from here who will be expressing themselves through this Forum Theatre? You mean the people are going to say what they think, say what they like, *they're* going to practise doing the actions they think necessary to liberate themselves?
> Yes.
> The people themselves?
> Exactly.

I have to admit that at this point the policeman had a rare moment of lucidity:

> Then it's even more subversive and much more dangerous than I thought. It's absolutely impossible.

The only solution was to talk to the *Sindaco* (the leader of the council and the mayor rolled into one). In the name of culture and free expression of thought, the *Sindaco* decided to take full responsibility and we got back to work.

The oppressed and the oppressors

Come the Saturday, we were all in the square. The whole town had got to know about the show; many took part, others were happy just watching, still others watched from a distance, from their window or their doorstep.

It was a wonderful experiment for a number of reasons. Apart from anything else, this was the first time in my experience that Forum Theatre was being done with an audience composed of oppressed and oppressors at one and the same time. In Latin America and in Europe, I had done lots of Forum Theatre, but always with the oppressed. At Godrano the adversaries were face to face.

1 The family

First we did a few exercises and games. Then we started the first scene.

1st action

Giuseppina, a young woman of 20, wants to got out after supper. She asks her Mother's permission. The latter answers that it is up to the Father. Giuseppina says that one of her Brothers will accompany her. The two women prepare supper.

2nd action

The Father arrives in a foul mood with everything and everyone – the increase in the cost of living, his wife who isn't bringing his children up right, the children who are all good-for-nothings, the co-operative they were intending to set up and which is making no progress. Enter the sons. Towards Giuseppina each practises a different species of oppression. The first, the violent one, is of the opinion that a woman's place is in the home, and that the stupider and more ignorant she is, the better she is. The second, who is younger, tries to tell on all his sister's smallest misdemeanours: she looked at the neighbour's son, etc. As for the third, he plays the nice guy; he accompanies his sister as long as she behaves as he thinks fit. Giuseppina asks if she can go out that evening, but it so happens they are all busy: one is going to play football, another is going to play cards and the third isn't available.

3rd action

The Father forbids his daughter to go out for a walk. The three Brothers go and do what they want, because they're men. Giuseppina gets back to the washing-up because she is a woman.

The forum

Immediately after the presentation of the play, the model which was to be the starting point of the forum, there were some very masculine reactions. Two husbands ordered their wives to leave their places to go home. The two women refused and stayed to the end. They didn't dare come on stage, but they were brave enough to stay, against their husbands' wishes.

Other men started to say that this was not a serious problem and that we should be discussing serious problems. The women protested, saying that as far as they were concerned, it was very serious.

Then the forum began, with the supper table right in the middle of the stage. Three young women decided to replace Giuseppina and tried to break the oppression. But the oppressors were well coached and on every occasion the women eventually found themselves back at the washing-up. They said just about everything they wanted to say, but in the end they were beaten. Then a fourth young woman came along and showed what was for her the only solution: force. Going against the paternal will, she went out for her walk; and the others accepted this as a solution. The *Sindaco*, who had no daughter of his own, was enchanted with this new form of theatre.

Then the second part of the forum started – the spectators were now encouraged to take the place of other characters as well, to show actors and audience new forms of oppression. Immediately a corpulent man appeared and played out his solution: he ordered his children out of his house and in the end threw his wife out, saying:

Yes, you too, go and find your boyfriend!

Thus he revealed the root of his reactionary thinking: if the girl had committed 'a sin' it was because the Mother was a *putana* (a whore). The women vigorously challenged this.

At the end of the 'forum' of this scene, one of the young women spect-actors commented:

We have dared to say things here, in the main square, in front of everybody, which we sometimes don't dare say at home. But for our parents the opposite has been true; things they say over and over at home, they haven't had the guts to say once here, in front of other people.

The transplanting of the dining-room into the middle of the street had other effects as well. There was another important moment when a young man took the place of the protagonist. We were then able to make the following observation: when a young woman took Giuseppina's place, she immediately excited a feeling of identification, which was experienced by all the other young women present. By contrast, with the young man's performance, there was no identification. The young women watched him, but didn't identify themselves with him.

What are the practical consequences of this non-identification? The male actor (even if he was a spectator at the beginning) was still, as far as the women were concerned, a male actor; the woman spect-actor on the other hand was one of them, a woman on stage, standing there in the name of other women.

It clearly follows that when an *actor* carries out an action of liberation, he or she does it in place of the spectator, and thus is, for the latter, a catharsis. But when a *spect-actor* carries out the same act on stage, he or she does it in the name of all other spectators, and is thus for them not a *catharsis* but a *dynamisation*.

It is not enough for a theatre to avoid catharsis – what is needed is theatre which produces dynamisation.

In the end, if the men weren't happy, the women, well, they were overjoyed. The next day, when we asked Giuseppina's mother how she liked the show, she answered:

> I thought it was sensational. And all my friends admired my daughter's performance. They told me that it's just the same in their homes. The problems are the same. And one of my friends said that we should look for the solutions together . . .

NOTE

1   Godrano: a small village in Sicily, some twenty-five miles from Palermo.

Augusto Boal (b. 1931), Brazilian writer, playwright, director and theatre activist, worked in the 1950s and 1960s with the Arena Theatre of Sao Paolo. An account of his work there can be found in his book, *The Theatre of the Oppressed*, London, Pluto Press, 1979. Like Buenaventura, he was strongly affected by the plays and theory of Brecht, and following shows like his *Revolution in South America*, and his development of methods aiming at popular empowerment, he was imprisoned. On his release, he moved into exile (1971). 'Forum Theatre' is his name for one of the methods he first developed with the Arena. He now works widely in Europe.

83

HÉLÈNE CIXOUS

FROM The place of Crime, the place of Pardon
(1986–7)

How can the poet open his universe to the destinies of peoples? How could he who is first of all an explorer of the Self, in what language foreign to his self, by what means could he write what is much more and altogether other than Myself?

And another question: how could I myself, of the species of people of letters, ever give speech to an illiterate peasant woman without taking it back from her, in a stroke of my word, without burying it with one of my fine phrases? So in my texts there can only be people who know how to read and write, how to juggle with signs? And yet I love this Khmer peasant man, I love this royal mother of a village in Rajasthan who knows so many things and does not know she lives in a country I call India.

For a long time I believed my texts would only inhabit those rare and desert places where only poems grow.

Until I arrived at the Theatre. There was the stage, the earth, where the self remains imperceptible, the country of others. There do their words, their silences, their cries, their song, make themselves heard, each one according to a particular world and in a particular foreign language.

Having arrived, a woman, everything begins to become clearer, and first of all the nature of my need for theatre.

I need a *certain* Theatre, whose first name was Shakespeare or Verdi, or Schönberg or Sophocles or Rossini. I need this theatre to tell me stories, and to tell them to me as it alone can tell them: as legends and yet looking me straight in the eye.

For if this Theatre is necessary it is because it allows us to live what no 'genre' allows us: the difficulty, the pain we have being human. Evil. What happens at the theatre is the Passion, but the passion according to Oedipus, according to Hamlet, according to you, according to Woyzeck, according to me, according to Othello, according to Cleopatra, according to Marie,[1]

340

according to this enigmatic, tortured, criminal, innocent human being that I am, I who am thou or you.

I believe that today more than ever we need our own theatre, the theatre whose stage is our heart, on which our destiny and our mystery are played, and whose curtain we very rarely see rise.

In truth we go as little to the Theatre as to our heart, and what we feel the lack of is going to the heart, our own and that of things. We live exterior to ourselves, in a world whose walls are replaced by television screens, which has lost its thickness, its depths, its treasures, and we take the newspaper columns for our thoughts. We are printed daily. We lack even walls, true walls on which divine messages are written. We lack earth and flesh.

We live before the curtain of paper, and often even as the curtain. But what matters to us, what wounds us, what makes us feel we are the characters of an immense adventure, is what happens behind the curtain. And behind the curtain there is the *naked* stage.

We need this nakedness. We need to see the faces hidden behind the faces, these faces that the Theatre unveils.

And under the charm of costumes and make-up, under the mask, what comes to light is the truth, that is to say only the best or the worst. And behind the curtain of words, the naked voice. What relief, when on entering into this place the lie, which is our daily politeness, comes to an end and we begin to hear the dialogue of the hearts! It could make us cry out. And we rejoice that it is not forbidden, in this marvellous land, to cry out, to strike blows, to translate into breath, into sweat, into song, the suffering of being a human inhabitant of our time.

We are the characters of an epic which we are forbidden, by the laws of mediocrity and of prudence, to live. And yet it is an epic. And what is frightening and beautiful is that, as majestic as the epic of nations appears, its moving forces – what causes the wars, the peace, the massacres, the heroisms – if one looks closely, in parting the curtain, are the minute and powerful humans. The world is a theatre. Each character who enters believes himself to be the centre of the world. And in a certain sense, because he believes it, he is. Each one of us is the Centre. And each Centre is beseiged by the other Centres.

The Theatre has kept the secret of History that Homer sang: History is made of stories of husbands, of lovers, of fathers, of daughters, of mothers, of sons, of jealousy, of pride, of desire. And there are faces which launch fleets of a thousand sails and destroy cities.

The human being needs to become human. Human? I mean that he is the scene of the war between good and evil. That there is war is a lucky chance for good: a chance to distinguish itself and to vanquish.

And he needs destiny: he needs to tell himself a story with a beginning and an end, in order to move forward from one day to the next. What is our destiny today? Since Shakespeare it has changed a bit. I am an island. Am I still only an island? My island, even England, is shaken by explosions, I hear bombs burst, cannons fire, I am surrounded by wars, I am haunted by the suffering of hostages. The last bomb did not kill me, we live under a heaven of injustice, of which we are the victims or the miraculous survivors. It is not through our home that madness passes with its scythe? But yes, it is our home, Paris, New Delhi, Beirut, Stockholm, we walk under the same sun of blood. Sometimes death approaches and strikes one street away from me, sometimes I do not hear it, one time it strikes. . .and it will be me. It is already me.

Yes, at times we have this thought I speak of here but most often we chase it away because it would prevent us from living. But in chasing it away we lose a large part of life. It is this part that the Theatre returns to us: the living part of death, or the mortal part of life.

I go to the Theatre because I need to understand or at least to contemplate the act of death, or at least to accept it, to meditate on it. And also because I need to cry.

To laugh also: but the laugh is only the sigh of relief at the scythe's passage: it missed us by a hair!

I admit that the Theatre is a form of religion: I mean that together one experiences there, in the re-ligere, the re-ligation, the re-collective meditation of emotions. I say 'I admit' because this is one of the reasons for which I sometimes resist the call of the Theatre: out of anti-religion. Out of need for individualism.

But I declare that we need these temples without dogma and without doctrine (but not without a large number of gods) where our torments and above all our blindnesses are played.

We are blind. We do not see what we do. We do not hear ourselves say what we say. We do not understand ourselves. And we lie to ourselves. Because we fear ourselves. We fear our wickedness. It's that we have guessed, thought, suspected, or seen that we are wicked. A little bit or a lot. But we do not truly like to be wicked. And yet? Or else we are wicked without wickedness?

The enigma of wickedness, of human cruelty, that of others and my own: this is what we come asking the Theatre to reveal to us.

For the Theatre is the place of Crime. Yes, the place of Crime, the place of horror, also the place of Pardon.

What does it allow us to see? The primitive passions: adoration, assassination. All the excesses I throw out of my apartment: suicide, murder, the share of mourning there is in every passionately human relationship: thirst and hunger. Sacrifice, cannibalism.

Because one does not only kill what one hates. One also kills what one loves. We always kill a little the being we love.

And by twisted love, because love is twisted, we come to kill Desdemona, Marie, our people or another people or Indira Gandhi or Olof Palme.[2]

Why do we love certain works of theatre or opera so immediately, so eternally? Because by showing us our crimes at the Theatre, before witnesses, they accuse us and at the same time they pardon us.

We are all victims, but we are also executioners. The Beast and the Knife. What does the Theatre tell us? There is death. What does the Theatre give us? Death. We love Carmen and Don José equally. And by the magic of music we become the one and the other, we tolerate being a killing man and a killed woman, a killed man and a killing woman.

The stage gives us this death, returns it to us, this death we are ashamed of, we are frightened of, which we push away. It gives us this to live, in an instant or slowly, this source of so many senses, death, the share of death in every life, and up to the intoxicated desire to kill Marie, the young woman or the old, the mother, the father, the child, the people.

And then, in this moment when, no longer fleeing, we accept to look the victim or the murderer in the eyes – as Mychkine looks at Rogojine[3] – we recall that we are human, that it is a hardship, but that it is a trying joy. *Equally* human: humanity comes through you and through me, and through Macbeth and through the king and through the beggar, and we understand ourselves.

There are essential things which make us equal: it is arriving by such different trails, at the same door, death.

And there are moments when the monster (the mean one, the 'villain,' the bandit, the assassin) discovers his humanity. There is always the moment of hesitation, and of temptation: what if I killed? What if I were wrong? What if I were a monster? What if I were blind? This moment is given to us at the Theatre, it is the tragic instant where everything could be changed. No longer take place. This instant takes place also in our lives. And the Theatre reminds us that we must be extremely vigilant not to miss it. Because the step between the bad and the good is narrow as a blade.

The Theatre does not give us death brutally like a blow in the back. No, it does not assassinate us. Because essentially the Theatre has pity. It gives us one of the most rarefied times in the market of our daily existences, the time of pity. Is it not true that we have become capable of no longer crying before the cut-off legs of a small Asian beggar? Fortunately, the Theatre stops us and strikes us in the heart and brings us to tears. Suddenly I hear the moan and I discover my deafness. And in return for our refound suffering, the spectacle gives us tears, and the beauty of the song reminds us that pain can be beautiful when there is compassion. Beautiful I mean: human, shared.

Yes pity, terror, remain the most precious emotions in the world. They are what love is. And they need so much to be brought back into the hearts of our time.

If only we had pity . . .

To begin, let us take the Theatre seriously. I mean: it is good to go there seriously, like children. Because one can pretend to go to listen to an opera. And then nothing happens. But if one participates in *Woyzeck* or in *King Lear*, with a simplified, uncovered heart, and if by chance one sheds tears, then perhaps on the earth a woman will be saved, a prisoner will be liberated – and perhaps an innocent person justified, and a forgotten person will be recalled.

Translation by Eric Prenowitz

NOTES

1 Murdered in Büchner's *Woyzeck*.
2 UN peacemaker in the Iran–Iraq conflict, shot in Stockholm in 1986.
3 In Dostoevsky's *The Idiot*.

Hélène Cixous (b. 1938) grew up in Algeria, of Jewish parentage, her mother German-speaking (see p. 135). Her plays have followed different paths from her other writing, and she has 'opened up her universe to the destiny of peoples' in epic plays for Ariane Mnouchkine's Théâtre du Soleil on Cambodia (1985) and India (1987). The piece here comes from one of a series of essays printed with the second, *L'Indiade, ou l'Inde de leur rêves* (*The Indiad, or the India of their Dreams*). Ariane Mnouchkine's interest in the performance techniques of Asian theatre are long-standing, and both productions were an opportunity for a long exploration of Asian styles and techniques. Her latest play, in two parts, *La Ville parjure (ou le reveil des Erinyes)* (*The Perjured City (or the Awakening of the Furies)*), was produced by Ariane Mnouchkine and the Théâtre du Soleil in 1994.

84

EUGENIO BARBA

Eurasian Theatre (1988)

The influence of Western theatre on Asian theatre is a well-recognized fact. The important affect that Asian theatre has had and still has on Western theatre practice-is equally irrefutable. But there remains an undeniable embarrassment: that these exchanges might be part of the supermarket of cultures.

DAWN

Kathakali and noh, onnagata and barong, Rukmini Devi and Mei Lan-fang[1] – they were all there, side by side with Stanislavski, Meyerhold, Eisenstein, Grotowski, and Decroux[2] when I started to do theatre. It was not only the memory of their theatrical creations which fascinated me, but above all the detailed artificiality of their creation of the actor-in-life.

The long nights of kathakali gave me a glimpse of the limits which the actor can reach. But it was the dawn which revealed these actors' secrets to me at the Kalamandalam school in Cheruthuruty, Kerala. There, young boys, hardly adolescents, monotonously repeating exercises, steps, songs, prayers, and offerings, crystallized their ethos through artistic behavior and ethical attitude.

I compared our theatre with theirs. Today the very word "comparison" seems inadequate to me since it separates the two faces of the same reality. I can say that I "compare" Indian or Balinese, Chinese or Japanese traditions if I compare their epidermises, their diverse conventions, their many different performance styles. But if I consider that which lies beneath those luminous and seductive epidermises and discern the organs which keep them alive, then the poles of the comparison blend into a single profile: that of a Eurasian theatre.

ANTITRADITION

It is possible to consider the theatre in terms of ethnic, national, group, or even individual traditions. But if in doing so one seeks to comprehend one's own identity, it is also essential to take the opposite and complementary

345

point of view: to think of one's own theatre in a transcultural dimension in the flow of a "tradition of traditions."

All attempts to create "antitraditional" forms of theatre in the West, as well as in the East, have drawn from the tradition of traditions. Certain European scholars in the 15th and 16th centuries forsook the performance and festival customs of their cities and villages and rescued the theatre in Athens and ancient Rome from oblivion. Three centuries later the avant-garde of the young romantics broke with the classical traditions and drew inspiration from new, distant theatres: from the "barbarous" Elizabethans and the Spaniards in the Siglo de Oro, folk performances, the commedia dell'arte, "primitive" rituals, medieval mysteries, and Oriental theatre. These are the theatrical images that have inspired the revolutions led by all "antitraditional" Western theatres in the 20th century. Today, however, the Oriental theatres are no longer approached through tales but are experienced directly.

WHY

Why in the Western tradition, as opposed to what happens in the Orient, has the actor become specialized: the actor-singer as distinct from the actor-dancer and, in turn, the actor-dancer as distinct from the actor-interpreter?

Why in the West does the actor tend to confine herself within the skin of only one character in each production? Why does she not explore the possibility of creating the context of an entire story, with many characters, with leaps from the general to the particular, from the first to the third person, from the past to the present, from the whole to the part, from person to things? Why, in the West, does this possibility remain relegated to masters of storytelling or to an exception like Dario Fo, while in the East it is characteristic of every theatre, every type of actor, both when she acts-sings-dances alone and when she is part of a performance in which the roles are shared?

Why do so many forms of Oriental theatre deal successfully with that which in the West seems acceptable only in opera, that is, the use of words whose meaning the majority of the spectators cannot undertstand?

Clearly, from the historical point of view, there are answers to these questions. But they only become professionally useful when they stimulate us to imagine how we can develop our own theatrical identity by extending the limits which define it against our nature. It is enough to observe from afar, from countries and uses which are distant, or simply different from our own; to discover the latent possibilities of a Eurasian theatre.

Every ethnocentricity has its eccentric pole, which reinforces it and compensates for it.

Even today, in the Asian countries – where often the value of autochthonous tradition is emphasized vis-a-vis the diffusion of foreign models or

346

the erosion of cultural identity – Stanislavski, Brecht, agitprop, and "absurd" theatre continue to be means of repudiating scenic traditions which are inadequate to deal with the conditions imposed by recent history.

In Asia, this breach with tradition began at the end of the 19th century: Ibsen's *A Doll's House*, the works of Shaw and Hauptmann, the theatrical adaptations of Dickens's novels or of *Uncle Tom's Cabin* were presented not as simple imports of Western models, but as the discovery of a theatre capable of speaking to the present.

In the meeting between East and West, seduction, imitation, and exchange are reciprocal. We in the West have often envied the Orientals their theatrical knowledge, which transmits the actor's living work of art from one generation to another; they have envied our theatre's capacity for confronting new themes, the way in which it keeps up with the times, and its flexibility that allows for personal interpretations of traditional texts which often have the energy of a formal and ideological conquest. On one hand, then, stories that are unstable in every aspect but the written; on the other hand, a living art, profound, capable of being transmitted, and implicating all the physical and mental levels of actor and spectator, but anchored in stories and customs which are forever old. On the one hand, a theatre which is sustained by *logos*. On the other hand, a theatre which is, above all, *bios*.[3]

ROOTS

The divergent directions in which Western and Eastern theatres have developed provokes a distortion of perception. In the West, because of an automatic ethnocentric reaction, ignorance of Oriental theatre is justified by the implications that it deals with experiences that are not directly relevant to us, that are too exotic to be usefully known. This same distortion of perception idealizes and then flattens the multiplicity of Oriental theatres or venerates them as sanctuaries.

Defining one's own professional identity implies overcoming ethnocentricity to the point of discovering one's own center in the tradition of traditions.

Here the term "roots" becomes paradoxical: it does not imply a bond which ties us to a place, but an ethos which permits us to change places. Or better: it represents the force which causes us to change our horizons precisely because it roots us to a center.

This force is manifest if at least two conditions are present: the need to define one's own traditions for oneself; and the capacity to place this individual or collective tradition in a context which connects it with other, different traditions.

VILLAGE

ISTA (the International School of Theatre Anthropology) has given me the opportunity to gather together masters of both Eastern and Western theatre, to compare the most disparate work methods, and to reach down into a common technical substratum – whether we are working in theatre in the West or in the East, whether we consider ourselves as experimental or "traditional" theatre, mime or ballet or modern dance. This common substratum is the domain of pre-expressivity. It is the level at which the actor engages her own energies according to an extradaily behavior, modeling her "presence" in front of the spectator. At this pre-expressive level, the principles are the same, even though they nurture the enormous expressive differences which exist between one tradition and another, one actor and another. They are *analogous* principles because they are born of similar physical conditions in different contexts. They are not, however, *homologous*, since they do not share a common history. These similar principles often result in a way of thinking which, in spite of different formulations, permits theatre people from the most divergent traditions to communicate with each other.

The work of more than 20 years with Odin Teatret has led me to a series of practical solutions: not to take the differences between what is called "dance" and what is called "theatre" too much into consideration; not to accept the character as a unit of measure of the performance; not to make the sex of the actor coincide automatically with the sex of the character; to exploit the sonorous richness of languages, which have an emotive force capable of transmitting information above and beyond the semantic. These characteristics of Odin Teatret's dramaturgy and of its actors are equivalent to some of the characteristics of Oriental theatres, but Odin's were born of an autodidactic training, of our situation as foreigners, and of our limitations. And this impossibility of being like other theatre people has gradually rendered us loyal to our diversity.

For all these reasons I recognize myself in the culture of a Eurasian theatre today. That is, I belong to the small and recent tradition of group theatres which have autodidactic origins but grow in a professional "village" where kabuki actors are not regarded as being more remote than Shakespearean texts, nor the living presence of an Indian dancer-actress less contemporary than the American avant-garde.

CREATING CONTEXTS

It often occurs in this "village" that the actors (or a single actor) not only analyze a conflict, let themselves be guided by the objectivity of the logos, and tell a story, but dance *in* it and *with* it according to the growth of the bios. This is not a metaphor: concretely, it means that the actor does not

348

remain yoked to the plot, does not interpret a text, but *creates a context*, moves around and within the events. At times the actor lets these events carry her, at times she carries them, other times she separates herself from them, comments on them, rises above them, attacks them, refuses them, follows new associations, and/or leaps to other stories. The linearity of the narrative is shattered by constantly changing the point of view, anatomizing the known reality, and by interweaving objectivity and subjectivity (i.e., exposition of facts and reactions to them). Thus the actor uses the same liberty and the same leaps of thought in action, guided by a logic which the spectator cannot immediately recognize.

That which has often created misunderstandings about Oriental theatre, has confused it with "archaic" ritual, or made it appear as perfect but static form, is in fact that which renders it closest to our epoch's most complex concepts of time and space. It does not represent a phenomenology of reality, but a phenomenology of thought. It does not behave as if it belonged to Newton's universe. It corresponds to Niels Bohr's sub-atomic world.

This phenomenology of thought, this objective behavior of the bios, which proceeds by leaps, is what I have tried to render perceptible in *The Romance of Oedipus* with Toni Cots, *Marriage with God* with Iben Nagel Rasmussen and Cesar Brie, and *Judith* with Roberta Carreri.

SPECTATOR

Eurasian theatre is necessary today as we move from the 20th into the 21st century. I am not thinking of Oriental stories interpreted with an Occidental's sensibility, nor am I thinking of techniques to be reproduced, nor of the invention of new codes. Fundamentally, even the complex codes which seem to make sense of many Oriental traditions remain unknown or little known to the majority of spectators in India as well as in China, Japan, and Bali.

I am thinking of those few spectators capable of following or accompanying the actor in the dance of thought-in-action.

It is only the Western *public* which is not accustomed to leaping from one character to another in the company of the same actor; which is not accustomed to entering into a relationship with someone whose language it cannot easily decipher; which is not used to a form of physical expression that is neither immediately mimetic nor falls into the conventions of dance.

Beyond the public there are, in the West as well as in the East, specific *spectators*. They are few, but for them theatre can become a necessity.

For them theatre is a relationship which neither establishes a union nor creates a communion, but ritualizes the reciprocal strangeness and the laceration of the social body hidden beneath the uniform skin of dead myths and values.

Translated by Richard Fowler

NOTES

1 *Kathakali* is the ancient dance-drama form of southern India as *noh* is of Japan, where the *onnagata* practice female impersonation. The *barong* dance-dramas of Bali are so-called after the mythical, variously masked two-man monster who features in them. Rukmini Devi founded the pioneer dance school Kalashetra in Madras in 1936, and helped revive traditional Indian dance forms from near extinction. On Mei Lan-fang see Brecht, p. 304, and note p. 305.

2 Etienne Decroux is the founding father of modern mime. See his book, *Words on Mime*, Claremont, California, Mime Journal, 1985.

3 *Bios*, life and its processes as distinct from *logos*, speech, or the word as creative ordering idea. See the section 'Logos and bios' in Grotowski's article 'Pragmatic Laws' in *Dictionary of Theatre Anthropology* by Eugenio Barba and Nicola Savarese, London, Routledge, 1991.

Eugenio Barba (b. 1936), Italian director, landed in Norway as a sailor at the age of 17, and there gained a scholarship to study theatre in Poland. Three years with Grotowski (1961–4) and a book on his work followed (*In Search of the Lost Theatre*). He then travelled to India to study and write on Kathakali (the ancient dance-theatre form of southern India). In 1964 he founded Odin Teatret. The group shortly moved to Holstebro, Denmark. As well as mounting productions, Odin also became an international contact point, organising workshops by invited performers, sponsoring visits from foreign companies, and publishing work dealing with a wide range of theatre practice, from Commedia to Piscator, and including the first English edition of Grotowski's *Towards a Poor Theatre*. In the 1970s Odin began performing in villages and city outskirts in Europe and South America, developing new outdoor skills. ISTA, the International School of Theatre Anthropology, was founded by Barba in 1979, and studies performance in the wide intercultural perspective suggested above.

85

GUILLERMO GÓMEZ-PEÑA

The Border as Performance Laboratory
(1991)

In 1980, choreographer Sara-Jo Berman and I founded Poyesis Genetica performance troupe, a fluctuating core of eight to ten artists from various disciplines and ethnic backgrounds, all studying at Cal-Arts. Poyesis was my first conscious attempt to make art in a culturally pluralistic, collaborative and interdisciplinary mode.

The original objective was, and I quote an early press release: "to create an inter-cultural space in which to fuse, hybridize and juxtapose the various artistic and performing traditions brought by the members." Perhaps the only thing we had in common was our willingness to step outside of our cultures and experiment. In a sense we were a bunch of rejects from monoculture, a kind of club for the culturally deterritorialized.

During the first year we developed a *sui-generis* performance style which resulted from "the blend of Mexican *carpa* [Mexican tradition of urban popular theater], magical realism, kabuki and U.S. multimedia." Where else but in California could this lunatic pastiche have happened? Though most of the scripts were written by me, the images and movement were conceived collectively through long discussions that would often take place in more than three languages.

Most scripts were based on the following metafiction: Mister Misterio, a Mexican detective/poet and his friend Salome, a burnt-out ballerina, underwent a series of crosscultural adventures. They belonged to the Tribe of the Fiery Pupils, an international group of radicals devoted to the dismantling of a monocultural order.

Each performance was a different episode in the Misterio-Salome saga, and their friends and enemies included hybrid characters such as "the wrestler shaman," "multi-media Pachuco,"[1] an Aztec Princess who worked as a cabaret chanteuse and an androgynous Maori warrior who sang opera.

Before every performance we underwent a series of elaborate "ritual steps to reach a trance-like state" that included fasting, chanting, exercise and consumption of exotic substances. We also built multi-media altars with a video monitor as main icon. These altars functioned as both set design and "nerve center of the ceremonial space."

On stage, we practiced ritual nudity and slow-motion movement juxtaposed with film and slides. According to a critic, the result was "a kind of techno-magical realism, that contrasted with the prevailing minimalist performance style" of the time. More than "techno-magical realists," I think we were a bunch of orphans trying to come to terms with a new culture, not quite yet ours. . . .

Since the success of our first show at the Galeria de la Raza in January of 1985, we knew that the Border Arts Workshop/El Taller de Arte Frontenzo (BAW/TAF) was a paradigmatic experiment. This success wasn't due to the quality of the art work, but to the intercultural nature of the collaborative process.

The sense of belonging to a larger cause had almost totally broken down in the 80s, specially within the art world. And the perspective of an interdisciplinary group of artists from the U.S. and Mexico working together to generate binational dialogue was not just a romantic but an extremely necessary idea.

We must remember that 1984 was a key year for the Chicano cultural movement. Institutions such as La Galeria de la Raza (San Francisco), SPARC (Los Angeles), and The Centro Cultural de la Raza (San Diego) began a process of redefinition of their relationship with the larger society which led to the shedding of separatism and the creation of multicultural alliances wih other Latinos as well as Blacks, Asians, feminists and gays.

BAW/TAF was a child of this original impulse. Its original members include Chicanos David Avalos and Victor Ochoa, Trinidadian Jude Eberhard, Americans Michael Shnorr, Sara-Jo Berman and Philip Brookman and Mexicans Isaac Artenstein and myself. We proclaimed the border region as our "intellectual laboratory," and immediately undertook action.

We began gathering weekly to discuss human rights violations by the border patrol, media depictions of Mexico and Mexicans and U.S. policy toward the South. In these lengthy discussions, we developed a very effective set of strategies to "broadcast" our point of view and to "intervene directly in the social landscape of the border." Unlike the unimaginative methods of straight political groups, we used experimental art techniques and performance-derived practices to garner the attention of the media.

One of our early performances, titled *End of the Line*, took place on October 12, 1986 at the intersection of Border Field Park and Playas de Tijuana, right where the U.S. meets with Mexico in the Pacific. Dressed as "border stereotypes," the members of the workshop and friends sat in a huge binational table bisected by the borderline.

The Mexicans were in Mexican territory and the Chicanos and Anglos on the U.S. side. We began to "illegally" hold hands and exchange food across the line. At one point we turned the table 180 degrees and entered "illegally" into each other's countries. The three *carabelas* of Columbus made out of flammable material were set on fire on the seascape.

The national Mexican media reported the event as news, and we became aware of the political power of site-specific performance.

Many other performance actions were staged in politically sensitive sites such as the border check-point, the legendary "soccer-field," the San Diego Federal building (which hosts the offices of the INS), and the streets of downtown San Diego. We also organized performance pilgrimages across the border and *tertulias* (town meetings) involving artists, journalists and activists from both cities. . . .

When Mexican political hero Superbarrio visited the border we organized a huge performance town meeting with representatives of the various political, cultural and media sectors of San Diego and Tijuana. We built a barbed wire wrestling ring and impersonating border heroes such as Supermojado, Superviviente, Chicanosaurio and Saint Frida (Kahlo), we welcomed Superbarrio and presented him with a pair of pliers "to cut the border fence."

We still had to rely on the artworld to protect our backs. And every now and then we would create installation pieces and performances in the safe environment of galleries and museums. Our strictly art activities were important in the sense that they provided us with the space and safety to reflect on the other contexts.

We shared a lot in common with ACT UP and the L.A.P.D. performance troupe. We walked back and forth from the art world to the real world, and the prestige of the group was precisely built around these dynamics. . . .

If we want to be makers of the culture of the 90s in a country that constantly pushes us to the margins, we have to constantly fight for the right to have a public voice. The European romantic myth of marginality has been shattered. We must try to speak from the center not the margins, and we must do it in large scale formats and for large audiences. The new objective as Karen Finlay[2] put it is "mainstreaming radical aesthetics and ideas."

We must also challenge the anachronistic myth that as "multicultural artists" we are only meant to work within the boundaries of our "community." Our place is the world and our "community" has multiplied exponentially.

In the 1990s, I feel a strong kinship with everyone in this and other continents who is trying to find new forms of interpreting and articulating the dangers and changes of the times: the true border artists; the Latinos, blacks, Asian-Americans, Native Americans, gays and feminists who are establishing cross-cultural alliances with one another, the performance activists, the non-aligned intellectuals and journalists; the post-earthquake Mexico City rockers, poets and cartoonists; the "Third World" collectives in Europe and the Latin American conceptual artists and writers who are so intelligently analyzing postcolonial relations, they all are my brothers and sisters of vision.

Their communities are also mine; and I hope my work will contribute to the creation of axes of thought and action among them.

NOTES

1 Sharp dresser (Mexican term).
2 American performance artist.

Guillermo Gómez-Peña (b. 1955), Mexican performer, writer and interdisciplinary artist, 'crossed the border' in 1978, but spends time in both Mexico and the US and describes himself as 'a Mexican part of the year, and a Chicano, the other part'. In Mexico he was part of a group dedicated to 'interdisciplinary trouble-making' in public situations, unaware of historical European performance-art parallels. At the California Institute of the Arts he discovered a reverse ignorance – of Latin American arts. The Poyesis Genetica group he describes here worked against this background. Development of 'border' work followed: in 1984, a bilingual radio show, 'Border Dialogues'; in 1986 a bilingual experimental magazine, exploring a border aesthetics. Border Arts Workshop eventually succumbed to stresses between the cultures involved – Chicano/Mexican as well as Chicano/American. Since then Gómez-Peña has worked as a solo performer or with Coco Fusco. He has presented his work widely, from the Soviet Far East (as member of a human rights commission), to Scotland (in the National Review of Live Art). He has also pioneered 'performance radio' akin to his live performances, involving poems, interventions, and layerings of 'poetical voices, musical juxtapositions and sound effects'.

SOURCES AND FURTHER WRITINGS

CONTRIBUTORS: SOURCES AND SELECTED WRITINGS

(The items listed under each name commence with the source of the writings in this book.)

ANDRÉ ANTOINE, translated from *Le Théâtre libre*, Paris, 1890. On his work, see Jean Chothia, *André Antoine*, Cambridge University Press, 1991.

GUILLAUME APOLLINAIRE, translated from *Les Mamelles de Tirésias*, Paris, Éditions Sic, 1918; reprinted in *Œuvres Complètes*, Paris, Gallimard, 1965–6. For the whole play, see *Modern French Plays: An Anthology from Jarry to Ionesco*, eds Michael Benedikt and George E. Wellwarth, London, Faber & Faber, 1965. See too Annabelle Henkin Melzer, 'The Premiere of Apollinaire's *The Breasts of Tiresias* in Paris', *Theatre Quarterly*, vol. VII, no. 27, Autumn 1977.

ADOLPHE APPIA: 'How to Reform Our Staging Practices', *La Revue des Revues*, 1, no. 9, 1 May 1904, and 'A New Art-Material' translated from *Œuvres Complètes*, vol. 2, 1895–1905, Lausanne, L'Age d'Homme, 1986. Further translations: *Music and the Art of the Theatre*, ed. Barnard Hewitt, Coral Gables, Fla., University of Miami, 1962; *Staging Wagnerian Drama*, Basel and Boston, Birkhäuser, 1982; *Adolphe Appia 1862–1928: Actor–Space–Light*, eds Denis Bablet and Marie-Louise Bablet, London, Calder, 1982; *Adolphe Appia: Essays, Scenarios and Designs*, eds W. R. Volbach and R. C. Beacham, Ann Arbor, Mich., and London, UMI Research Press, 1989; *The Work of Living Art*, ed. Barnard Hewitt, Coral Gables, Fla., 1960; *The Essays of Adolphe Appia*, ed. R. C. Beacham, Ann Arbor, Mich., and London, UMI Research Press, 1989; and R. C. Beacham, *Adolphe Appia: Texts on Theatre*, London and New York, Routledge, 1993. On his work, see Richard C. Beacham, *Adolphe Appia: Theatre Artist*, Cambridge University Press, 1987.

ANTONIN ARTAUD: 'Letter to *Comœdia*' translated from *Antonin Artaud: Œuvres Complètes*, vol. 5, Paris, Gallimard, 1964; other pieces are from *Collected Works*, vol. 4, London, Calder & Boyars, 1974; See also vol. 2, 1971, for much interesting theatre material. For an alternative translation, see *The Theatre and Its Double*, New York, Grove Press, 1958.

EUGENIO BARBA, from the *Drama Review*, vol. 32, no. 3 (T119), Fall 1988. See too *The Floating Islands*, Holstebro, Denmark, Odin Teatret, 1979; *Beyond the Floating Islands*, New York, PAJ, 1986; Eugenio Barba and Nicola Savarese, *Dictionary of Theatre Anthropology*, London, Routledge, 1991; and *The Paper Canoe: A Guide to Theatre Anthropology*, London, Routledge, 1994. For discussion by Odin performers, see Erik Exe Christoffersen, *The Actor's Way*, London, Routledge, 1993; for photo record, see Tony d'Urso and Ferdinando Taviani, *L'Étranger qui danse: l'album de l'Odin Teatret 1972–77*, Maison de la Culture de Rennes, 1977.

BLUE BLOUSE, from the Blue Blouse magazine *Sinyaya Bluza*, Moscow, 1925, no. 18, translated in Richard Stourac, *Revolutionary Workers' Theatre in the Soviet Union, Germany and Britain (1918–1936)*, Ph.D. dissertation, Bristol University, 1978, privately distributed; revised (with the loss of much documentation including the piece printed here) as *Theatre as a Weapon: Workers' Theatre in the Soviet Union, Germany and Britain, 1917–34*, by Kathleen McCreary and Richard Stourac, London, Routledge, 1986.

AUGUSTO BOAL, from *Games for Actors and Non-Actors*, London, Routledge, 1992, based on *Jeux pour acteurs et non-acteurs*, Paris, La Decouverte, 1979, and *Stop! C'est magique*, Paris, Hachette, 1980. See too his *The Theatre of the Oppressed*, London, Pluto Press, 1979; and *The Raindow of Desire: the Boal Method of Theatre and Therapy*, London, Routledge, 1995. For recent applications of his methods by others, see *Playing Boal: Theatre, Therapy and Activism*, eds Mady Schutzman and Jan Cohen-Cruz, London, Routledge, 1993.

EDWARD BOND, from *The War Plays*, London, Methuen, 1991. Prefaces, notes, poems and essays on theatre are included with many of his plays; of particular interest: 'On Brecht: A Letter to Peter Holland', *Theatre Quarterly*, vol. 8, no. 30, Summer 1978; 'A Note on Dramatic Method' (*The Bundle*, 1978); 'Types of Drama' in 'The Activist Papers' (*The Worlds*, 1979), 'Notes on Acting *The Woman*', (*The Woman*, 1979), and 'Notes on Post-Modernism' (*Two Post-Modern Plays*, 1990).

BERTOLT BRECHT: Prologue to *The Exception and the Rule* from *The Measures Taken and Other Lehrstücke*, London, Eyre Methuen, 1977. All other pieces are from *Brecht on Theatre: The Development of an Aesthetic*, London, Methuen, 1964. See too: *The Messingkauf Dialogues*, London, Methuen, 1965; *Diaries 1920–1922*, London, Eyre Methuen, 1979; *Letters*, London, Methuen, 1990; and *Journals 1934–1955*, London, Methuen, 1994. See too his poems on theatre in *Poems 1913–1956*, revised edn, London, Methuen, 1979.

PETER BROOK, from *The Shifting Point*, London, Methuen, 1988. See too *The Empty Space*, London, McGibbon & Kee, 1968, and London, Penguin Books, 1972; *There are no Secrets: Thoughts on Acting and Theatre*, London, Methuen, 1993; and *Peter Brook – a Theatrical Casebook*, ed. David Williams, rev. ed., London, Methuen, 1988.

ENRIQUE BUENAVENTURA, from the *Drama Review*, vol. 14, no. 2, (T46), Winter 1970. See too vol. 24, no. 2 (T86), June 1980, for an interview with Roberta Sklar; and Roman de la Campa, 'The New Latin American Stage: An Interview with Enrique Buenaventura', *Theater*, vol. 12, no. 1 Fall/Winter 1980.

JUDY CHICAGO, from *Through the Flower: My Struggle as a Woman Artist*, New York, Doubleday, 1975; reprinted London, The Women's Press, 1982.

HÉLÈNE CIXOUS: 'Aller à la mer' from *Modern Drama*, vol. 27, 1984. 'The Place of Crime' translated from *L'Indiade ou l'Inde de leurs rêves; et quelques écrits sur le théâtre*, Paris, Théâtre du Soleil, 1987. See too *The Newly Born Woman*, Manchester University Press, 1986. Plays in translation: *Portrait of Dora* in *Benmussa Directs*, London, John Calder, 1979; and *The Conquest of the School at Madhubai*, in *Women and Performance*, vol. 3 (1986), pp. 59–96. For bibliography of further translations, see Morag Shiach, *Hélène Cixous: A Politics of Writing*, London, Routledge, 1991.

GORDON CRAIG: 'Rearrangements' from *The Theatre Advancing*, 1919, re-printed New York, Benjamin Blom, 1963; 'One Word about the Theatre' from *The Art of the Theatre*, Edinburgh and London, T. N. Foulis, 1905; 'Study for Movement' from *Towards a New Theatre: Forty Designs for Stage Scenes with Critical Notes by the Inventor Edward Gordon Craig*, London and Toronto, J. M. Dent, 1913; 'The Artists of the Theatre of the Future' from *On the Art of the Theatre*, London, Heinemann, 1911. For selections see *Gordon Craig on Movement and Dance*, ed. Arnold Rood, New York, Dance Horizons, 1977, and *Craig on Theatre*, ed. J. Michael Walton, London, Methuen, 1983. On his work, see Christopher Innes, *Edward Gordon Craig*, Cambridge University Press, 1983.

ISADORA DUNCAN, from *The Art of the Dance*, ed. Sheldon Cheney, New York, Theatre Arts Books, 1969; see too: *My Life*, London, Sphere, 1988; *Isadora Speaks*, San Francisco, City Lights, 1986.

SERGEI EISENSTEIN: 'A Personal Statement' from *Film Essays, With a Lecture*, London, Dobson, 1968; other passages from *Selected Works, Vol. 1: Writings 1922–34*, ed. Richard Taylor, London, BFI, 1988. See too Robert

Leach, 'Eisenstein's Theatre Work', in *Eisenstein Rediscovered*, eds I. Christie and R. Taylor, London and New York, Routledge, 1993.

DARIO FO, from 'Aspects of Popular Theatre', *New Theatre Quarterly*, vol. 1, pt. 2, May 1985. See too his 'Popular Culture', *Theater*, vol. 14, no. 3, Summer/Fall 1983, pp. 50–4; 'Dialogue with an Audience', *Theatre Quarterly*, vol. IX, no. 35, Autumn 1979; *The Theatre Workshops at Riverside Studios, London*, ed. R. McEvoy, London, Red Notes, 1983; *Tricks of the Trade*, London, Methuen, 1991. On the *giullare*, see *Mistero Buffo*, London, Methuen, 1988. For further bibliography, see Tony Mitchell, *File on Dario Fo*, London, Methuen, 1989.

HONOR FORD-SMITH, from *Cultures in Contention*, eds Douglas Kahn and Diane Neumaier, Seattle, Real Comet Press, 1985; originally published in *FUSE*, November/December 1981. See too Sistren Theatre Collective, *Lionheart Gal: Lives of Women in Jamaica*, ed. Honor Ford-Smith, London, The Women's Press, 1986; and Elean Thomas, 'Lionhearted Women: Sistren Women's Collective', *Spare Rib*, no. 172, Nov. 1986.

RICHARD FOREMAN, from *Unbalancing Acts: Foundations for a Theater*, New York, Pantheon Books, 1992. See too *Plays and Manifestos*, New York University Press, 1976; *Reverberation Machines: The Later Plays and Essays* (i.e. 1976–83), Barrytown, NY, Station Hill Press, 1985; and *Love and Science: Selected Music-Theatre Texts*, New York, Theater Communications Group, 1991.

JOHN FOX, from *Engineers of the Imagination: The Welfare State Handbook*, eds Tony Coult and Baz Kershaw, London, Methuen, 1983; see too John Fox and Sue Gill, 'Welfare State International: 17 Years on the Street', *Drama Review*, vol. 29, no. 3 (T107), Fall 1985.

ATHOL FUGARD, from *Notebooks 1960/1977*, London, Faber & Faber, 1983. For *The Coat* see *The Township Plays*, Oxford University Press, 1993. For a selective bibliography, see *File on Fugard*, compiled by Stephen Gray, London, Methuen, 1991.

LOIE FULLER, from *Fifteen Years of a Dancer's Life, with Some Account of Her Distinguished Friends*, London, H. Jenkins, 1913.

FEDERICO GARCÍA LORCA, from *Deep Song and Other Prose*, London, Marion Boyars, 1980. His *Plays* are published in three volumes by Methuen. For a selective bibliography, see *File on Lorca*, compiled by Andy Piasecki, reprinted London, Methuen, 1995.

ARMAND GATTI, translated from Marc Kravetz and Armand Gatti, *L'Aventure de la parole errante*, Toulouse, Patrice Thierry, L'Ether Vague, 1987. For survey and bibliography see Dorothy Knowles, *Armand Gatti in the Theatre: Wild Duck against the Wind*, London, Athlone Press, 1989. His plays have since been collected in three volumes: *Œuvres Théâtrales*, Toulouse, Verdier, 1991.

VALESKA GERT, translated from *Ich bin eine Hexe*, 1950, in *Cabaret Performance, Vol. 2: Europe 1920–1940*, ed. Laurence Senelick, Baltimore, Johns Hopkins University Press, 1993. See too her 'Dancing' in *Schrifttanz: A View of German Dance in the Weimar Republic*, eds Valerie Preston-Dunlop and Susanne Lahusen, London, Dance Books, 1990.

IVAN GOLL, from *Seven Expressionist Plays*, London, Calder & Boyars, 1968. See too 'Two Super-dramas' in *Anthology of German Expressionist Drama*, Ithaca, NY, Anchor, 1963.

GUILLERMO GÓMEZ-PEÑA, from *California Performance, Volume 2, Interviews and Essays, Mime Journal 1991/1992*, Claremont, Calif., Pomona College Theatre Department, 1991. For his 'performance chronicle' *1992*, see *Walks on Water*, ed. Deborah Levy, London, Methuen, 1992. See too his 'A New Artistic Continent' in *Art in the Public Interest*, Ann Arbor, Mich., UMI Research Press, 1989; 'The Multicultural Paradigm', *High Performance*, no. 47, Fall 1989; 'Border Brujo: A Performance Poem', *Drama Review*, vol. 35, no. 3 (T131), Fall 1991; 'From Artmaggedon to Gringostroika', *High Performance*, no. 55, Fall 1991; 'The New World Border: Prophecies for the End of the Century', and Coco Fusco, 'The Other History of Intercultural Performance', *The Drama Review*, vol. 38, no. 1 (T141), Spring 1994.

JERZY GROTOWSKI, from *Towards a Poor Theatre*, Holstebro, Denmark, Odin Teatrets Forlag, 1968, reprinted London, Methuen, 1969. See too 'Tu es le fils de quelqu'un', *Drama Review*, vol. 31, no. 3 (T115), Fall 1987; and Thomas Richards, *At Work with Grotowski on Physical Actions*, London, Routledge, 1995.

WALTER HASENCLEVER, translated from 'Die Aufgabe des Dramas', *Der Zwinger*, Dresden, 15 October 1920. See too 'The Nature of Tragedy', *English Review*, pt. 33, November 1921.

DOROTHY HEATHCOTE, from *Collected Writings on Education and Drama*, eds Liz Johnson and Cecily O'Neill, London, Hutchinson, 1984 (includes list of filmed records of her work). 'Drama as a Process for Change' originally printed by Cleveland State University, 1976.

ERROL HILL, from *Caribbean Quarterly*, vol. 18, no. 4, December 1972. See too his 'Towards a National Theatre' in *Cultures in Contention*, eds Douglas Kahn and Diane Neumaier, Seattle, Real Comet Press, 1985; *The Trinidad Carnival: Mandate for a National Theatre*, Austin and London, University of Texas Press, 1972; and *The Theatre of Black America*, 2 vols, ed.

359

Errol Hill, Englewood Cliffs, NJ, Prentice-Hall, 1980, reprinted New York, Applause Theatre Book Publishers, 1987.

EUGENE IONESCO, from *Notes and Counternotes*, London, Calder & Boyars, 1964. See too *Present Past, Past Present*, London, Calder & Boyars, 1972. *L'Impromptu à l'Alba* appears as *Improvisation, or the Shepherd's Chameleon* in his *Plays*, vol. III, London, Calder & Boyars, 1960.

ALFRED JARRY, translated from 'De l'inutilité du théâtre au théâtre', *Mercure de France*, September 1896; reprinted in *Œuvres Complètes*, Paris, Gallimard, 1972. For his plays, see *The Ubu Plays*, London, Methuen, 1968, rev. ed. 1993, and *Caesar Antichrist*, Tucson, Ariz., Omen Press, 1971.

WASSILY KANDINSKY, translated from the almanac *Der Blaue Reiter*, Munich, Piper, 1912. For *The Yellow Sound* see *Arnold Schoenberg, Wassily Kandinsky: Letters, Pictures and Documents*, ed. Jelena Hahl-Koch, London, Faber & Faber, 1984.

TADEUSZ KANTOR: 'Impossible Theatre' translated from 'Le Théâtre impossible', *Lettres françaises*, 12 July 1972; 'Elementary School of Theatre' from *Lezioni Milanesi 1: Scuola elementare del teatro*, La Scuola d'Arte Drammatica Paolo Grassi/Ubulibri, Milan, 1988. See too: *Wielopole/Wielopole*, London, Marion Boyars, 1990 (includes selection of his writings on theatre); *A Journey Through Other Spaces: Essays and Manifestos, 1944–1990*, Berkeley and Los Angeles, University of California Press, 1993; and *Lovelies and Dowdies*, 30-minute film by Ken McMullen, 1974.

ALLAN KAPROW, from *Assemblages, Environments and Happenings*, New York, Harry N. Abrams, 1966. For script/productions by Kaprow, see *Happenings*, ed. Michael Kirby, New York, Dutton, 1965. See too *Echo-Logy* and *Satisfaction*, New York, D'Arc Press, 1975; and *Happenings and other Acts*, ed. Mariellen Sandford, London, Routledge, 1994.

DANIIL KHARMS, from *Russia's Lost Literature of the Absurd: Selected Works of Daniil Kharms and Alexander Vvedensky*, ed. George Gibian, Ithaca, NY, Cornell University Press, 1971; reissued as *The Man in the Black Coat: Russia's Lost Literature of the Absurd*, Evanston, Ill., Northwestern University Press, 1987. For further work and brief bibliography, see *Incidences*, London, Serpent's Tail, 1993.

PAUL KORNFELD, translated from 'Der beseelte und der psychologische Mensch: Kunst, Theater und Anderes', *Das junge Deutschland*, no. 1, 1918. His 'Epilogue to the Actor' is in *Actors on Acting*, eds Toby Cole and Helen Krich Chinoy, New York, Crown Publishers, 1949; and in *An Anthology of German Expressionist Drama*, ed. Walter Sokel, New York, Anchor Books, 1973.

360

GRIGORI KOZINTSEV, from *Futurism, Formalism, FEKS: 'Eccentricism' and Soviet Cinema 1918–36*, eds Ian Christie and John Gillett, London, BFI, 1978.

SUZANNE LACY and LESLIE LABOWITZ, from *Cultures in Contention*, eds Douglas Kahn and Diane Neumaier, Seattle, Real Comet Press, 1985; for bibliography see *Drama Review*, vol. 32, no. 1 (T117), Spring 1988.

EL LISSITZKY, from *Art and the Stage in the Twentieth Century*, ed. Henning Rischbieter, Greenwich, Conn., New York Graphic Society, 1968. Further writings are in *The Tradition of Constructivism*, ed. Stephen Bann, New York, Viking Penguin, 1974. See too his 'The Electro-Magnetic Spectacle', *Form*, no. 3, Cambridge UK, 1966. For a critique of constructivism in theatre, see Kazimir Malevich, 'Letter to Meyerhold', in *Art in Theory 1900–1990*, eds Charles Harrison and Paul Wood, Oxford, Blackwell, 1992.

CHARLES LUDLAM, from *Ridiculous Theatre, Scourge of Human Folly: The Essays and Opinions of Charles Ludlam*, ed. Steven Samuels, New York, Theater Communications Group, 1992. See too *The Complete Plays of Charles Ludlam*, eds Steven Samuels and Everett Quinton, New York, Harper & Row, 1989.

JUDITH MALINA, from *Women in Theatre*, ed. Karen Malpede, New York, Limelight Editions, 1985. See too: *The Diaries of Judith Malina 1947–1957*, New York, Grove Press, 1984; Aldo Rostagno with Julian Beck and Judith Malina, *We, the Living Theatre*, a pictorial documentation by Gianfranco Mantegna, New York, Ballantine, 1970; and *Paradise Now: Collective Creation of the Living Theatre*, 'written down by Judith Malina and Julian Beck', New York, Random House, 1971; and *The Enormous Despair*, New York, Random House, 1972.

F. T. MARINETTI, 'The Variety Theatre', and F. T. MARINETTI, E. SETTIMELLI and B. CORRA, 'The Futurist Synthetic Theatre', from *Marinetti: Selected Writings*, ed. R. W. Flint, London, Secker & Warburg, 1972. Playscripts by them can be found in Michael Kirby, *Futurist Performance*, New York, E. P. Dutton, 1971; and in *Cabaret Performance, Vol. 1: Europe 1890–1920*, ed. Laurence Senelick, New York, PAJ, 1989.

VLADIMIR MAYAKOVSKY: 'Letter to the Workers' from Wiktor Woroszylski, *The Life of Mayakovsky*, London, Victor Gollancz, 1972; 'Prologue to Mystery-Bouffe' from *The Complete Plays of Vladimir Mayakovsky*, New York, Simon & Schuster, 1968. See too V. Shklovsky, *Mayakovsky and his Circle*, London, Verso, 1974.

JOHN McGRATH, from *A Good Night Out*, London, Methuen, 1981. See too *The Bone Won't Break*, London, Methuen, 1990; and Elizabeth McLennan, *The Theatre Belongs to Everyone: Making Theatre with 7:84*, London, Methuen,

1990. His plays for 7:84 include *Fish in the Sea* and *Little Red Hen*, London, Pluto, 1977; *The Cheviot, the Stag and the Black, Black Oil*, London, Eyre Methuen, 1981; *Two Plays for the Eighties: Blood Red Roses and Swings & Roundabouts*, 7:84 and Aberdeen People's Press, 1981.

VSEVOLOD MEYERHOLD, from *Meyerhold on Theatre*, ed. Edward Braun, London, Methuen, 1969. See too 'Vsevolod Meyerhold on the Russian Theater' in Andrew Field, *The Complection of Russian Literature*, London, Allen Lane, 1971. For first hand accounts by those who worked with him, see *Meyerhold at Work*, ed. Paul Schmidt, Austin, University of Texas Press, 1980. See too: Konstantin Rudnitsky's pioneering study, *Meyerhold the Director*, Ann Arbor, Mich., Ardis, 1981; Edward Braun, *The Theatre of Meyerhold*, London, Eyre Methuen, 1979; and on his 'system', Robert Leach, *Vsevolod Meyerhold*, Cambridge University Press, 1989. For a wider lavishly illustrated survey, see Konstantin Rudnitsky, *Russian and Soviet Theatre: Tradition and the Avant-Garde*, London, Thames & Hudson, 1988.

ARIANE MNOUCHKINE, translated from 'Rencontres avec le Théâtre du Soleil', *Travail théâtrale*, no. 18/19, January–June 1975. See too: *L'Age d'or*, Paris, Stock, 1975; and '*L'Age d'or*: the long journey from 1793–1795', *Theatre Quarterly*, V, no. 18, 1975. On her work, see Adrian Kiernander, *Ariane Mnouchkine and the Théâtre du Soleil*, Cambridge University Press, 1993.

KWESI OWUSU, from *The Struggle for Black Arts in Britain*, London, Comedia, 1986. See too Kwesi Owusu and Jacob Rees, *Behind the Masquerade: The Story of the Notting Hill Carnival*, London, Arts Media Group, 1988; and Kwesi Owusu, *Storms of the Heart: Anthology of Black Arts and Culture*, London, Camden Press, 1988. For more on carnival, see under Errol Hill.

ERWIN PISCATOR, from *The Political Theatre*, London, Eyre Methuen, 1980. On his work, see John Willett, *The Theatre of Erwin Piscator*, London, Eyre Methuen, 1978.

ENRICO PRAMPOLINI, from Michael Kirby, *Futurist Performance*, New York, E. P. Dutton, 1971. See too 'The Futurist Pantomime' in *Art and the Stage in the Twentieth Century*, ed. Henning Rischbieter, Greenwich, Conn., New York Graphic Society, 1968; and 'The Magnetic Theatre and the Futurist Scenic Atmosphere', *Little Review*, Winter 1926.

SERGEI RADLOV, from *Drama Review*, vol. 19, no. 4 (T68), 1970. On his work, see in the same issue 'Radlov's Theatre of Popular Comedy' by Mel Gordon.

RACHEL ROSENTHAL, from *California Performance, Volume 2, Interviews and Essays, Mime Journal 1991/1992*, Claremont, Calif., Pomona College Theatre Department, 1991. Her performance text *My Brazil* is in *Out from Under: Texts by Women Performance Artists*, ed. Lenora Champagne, New

York, Theater Communications Group, and London, Nick Hern, 1990. For bibliography, see *Drama Review*, vol. 32, no. 1 (T117), Spring 1988.

OSKAR SCHLEMMER, translated from 'Neue Formen der Bühne', *Schünemanns Monatshefte*, October 1928, Bremen. See too *The Theatre of the Bauhaus*, ed. Walter Gropius, London, Eyre Methuen, 1979, for essays and photos; and *The Letters and Diaries of Oskar Schlemmer*, Evanston, Ill., North Western University Press, 1990.

CAROLEE SCHNEEMANN, from *Artforum*, vol. xxii, no. 2, October 1983. See too: *Parts of a Body House*, Devon, UK, Beau Geste Press, 1972; *Cézanne, She was a Great Painter*, New York, Trespass Press, 1974; *ABC — We Print Anything in the Cards*, Beuningen, Holland, Brummense Uitgeverij Van Luxe Werkjes, 1977; *More than Meat Joy: Complete Performance Works and Selected Writings*, New York, McPherson/Documentext, 1979; and *Early and Recent Work*, New York, McPherson/Documentext, 1983. 'Carolee Schneemann II: Recent Work', New Paltz, NY, Max Hutchinson Gallery Documentext, 1983, includes list of performance works and selected bibliography.

PETER SCHUMANN, from Stefan Brecht, *The Bread and Puppet Theatre*, vol. 2, London, Methuen, 1988. See too Helen Brown and Jane Seitz, 'With the Bread and Puppet Theatre: An Interview', *Drama Review*, vol. 12, no. 2 (T38), Winter 1968. More recent writings include *The Radicality of the Puppet Theater* (1990), and *The Old Art of Puppetry in the New World Order* (1993). Current mail-order publications list available from Bread and Puppet Theater, att. Elka Schumann, R.D. #2, Glover, VT, USA.

NTOZAKE SHANGE, from *Three Pieces*, New York, St Martin's Press, 1981. Further scripts include *for coloured girls who have considered suicide/when the rainbow is enuf*, New York, Macmillan, 1977; *From okra to greens: a different kinda love story*, New York, French, 1983; and *The Love Space Demands* in *Plays: One*, London, Methuen, 1994. See too *See No Evil: Prefaces, Essays and Accounts 1976–1983*, San Francisco, Momo's Press, 1984.

BERNARD SHAW, from *Complete Prefaces*, London, Paul Hamlyn, 1965. See too *The Quintessence of Ibsenism*, London, Walter Scott, 1891; 'A Dramatic Realist to His Critics', *New Review*, 11, 1894; *Bernard Shaw's Letters to Granville Barker*, ed. C. B. Purdom, London, Phoenix House, 1956; and *Shaw on Theatre*, ed. E. J. West, London, McGibbon & Kee, 1960.

WOLE SOYINKA, from *Myth, Literature and the African World*, Cambridge University Press, 1976. See too: *Art, Dialogue and Outrage: Essays on Literature and Culture*, Oxford University Press, 1988; 'Drama and the Revolutionary Ideal', in *In Person: Achebe, Awoonor, and Soyinka*, ed. Karen L. Morell, Seattle, University of Washington Press, 1975; 'The Fourth Stage: Through the Mysteries of Ogun to the Origin of Yoruba Tragedy' in *The Morality of Art*, ed. D. W. Jefferson, London, Routledge & Kegan Paul, 1969; 'Shakespeare and the Living Dramatist', *Shakespeare Survey 36*, Cambridge University Press, 1983; and his *Collected Plays*, Oxford University Press, vol. 1, 1973, vol. 2, 1974.

CONSTANTIN STANISLAVSKI, from *Creating a Role*, translated by Elizabeth Reynolds Hapgood, New York, Theater Art Books, 1961. See too: *My Life in Art*, London, Geoffrey Bles, 1924; *An Actor Prepares*, London, Geoffrey Bles, 1937; *Building a Character*, London, Max Reinhardt, 1950; *Stanislavski's Legacy*, London, Max Reinhardt, 1959; and *Stanislavski Directs*, New York, Limelight Editions, 1986. His *Collected Works* are to be published by Methuen.

GERTRUDE STEIN, from *Lectures in America*, New York, Random House, 1935; reprinted London, Virago, 1988. Her Plays and Operas have been published in three volumes.

LOUISE STEINMAN, from *The Knowing Body*, Boston and London, Shambhala, 1986 (includes material by Trisha Brown, Wendy Perron, Meredith Monk, Whoopi Goldberg, Spalding Gray and Ping Chong).

AUGUST STRINDBERG, from *Plays: First Series*, London, Duckworth, 1912. See too his *Open Letters to the Intimate Theater*, Seattle, University of Washington, 1966. See too 'The Role of Chance in Artistic Creation' in *Inferno, Alone and Other Writings*, New York, 1968.

VESTA TILLEY, from Lady de Frece, *Recollections of Vesta Tilley*, London, Hutchinson, 1934.

ERNST TOLLER, from *Nation*, no. 127, 7 November 1928. His play *The Transfiguration* is in Mel Gordon, *Expressionist Texts*, New York, PAJ, 1986. See too his *Seven Plays*, London, John Lane, 1935; *and Pastor Hall by Ernst Toller*, trans. Stephen Spender and Hugh Hunt, New York, Random House, 1939.

TRISTAN TZARA, translated from *Œuvres Complètes*, vol. 1, Paris, Flammarion, 1975. His play *The Gas Heart* (1920) is in *Modern French Plays: An Anthology from Jarry to Ionesco*, eds Michael Benedikt and George E. Wellwarth, London, Faber & Faber, 1965. On Dada and surrealist performance, see Annabelle Henkin Melzer, *Latest Rage the Big Drum*, UMI Press, Ann Arbor, Mich., 1981, and John H. Matthews, *Theatre in Dada and Surrealism*, Syracuse, New York, Syracuse University Press, 1974. See too *The Dada Painters and Poets: An Anthology*, ed. Robert Motherwell, Cambridge, Mass., Belknap, 1989.

EVGENY VAKHTANGOV, from *Evgeny Vakhtangov*, compiled by Lyubov Vendrovskaya and Galina Kaptereva, Progress Publishers, Moscow, 1982. See too *Acting: A Handbook of the Stanislavsky Method*, compiled by Toby Cole,

New York, Lear, 1947. On Vakhtangov's work, see Nick Worrall, *Modernism to Realism on the Soviet Stage*, Cambridge University Press, 1989.

LUIS VALDEZ, from John Weisman, *Guerilla Theatre*, New York, Doubleday; 1973. This volume also includes two Campesino scripts. One more and his article 'Actos' are in *Guerilla Street Theater*, ed. Henry Lesnick (listed on p. 367). All these pieces originally published in *Actos*, by Luis Valdez and El Teatro Campesino, San Juan Bautista, Calif., El Centro Campesino Cultural, 1971. See too Beth Bagby, 'El Teatro Campesino: Interviews', *Drama Review*, vol. 11, no. 4 (T36), Summer 1976.

KARL VALENTIN, translated from 'Zwangvorstellungen' in *Sturzflüge im Zuschauerraum; der gesammelten Werke andere Teil*, Munich, R. Piper Verlag, 1969. Further sketches can be found in *Cabaret Performance, Vol. 2: Europe 1920–1940*, ed. Laurence Senelick, Baltimore, Johns Hopkins University Press, 1993. For a historical survey of cabaret, see Lisa Appignanesi, *Cabaret: The First Hundred Years*, London, Studio Vista, 1975; revised edn London, Methuen, 1984.

JEAN VILAR, translated from *Le théâtre, service publique*, Paris, Gallimard, 1975. For accounts of his work, see David Bradby and John McCormick, *People's Theatre*, London, Croom Helm, 1978; and David Whitton, *Stage Directors in Modern France*, Manchester University Press, 1987.

ROBERT WILSON, from Stefan Brecht, *The Theatre of Visions: Robert Wilson*, Frankfurt am Main, Suhrkamp Verlag, 1978, and London, Methuen, 1982. See too: Robert Wilson, '. . . I thought I was Hallucinating', *Drama Review*, vol. 21, no. 4 (T76), December 1977; 'The $ Value of Man', *Theater*, vol. 9, no. 2, Spring 1978, Yale School of Drama; and *Robert Wilson: The Theater of Images*, Cincinnati, Contemporary Arts Center, 1980, rev. ed. New York, Harper & Row, 1984 – exhibition catalogue with contributions by John Rockwell, Robert Stearns, Calvin Tomkins and Laurence Shyer.

STANISLAS IGNACY WITKIEWICZ, from *The Madman and the Nun*, Seattle, University of Washington Press, 1968. See too: *The Mother and Other Unsavoury Plays*, New York, Applause Books, 1993; *The Witkiewicz Reader*, ed. Daniel Gerould, Evanston, Ill., Northwestern University Press, 1992, and London, Quartet Books, 1993; 'A Few Words about the Actor in the Theater of Pure Form' in *20th Century Polish Avant-Garde Drama*, ed. Daniel Gerould, Ithaca, NY, Cornell University Press, 1977; and *Theatre Quarterly*, 5, 1975 (special Witkiewicz issue).

WORKERS' THEATRE MOVEMENT, from Raphael Samuel, Ewan McColl and Stuart Cosgrove, *Theatres of the Left 1880–1935*, London, Routledge & Kegan Paul, 1985 (contains scripts and documents from Britain and the US). See too: Howard Goorney, *The Theatre Workshop Story*, London, Eyre

Methuen, 1981; *Agit-Prop to Theatre Workshop: Political Playscripts, 1930–1950*, eds Howard Goorney and Ewan McColl, Manchester University Press, 1986; and Joan Littlewood, *Joan's Book*, London, Methuen, 1994.

W. B. YEATS, from *The Irish Dramatic Movement 1901–1919*, in *Explorations*, London, Macmillan, 1962. See too 'Dramatis Personae 1896–1902' and 'The Death of Synge', 1909, in *Autobiographies*, London, Macmillan, 1955.

FURTHER USEFUL COLLECTIONS

Aesthetics and Politics: Debates between Ernst Bloch, Georg Lukacs, Bertolt Brecht, Walter Benjamin, Theodor Adorno, London, New Left Books, 1977.

Ayers, Robert and David Butler (eds), *Live Art*, Sunderland, AN Publications, 1991. Accounts and tips by performance artists and organisers working in Britain.

Bentley, Eric (ed.), *The Theory of the Modern Stage*, London, Penguin Books, 1968; includes material by Artaud, Brecht, Craig, Piscator, Shaw and Yeats; and on Appia and Stanislavski; among others.

Betsko, Kathleen and Rachel Koenig, *Interviews with Contemporary Women Playwrights*, New York, Beech Tree Books, 1986. Includes interviews with Ntozake Shange, Maria Irene Fornes, Beth Henley, Caryl Churchill, etc.

Brown, Jean Morrison (ed.), *The Vision of Modern Dance*, Princeton, NJ, Princeton Book Co., 1979; includes writings from Duncan, Fuller, Mary Wigman, Martha Graham, etc., to Trisha Brown and Rod Rodgers.

Champagne, Lenora (ed.), *Out from Under: Texts by Women Performance Artists*, New York, Theater Communications Group, and London, Nick Hern, 1990; contains pieces by Rachel Rosenthal, Laurie Anderson, Karen Finlay, Holly Hughes and others.

Cole, Toby and Helen Krich Chinoy (eds), *Actors on Acting*, New York, Crown, 1949; contains writings by Antoine, Brecht, Copeau, Eisenstein, Kornfeld, Meyerhold, Piscator, Shaw, Stanislavski, Vakhtangov and others.

Cole, Toby and Helen Krich Chinoy (eds), *Directors on Directing*, revised edition, Indianapolis, Bobbs-Merrill, 1963.

Corrigan, Robert W. (ed.), *Theatre in the Twentieth Century*. Essays by playwrights, directors and critics from Hofmannsthal to Arthur Miller.

Duerdon, D. and C. Pieterse (eds), *African Writers Talking*, London, Heinemann, 1972; includes interviews with Wole Soyinka and Ngugi wa Thiong'o.

Green, Michael (ed.), *The Russian Symbolist Theatre: An Anthology of Plays and Critical Texts*, Ann Arbor, Mich., Ardis, 1986. Texts by Bryusov, Blok, Ivanov and others.

Hart, Lynda (ed.), *Making a Spectacle: Feminist Essays on Contemporary Women's Theatre*, Ann Arbor, University of Michigan Press, 1989.

Kidd, Ross (ed.), *Third World Popular Theatre*, Toronto, International Popular Theatre Alliance, 1984.

Kirby, E. T. (ed.), *Total Theatre*, includes pieces from Wagner onwards.

Kirby, Michael, *Happenings*, New York, E. P. Dutton, 1965; includes scripts for productions by Jim Dine, Red Grooms, Allan Kaprow, Claes Oldenburg and Robert Whitman.

Lesnick, Henry (ed.), *Guerilla Street Theater*, New York, Avon Books, 1973. Texts and scenarios by numerous American groups.

Loeffler, Carl E. (ed.), *Performance Anthology: Source Book for a Decade of California Performance Art*, San Francisco, Contemporary Arts Press, 1980.

Luzuriaga, Gerardo (ed.), *Popular Theater for Social Change in Latin America: Essays in Spanish and English*, Los Angeles, UCLA Latin American Center Publications, UCLA Latin American Studies, vol. 41, 1978; (includes essays by Boal and Buenaventura).

Malpede, Karen (ed.), *Women in Theatre*, New York, Limelight Editions, 1985. A collection of texts by women on their work for theatre.

Miesel, Victor H. (ed.), *Voices of German Expressionism*, Englewood Cliffs, NJ, Prentice Hall, 1970; includes some theatre material by Barlach, Kandinsky and Kokoschka.

Rees, Roland, *Fringe First: Pioneers of Fringe Theatre on Record*, London, Oberon Books, 1992. First-hand accounts by the creators of the British alternative theatre scene.

Rolfe, Bari (ed.), *Mimes on Miming*, Los Angeles, Panjandrum Books, 1980, repr. London, Millington Books, 1981.

Sainer, Arthur, *The Radical Theatre Notebook*, New York, Avon, 1975. Part II samples the work of a number of American groups, offering 'Scripts, Notes, Logs, Dialogues'.

Senelick, Laurence (ed.), *Cabaret Performance, Vol. 1: Europe 1890–1920*, New York, PAJ, 1989; *Vol. 2: Europe 1920–1940*, Baltimore, Johns Hopkins University Press, 1993.

Senelick, Laurence (ed.), *Russian Dramatic Theory from Pushkin to the Symbolists*, Austin, University of Texas Press, 1981.

Tolstoy, Vladimir, Irina Bibikova and Catherine Cooke, *Street Art of the Revolution: Festivals and Celebrations in Russia 1918–33*, New York, The Vendome Press, and London, Thames & Hudson, 1990.

ACKNOWLEDGEMENTS

For material reproduced or translated in this volume, thanks are due to the following:

HARRY N. ABRAMS for excerpt from Allan Kaprow, *Assemblages, Environments and Happenings*, New York, Abrams, 1966. © 1966 by Allan Kaprow, New York.

ARCADE PUBLISHING for the Prologue to *The Exception and the Rule*, by Bertolt Brecht.

ARTFORUM and CAROLEE SCHNEEMANN for 'Letter to the Editor' by Carolee Schneemann, *Artforum*, October 1983, © *Artforum*, by permission of Carolee Schneemann.

BFI PUBLISHING for excerpts from *S. M. Eisenstein: Selected Works, Volume I, Writings, 1922–34*, edited and translated by Richard Taylor (London: BFI, 1988 and Bloomington and Indianapolis: Indiana University Press, 1988); and 'AB: Parade of the Eccentric', by Grigori Kozintsev, translated by Richard Sherwood, from *Futurism/Formalism/FEKS*, edited by Ian Christie and John Gillett, London, BFI, 1978.

MARION BOYARS and NEW DIRECTIONS for 'Play and Theory of the Duende' from Federico García Lorca, *Deep Song and Other Prose*. Copyright © 1975 by The Estate of Federico García Lorca, translated by Christopher Maurer, © Marion Boyars Publishers Ltd, 1980. Reprinted by permission of Marion Boyars and New Directions Publishing Company.

THE CALDER EDUCATIONAL TRUST for 'The Theatre of Cruelty', 'An Affective Athleticism' and 'On Balinese Theatre' by Antonin Artaud from *Collected Works*, volume 4, translated by Victor Corti, Calder & Boyars Limited, London. Copyright © Calder & Boyars Ltd 1974. 'Letter to Comœdia' translated by Richard Drain and Micheline Mabille, reproduced for this edition only by permission of the Calder Educational Trust, London. Also for 'Preface to *Methusalem*' by Ivan Goll from *Seven Expressionist Plays*, edited and translated by J. M. Ritchie, John Calder (Publishers) Ltd, and Riverrun Press, New York. Copyright © this translation John Calder

ACKNOWLEDGEMENTS

(Publishers) Ltd, 1968, 1980. And for 'Notes on the Theatre' by Eugene
Ionesco from his *Notes and Counter Notes*, translated by Donald Watson,
John Calder (Publishers) Ltd, London. Copyright © this translation by
John Calder (Publishers) Ltd, 1964. All items reprinted by permission of
The Calder Educational Trust, London.

CAMBRIDGE UNIVERSITY PRESS and WOLE SOYINKA for 'Drama and the African
World View' by Wole Soyinka from *Myth, Literature and the African
World*, Cambridge University Press, 1976. © Cambridge University
Press 1976. By permission of Wole Soyinka.

CARIBBEAN QUARTERLY for 'The Emergence of a National Drama in the West
Indies' by Errol Hill, from *Caribbean Quarterly*, vol. 18, no. 4, December
1972, University of West Indies, Mona Campus.

JUDY CHICAGO for excerpts from *Through the Flower: My Struggle as a Woman
Artist*, copyright Judy Chicago, 1975, Doubleday & Company, Inc.,
Garden City, New York. By permission of Through the Flower.

LA CITE for excerpts translated from Adolphe Appia, *Œuvres Complètes*, vol. 2,
1895–1905, Lausanne, La Cité, L'Age d'Homme, 1986.

COMEDIA for excerpts from *The Struggle for Black Arts in Britain* by Kwesi
Owusu, London, Comedia, 1986.

THE EDWARD GORDON CRAIG C. H. ESTATE for excerpts from *The Theatre Advancing*, *The Art of the Theatre*, and 'Study for Movement' by Edward Gordon
Craig, by kind permission of Ellen T. M. Craig and Marie J. Taylor, joint
executors.

DOBSON BOOKS for excerpt from *Film Essays, With a Lecture* by Sergei
Eisenstein, London, Dobson, 1968.

DOUBLEDAY and JULIAN BACH for 'Notes on Chicano Theater' by Luis Valdez,
from *Guerilla Theatre*, by John Weisman. Copyright © 1973 by John
Weisman. Used by permission of Doubleday, a division of Bantam
Doubleday Dell Publishing Group, Inc.

THE DRAMA REVIEW, MIT PRESS, ENRIQUE BUENAVENTURA and EUGENIO BARBA for
'Theatre and Culture' by Enrique Buenaventura, translated by Joanne
Potzlitzer, *The Drama Review*, vol. 14, no. 2 (T46), by permission of the
MIT Press, Cambridge, Massachusetts, and Enrique Buenaventura ©
1970 The Drama Review; 'Eurasian Theatre' by Eugenio Barba, trans-
lated by Richard Fowler, *The Drama Review*, vol. 32, no. 3 (T119) by
permission of the MIT Press, Cambridge, Massachusetts, and Eugenio
Barba, copyright © 1988 New York University and the Massachusetts
Institute of Technology; and 'On the Pure Elements of the Actor's Art' by
Sergei Radlov, translated by Lynn Ball, *The Drama Review*, vol. 19, no. 4

ACKNOWLEDGEMENTS

(T68), by permission of the MIT Press, Cambridge, Massachusetts, © 1970 The Drama Review.

ELLEN LEVINE LITERARY AGENCY on behalf of Louise Steinman for excerpts from *The Knowing Body* by Louise Steinman, Shambhala, 1986, © Louise Steinman.

FABER & FABER and ATHOL FUGARD for excerpts from *Notebooks 1960/1977* by Athol Fugard, edited by Mary Benson, Faber and Faber, 1983, with permission from the author and 'Faber and Faber Ltd' and 'Ad Donker (Pty) Ltd'. Text © Athol Fugard 1983.

FARRAR, STRAUS & GIROUX for excerpts from *Marinetti: Selected Writings* by F. T. Marinetti, edited by R. W. Flint. Copyright © 1971, 1972 by Farrar, Straus & Giroux, Inc. Reprinted by permission of Farrar, Straus & Giroux, Inc.

FLAMMARION for excerpts translated from *Tristan Tzara – Œuvres Complètes*, tome 1, Flammarion, 1975.

HONOR FORD-SMITH for excerpts from 'Sistren: Jamaican Women's Theatre'.

EDITIONS GALLIMARD for article translated from *Le théâtre, service publique*, by Jean Vilar, © Editions Gallimard 1975.

GEORGE GIBIAN for 'The Oberiu manifesto' by Daniil Kharms from George Gibian ed., *The Man in the Black Coat: Russia's Lost Literature of the Absurd*, Northwestern University Press, 1987. Originally published in *Russia's Lost Literature of the Absurd: Selected Works of Daniil Kharms and Alexander Vvedensky*, translated and edited by George Gibian, Cornell University Press, Ithaca, NY, 1971. By permission of George Gibian. Copyright George Gibian.

JERZY GROTOWSKI for 'Methodical Exploration' translated by Amanda Pasquier and Judy Barba, from *Towards a Poor Theatre* by Jerzy Grotowski, Odin Teatrets Forlag, 1968. By permission of Jerzy Grotowski. Copyright © 1968 Jerzy Grotowski and Odin Teatrets Forlag.

MICHAEL IMISON for 'Aspects of Popular Theatre' by Dario Fo, translation copyright © 1985 by Tony Mitchell; by permission of Michael Imison Playwrights Ltd, 28 Almeida Street, London N1 1TD.

VICTORIA KIRBY for translation by Victoria Kirby from Italian of Enrico Prampolini, in *Futurist Performance* by Michael Kirby, New York, E. P. Dutton, 1971, © 1971 by Victoria Kirby. By permission of Victoria Kirby.

JUDITH MALINA for permission to reprint 'Notes on a Ritual Tragedy'.

MIME JOURNAL, GUILLERMO GÓMEZ-PEÑA and RACHEL ROSENTHAL for excerpts from their articles in *Mime Journal 1991/1992: California Performance*,

Vol. 2; by permission of *Mime Journal*, Pomona College, Claremont, Calif., Guillermo Gómez-Peña and Rachel Rosenthal. © *Mime Journal* 1991.

MODERN DRAMA for 'Aller à la mer' by Hélène Cixous, translated by Barbara Kerslake, *Modern Drama* 27, 1984.

PANTHEON BOOKS for excerpts from *Unbalancing Acts*, by Richard Foreman. Copyright © 1992 by Richard Foreman. Reprinted by permission of Pantheon Books, a division of Random House, Inc.

R. PIPER VERLAG for excerpts translated from Karl Valentin, *Sturzflüge im Zuschauerraum*, © R. Piper & Co. Verlag, München, 1969.

PROGRESS PUBLISHERS for excerpts from *Evgeny Vakhtangov*, comp. L. Vendrovskaya and G. Kaptereva, translated by D. Bradbury, English translation © Progress Publishers, 1982.

RANDOM HOUSE and DAVID HIGHAM ASSOCIATES for excerpts from *Lectures in America* by Gertrude Stein. Copyright 1935 and renewed 1963 by Alice B. Toklas. Reprinted London, Virago, 1988; by permission of Random House, Inc. and David Higham Associates.

REED CONSUMER BOOKS for excerpts from Edward Bond, *The War Plays*, Methuen, 1991, by permission of Edward Bond; and *Engineers of the Imagination* edited by Tony Coult and Baz Kershaw, Methuen, London, 1983. Both by permission of Reed Consumer Books.

REED CONSUMER BOOKS and ARCADE PUBLISHING for excerpt from *The Exception and the Rule* © 1957 by Suhrkamp Verlag, Berlin. Translation by Ralph Manheim © 1977 by Stefan S. Brecht. Reprinted from *The Measures Taken and Other Lehrstücke*, translation by Bertolt Brecht, published by Methuen London and Arcade Publishing, Inc., New York.

REED CONSUMER BOOKS and SANFORD J. GREENBURGER ASSOCIATES for excerpts from *The Political Theatre* by Erwin Piscator, translated and edited by Hugh Rorrison, Eyre Methuen, 1980. Copyright © by Rowohlt Verlag Publishing Co., Reinbek bei Hamburg, 1963. By permission of Reed Consumer Books.

REED CONSUMER BOOKS and HARPER COLLINS for pp. 129–32 from *The Shifting Point* by Peter Brook, London, Methuen, 1988. Copyright © 1987 by Peter Brook. Reprinted by permission of Reed Consumer Books and HarperCollins, Publishers, Inc.

REED CONSUMER BOOKS and ROUTLEDGE (NEW YORK) for excerpts from Bertolt Brecht, *Brecht on Theatre*, translated and edited by John Willett, Methuen (London) and Hill & Wang (New York), 1964, by permission of Reed Consumer Books, Routledge, New York, and the Brecht Estate, copy-

ACKNOWLEDGEMENTS

right © 1957, 1963 and 1964 by Suhrkamp Verlag, Frankfurt am Main, translation and notes © 1964 by John Willett; from *On the Art of Theatre* by Edward Gordon Craig, Heinemann 1911 and Theatre Art Books, 1925; from *Creating a Role* by Constantin Stanislavski, translated by Elizabeth Hapgood (1980), by permission of the publisher, Routledge, Chapman & Hall, Inc., and Eyre Methuen, © by Elizabeth Reynolds Hapgood 1961; from article by Peter Schumann reprinted from *The Bread and Puppet Theatre*, vol. 2 (1988) by Stefan Brecht, copyright © Stefan Brecht 1988, by permission of the publisher, Routledge, New York, Reed Consumer Books and Peter Schumann.

THE REAL COMET PRESS for Suzanne Lacy & Leslie Labowitz, 'Feminist Media Strategies for Political Performance' © 1980 by Leslie Labowitz. From *Cultures in Contention*, Kahn & Neumaier, eds, 1985, The Real Comet Press. Reprinted by permission of The Real Comet Press, Seattle.

MRS RODRIGUEZ-DANIELS for excerpt from *The Complete Plays of Vladimir Mayakovsky*, translated by Guy Daniels, New York, Simon & Schuster, 1968. © Estate of Guy Daniels. By permission of Mrs Josiane Rodriguez-Daniels.

ROUTLEDGE for excerpts from *Games for Actors and Non-Actors* by Augusto Boal, translated by Adrian Jackson, Routledge, 1992; and for 'Agit-Prop Style' from *Theatres of the Left* by Raphael Samuel, Ewan McColl and Stuart Cosgrove, Routledge & Kegan Paul, 1985. Both by permission of Routledge.

ROUTLEDGE NEW YORK for 'Depth' by Isadora Duncan, reprinted from *Isadora Duncan: The Art of the Dance*. Copyright 1928 by Helen Hackett, Inc. Copyright renewed 1956. Sheldon Cheney, editor, by permission of the publisher, Theatre Arts Books, New York. Copyright © 1969 by Theatre Art Books.

ST. MARTIN'S PRESS and A. M. HEATH on behalf of NTOZAKE SHANGE for 'unrecovered losses/black theater traditions' by Ntozake Shange, copyright © 1972, 1974, 1975, 1976, 1977, 1978 by Ntozake Shange. From the book *Three Pieces* and reprinted with permission from St. Martin's Press, Inc., New York.

SCUOLA D'ARTE DRAMMATICA PAOLO GRASSI for 'Elementary School of Theatre' by Tadeusz Kantor from *Lezioni Milanesi 1: Scuola elementare del teatro*, one of a series of texts published by the Scuola d'Arte Drammatica 'Paolo Grassi' in conjunction with Ubulibri, Milan, 1988, following a series of seminars by Kantor at the Scuola d'Arte Drammatica 'Paolo Grassi' of Milan given in June/July 1986. Copyright © Ubulibri under licence from Scuola d'Arte Drammatica Paolo Grassi.

372

ACKNOWLEDGEMENTS

LAURENCE SENELICK for extract translated by Laurence Senelick from *Ich bin eine Hexe* by Valeska Gert, included in his *Cabaret Performance, Volume 2: Europe 1920–1940*, Baltimore, Johns Hopkins University Press, 1993. By permission of Laurence Senelick.

SOCIETY OF AUTHORS AND BERNARD SHAW ESTATE for excerpts from Preface to *Mrs. Warren's Profession* by Bernard Shaw, by permission of the Society of Authors on behalf of the Bernard Shaw Estate.

THEATRE COMMUNICATIONS GROUP for excerpts from *Ridiculous Theatre: Scourge of Human Folly. The Essays and Opinions of Charles Ludlam*, edited by Steven Samuels. Copyright 1992 by the Estate of Charles Ludlam. Introduction and chronological copyright 1992 by Steven Samuels.

LE THÉÂTRE DU SOLEIL, ARIANE MNOUCHKINE and HÉLÈNE CIXOUS for excerpts translated from 'Rencontres avec le Théâtre du Soleil', by Ariane Mnouchkine and Denis Bablet, and from *L'Indiade, ou l'Inde de leurs rêves; et quelques écrits sur le théâtre*, by Hélène Cixous, Théâtre du Soleil, 1987, by permission of the publishers and Hélène Cixous.

PATRICE THIERRY for excerpts from *L'aventure de la parole errante*, by Armand Gatti and Marc Kravetz, Toulouse, Patrice Thierry, 1987, © L'Ether Vague 1987.

INTERNATIONAL THOMSON PUBLISHING SERVICES for excerpt by the WTM from *Theatres of the Left 1880–1935* by Raphael Samuel, Ewan McColl & Stuart Cosgrove, Routledge & Kegan Paul, 1985.

STANLEY THORNES and THE MARTHA HOLDEN JENNINGS FOUNDATION for excerpts from *Collected Writings on Education and Drama* by Dorothy Heathcote, published by Stanley Thornes. 'Drama as a Process for Change' also by permission of the Martha Holden Jennings Foundation, Cleveland.

UNIVERSITY OF WASHINGTON PRESS for 'On a New Type of Play' from *The Madman and the Nun* by S. I. Witkiewicz, translated by Daniel C. Gerould and C. S. Durer, University of Washington Press, 1968. Copyright © 1966, 1967, 1968 by Daniel C. Gerould and C. S. Durer.

VIKING PENGUIN for 'Open Letter to the Workers', by Vladimir Mayakovsky, from *The Life of Mayakovsky*, by Wiktor Woroszylski, translated by Boleslaw Taborski, translation copyright © 1971 by Grossman Publishers, Inc. Used by permission of Viking Penguin, a division of Penguin Books USA, Inc.

A. P. WATT and SIMON & SCHUSTER for excerpt from 'A People's Theatre: A Letter to Lady Gregory'; excerpted with permission of Simon & Schuster, Inc., and A. P. Watt Ltd on behalf of Michael Yeats, from *Explorations* by W. B. Yeats. Copyright © 1962 by Mrs W. B. Yeats.

373

ACKNOWLEDGEMENTS

ROBERT WILSON and THE BYRD HOFFMAN FOUNDATION for excerpts from 'Speech introducing *Freud*', from *The Theatre of Visions: Robert Wilson*, by Stefan Brecht.

Every attempt had been made to trace and contact known copyright holders before publication. If any copyright holders have any queries they are invited to contact the publishers.

INDEX